AIR TIME

Also by Gary Paul Gates

The Palace Guard *(with Dan Rather)*

AIR TIME

The Inside Story of CBS News

by Gary Paul Gates

HARPER & ROW, PUBLISHERS

1817

NEW YORK

HAGERSTOWN

SAN FRANCISCO

LONDON

For
John Merriman
(1924–1974)

FIRST EDITION

Designed by Sidney Feinberg

Library of Congress Cataloging in Publication Data

Gates, Gary Paul.
  Air time.
  Includes index.
  1. Columbia Broadcasting System, inc. CBS News.
2. Television broadcasting of news—United States.
I. Title.
PN4888.T4G37   791.45'7   77–3750
ISBN 0–06–011477–0

78 79 80 81 82 10 9 8 7 6 5 4 3 2 1

Contents

1   "Kennedy's Been Shot!"   1

2   Higher Murrow and Lower Murrow   14

3   The Outcast, the Gray Eminence, and the Duke   35

4   "We Have to Make Air!"   50

5   An Accident of Casting   71

6   Anchorman   82

7   Friendly Fire   97

8   Martyrdom and Restoration   118

9   Discussing the Lineup with God   137

10   Living-Room War   155

11   On the Road and Other Beats   167

12   Off-Camera Cadre   181

13   Uncle Walter   198

14   Wild about Harry   214

15   The Trouble with Harry   230

16   Marathon Man   242

17   Weekend Update   256

18   Morning Blues   269

19   "Don't Let the Bastards Scare You"   288

20   Kill the Messenger   301

21   Rooks and Bishops, Knights and Pawns   317
22   A Little More Tabloid in the Blood   336
23   Small Reward   356
24   Character Studies   378
25   "We Are No Longer Starvelings . . ."   397

Author's Note   425
Index   429

The name of the game in this business is time on the air.

Les Midgley, executive producer, CBS News

1   "Kennedy's Been Shot!"

Some of the things he did that day would pass into folklore and become part of the legend. More than a decade later, journalism professors would still be telling their students, who were mere children at the time, how Walter Cronkite cried on air when he had to report the official announcement that President John F. Kennedy was dead. While on the subject, they might also relate that the afternoon of the Kennedy assassination was the only time, as far as anyone could remember, that Walter Cronkite appeared on air in his shirt-sleeves.

He arrived at his office that day around 10:00 A.M., as was his custom, and promptly settled into the routine preparations for that evening's broadcast. There wasn't very much going on in the world. The news had been on the dull side all week, and now, on this Friday morning in November, the outlook was for more of the same. Things were so quiet that some members of his news staff were hoping, as journalists often do, that a major story of some kind would break in the next few hours. Then they wouldn't have to worry about what to lead with that night on the *CBS Evening News with Walter Cronkite.*

The previous evening—November 21, 1963—the lead item was about the wreckage of a U-2 spy plane, which had been located in the Gulf of Mexico. But it wasn't really much of a story. American U-2 flights over Cuba had long been an open secret, and Cronkite was careful to point out that the plane was *not* shot down. The crash had been caused by a mechanical failure.

Fairly deep into the Thursday evening broadcast, there was a film report by Dan Rather from San Antonio on President Kennedy's visit

1

to Texas. But that also fell into the category of a routine story. Rather noted that the purpose of the trip was political fence-mending, and that Kennedy was aware he might have trouble carrying Texas in the 1964 election, especially if the Republicans nominated the conservative Barry Goldwater. The only fresh angle, which Rather emphasized, was that this was Jackie Kennedy's first appearance before large crowds since the victorious 1960 campaign.

On his first day in Texas, Kennedy had visited three cities—San Antonio, Houston, and Fort Worth—and had received a warm and enthusiastic welcome. On this second day, he would be in Dallas, and there were many at CBS News who felt the situation there might be altogether different. In recent years, Dallas had become a city boiling over with antiliberal (and, therefore, anti-Kennedy) feeling. Emotions there ran high and sometimes took ugly turns. Just a few weeks earlier, UN Ambassador Adlai Stevenson had visited Dallas and was jeered at and jostled by an angry crowd of pickets. At one point, a woman hit him on the head with a picket sign and a man spat on him. So there was some concern that Friday morning that Kennedy could run into trouble in Dallas, and by "trouble," of course, what everyone had in mind was a few hecklers or, at worst, hostile protesters similar to the group that had greeted Stevenson. American journalists had not yet become accustomed to thinking of assassination as a real possibility.

At lunchtime, many of the people on Cronkite's news staff began drifting out to nearby restaurants. But Cronkite himself was not among them. He often passed up the opportunity to go out for lunch, a habit dating back to his years as a reporter for the United Press, when lunching out was generally viewed with suspicion, as an excuse to goof off. Also, Cronkite had recently turned forty-seven, and he was conscious of the need to keep a firm check on his waistline. So instead of going out that day, he had his secretary bring him a light snack of cottage cheese, a slice of canned pineapple, and some hot tea, which he ate at the anchor desk, the same desk where each evening he broadcast the news.

After finishing his snack, Cronkite decided to take advantage of the early-afternoon lull. He leaned back in his chair, put his feet up on the desk, and began skimming through the bulldog edition of the *World-Telegram & Sun*, then one of New York City's three evening newspapers. This is the position he was in when his news editor, Ed Bliss, dashed in from the main CBS newsroom with a bulletin that had just moved on the UPI wire. "Kennedy's been shot!" hollered Bliss. It was 1:40 P.M. in New York, an hour earlier in Dallas.

Cronkite jumped up from his chair, grabbed the UPI copy from a nearby printer, and headed for a small announcer's booth a few feet down the hall. At that time, CBS did not have the facility for putting a correspondent on camera immediately. When Cronkite broke into the soap opera *As the World Turns* with the first, fragmentary news from Dallas, it was with an audio report only. A bulletin slide filled the television screen as he relayed to CBS viewers the UPI report that the President's wounds were serious and "perhaps could be fatal." It took nearly twenty minutes to set up the cameras so Cronkite's voice could be joined by his face, and because of that experience, CBS would later install a special "flash studio" to enable visual, as well as audio, bulletins to be transmitted immediately.

By the time Cronkite appeared on the screen, he was back in his customary slot in the combination studio-newsroom from which his regular evening newscast originated. By this time, too, details of the story were pouring in from a confusing variety of sources and, like every other newsroom in the country, CBS News headquarters in New York was a bedlam of activity. Writers and producers had formed a kind of bucket brigade to make sure that the crush of wire copy, now clattering away on all printers, quickly reached the editor's desk. There, Ed Bliss sifted through it, eliminating duplication, then passed it on to Cronkite. Whatever coherence the broadcast had during that first hectic hour or so (and the transcript reads surprisingly well) was due largely to Cronkite's own expert ability to ad-lib and maintain order in the midst of chaos.

Within moments after the first UPI report of the shooting, CBS's own correspondents in the field were moving in on the story. Both Dan Rather, who was in Dallas, and Eddie Barker, news director of the CBS affiliate in Dallas, soon received word, from separate sources, that Kennedy was dead. Cronkite passed on these reports, but he went out of his way to stress that they were not official, that there was as yet no confirmation. During the last minutes of uncertainty, he seemed, at times, almost to be straining to have it *not* be so. Then, at 2:33 P.M., New York time, the official announcement came in. As Cronkite broadcast the announcement, his voice broke and his eyes filled up with tears.

Quickly, however, he regained his composure. This was, after all, Walter Cronkite, who had a reputation for being the coolest, most detached of broadcast journalists. The tragedy was now a *fait accompli*, but other aspects of the story were now unfolding, and Cronkite remained seated at the anchor desk broadcasting each new development: the transition of power to Lyndon Johnson, the arrest of a suspect named Lee Harvey Oswald, the stunned reaction of government leaders in Washington and in other capitals around the world, and the preparations for a weekend of mourning, to be followed by the funeral and burial. After he had been on the air steadily for about three hours, Cronkite decided he needed a break and turned the anchor slot over to Charles Collingwood. As he stood up, he caught sight of his suit coat draped over the back of his chair, and it was then, and only then, that he realized he had been on the air all this time in his shirt-sleeves with his tie askew and his hair uncombed. Such minor neglects were not at all in character.

The first thing Cronkite did, after Collingwood relieved him, was to go to his office to call his wife. But the CBS switchboard was jammed. While he was waiting for a line to clear, his other phone rang. He picked it up, and before he had a chance to identify himself, a woman's strident voice came on: "May I have the news department of CBS?" Cronkite replied, "This *is* the news department of CBS." The woman then said, "Well, I think it is absolutely criminal for CBS to have that man Cronkite on the air at a time like this, when everybody knows that he hates the Kennedys. But there he is, in shirt-sleeves, crying his crocodile tears."

Cronkite took a deep breath and then roared back, "Madam, *this* is Walter Cronkite and you are a goddamn idiot!" He then slammed the receiver down so hard that for a moment he thought he had damaged it.

Cronkite was back on the air later that afternoon, and by the end of the day the decision had been made, by all three networks, to suspend all commercials and entertainment programs until after Kennedy's funeral. Thus, by nightfall, the nation was locked into what, in retrospect, still stands out as the most extraordinary weekend in the history of television.

With the decision to turn continuous air time over to the network news departments, TV journalism was suddenly faced with a challenge far greater than any it had previously experienced. Because of the triumph it achieved in meeting that challenge, television news would never be regarded in quite the same way again. It is no exaggeration to say that during those four days in November 1963, TV journalism came into its full maturity. What's more, its performance that weekend provided a clear glimpse into the future. In the years ahead, television would come to be recognized as the dominant voice in American journalism, the prime source from which the majority of Americans received their news.

To appreciate the significance of this historic shift from newspapers to television, it may be useful to recall how TV's role in the world of journalism was perceived up to the time of the Kennedy assassination. Prior to the 1960s, television news was given credit for being able to provide thorough coverage of certain live events that were scheduled well in advance, thus allowing plenty of time for preparation—the best example being the political conventions. It was also acknowledged that, on rare occasions, one of the networks might come up with an excellent documentary worthy of comparison with the best reporting in print journalism. But once those exceptions were conceded, TV news was generally dismissed as a journalistic frivolity, a cumbersome beast unequipped to meet the demands of breaking news on a day-to-day basis. By the early 1960s, there already were signs that this attitude was beginning to change as technological advances (for example, the use of videotape, the communications satellites), along with a general strengthening of editorial skills, helped improve the quality of television newscasts. Indeed, news executives at two of the networks, CBS and NBC, were so confident that TV journalism was ready to step up in class that in September 1963—just a few weeks before the Kennedy assassination—they had expanded their evening news programs from fifteen minutes to a half hour. The effect of that move was not immediate; only later would its impact be fully recognized.

But this was not the case with the coverage of those four days in November. The impact of that *was* immediate. The critical acclaim that followed television's performance that weekend was almost startling in its extravagance. From Senator William Proxmire of Wisconsin came this fervent tribute: "Not only was the coverage dignified and immaculate in taste, it was remarkably competent and frequently it soared with imaginative, if tragic beauty. The intelligence and sensitivity of commentary and continuously expressed dedication to this country's strength and solidity in its hour of terrible grief was superb."

Even some of the participating newsmen thought this tribute was a bit much. Journalists, a rather gruff breed, tend to be embarrassed by expressions like "tragic beauty." But there is no doubt that Proxmire's sentiments were shared by millions of other Americans who sat, transfixed, for hours on end in front of their sets that weekend.

If television news, as an entity, enhanced its reputation that weekend, then so did its chief practitioners—the most notable example being Walter Cronkite. From the time of that first bulletin on Friday until Kennedy's burial at Arlington on Monday, Cronkite was the mainstay of CBS's live and continuous coverage. As a result, his was the presence with which millions of Americans most strongly identified. Later, when critics and other viewers expressed admiration for the restraint, the taste, and the all-around professionalism of TV's coverage that weekend, it was Cronkite's performance that was invariably cited. And in the process, a subtle change had begun to take place in the way Cronkite was perceived by the viewing public.

Walter Cronkite was, of course, no stranger to the television audience in 1963. A veteran broadcaster, he had been the TV anchorman for CBS at every political convention since 1952. In addition, he was known to millions as the regular narrator on a series of popular Sunday afternoon broadcasts, starting with the pseudohistorical *You Are There* programs in the early 1950s. By the time he took over as anchorman on the *CBS Evening News* in April 1962, he had established himself as the workhorse of the CBS News team, the correspondent who covered all the major stories, from election nights to space shots. Yet for all his diligence and constant exposure, Cronkite had never acquired, during those early years, the kind of prestige that attached itself to the name of his older CBS colleague, Edward R. Murrow. Nor had he been able to achieve in the early 1960s the popularity of the excellent NBC team of Chet Huntley and David Brinkley. As a matter of fact, there was a growing belief that Cronkite was becoming passé, that his broadcasting style—straightforward reporting with a minimum of adornment—was no longer in tune with the hip and swinging 1960s.

But on the weekend of the Kennedy assassination, Cronkite's sober mien—his natural strength—reflected the mood of the country. His earnest, almost reverent approach, often criticized as being stuffy, now struck many viewers as solid and reassuring. This was the start, for Cronkite, of a new persona or, to be more precise, what was *perceived* as a new persona. In the years ahead, as the country continued to reel through difficult times (a despised war, urban riots, more political assassinations), Cronkite always seemed to be there, on the TV screen, in moments of crisis or travail. Thus the image of solid integrity was steadily reinforced until, eventually, his reputation grew so immense that it extended well beyond the limits of broadcast journalism.

Needless to say, what was sauce for Cronkite was sauce for his network. At the time of the Kennedy assassination, CBS News was in the midst of a severe losing streak. For years, ever since Ed Murrow and his cohorts broke new ground with their radio coverage of World War II, CBS had been the acknowledged leader in broadcast journalism. But by the early 1960s, it had fallen far behind NBC, both in the coverage of such special events as political conventions and in the nightly "ratings war" with *The Huntley-Brinkley Report.* All that was destined to change, and the person most responsible for leading CBS News back to the top was, of course, Walter Cronkite.

Yet there was more to it than that. The people in power at CBS News have always insisted over the years that Cronkite was simply the lead horse in an impressive stable of talent. They would argue that as important as Cronkite was in the struggle to take the play away from NBC, the turnabout could not have been accomplished without the strong bench behind him, the team of gifted reserves. And invariably during the late 1960s, whenever CBS executives talked about the backup strength in their news operation, the first name to be mentioned was Harry Reasoner's.

On the afternoon of November 22, 1963, at the time Cronkite was going on the air with the first bulletin from Dallas, Harry Reasoner was having lunch at a restaurant in midtown Manhattan. Unlike Cronkite, Reasoner viewed going out for lunch as a daily ritual never to be missed except in case of illness or some meteorological calamity. As a rule, his taste ran to stylish, out-of-the-way French restaurants where the emphasis was on good food and quiet talk. But he had spent the morning with a camera crew filming a *CBS Reports* documentary, and at lunchtime he found himself near Lindy's, the raffish Broadway establishment made famous by Damon Runyon. Not at all Reasoner's sort of place, but he decided to give it a try. It proved to be the last as well as the first time in his life that Harry Reasoner dined at Lindy's.

On leaving the restaurant, he caught a taxi. It was the driver who first told him that Kennedy had been shot and might well be dead. Reasoner knew there would be no more work that day on the *CBS*

Reports documentary. He told the cabdriver to stop, then scurried around for the nearest phone to call the office. He was instructed to come in at once to help write and put together a full-length obituary on Kennedy, which he would broadcast sometime that evening. It was a major undertaking; because Kennedy was so young, CBS News did not have a prepared film biography of him, as it did of prominent older public figures, such as Eisenhower, Truman, or Charles de Gaulle. Later in the afternoon, Reasoner was given another important assignment. He was told he would be the anchorman throughout the prime-time hours that evening. He was also told to keep himself available to sit in for Cronkite at other intervals in the days and nights ahead. This came as no great surprise, for by the fall of 1963, Harry Reasoner had become quite accustomed to the role of sitting in for Walter Cronkite.

Reasoner took over the anchor slot that Friday evening, most of which was devoted to the long and moving biography of Kennedy he had helped prepare. He was back on the air the next night to broadcast a wrap-up report on the day of mourning in Washington and elsewhere. But the most dramatic moment for Reasoner came early Sunday afternoon. Again he was at the anchor desk, filling in for Cronkite, when Jack Ruby shot and killed Lee Harvey Oswald in the basement of the Dallas city jail. Those who remember seeing that grisly event *live* were not watching CBS at the time. The only network to broadcast the murder when it actually happened was NBC.

At the moment Oswald was shot, CBS was broadcasting a live report from Washington by Roger Mudd on the preparations for the arrival of Kennedy's body at the Capitol rotunda, where it would lie in state until the next morning. But CBS reporters and cameras were on the scene in Dallas, and Reasoner, who was watching the Oswald story on a closed-circuit monitor, saw it happen—or saw, at least, that *something* had happened. Although seldom given to emotional outbursts, Reasoner began jumping up and down in his chair, screaming for the control room to "switch to Dallas." A few seconds later, the switch was made, and once the confusion began to clear up, details of the story were pieced together. Thanks to videotape, CBS soon was able to broadcast an "instant replay" of the shooting, but later there would be angry postmortems within the network because of the "beat" NBC scored on the event itself.

In the meantime, while there was still widespread confusion over what had happened, Reasoner was handed a wire-service story quoting

Dallas police as saying that Oswald had been shot by a "black man." Reasoner did not remember seeing a black man in all the melee on the closed-circuit monitor, and his instincts told him it would be better not to broadcast the item until more details were known. Later, he would look back on that decision with a considerable sense of satisfaction.

Around the time that Harry Reasoner was calling for his check at Lindy's in New York, Roger Mudd was having lunch in the Senate Dining Room in Washington with two wire-service reporters who also covered Capitol Hill, Warren Duffy of AP and Bill Theis of UPI. Thier meal was interrupted when somebody rushed in with the news that Kennedy had been shot in Dallas. All three men instantly jumped up and headed for the nearest telephones to call their respective offices. Mudd's assignment that afternoon was to round up prominent senators and congressmen for reaction reports to be broadcast later in the day.

He went to the Marble Room in the Senate building, where the wire-service printers were located, and the first sight to greet him there was a cluster of senators gathered around the UPI printer. In the center of the group was Richard Russell of Georgia, then the most prestigious member of the Senate and a bitter foe of President Kennedy on a number of issues, especially civil rights. As the details of the story from Dallas appeared on the printer, Russell hollered them out for all to hear, and as he did so, his voice trembled and tears came streaming down his cheeks. That particular scene would remain vivid in Roger Mudd's memory for many years.

His next major assignment came on Sunday, when he reported on the lying-in-state of Kennedy's body at the Capitol rotunda. Much of the time during those long hours, his own feelings were torn between the banality of trying to stay warm in the chill November air (his vantage point was outside the rotunda) and the solemn grandeur of the event he was reporting.

Mudd had reported on grandeur of another sort three months earlier when he anchored CBS's live coverage of what, up until then, was the biggest domestic story of 1963: the massive civil rights March on Washington, an event highlighted by Martin Luther King's famous "I have a dream" speech. But even though he already was taking on important assignments, Mudd was a relative newcomer to CBS News, having joined the network's Washington bureau in 1961. In the fall of 1963, his rise to journalistic prominence had just begun. And as he stood outside the Capitol rotunda that bleak November weekend, reporting on the crowds that had gathered to mourn the death of one Kennedy, Roger Mudd had no way of knowing what a personal and poignant role he would play at the scene of another tragic event—the second Kennedy assassination, five years later.

For CBS News, the key man at the scene of the first Kennedy assassination was Dan Rather. In the fall of 1963, Rather was even more of a newcomer to the network than Mudd. He was hired in February 1962, and after a few weeks of apprenticeship in New York, he was sent to Dallas to open a new CBS bureau. In working out of Dallas, Rather had acquired a perceptive understanding of the city's prevailing moods and, in particular, of its harsh political climate. Thus, in the fall of 1963, he persuaded his editorial superiors in New York to lay on extra coverage for the President's visit to Dallas. Rather was among those who felt, most acutely, that "something unusual" might happen while Kennedy was in Dallas. And when it was all over, CBS News executives in New York would remember his foresight.

On the day Kennedy arrived in Dallas, Rather's main responsibility was to supervise the overall coverage. Other reporters were assigned to specific aspects of the story, such as the motorcade and the speech Kennedy was scheduled to deliver at the Dallas Trade Mart. But shortly before noon, Rather learned that one of the CBS camera crews was planning to make a "film drop" at a certain point along the motorcade. Having nothing better to do at the moment, he decided to go over to the designated site and wait for it. Hence, it was largely a whim that accounted for Rather's presence on the route of the Presidential motorcade a block or so beyond the Texas School Book Depository.

For Rather, the motorcade, as such, never came. While he stood there waiting, a police car and an open limousine zoomed by at extremely high speed and turned not toward Kennedy's destination, the Dallas Trade Mart, but onto another expressway heading out toward the airport. Only a few seconds passed before it dawned on him that the route to the airport was also the route to the nearest medical facility, Parkland Memorial Hospital. At that moment, Rather felt his first tremor of concern.

He jogged up the hill in the direction from which the limousine had come, and by the time he reached the top he knew that something terrible had happened. Looking down toward the School Book Depository, all he saw was chaos: women on the ground shielding children with their arms, policemen standing with guns drawn and perplexed expressions on their faces, crowds of people shouting and running around in confusion. Rather turned and ran, at full speed, the five blocks back to television station KRLD, the CBS affiliate in Dallas. As he rushed in past the telephone switchboard, he shouted to the operator, "Open the lines to New York and keep them open!" Then, grabbing a phone himself, Rather called Parkland Hospital. The operator there told him she had "heard" that the President had been shot, but she didn't know if it was true or not. She connected him with a doctor who was standing nearby. Rather identified himself, then said, "The lady on the switchboard says that the President has been shot, and I'd like to verify that with you."

"Yes," the doctor replied, "the President has been brought in, and it is my understanding that he's dead."

That statement, along with the eerily calm way the doctor had uttered it, hit Rather with such stunning force that for a moment his mind went blank. Recovering, he asked the doctor to identify himself.

"I'm not the person you need to talk with," came the reply, and with that the doctor hung up. Rather frantically dialed back, but by then the switchboard was jammed and it took what seemed to him an agonizingly long time before he could get through. The doctor he talked to earlier could not be found, so this time a Catholic priest was put on the line. The priest informed Rather that he had seen Kennedy and that he was certain the President was dead.

As Rather hung up the phone, the bulletin slide appeared on the television screen in the KRLD newsroom, and he heard Walter Cronkite's voice broadcasting the UPI report that Kennedy had been shot and that his wounds "perhaps could be fatal." It was as far as anyone was prepared to go at that point. Rather's next move was to get on the direct line to the CBS radio desk in New York. He told the radio editor that he expected to have something in "another minute or so" and to "just hang on." Hunching his shoulder to hold the New York receiver to one ear, Rather then got on a second phone to talk to Eddie Barker, the news director of KRLD, who was at the Trade Mart. Barker said that a Parkland Hospital official who was also at the Trade Mart was telling everyone that Kennedy was dead.

"Yes," said Rather, "that's what I hear, too. That he's dead."

"What was that?" The question came over the other phone from the radio editor in New York, but in his excitement Rather thought it had come from Barker.

"I said that's my information, too. That he's dead."

"Did you say 'dead'?" the radio editor in New York asked. "Are you sure, Dan?"

"Right, dead," said Rather, still thinking he was talking to Barker. "That's the word I get from two people at the hospital."

A few seconds passed, and then Rather heard, through the receiver connected to New York, the voice of Allan Jackson on the CBS radio network with the bulletin that Kennedy was dead. To Rather's horror, Jackson was naming *him* as the source. He began screaming into the phone to New York, "What the hell's the matter with you people? I never authorized that! I never—"

The radio editor, interrupting, recalled the previous conversation in which Rather had said, then had repeated, that Kennedy was dead. Rather now understood what had happened, now realized that it was not Barker's questions he had been answering but the radio editor's. Still, that did not strike him as a legitimate excuse. In loud and angry tones, he accused the New York radio desk of jumping the gun, of acting irresponsibly, of squeezing him into a terrible corner. Then he realized there was no point in arguing. The deed was done. There could be no pulling back.

Tense would be a fairly accurate word to describe the next few minutes in Dan Rather's life. As he wrote many years later, in recalling the queasy sensation that gripped him that afternoon: "It dawned on me that it was possible I had committed a blunder beyond comprehension, beyond forgiving." About fifteen minutes after Allan Jackson had gone on the air with Rather's story, the other two networks, citing their sources, also reported that Kennedy was dead. Rather's period of anxiety was over.

Dan Rather went on from there to provide thorough and accurate coverage of that weekend in Dallas, and his performance was duly noted at network headquarters. That tragic weekend in November 1963 brought an end to Rather's career as a regional journalist who mainly covered stories in the South. Only a few weeks after the assassination, he was appointed CBS News White House correspondent over the heads of several more experienced reporters in Washington.

Beyond Cronkite, Reasoner, Mudd, and Rather, there were many other correspondents who contributed to CBS's coverage of that long weekend. And beyond the on-camera faces, there was a host of other men and women: producers, directors, camera crews, film editors, writers, researchers, and various technicians. Without them, the complex craft of TV journalism could not have come into being at CBS or continued to exist. And hovering over all of them, the "star" correspondents and the off-camera operatives, was another man. For it may also be said that most of the people who have been a part of the CBS News story over the past two decades or so have been conscious, in varying degrees, of a sense of legacy. This legacy or tradition can best be summed up in one word: Murrow.

By the fall of 1963, Edward R. Murrow had been out of television for nearly three years. A few weeks after his election in 1960, John Kennedy had offered Murrow a job as director of the United States Information Agency (USIA). And Murrow, for reasons that had more to do with the internal problems he was having at CBS than with any desire to be a part of Kennedy's New Frontier, accepted the post. But in November 1963, Murrow was seriously ill, having been stricken with lung cancer earlier in the year. He received the news of the assassination in bed at his home in Washington, where he was trying to recuperate from surgery. Murrow never regained his health. The following year, while he was still convalescing, the cancer hit him again; this time it had spread to the brain. He died on April 27, 1965.

Murrow's towering reputation as a broadcast journalist did not die with him. In fact, just the opposite was true. In the years since his death, he has become the stuff of legend, a figure of Olympian stature. Many of the people in power at CBS, some no doubt acting in their own self-interest, have done everything they could to perpetuate the Murrow myth. Since his death, it has been an article of faith at CBS that Murrow's sterling qualities of courage and integrity should serve as the model for broadcast journalists everywhere. Seldom, if ever, on such occasions does anyone mention how CBS agonized over those qualities when Murrow was around, dragging the network into battles it would have preferred to avoid.

It does no great honor to Ed Murrow's memory to enshrine him in myth and platitude. Like all great men, he was both more and less than his legend. What should not be forgotten is that before he was taken over by the mythmakers, there was simply the man and his work, which, by any conceivable standard, was impressive enough.

2 Higher Murrow and Lower Murrow

His presence was so strong, so clearly defined, that it is still easy to recall in vivid detail his most characteristic pose. First of all, there was the inevitable cigarette clutched in his fingers, sending smoke swirling up in front of his face; then, through the smoke, the furrowed brow reflecting his generally bleak view of the world and its future; and beneath the brow, the dark, piercing eyes staring straight into the camera, or into the face of the person he was speaking to at the moment. After his lung cancer, the cigarette was remembered with head-shaking poignancy, but at the time it gave him a certain cachet. It was more than an addiction, and more than a prop. It was an essential extension of his personality, an integral part of his identity, as if were he to appear for any length of time without it, he would somehow cease to be Edward R. Murrow.

The burning cigarette, the creased brow, the steady gaze, in conjunction with his long, thoughtful pauses, helped create the quiet little dramas Murrow was capable of producing on a moment's notice. At the time of the famous *See It Now* broadcast on Senator Joseph McCarthy, the weekly program was being sponsored exclusively by the Aluminum Company of America. During the controversy that followed, a group of Alcoa executives met with Murrow to discuss the situation, and at one point an Alcoa man asked the blunt question: "Mr. Murrow, what are your personal politics?" There followed the long, reflective drag on the cigarette, the rising plumes of smoke, the familiar frown, and finally, after a long, *long* silence, he intoned, "That's none of your damn business." The Alcoa executives smiled at each other and agreed that Mur-

14

row had given the right and proper answer. Yet one of Murrow's CBS colleagues present at the meeting was convinced it wasn't the answer itself that impressed them, but the intense scene preceding it, the taut manner in which Murrow seemed to weigh the question as if his very life depended on the answer he gave.

So there was that about him: an innate and shrewd sense of drama. As a speech major in college in the 1920s, he had played the lead in several campus productions, and many of the gifts he developed then, he later put to use in his broadcasting career. In fact, much of his strength as a personality, as opposed to his strength as a journalist, was the result of his having mastered the art of *playing* himself—Edward R. Murrow. It also is true that it was on the advice of his college drama coach that he injected the famous dramatic pause in his World War II radio broadcasts from London. Thus a rather bland and routine opening line became the celebrated Murrow trademark: "This—is London."

It would be a mistake to make too much of that, however. If Murrow indulged in a bit of theatrical flair, it was never intended as an end in itself. Whether working in radio or television, he would have rejected the notion that the medium is the message. For Murrow, the message, the subject matter of a broadcast, was always the supreme concern. When he resorted to dramatic techniques, it was in an effort to give the message a greater sense of urgency. In a revealing letter to his parents during World War II, he wrote: "I remember you once wanted me to be a preacher, but I had no faith, except in myself. But now I am preaching from a powerful pulpit. Often I am wrong but I am trying to talk as I would have talked were I a preacher. One need not wear a reversed collar to be honest."

So even then, at the outset of his broadcasting career, Murrow saw his role in evangelical terms. From beginning to end, it was his desire to enlighten, to awaken, that distinguished him as a journalist. To cite just one example, consider the closing lines he wrote for the *See It Now* broadcast on McCarthy:

> This is no time for men who oppose Senator McCarthy's methods to keep silent, or for those who approve. We can deny our heritage and our history, but we cannot escape responsibility for the result. There is no way for a citizen of a republic to abdicate his responsibilities. As a nation we have come into our full inheritance at a tender age. We proclaim ourselves —as indeed we are—the defenders of freedom, what's left of it, but we

cannot defend freedom abroad by deserting it at home. The actions of the junior senator from Wisconsin have caused alarm and dismay amongst our allies abroad and given considerable comfort to our enemies, and whose fault is that? Not really his. He didn't create this situation of fear; he merely exploited it, and rather successfully. Cassius was right: "The fault, dear Brutus, is not in our stars but in ourselves." Good night, and good luck.

Those are the words of a man trying to prod his viewers to think, to open their minds to the peril he felt threatened the country. In fact, given everything he later became, it is hardly surprising that it was a consuming interest in education that launched Murrow on his career.

At the time of his graduation from college in 1930, Murrow was president of the National Student Federation of America, and for the next five years he continued to work with student and education organizations, at home and abroad. Then, in 1935, a new job—"director of talks"—was created at the still-fledgling CBS radio network, and on the recommendation of a friend from Student Federation days, it was offered to Murrow. As director of talks, his main responsibility was to line up important guests for serious, informational broadcasts on CBS. He had no interest in broadcasting news himself at this time, although he did dabble a bit in it. One Christmas Eve, following a spirited office party, he spontaneously volunteered to sit in for Robert Trout on his evening news program, wrestling the script away from him with the giddy explanation that Trout was in no condition to read the news. In truth, it was Murrow, and not Trout, who had overindulged at the party. Trout, the top CBS newscaster at the time, sat back, gleefully anticipating a mishmash of slurred words and other flubs. But to his amazement, Murrow proceeded through the broadcast with clarity and zest, never missing a beat—a flawless performance.

Nevertheless, the fact that Murrow went on to become a full-time broadcaster was entirely an accident, and the accident was World War II. In 1937, at the age of twenty-nine, he was sent to London as CBS's European director. Like his previous job, this was essentially an administrative post: setting up speeches and other "special events" for broadcast back home. Then, in March 1938, Hitler swept into Austria. At the time, Murrow was in Poland, where he had gone to set up a CBS *School of the Air* program. He chartered a plane and reached Vienna in time to describe the arrival of the Nazi troops: "Hello, America. . . . Herr Hitler is now at the Imperial Hotel." That was the start, and from there he went on to cover the Munich crisis, the fall of Czechoslovakia, the London blitz, and some of the major European battles of the war.

It is not precisely true that Ed Murrow created radio journalism. By the late 1930s, newscasts had become an established part of network programming. But along with the fine team of reporters he hired (a group that became known, inevitably, as "Murrow's boys"), he greatly advanced the form. His most impressive contribution was to shift the emphasis away from the static world of studio newscasts to the "beat" reporter at the scene. No longer did radio journalism primarily consist of reading or rephrasing information that came from other sources. Murrow and his "boys" covered the news themselves.

Some of the reporters he hired away from newspapers and wire services in those early years had trouble adjusting to radio. But Murrow himself was a natural. It is no doubt true that his lack of newspaper experience worked to his advantage, for to borrow a favorite phrase of his, he was not "contaminated by the conventions of print." Nevertheless, Elmer Davis, one of the first journalists to go from a distinguished career in print to a distinguished career in radio, once wrote that he was "faintly scandalized" that such good reporting could be done by a man who had never worked on a newspaper. Early on, Murrow developed the habit of dictating his pieces instead of writing them down. The words and rhythms were thus shaped, from the start, to engage the ear rather than the eye. Some of his touches were nothing less than inspired. On one occasion during the blitz, seeking to convey the quiet courage of Londoners under siege, he held a microphone on the sidewalk to pick up the sound of footsteps moving calmly toward the bomb shelters.

When he finally came home after the war, it was as a celebrity. He had elevated radio journalism to new levels of respectability, and, in the years ahead, he would leave just as strong an imprint on television.

Murrow greeted the arrival of television with all the wariness of a foot soldier entering an enemy mine field. To the end of his life, he remained firm in his belief that radio was the purer medium, the more honest medium. Television, he thought, was overly collaborative; a TV reporter had to rely too much on camera crews and other technicians who were not necessarily motivated by journalistic concerns. Nor was he happy with the "show-biz" aspects of television, the tendency to use visual effects to heighten and exaggerate, thus leaving the viewer with a misleading impression. Still, Murrow recognized that television was destined to become a medium of awesome power and that, given his position, he had no choice but to try to channel some of that power in the right direction. But his move into TV was cautious and restrained. He did some on-camera reporting at the 1948 political conventions, but it wasn't until three years later that he committed himself to television on a regular basis.

By this time, he had hooked up with Fred Friendly, an ebullient and energetic man whose interest in news and public affairs was more than matched by his enthusiasm for the technological advances in radio and television. The Murrow-Friendly association began in 1947, when they collaborated on a record album of recent historical events that had been broadcast on radio. Murrow's narrative skill and Friendly's technical ability proved to be a winning combination. The album, called *I Can Hear It Now,* enjoyed spectacular success and led to several sequels. Coming off that experience, Friendly went to work for CBS as Murrow's producer on a weekly radio documentary program called, naturally enough, *Hear It Now.* From there, the obvious next step for both men was to television, and *See It Now.*

The first *See It Now* broadcast, in November 1951, was basically a "media event," as television took the opportunity to rejoice in its own technology. In September of that year, engineers had succeeded in splicing together, by microwave relay and coaxial cable, the nation's first coast-to-coast television system. In its eventual impact, this technological feat was comparable to the driving of the Golden Spike in 1869 that linked America's railways from one coast to the other. So the first *See It Now* broadcast was a celebration of that achievement. Seated in a swivel chair, Murrow invited his viewers to enjoy the privilege of seeing—live and simultaneously—pictures of the Golden Gate Bridge in San Francisco and the Brooklyn Bridge in New York. More than anything else, that first *See It Now* program drove home the message that the country had entered a new era of communications.

In his introductory remarks on that first broadcast, Murrow told his viewers that "this is an old team trying to learn a new trade." The learning process would extend over the next two years or so, and, during that time, *See It Now* offered little in the way of memorable television. There were some exceptions, a notable one coming in December 1952, when *See It Now* did an hour-long piece on what Christmas was like for the troops fighting in Korea. But for the most part, as the Murrow-Friendly team struggled to learn its new trade, those early TV efforts lacked both the force and the imagination that had character-ized Murrow's great radio broadcasts during World War II.

From the vantage point of later years, when Murrow became en-gulfed in controversy, some of his friends at CBS looked back on the early 1950s as a period of innocence and happy times. Working on the formative *See It Now* broadcasts was not unlike playing with a new toy, and there was a great sense of fun. Murrow had his lighter side, and it surfaced from time to time. But even in those relatively easygoing days, he was never much of a mixer, never really one of the boys. In a profession known for its brashness, he was genuinely shy and reserved, a deeply private person. Surrounded by garrulous men, he was given to reticence and long bouts of brooding. Even when he did make a gesture toward familiarity, he often did so in a somber and portentous way. For example, one day during this period, Murrow joined a group of young CBS reporters who were engaged in a casual bull session. His contribution dramatically changed the tone of their conversation. "Gentlemen," he asked, "what do you think is the most important problem facing the world today?"

The compassion that people recognized in his voice and manner stemmed from a deep sense of melancholy and foreboding. Not every-one who worked with Murrow appreciated his "gloom-and-doom" atti-tude, as one critic called it. Once, during World War II, a CBS executive in New York, who was urgently trying to locate Murrow, called the BBC office in London and asked if he was there. "Oh, yes," said the English-man who took the call, "he's somewhere around here wearing his cus-tomary crown of thorns." When Murrow was courting his wife, he warned her to beware of his depressions and black moods. Years later, Janet Murrow said of him, "Ed is a sufferer."

On the air, he always came across as fluent and firmly in control, but it was a triumph of will over temperament. His viewers or listeners had no inkling of the private tension that often preceded a broadcast. It was his habit to keep a bottle of Scotch at his feet, from which he almost always took at least one healthy belt before going on the air. Even when doing a routine radio newscast, his foot jiggled up and down in a nervous spasm, and often, by the time he bade his listeners "Good night, and good luck," his shirt would be damp with perspiration. For all his natural gifts as a broadcaster, he never succeeded in conquering the jitters, the stage fright of his profession, which is one reason why he was never a facile ad-libber. On the other hand, a case of the jitters would have been understandable on the night of March 9, 1954. But never did Murrow appear more calm and intent on his purpose than that night when he looked into the camera and said, "Good evening. Tonight, *See It Now* devotes its entire half hour to a report on Senator Joseph R. McCarthy, told mainly in his own words and pictures."

Strictly on its own terms, the McCarthy broadcast was a major milestone in the history of TV journalism. But that apparently has not been enough to satisfy some of Murrow's more ardent mythologizers, who have seen fit to embellish the event and make of it something it was not. Hence, the need to try to set the record straight.

First of all, Murrow was never the flaming liberal he has become in retrospect to some of those who revere the legend. Like so many other Americans at that time, he was a dedicated cold-warrior whose concern over the threat of Communism, at home and abroad, was as great as that of some of McCarthy's most loyal supporters. On the issue of civil rights, Murrow leaned toward a progressive view, but in doing so, he constantly had to struggle with his Southern heritage. (Although he spent most of his early years in the Pacific Northwest, Murrow was born in North Carolina, and he generally looked upon that region as his native soil.) Once, when Joe Wershba, a talented young reporter on the *See It Now* unit, gently chided him about his cautious approach to civil rights, a pained expression came over Murrow's face and he said, "Joe, you have to understand that I'm a Southern boy. It's harder for me." Nevertheless Murrow was passionately committed to civil liberties, and this meant, among other things, that he firmly believed in the right of free men to speak out, on any issue, without fear of reprisal. That alone was enough to convince him that McCarthyism could not be tolerated in silence.

Furthermore, it's one thing to say that McCarthy was badly cut up by the Murrow broadcast (which he was), but quite another to claim that the senator and his cause were destroyed by it. McCarthy himself still had a few innings left, even though he was, by this time, clearly on the wane. More to the point, the poison associated with his name continued to fester over the next several years. Certainly the infamous "blacklist," which left such an indelible stain on Murrow's own broadcasting industry, was unaffected by the McCarthy program. It continued to operate at full force, ruining lives and careers, until the early 1960s.

Finally, Murrow was *not* the first major journalist to take on McCarthy. By 1954, the senator had been denounced in any number of newspaper columns and magazine articles. Even within the narrower confines of broadcast journalism, Elmer Davis and Eric Sevareid, as well as others, had been putting the wood to McCarthy in their radio commentaries during the years leading up to the *See It Now* program. As Sevareid remarked many years later, "We were trying, on radio, to keep the salient open so that when the time came, Ed and Friendly could drive their big tank through."

That was the difference: television was the big tank, the one with the cannon. And no one was more acutely aware of that than Murrow himself. For well over a year before the broadcast, his friends and colleagues had been urging him, with steadily diminishing patience, to bring his personal prestige and the power of television into the fight against McCarthyism. They argued that Murrow's own reputation was at stake, that his fine record of heroism under fire during World War II was now being questioned. His detractors, they told him, were saying that physical courage in the face of a common enemy was one thing, but that the kind of moral courage required to speak out against McCarthy was something else again.

Still, Murrow held back. He rejected as inappropriate the suggestion that he simply go on television and make a speech attacking McCarthy. If he was going to use the power of television and his own prestige against McCarthy, then he had to have the right format. He believed that the most effective way to expose McCarthy was to let McCarthy expose himself, in clips and footage gleaned from the senator's own public performance. That required time and patience. Finally, in early 1954, the elements he wanted had been pulled together, and *See It Now* was ready to tell the story of Joe McCarthy "in his own words and pictures."

Even with this shrewd approach, Murrow fully anticipated the storm that followed. A few seconds before the McCarthy broadcast began, Friendly leaned over and whispered to him, "This is going to be a tough one." His face set in a taut expression, Murrow replied, "Yes, and after this one they're all going to be tough."

The McCarthy broadcast drastically changed Ed Murrow's life and career. Up until then, he had been an unequivocal asset to CBS, the network's "great ornament," as he was called. He emerged from the McCarthy program with a more formidable reputation than ever, but while most of the reaction to the broadcast was favorable, some of it was not, and, as a result, Murrow suddenly became a divisive influence. Not long after the broadcast, a public-opinion poll, commissioned by CBS president Frank Stanton, disclosed that of those questioned, 33 percent said they believed Murrow was pro-Communist. In Stanton's view, this was extremely distressing news, not only for Murrow but for CBS.

Nevertheless, the storm might well have blown itself out if after the McCarthy show *See It Now* had reverted to the routine interviews and innocuous subjects of its early years. As Fred Friendly later wrote about those early programs: "The missing ingredients were conviction, controversy and a point of view." By the night of the McCarthy broadcast, those ingredients were there, and from then on, there was no turning back. In the months that followed, there were broadcasts on other sensitive subjects, including an interview with the brilliant but controversial physicist J. Robert Oppenheimer, the first hard look by a TV network at school segregation in the South, and a grimly prophetic two-part report on the relationship between smoking and lung cancer. So the heavy flak over *See It Now* continued, and among those caught in the middle of it was the all-powerful Chairman of CBS—William S. Paley.

The vast CBS broadcasting empire was Paley's personal creation. His father, a Russian-Jewish immigrant, had made a fortune in the cigar business, and young Bill Paley was expected to follow in his footsteps. But in 1928, he decided instead to pursue a career in radio, then a new industry with an uncertain future. Sam Paley put up the $400,000 his twenty-seven-year-old son needed to buy a controlling interest in the Columbia Broadcasting System, a financially frail network struggling through the first year of its existence. At the time, CBS consisted of sixteen radio stations, all east of the Mississippi and north of the Mason-Dixon line. By the end of 1928, it had in its fold forty-nine affiliate stations. Bill Paley and CBS were on their way.

But CBS did not have an easy time of it during those early years. NBC, the older and far more powerful network, completely dominated entertainment programming and had a tight hold on almost all the big sponsors. Faced with that situation, Paley chose to concentrate on news and public affairs. More than anything else at that point, Paley wanted to infuse CBS with an aura of class and respectability, and an emphasis on news and other "serious" programs was the quickest and surest way to accomplish that. He also reasoned, with customary shrewdness, that such prestige, once attained, could later be parlayed into power and profits.

So the strong commitment to news was there from the start, even before the emergence of Murrow and his group. But their work during World War II greatly enhanced CBS's reputation as the leader in broadcast journalism. The war also brought Paley and Murrow together in a more personal way. Until then they scarcely knew each other, but in 1943, Paley took a leave of absence from his CBS executive suite and went to London to serve on General Eisenhower's psychological warfare staff. He was already an admirer of Murrow's radio broadcasts and, as the two men moved through the same social circles in wartime London, they became close friends. The friendship, which continued in New York after the war, was a mutually advantageous one: Paley enjoyed being on intimate terms with his network's "great ornament," and Murrow relished the power that came with easy and direct access to the corporate lion of CBS.

But the postwar years also brought sweeping changes that eventually complicated the Murrow-Paley relationship. In 1948, as the networks began shifting the emphasis from radio to television, Bill Paley decided that two decades of being second to NBC in entertainment programming were enough. He realized that drastic measures were required to make CBS number one, but that didn't faze him. The time had come for bold action. No more Mr. Nice Guy. So, in a dazzling coup that stunned the broadcasting industry, Paley managed, through an artful combination of financial inducement and personal charm, to lure Jack Benny and other top stars away from NBC. In effect, he stole the nucleus of NBC's prime-time talent. In doing so, Paley violated a long-standing gentlemen's agreement he had with his NBC counterpart, General David Sarnoff, not to steal each other's stars. A few days after the talent raid, an enraged General Sarnoff called Chairman Paley to ask how he could have stooped to such a low and larcenous tactic. Paley's reply was concise and imperious: "Because I needed them."

The raid on NBC accomplished its purpose. With Jack Benny and other big stars in its lineup, CBS went on to become the perennial leader in prime-time television ratings. This meant, among other things, that the network no longer had to rely quite as much on the prestige of its news department. Paley continued to esteem Murrow and the news operation in general, but he knew it was the entertainers —Benny, Lucille Ball, Jackie Gleason, et al—who accounted for the huge, escalating profits that began pouring in as soon as Madison Avenue discovered that television was the greatest advertising medium ever invented. The profits, in turn, enabled CBS to diversify, to expand its power beyond broadcasting into other influential areas, such as publishing. And Bill Paley, the man astride this incredible tidal wave of success, wanted it all: the prestige and the profits and the enormous power that resulted from CBS's growth into a vast conglomerate.

A heavy reliance on entertainment programming had the further advantage of being safe, and that, too, was an important corporate consideration. For the postwar era also brought about a significant change in the nation's political climate. During World War II, when Murrow was building up his reputation as a courageous reporter, the overriding issue was clear-cut, the battle line precisely drawn. On one side were Ed Murrow, Bill Paley, and the U.S. government, plus all decent and patriotic Americans and their allies abroad. On the other were Hitler's *Wehrmacht* and the imperial forces of Japan. Never again, in the decades to come, would the country be so unified in a common purpose. Indeed, the rise of McCarthyism was one of the first manifestations of the discords and passions that began to fragment America in the postwar era. In taking a strong stand on that issue on television, Murrow inevitably antagonized many viewers even as he heartened many others. For that reason alone, such a controversial program did not sit well with those CBS executives who, with their focus on ratings and sales and commercial profits, were primarily committed to the dubious goal of trying to please everyone, and in as inoffensive a way as possible.

Finally, there was television itself—the big tank. With its visual impact and its power to engage the full attention of its audience, television hit nerves and emotions seldom reached by radio. In the years ahead, Paley and other CBS officials would become reconciled to the heightened, provocative effect of TV journalism. With the exception of a couple of regrettable lapses, they would support the network's television coverage of controversial issues and events. But in the 1950s, that was a new and disturbing phenomenon. Murrow's *See It Now* program was the bold pioneer—the first that ever burst into that silent sea—and both Murrow and *See It Now* were destined to pay a heavy price for that breakthrough.

On the evening of the McCarthy broadcast, Bill Paley called his good friend Ed Murrow and gave him a personal message: "Ed, I'm with you today, and I'll be with you tomorrow." It was a thoughtful gesture. A touching show of support. But the real question was whether Paley would be with Murrow the day *after* tomorrow, and in the years ahead. The answer was no.

In the months following the McCarthy show, as Murrow and Friendly delved into other sensitive subjects, Paley and others on the corporate level became increasingly irritated by all the furor *See It Now* was causing. As Friendly later wrote: "The attitude at CBS was: 'Why does Murrow have to save the world every week?' " Clearly overlooked was the fact that many of the post-McCarthy *See It Now* broadcasts— for example, an affectionate portrait of Carl Sandburg, a casual look at Las Vegas, a report on the Salk polio vaccine—weren't at all controversial. Still, the impression persisted within the corporate hierarchy that Murrow had become a weekly messiah. And eventually, the nervous desire to dilute *See It Now*'s impact, along with the related push for more popular programming and ever-higher ratings, led to the decision to reduce the frequency of Murrow's sermons.

In the summer of 1955, a little more than a year after the McCarthy broadcast, Paley ordered that *See It Now* be changed from a weekly half-hour program to a one-hour show, to be broadcast only eight times over the course of a year. He explained to Murrow and Friendly that this leisurely schedule would give them more time to prepare stories in depth, but he neglected to explain that they would lose the relevance and continuity of a weekly broadcast, that had been so much a part of *See It Now*'s strength. (Wags on Madison Avenue soon began calling it *See It Now and Then.*) Then, in 1956, Paley moved *See It Now* out of prime time altogether, consigning it to a far more harmless slot on Sunday afternoon. In spite of this, the program continued to make waves, to stir up trouble, until finally, in the spring of 1958, the day of reckoning came.

Murrow and Friendly were summoned to Paley's office to discuss a dispute that had arisen over a recent broadcast. In the course of the meeting, they suddenly realized that Paley wanted to take *See It Now* off the air entirely, and that he was merely using this latest squabble as a pretext for doing so. A spirited argument followed, according to Friendly, who recalled the confrontation in his book, *Due to Circumstances Beyond Our Control:* "A forty-five minute scene ensued in which these commanding figures, the industry's foremost reporter and its top executive . . . faced each other in a blazing showdown with all guns firing."

At one point, Murrow demanded, "Bill, are you going to destroy all this? Don't you want an instrument like the *See It Now* organization to continue?"

"Yes," said Paley, "but I don't want this constant stomachache every time you do a controversial subject."

"I'm afraid that's a price you have to be willing to pay," said Murrow. "It goes with the job."

Not with Bill Paley's job, it didn't. The subject was closed, and *See It Now* was dead.

Murrow may have lost the battle over the survival of *See It Now*, but he wasn't through fighting. Indeed, his next move was hardly designed to bring comfort to Paley's sensitive stomach. In the fall of 1958, just three months after the last *See It Now* broadcast, he went to Chicago to address a national meeting of radio and television news directors. His speech there turned out to be nothing less than a blistering attack on his own industry and, by implication, on his friend and superior, Bill Paley. Future historians looking at television, he said, "will find recorded, in black and white or color, evidence of decadence, escapism, and insulation from realities of the world in which we live. . . . If we go on as we are, then history will take its revenge." Paley was furious. This was treachery. In his view, Murrow had betrayed him and the industry that had brought him so much fame and fortune.

Yet Murrow's Chicago speech could not have been more prescient, for the following year, 1959, was the year of the great TV quiz-show scandals. The evidence of decadence and escapism was there for all to see. The television networks were found to be involved in an outrageous scheme of fraud and deception.

The crisis of the quiz-show scandals brought out the best in Frank Stanton. By the late 1950s, Stanton was as firmly ensconced in his position as the number two man in the corporation as Paley was in his at the top of the executive structure. If Paley was the Chairman Mao of CBS, then Stanton was very much its Chou En-lai: the administrative technician and suave negotiator with both friends and foes in the world outside broadcasting. He came to CBS in 1935 with a doctorate in psychology from Ohio State University, an academic achievement that meant a great deal to him. (During his years of eminence at CBS, he invariably was referred to as *Dr.* Stanton, a practice he quietly encouraged.) His Ph.D. dissertation—an august tome entitled *A Critique of Present Methods and a New Plan for Studying Radio Listening Behav-*

ior—had come to the attention of CBS executives in New York, and he was hired as a $55-a-week audience research specialist. Over the next ten years, he steadily advanced through the CBS hierarchy, and when Paley came marching home from the war in 1945, he anointed himself Chairman and made Stanton president of the corporation.

Like Paley, Stanton was an adroit businessman who was profoundly committed to the welfare and growth of CBS. But the two men differed in other respects. Paley was essentially a showman, an impresario, whose great love was programming. He had an exceptional eye and ear for talent, or at least the kind of talent that appealed to mass audiences. Most shows that made their way into the CBS schedule bore his personal stamp of approval, his instinctive feel for the national taste. And over the years, Paley became attached to many of his network's big hits, doting on such long-running winners as *I Love Lucy* and *Gunsmoke.*

Frank Stanton also had a clear idea of what viewers liked to watch. His approach, however, was not that of an impresario, but of a highly skilled researcher. He was primarily a man of charts and data and statistical analysis. The research methods he developed back in the 1930s were established to determine, in advance, how big an audience a specific program was likely to attract, and that information was used as a selling point to potential sponsors. Inevitably, both advertisers and network officials opted for shows that would appeal to the largest possible audience, and thus began the systematic process of catering to the lowest common denominator of taste. So Stanton's meticulous research procedures also contributed, first in radio and then in television, to the kind of programming that, twenty years later, Murrow would denounce as decadent and escapist. Indeed, when the quiz-show mania struck in the mid-1950s, Stanton said in defense of it, "A program in which a large part of the audience is interested is by that very fact . . . in the public interest."

Yet Stanton himself was certainly no fan of quiz shows or, for that matter, of most prime-time television programs. While he studied and justified mass-audience preferences, he had almost none of Paley's enthusiasm for programming, and he generally kept as much distance as possible between himself and the show-biz world of CBS. As a matter of fact, Stanton's personal distaste for that world was such that he fought a stubborn and largely futile battle over the years to dissuade people from calling news offerings "shows." He even thought the word "program" was a shade too vulgar for such a serious and uplifting exercise.

The correct term, in his stern judgment, was "news broadcast."

This austere and fastidious attitude made Stanton an ideal choice for the role Paley delegated to him in the early years of television. For all his zest for power and sense of showmanship, Paley was in many ways a retiring man who shunned the limelight and, in particular, the arena of government inquiry into the policies and practices of broadcasting. So, at Paley's urging, Stanton became CBS's chief lobbyist and spokesman, representing the company at Congressional hearings and at other public forums. It proved to be a master stroke on Paley's part and a boon to Stanton's own reputation. With his academic title, his reserved and stately manner, and his persuasive sincerity, Frank Stanton made an excellent front man, a superb Mr. Clean. The more time he spent in Washington dealing with sublime, abstract questions, such as censorship and television's rights under the First Amendment, the farther he moved away from the world of garish commercials and pedestrian programming. As the years passed, Stanton came to be regarded as broadcasting's foremost statesman, and, more than anything else, it was his vigorous and admirable response to the 1959 quiz-show scandals that elevated him to that stature.

While other network executives tried to make self-serving excuses or merely cringed before the scorn of Congressional interrogators, Stanton forthrightly acknowledged that CBS had been remiss in not keeping a tighter rein on its quiz shows. Yet he also insisted, with some eloquence, that it was up to the television industry to clean up its own mess, and he vowed that his network would take every possible step in that direction. There are many who believe that it was Stanton's performance that saved the networks from being brought under government control at that time.

In the fall of 1959, one year after Murrow's attack on the TV industry, Stanton addressed the same group of radio and television news directors. Reacting to the scandals, he promised to impose tighter restrictions on all CBS television shows. There would be no more rigging of any kind, no more "hanky-panky," as he called it. Later, when asked in an interview to be more specific about just what he meant by "hanky-panky," Stanton cited, among other examples, the popular program *Person to Person*. That show, he said, gave the false impression that its interviews were spontaneous when, in fact, they were rehearsed in advance. It was not necessary for him to add that for six years the star on *Person to Person* had been Edward R. Murrow. It had been awhile in coming, but if Murrow could take a slap at the corporate power of CBS, then CBS could take a slap at Murrow. *Quid pro quo.*

At the time, Murrow was in London on a sabbatical. When he learned about Stanton's remarks, it was his turn to be furious. His public reply, a model of intemperance, said, in part: "Dr. Stanton has finally revealed his ignorance both of news and of requirements of television production." The Murrow-Stanton dispute made front-page headlines as CBS seemed to be trying to set some kind of record for washing its dirty linen in public. Paley and Stanton sent a CBS lawyer to London to obtain from Murrow a face-saving apology or his resignation. Murrow refused to give either.

The quarrel over *Person to Person* brought to a head the strains and frictions that had long been simmering between Murrow and Stanton. Years later, Stanton would insist that the problems between them were never as severe as others made them out to be, but he did not deny that there had been problems. The pity of it was that Stanton and Murrow had much in common. They were the same age, they had begun their CBS careers at the same time, and, although they took divergent paths, they both were brilliant enough to rise rapidly to the top of their profession. Even more to the point, the two men ultimately came to share the same ideals and concerns about broadcasting. But whatever respect they had for each other was marred by a mutual jealousy, a sense of rivalry that centered on Bill Paley.

The problems began shortly after Stanton became president of CBS. As he acquired more and more executive power, Murrow grew to resent his influence over the corporate side of Paley. Whenever network decisions were made that Murrow didn't like, he privately blamed Stanton—whom he derisively called "the Bookkeeper"—and not his friend, Paley. For his part, Stanton resented the fact that Murrow was much closer to Paley, in personal terms, than he was. For example, he was deeply hurt when he discovered that Paley had invited Murrow to his second wedding in 1947, to the beautiful socialite Barbara "Babe" Cushing, while he, Stanton, was not invited. The wound from that snub rankled him for many years.

Then, too, there was the new situation that had developed by 1959. In the aftermath of the McCarthy program, Murrow was often hailed as "the conscience of the broadcasting industry," an esteem he richly enjoyed. But later, in the wake of the quiz scandals, Stanton suddenly became the voice of reform and high purpose in television. Moreover, Stanton believed that the chief spokesman for integrity in broadcasting should be a top executive and not a working journalist, even one of Murrow's stature. Hence, a subtle rivalry developed between them on that front, which further aggravated their relationship.

This was the uneasy background against which the *Person to Person* fight erupted. Still, there was more to it than that.

The truth is that *Person to Person* was not the most edifying chapter in Ed Murrow's career. What the mythmakers tend to overlook is the fact that to the majority of Americans in the 1950s, Murrow was principally known not as the crusading journalist on *See It Now* but as the urbane "houseguest" on *Person to Person*, which was, in essence, a gossipy talk show. Most of the homes the *Person to Person* cameras visited once a week were those of tabloid celebrities, movie stars and the like. Marilyn Monroe, clad in a tight-fitting sweater, was a much-ballyhooed "hostess" on one program, while on another, Mickey Spillane bounced around his rumpus room on a pogo stick. Some of the celebrities were more substantial figures, such as statesmen or religious leaders, but the nature of the show was such that it called, almost exclusively, for light banter and trivia. Since Murrow was Murrow, he was able to bring to this piffle more dignity than it deserved, but most of the time on *Person to Person* he seemed to be going against the grain of his true identity and vocation. The critic John Lardner dubbed the news broadcasts "Higher Murrow," and *Person to Person* "Lower Murrow."

From the time it first went on the air in 1953, Murrow was deeply ambivalent about *Person to Person*. It was the brainchild of his two radio writers, Jesse Zousmer and Johnny Aaron, and he was fond of saying he did the show to help "Jesse and Johnny pick up a little change." Actually, Murrow himself picked up an impressive pile of change from *Person to Person*. Under an unusual arrangement, he and the two writers owned the show themselves and took in huge profits; later, when it was sold to CBS, Paley paid an estimated $1 million for it.

Murrow was fascinated by the show's enormous popularity. When Bill Downs, a colleague from the World War II days, accused him of "whoring" on *Person to Person*, Murrow just smiled and said, "Yes, but look at all those voyeurs." In the uproar that followed the McCarthy broadcast, "all those voyeurs" proved to be a blessing. One reason Murrow was able to withstand that storm was that millions of Americans simply refused to believe that this nice man who talked to Marilyn Monroe in her boudoir could be, of all things, a Communist. Yet at other times Murrow clearly regarded *Person to Person* as an embarrassment. "I hate that goddamn show," he once said in a flash of temper, "it's so damn demeaning." Then, a moment later, he added, "But it really makes a lot of money."

The point can be made that Murrow wanted it both ways. If in his role as "conscience of the industry" he attacked the "decadence" in network television, he was also making a bundle as the star of a show as crassly commercial, in its way, as the drivel he denounced.

From the start, Frank Stanton was opposed to the idea of Murrow doing *Person to Person* and becoming involved in the "show-business" side of television. Perhaps that was in the back of his mind when he singled out *Person to Person* as a show that employed deceptive techniques. His criticism of *Person to Person* was basically a cheap shot, for whatever fakery went into that program was kid stuff compared to the tawdry deceits of the quiz shows. But Stanton surely knew what he was doing. More than anything else, the slap at *Person to Person* served to remind Murrow what it is that people who live in glass houses are not supposed to do.

In June 1959, Fred Friendly was offered the job of producing a new CBS documentary series, to be broadcast once a month in prime time. Plans for the new program, to be called *CBS Reports*, had been unveiled by Stanton in a speech earlier that spring, but Friendly never dreamed he would be asked to take charge of the project. It meant, he assumed, the resurrection of the Murrow-Friendly team on a large scale; the good old days of *See It Now* were to be revived. Well, no, he was told, not exactly. Murrow was about to go on his leave of absence, and in order to get the new show off the ground and on a steady course, Friendly would need to use other correspondents as well. Although he was nervous about this stipulation, Friendly agreed to it—on a temporary basis.

When Murrow returned from his sabbatical in the summer of 1960, Friendly went back to Paley and Stanton to say that it was his understanding that Murrow now would assume a dominant role in the *CBS Reports* series, just as he had on *See It Now*. No, he was told, he had misunderstood. He was, of course, free to use Murrow on *some* of the programs, but on others, he must continue to employ the services of other correspondents. Paley and Stanton made it clear that *CBS Reports* was not going to become a Murrow-Friendly operation the way *See It Now* had been. When Friendly protested and began to talk about Murrow's unique status in broadcast journalism, Paley interrupted him to ask what it was that he, Friendly, had against Howard K. Smith, who had been the anchorman on many *CBS Reports* programs during Murrow's absence. Or if he was not all that happy with Smith, what did he have against Eric Sevareid or Charles Collingwood?

The corporate screws were being turned. By insisting that *CBS Reports* be centered around Murrow, Friendly was being maneuvered into the awkward position of seeming to thwart the careers of other top CBS correspondents, all of whom had been close friends and colleagues of Murrow since the World War II days. Friendly naturally had his own ambitions, and he knew that if he protested too vehemently, *CBS Reports* might be taken away from him altogether and given to a less troublesome producer. For Fred Friendly, who owed his entire television career to Murrow, the situation was not a pleasant one.

Actually, Murrow was the correspondent on the major *CBS Reports* program in the fall of 1960, and it turned out to be one of the best documentaries of his entire career. Called *Harvest of Shame*, it was a piercing and poignant report on the plight of America's migrant workers. When it was broadcast, Frank Stanton called Friendly to say he had "never been so proud of CBS." But if *Harvest of Shame* added still another laurel to Murrow's list of achievements, it was, for him, a bittersweet triumph. For despite this latest success, Murrow was fully aware that things were not the same as they had been before.

The days of frequent and direct access to Paley were over. Worse, his quarrel with Stanton had never been resolved, and relations between them were now cooler than ever. What made that situation so difficult for Murrow (in *his* view, at least) was the fact that Stanton was exerting more and more influence on the news operation. *CBS Reports* had been Stanton's idea, and it had been his decision to entrust the series to Friendly. Moreover, by the fall of 1960, Stanton's corporate protégé, a tough-minded lawyer named Richard Salant, was on the verge of taking over as president of the CBS news division. Clearly, a new regime was settling in at the controls of CBS News, and with it would come a new era. Whatever role Murrow might have in that era would be greatly reduced from the one he had enjoyed in the "good old days" of World War II and the early *See It Now* years. So, in early 1961, when the newly elected John Kennedy offered him the USIA post, Murrow welcomed it with a sense of relief and gratitude. Years later, his widow would remember Kennedy's offer as "a brilliant and timely gift."

But Murrow's personal frustrations at CBS, which had so much to do with his decision to leave network journalism, were only part of a larger and more depressing concern. By 1960, he had become more pessimistic than ever about the future of television. He was convinced that the networks had been taken over completely by hucksters, and, knowing what their values were, he believed that television had missed its opportunity to become an influential force in the area of news and public affairs. Given his own experience and the prevailing situation at the time, one can understand why Murrow felt this way. Yet the truth is, he could not have been more mistaken.

At the time Murrow left CBS, the prime-time documentary was regarded as TV journalism's most important and influential format. So when Paley decided to scrap *See It Now,* the most advanced documentary of its time, Murrow saw it as a mortal blow directed against the very best that television news had to offer. Moreover, he had no faith in *CBS Reports* as a long-term venture. He suspected it was little more than a public-relations ploy on Frank Stanton's part, and once the heat of the quiz scandals wore off, it would follow *See It Now* into the graveyard.

But what Murrow could not envision was the remarkable evolution, in quality and influence, of the evening news format. In the 1950s, the evening news on television was little more than a visual version of a radio newscast, and no one paid much attention to it. But by the middle 1960s, the evening news had become the showcase of TV journalism. In any number of areas—from civil rights to space exploration, from Vietnam to Watergate—the day-to-day thrust of the evening news would have more impact than any documentary could hope to achieve. So if the documentary diminished in importance in the 1960s, it was not because of any timidity on the part of network executives (although there was, as always, plenty of that), but because the documentary form simply could not compete with the cumulative force of the evening news.

As a matter of fact, even in Murrow's time, the so-called golden age of television, the impact of documentaries was greatly exaggerated. A case in point is *Harvest of Shame.* Like the McCarthy broadcast, it touched off a strong reaction. Public anguish was genuine, but the subject was soon forgotten and very little was done to alleviate the problem. So little, in fact, that ten years later, in 1970, NBC broadcast an excellent documentary on the same subject (called *Migrant*), and it revealed that almost nothing had changed: the migrant workers were still being brutally exploited. By way of contrast, TV journalism in the post-Murrow era would grow to have a devastating impact, and almost all of it came from the evening news format, the night-after-night pounding away at critical issues. How delighted Lyndon Johnson would have been if the coverage of the Vietnam War had been confined to a one-hour documentary with no immediate follow-up. And the mind can scarcely fathom the joy that would have coursed through Richard Nixon's veins if coverage of the Watergate scandal could have been similarly restricted.

Ironically, ten years after Murrow's 1958 speech attacking the networks for their "escapism and insulation from realities," the very opposite concern was being expressed: namely, that television now was giving the people *too much* reality. In 1968, Reuven Frank, then president of NBC News, met that accusation head-on. Speaking before the same forum of radio and television news directors that Murrow had addressed a decade earlier, Frank said, "I gather Americans are tired of television forcing them to look at the world they live in. I refuse to consider that we can do anything else."

By then, not only had television come to dominate journalism, but the real world—that is, news—had become a significant part of television. Far from being submerged and kept in fetters, as Murrow once feared, television news had acquired such power that it would play a major role in driving two strong-willed Presidents out of office. There is no way of knowing how Murrow would have reacted to this dramatic change in the TV journalism he helped to pioneer. For by the time all this was happening, Edward R. Murrow was dead.

3 The Outcast, the Gray Eminence, and the Duke

At the time of Murrow's death in 1965, the legend had already taken root, and in the years that followed, it proceeded to grow to epic proportions. Although journalists often lean toward cynicism (especially when dealing with legends), the overall tendency among those who worked at CBS News was to honor the Murrow tradition. They believed that CBS represented the very best in broadcast journalism, and they attributed its position of leadership in large part to the standards set by Murrow and their own efforts to measure up to those standards. This almost reverential attitude permeated the top management level as well. More than a decade after his death, Murrow's picture continued to grace the wall of Bill Paley's office, as it did those of other executive suites at CBS. Within that world, even the slightest disparagement of Murrow—a reference, say, to the inanity of the *Person to Person* series —was regarded as, at the least, a breach of taste, and at worst, an act of blasphemy. Nor did the principal members of the CBS family care to be reminded about the squabbles and frustrations that darkened Murrow's last years at the network. There was, throughout the corporate empire, a conscious effort to remember only the best about Murrow, and only the best about his association with CBS.

Nowhere was the Murrow legacy more evident, more tangible, than in the careers of those correspondents who were hired by Murrow in Europe and went on to become known as "Murrow's boys." For there is no question that next to his own gifts as a reporter, Murrow's greatest contribution to CBS was as a recruiter of other talent. The staff he assembled in Europe during the early days of World War II soon became recognized for its all-around excellence. By the end of the war, the reputation of CBS foreign correspondents was such that many government officials in Washington made it a policy to start their day with a transcript of the CBS *World News Roundup* as well as a copy of the *New York Times*.

But the *World News Roundup* was radio, and only a few of Murrow's World War II colleagues were able to parlay their skills as radio reporters into strong television careers. Insofar as the Murrow imprint was carried over into television (that is, beyond the work of Murrow himself), it was done so by three members of that original World War II team who did make the successful transition from one medium to the other: Howard K. Smith, Eric Sevareid, and Charles Collingwood.

A native of Louisiana, Howard Smith had Adolf Hitler to thank for the opportunity that sent him to Europe in 1936. The Nazi government was then offering scholarships to American students as part of an international propaganda campaign, and Smith, following his graduation from Tulane, accepted one to study at Heidelberg. He later won a Rhodes scholarship to Oxford. Turning to journalism in 1940, he was hired by the United Press and sent to Berlin at a salary of $25 a week. His work for the UP came to the attention of Murrow in London and CBS editors in New York, and in the spring of 1941, Smith became the network's man in Berlin. The day after Pearl Harbor, all American reporters in Berlin were interned by the Nazis, but Smith fortunately had left the German capital a few days earlier and was safely in Switzerland when the United States entered the war. He spent the next two years working out of Switzerland, covering the French underground and other guerrilla activities, and, in the process, he discovered a then unknown Yugoslav named Tito. After D-Day, Smith followed the Allied advance across Europe and was one of the first American newsmen to enter the conquered city of Berlin, which, in its devastation, bore no resemblance to the proud and triumphant capital he had left four years earlier. In the meantime, he did not meet Ed Murrow in person until 1944, when their paths crossed briefly in Paris, shortly after it was liberated. But Murrow obviously had a high regard for Smith's work. When the war ended and he decided to return to America, Murrow first asked Eric Sevareid to replace him as CBS's chief foreign correspondent. But Sevareid also wanted to go home, and when he turned down the offer, Murrow picked Smith as his successor in London.

Howard Smith remained overseas another twelve years, during which time he covered a host of major stories for CBS radio, from the Nuremberg war crimes trials in 1946 to the Suez crisis a decade later. Then, in 1957, at his request, CBS brought him back to the States and appointed him chief Washington correspondent. Soon after his arrival in the capital, Smith began doing news analysis on television as a regular assignment on the evening news show. His career received another boost in 1959 when *CBS Reports* went on the air; as Fred Friendly's favorite alternative to Murrow, Smith anchored many of those documentaries. Then, in 1961, he was named Washington bureau chief, a promotion that gave him some managerial power to augment his growing stature as a correspondent. On the surface, at least, everything was going his way, and so, when Murrow left CBS early that year, Smith seemed to be in an ideal position to inherit his role as the network's premier correspondent.

Yet at the same time, Smith was creating serious problems for himself, particularly with his television commentaries. He spoke out on the most controversial issues, and there were frequent complaints from viewers about his blunt and aggressive commentaries. Nevertheless, the CBS News executives were reluctant to terminate them because they also believed that when Smith wasn't raising hell about something, he was capable of thoughtful and concise analysis; in fact, in their view, he was the best analyst in all of TV journalism.

But if his superiors had a high opinion of Smith, it was nothing compared to Smith's opinion of himself. He had become, by this time, extremely arrogant and intractable. At one point, in early 1961, when a high-level CBS News executive urged him to tone down his more assertive commentaries, Smith said he couldn't do that because the country had just gone through eight years of weak leadership under Eisenhower, and now the President was Kennedy, whom Smith regarded as shallow and as inept as Ike. The country, he proclaimed, was desperately in need of leadership, the clear implication being that he, Howard K. Smith, was the one to provide that leadership, via the CBS television network. A man who could carry self-esteem to such lengths was no doubt destined for trouble, and it was not long in coming. In the spring of 1961, an incident occurred that brought matters to a head.

When Murrow was summoned by Kennedy to take on the USIA post, he had just begun work on a *CBS Reports* story on the tense racial situation in Birmingham, Alabama. Following his departure, the assignment was passed on to Smith, and so Smith was in Birmingham in May 1961 when Sheriff "Bull" Connor's police stood by and did nothing while local thugs beat up a group of civil rights activists. He was appalled by the violence he saw, and he later decided to end the Birmingham documentary with a quote from Edmund Burke: "The only thing necessary for the triumph of evil is for good men to do nothing."

The CBS executives were not going to have any of that. They were already nervous about the Birmingham broadcast and the howls of protest it was sure to arouse from the network's Southern affiliates. The Burke quote, they said, was an insult to all decent white Southerners, and they ordered it removed from Smith's script. Smith was incensed. For one thing, even though he had lived in other parts of the world for the past twenty-five years, he still felt close to his Louisiana roots and he resented the patronizing conception his New York bosses seemed to have of decent white Southerners. But his main concern was over the larger principle. Smith thought the deletion of the Burke quote represented managerial coercion of the worst sort, and he decided the time had come to force a showdown on the question of control over editorial content. He insisted on nothing less than a face-to-face encounter with the Chairman himself—William S. Paley. This was courageous of him, but not especially prudent. For Paley, having become increasingly annoyed with Smith's attitude, had decided that a sharp dressing-down was long overdue, and he was now waiting for him like a lion in ambush.

Smith's meeting with Paley was brief and bitter. (Stanton and other executives were also present, more or less as mediators. "We furnished the smelling salts," one of them later said.) Paley let Smith have his say about what kind of freedom he was entitled to as a journalist who did commentary as well as straight reporting. Then Paley hammered away at the point that broadcasting was licensed by the government and therefore did not have the freedom or luxury that privately owned newspapers and magazines did. In bristling tones, he told Smith that he didn't seem to understand what CBS's policy was and what it had to be. Smith countered with the engaging assertion that it was Chairman Paley who didn't understand what the company's policy should be in the area of news analysis. That, of course, was tantamount to telling Jehovah he needed to bone up on the Ten Commandments, and so Smith, a rebellious Moses, was told to take his talents elsewhere. His dismissal was announced in October 1961.

Smith promptly entered into negotiations with CBS's principal rival, NBC. The initial reaction there was most enthusiastic; NBC News officials welcomed the chance to acquire a correspondent of Howard Smith's caliber and reputation. But then, just as the contract was about to be signed, something went wrong and the deal fell through. A puzzled and embarrassed NBC News executive called Smith to apologize and inform him that the decision not to hire him had come down from the "very top." Smith strongly suspected that in reaching that decision, the very top at NBC had been influenced by a conversation it had with the very top at CBS. A few weeks later, Smith went to work for ABC, where, after several years of frustration and disappointment, he became, at the age of fifty-five, co-anchorman on its evening news show.

But the passage of time did little to alleviate the bitterness Paley and Smith felt toward each other. At Ed Murrow's funeral in 1965, Paley went out of his way to exchange condolences with *most* members of the old World War II team. When he saw Smith, however, he just stared right through him, declining to speak or nod or in any way acknowledge his presence. It was almost as if Paley thought that Smith —the black sheep, the outcast—had no proper business being there.

Smith's departure cleared the way for Eric Sevareid to become the top TV news commentator at CBS, and there was no small irony in *that*. Just four years earlier, in 1957, it was Sevareid who had had a run-in with Paley over the question of news analysis. At the time, Sevareid was doing regular radio commentary out of Washington, where he had been based since the end of World War II, and by the middle 1950s he had become sharply critical of John Foster Dulles's foreign policy. One piece, in particular, which dealt with Dulles's ban against newsmen entering Red China (as it was then called), so upset his superiors that they refused to allow it on the air. Sevareid was furious, and he retaliated by leaking the piece to a senator, who promptly read it into the *Congressional Record*. Soon thereafter, he was summoned to New York for a meeting with Paley.

If Sevareid's encounter with the Chairman produced fewer fireworks than the Paley-Smith clash four years later, it was only because Sevareid had a far less pugnacious temperament than Smith. The issues at stake were the same. Paley told Sevareid that he must exercise more care in analyzing the news. Sevareid, speaking with great calm and caution, tried to explain that analysis and interpretation were essential to the craft of journalism; without them, there could be no quality or depth in reporting. But Paley was in no mood to listen. Most of the time, as Sevareid talked, the Chairman just glared at him with severe disapproval. When the meeting ended, Sevareid left with the sour conviction that what Paley really wanted was his resignation.

No grapevine is more active than the one that winds through the broadcasting industry, and not long after his meeting with Paley, Sevareid received a call from Robert Kintner, who was about to take over as president of NBC, having just moved over to that network from ABC. If for any reason, Kintner slyly suggested, Sevareid was not happy at CBS, would he consider coming over to NBC where a revamped news operation would be built around his ability and prestige? Sevareid was flattered, but he declined the offer, at least in part because of his feelings of loyalty to Murrow and the old Murrow team, if not to CBS in general.

There was another reason. Sevareid was not at all sure he was truly suited for television, especially as a star attraction. He was having great difficulty making the adjustment from radio to television. It reminded him of a similar ordeal he went through eighteen years earlier when he made the transition from print journalism to radio. When Murrow hired him in 1939, Sevareid was twenty-seven years old. Like Smith, he was also working for the United Press, but in the Paris bureau. He was looking for a better job; he knew war was imminent, and he hoped to cover it for a major newspaper. That's what journalism meant to him: newspapers, the printed word. Now here was this man Murrow calling from London with the offer of a better job, but in *radio*. Sevareid had his doubts.

The doubts were justified. Sevareid's first broadcasts for CBS were comic disasters, replete with slurs, stammers, and ill-timed pauses. His hands often shook so violently that he was convinced his listeners heard more of his rattling script than they did of him. (Thirty-six years later, he still remembered the experience as "traumatic, like being on stage in Carnegie Hall with no pants on.") The CBS brass in New York would have rejected him on the spot had it not been for the intercession of Murrow, who, by some supreme act of faith, was confident that Sevareid would pull himself together and become a first-class radio reporter.

Which, of course, he did. Once he became adjusted to that alien creature, the microphone, he went on to cover some of the major stories of World War II, including the fall of France, the Italian campaign, and the first landing of American troops in southern France. By the end of the war, he had become, next to Murrow himself, the most respected member of the Murrow team. By then, however, a new electronic hurdle loomed ahead: television. Sevareid was even more wary than Murrow about television as a journalistic medium. Once, in the late 1940s, he said to Frank Stanton, "That damn picture box may ruin us all." Stanton just laughed and said, "No, no, don't worry. You'll survive it."

For the next several years, however, it was a very close call. Because Sevareid was perhaps the most brilliant (and certainly the most cerebral) of all "Murrow's boys," every effort was made during the 1950s to transform him into a television star. He was featured at the political conventions, on a Sunday afternoon news show called *The American Week*, and on various specials. But he did not have an on-camera presence. Most of the time he seemed stiff and awkward and ill at ease. Occasionally he tried his hand, in place of Howard Smith, at doing analysis on the evening news. But in those pre-videotape days, everything was broadcast live, and Sevareid's commentaries were often a hodgepodge of nervous glances, missed cues, and self-conscious mannerisms. No one was more aware of the problem than Sevareid himself. He once tried to describe to a newspaper reporter the anguish he felt on television: "A lot of people start blooming when that little light goes on. I start to die."

He survived. But by 1959 he was unhappy with the way his career was going and induced CBS to send him to London. It turned out to be a fortuitous move. Going to Europe took him back to his journalistic roots, the scene of his earlier triumphs, and that helped revive his spirits. In March 1961, he did a *CBS Reports* documentary called *Great Britain—Blood, Sweat and Tears Plus Twenty Years*. It was Sevareid's finest TV performance up to that time. Reviewing the program for the *New York Times*, Jack Gould wrote: "Mr. Sevareid always has been one of the ablest essayists in broadcasting, and last night he had many an excellent turn of phrase: pictures may be of prime importance to TV but they can be immeasurably enhanced by the right words." What's more, Sevareid's return from London could not have been better timed. He came home in September 1961, just as Howard K. Smith was about to wire himself into Bill Paley's electric chair.

So Sevareid took over as the main TV news analyst at CBS. By this time, videotape had come into common usage and he could record his pieces in advance instead of having to do them live, cold turkey. Still, there were problems to be resolved. The executive producer of the evening news was as picture-oriented as Sevareid was not, and he wanted to "dress up" the commentaries with film, still photos, and charts. But Sevareid would have none of that: no graphics or "gimmicks," as he called them, while he was on the air. His words, for better or for worse, would have to speak for themselves.

For the first few years, from 1961 to 1964, Sevareid worked out of New York, and his commentaries were aired on an irregular basis, an average of two or three times a week. Then, in 1964, three things happened. First, he was transferred to Washington, which put him in closer touch with most of his primary sources. Second, he began doing commentaries five nights a week, which made him a regular, built-in fixture on Cronkite's evening news show. And finally, since the broadcast was now a half hour instead of fifteen minutes, he had more time, which enabled him to give his essays more body and depth.

Sevareid's commentaries were far less abrasive than Smith's had been. Whereas Smith usually went in for the frontal attack, the verbal equivalent of a sock on the jaw, Sevareid was much more subdued and indirect, preferring subtle implication over blunt assertion. Smith's downfall, as well as Sevareid's unpleasant memory of his own close call with Paley, may well have worked as a deterrent. One CBS News producer, who had been around during the Smith years, put it this way: "Smith got into trouble because he refused to play the Sevareid game —analyze without saying anything." Yet the "Sevareid game" was more complicated than that. If Smith's commentaries were often full of bite and bile, reminiscent of columnist Joseph Alsop at his most combative, Sevareid's pieces more closely resembled the Walter Lippmann approach. This would have been his natural bent under any circumstances. A man of profound scholarly interests, he believed he should use his craft to elucidate, to clarify, to place in perspective. While this style was certainly safer in terms of corporate survival, it was also, at its best, more illuminating.

But if Sevareid brought to television a superior presence, it continued to be, in many ways, an alien presence: that of a thoughtful, often complex writer working in a milieu of action and dazzle and striking effects. This incongruity did not go unnoticed at CBS, least of all by members of Cronkite's news staff in New York, some of whom felt that Sevareid's pieces "slowed down" the pace of the show. A few people fell into the habit of referring to him, not at all flatteringly, as "the Gray Eminence" and "the Pontiff." Such terms were clearly inspired by his on-air presence: the stern voice and manner, the highbrow tone and language, the grave, elder statesman's face, and the graying hair so carefully slicked back that it looked as if, to borrow the old longshoremen's phrase, every strand had been "nailed into place."

His presence off camera, in person, was much the same. Although he had a lighter side (he was, in fact, the possessor of a fine, dry wit), there is no denying that Eric Sevareid, the grandson of a Norwegian immigrant, often came across as a Scandinavian cliché: aloof and forbidding in manner, somber and brooding in temperament. (He must have been a marvelous companion to Murrow when he was in one of *his* black moods: two dark princes lamenting the inescapable miseries of human existence.) His penchant for introspection was so strong that in conversation he frequently lapsed into whispers and mumbles that made it all but impossible to hear what he was saying. Once, when a relatively new member of the CBS News staff in Washington was going to have lunch with Sevareid, he rather pompously asked a senior correspondent what he might do to prepare himself for such a privileged event. "Oh, nothing, really," said the senior man. "All you'll need is an attentive gaze, and an ear trumpet." But those who worked closely with Sevareid also had great respect for his gifts as a writer and thinker—and for the way he was able, finally, to apply those gifts to an inhospitable medium without compromising his natural style or dignity. If he never quite became a headliner or anchorman, he did go on to establish himself, after his move to Washington in 1964, as the most distinguished commentator in TV journalism.

On that summer night back in 1939 when he was sitting in the United Press bureau in Paris and the call that changed his life came through from London, Ed Murrow had said to him, "I don't know very much about your experience, but I like the way you write and I like your ideas." It was Murrow's unorthodox view at the time that those qualities would more than compensate for any deficiencies he might have as an on-air personality. Four decades later, Eric Sevareid could look back on a career that, among other things, had been a vindication of that judgment.

In the fall of 1940, one year after he hired Sevareid, Murrow telephoned yet another young man who was working for the United Press

—this time in the London bureau—and a few weeks later, Charles Collingwood went to work for CBS. Unlike Sevareid, who had been drawn to journalism even as a boy growing up in rural North Dakota, Collingwood's early ambition had been to be a lawyer. The son of a college professor who became a top official in the U.S. Forest Service, Collingwood spent most of his early life in Washington. It was a Rhodes scholarship that brought him to England in 1939 on the eve of World War II. (At Oxford he met and became friends with Howard K. Smith.) The outbreak of war changed Collingwood's mind about pursuing a career in international law, and in 1940, at the age of twenty-three, he took a job with the United Press in London. One day, when he returned from an assignment, there was a message for him that a "Mr. Morrell" from CBS had called.

"Morrell," of course, turned out to be Murrow, and they met for lunch at the Savoy Hotel. That meeting went well, or at least Colling-wood *thought* it went well, and his trial broadcasts also went well. The only criticism of Collingwood, after his first encounter with the micro-phone, was that he was too loud. "It isn't necessary," Murrow told him, "to shout across the entire Atlantic Ocean."

So Collingwood joined "Murrow's boys" and soon became a solid member of the team. Among the major stories he covered during the war were the North African campaign and D-Day, when he landed on Omaha Beach in the first hours of the invasion. It wasn't until a year or so after he had gone to work for Murrow that Collingwood learned how close he had come to missing out on a career at CBS. One night when the two correspondents were having drinks, Murrow suddenly became serious and, recalling their first meeting at the Savoy, confessed, "You know, Charlie, I almost didn't hire you that day."

Collingwood was stunned and asked why. Was it something he had said?

"No, no," Murrow replied, "but when you walked in wearing those god-awful loud Argyle socks, I wondered if you were really right for us."

The story reveals still another side of Murrow. In addition to seek-ing intellect and strong writing ability, the two qualities that attracted him to Sevareid, he wanted his news team to have class, even a certain amount of elegance. Murrow himself was always impeccably groomed and tailored in the best Savile Row fashion, and in putting together his staff, he steered clear of the loudmouthed, rumpled-suit, squashed-hat type of newspaperman so common to the profession. One look at Col-lingwood's Argyle socks and he feared darkly that he was about to have lunch with a frivolous sport instead of a serious young journalist who might help him cover World War II. Murrow would come to appreciate the irony in that first impression. For in later years, Collingwood would be recognized, even more than Murrow, as the Beau Brummell of CBS News correspondents. One day, in fact, his sartorial elegance, and the grand manner that went with it, would prove, in various subtle ways, to be a hindrance to his career at CBS.

After the war, Collingwood returned to America, and by the late 1940s, he was covering the Truman White House. In contrast to what that beat would later become, it was a relaxing and extremely pleasant assignment. Truman himself mingled freely and informally with the "press boys." Those who were special favorites, as Collingwood was, were invited to join in the poker games Truman frequently played with some of the "cronies" on his White House staff. Collingwood, an inveterate gambler, welcomed the action because he was trying to recover from a long streak of bad luck. While in London, he had acquired an impressive collection of modern art at bargain prices, but in the years following the war he had to sell the paintings to cover his heavy losses at racetracks and in poker games. (Recalling the experience years later, he said, "Those pictures would be worth a fortune today." His voice, however, betrayed no sense of regret, in accordance with the code that a gentleman never grouses about his gambling losses.) Toward the end of the Truman years, Collingwood took a leave of absence from CBS to serve as special assistant to Averell Harriman, then Director for Mutual Security in Washington, and when he returned to the network in 1953, the emphasis had shifted from radio to television.

Of all "Murrow's boys," Collingwood came the closest to being ideally suited for television. He was, in many ways, a more fluent and polished broadcaster than Murrow himself, and while he didn't project Murrow's strength and intensity, he had all his mentor's on-air urbanity, and then some. Still another big plus was his looks. Murrow, Smith, and Sevareid were telegenic, each in his own way, but Collingwood had them all beat in that department. With his fine features and wavy hair, he was movie-star handsome, which was only appropriate since he had married the glamorous Hollywood actress Louise Allbritton shortly after the war. Nor was Collingwood in any way a lightweight, a mere tailor's dummy. If he wasn't quite in Sevareid's intellectual class, he still was very bright and serious and had sound reportorial instincts. In short, he was a natural for TV journalism.

When he rejoined CBS in 1953, the top news position in television was Murrow's *See It Now* showcase. But the second-best slot, even then, was the fifteen-minute evening news, which was being anchored by Douglas Edwards. There was, of course, no question of dislodging Murrow, but there was some talk in the mid-1950s of having Collingwood replace Edwards on the evening news. But Edwards and his show were doing well at the time, and his supporters (including his sponsor, Pall Mall cigarettes) quickly closed ranks in his defense. Still, Collingwood often filled in for Edwards on the evening news, and that assignment, along with others he was given, seemed to put him in an excellent position to benefit from future openings.

The openings came in rapid succession in the early 1960s. First Murrow left, then Howard K. Smith was fired, and in 1962, Douglas Edwards was taken off the evening news. Collingwood was not exactly overlooked during this period of transition. Even before Murrow's departure, he had inherited the *Person to Person* slot, and that alone, given the show's immense popularity, was enough to put him fully in the limelight. In addition, he was picked, in 1962, to anchor a weekly prime-time news program called *Eyewitness,* and he was also featured on several documentaries. But the big plum by this time was the evening news—and there Collingwood ran into constant frustration.

When the decision was made to remove Edwards, he was succeeded not by Collingwood but by Walter Cronkite. It was difficult to argue with that move, for by 1962, Cronkite—the workhorse, the good soldier who had covered all the political conventions and just about every other live news event—was the biggest name at CBS News. Collingwood nevertheless felt he at least was entitled to be regarded as next in line, to be the man who filled in regularly for Cronkite as, in the past, he had filled in regularly for Edwards. Instead, he now had to share that assignment with a relative newcomer to CBS, a younger correspondent named Harry Reasoner. In fact, as time went on, the balance shifted more and more to Reasoner until, by the end of 1962, the word had been quietly passed to Reasoner that he, not Collingwood, was to be Cronkite's regular substitute. It was all very subtle, but there was no doubt that when it came to anchorman status Collingwood was steadily losing ground.

The trouble was that Charles Collingwood, of all people, was having image problems. He was so handsome, so debonair, so infernally elegant that he was perceived by some of his superiors as being just a bit too soft and indolent. In this regard, *Person to Person* worked against him. The program brought ample rewards in extra income and viewer recognition, but it also hurt him in other ways. While there had been a tendency at CBS News to rationalize Murrow's involvement in *Person to Person*, Collingwood did not have comparable stature as a serious journalist. And whereas Murrow often appeared to be ill at ease in the gossipy format of *Person to Person*, Collingwood nattered his way through the interviews with such grace and charm that he usually seemed to be thoroughly enjoying the idle chitchat. His performance reinforced the notion that he was more comfortable in this milieu— tut-tutting with the celebrity set, the Beautiful People—than he was in the clenched-fist world of breaking news.

That was extremely unfair to Collingwood. The man, after all, had trudged through the mud of European battlefields as a reporter, which was a lot more dues than most of his detractors had ever paid. But his patrician clothes and manner set him apart from his colleagues. Harry Reasoner once said that whenever he stood next to Collingwood, he felt the discomfort of a man who's just noticed he has soup stains on his tie or that his fly is open. Yet Reasoner was among those who truly admired Collingwood, not only for his ability but for his classy presence as well. When Reasoner learned that the CBS executives preferred him over Collingwood as Cronkite's regular replacement, he was mildly puzzled —pleased, but still puzzled. So he asked an associate who had been around CBS longer than he had why the network didn't want to use more of Collingwood on the evening news. "Because," came the answer, "he's too fucking urbane."

By 1963, Collingwood knew he was being eased into the second echelon of CBS News correspondents, and such was his irritation that in the summer of that year he entered into negotiations with ABC. To help pull their news operation out of its perennial rut, the ABC people were prepared to make Collingwood their star attraction. But he ran into a snag in getting out of his CBS contract, and during the weeks it took to try to unravel the problem, he underwent a change of heart. He decided he would rather remain a semistar at a first-class network than become the headliner at an inferior one. Thus, when it came down to cases, the pull of the old Murrow tradition exerted its force on Collingwood just as it had on Sevareid six years earlier.

But he would not stay in New York. Collingwood's loyalty to CBS did not extend to the humiliation of sitting back and watching a parade of younger correspondents pass him by. He would take himself out of that savage pecking order. So, in 1964, he prevailed upon CBS to send him to London as chief foreign correspondent for CBS News. In the years that followed, Collingwood took the opportunity to remind his superiors (just in case they had forgotten) that beneath all the veneer and foppish airs, he was still a perceptive and intelligent reporter. Over the course of the next decade, he covered most of the major stories in Europe. He also reported on the 1967 Middle East war and made numerous trips to Vietnam. His biggest coup came in 1968: at a time when U.S. involvement in Vietnam was at its height, he became the first American network correspondent to be allowed into Hanoi.

Yet during these years, his other reputation—as a dandy, as a man of elegance—continued to grow. When Morley Safer joined CBS News in London in 1964, Collingwood took him under his wing and became, to some extent, Safer's mentor. In the process, Safer came to know a warm and generous side of Collingwood that very few other people at CBS ever saw. At the same time, Safer fully appreciated the way Collingwood was viewed by others, and never more so than on one occasion when he went to Paris. There, in the lobby of the Ritz Hotel, he ran into Janet Flanner, who, under the pseudonym "Genet," had been writing about Paris and London for *The New Yorker* magazine since the 1920s. When Safer introduced himself to Flanner, her eyes lit up and she exclaimed, "Oh, really, CBS? How marvelous for you. You must tell me, young man, how is the Duke these days?" Safer leaned his head back and roared with laughter. For although he had been with the network just a short time, he was aware that in all the world of CBS News, there was only one Duke—the Duke of Collingwood.

So while Smith, Sevareid, and Collingwood went farther in television at CBS than any of Murrow's other World War II recruits, they did not quite make it to the top. Smith, it's true, eventually rose to the anchorman level in the waning years of his career, but he achieved that status at ABC, where, it must be said, the internal competition was far less keen. As for the big television news stars at CBS during the 1960s and 1970s—Cronkite, Reasoner, Mudd, Rather, et al—they did not come out of the old radio tradition established by Murrow. Instead, they made their reputations in television itself, and they did so by following another route, a route charted in the 1940s by a young man who also had never been a member of Murrow's World War II clique. What this man did was to embrace television at a time when the Murrow group would have nothing to do with the "damn picture box." Hence, in his own way, he was the real pioneer of television news. For the truth is that Cronkite and all the other TV anchormen who have come along since are the direct descendants of Douglas Edwards.

4 "We Have to Make Air!"

For fourteen years, from 1948 to 1962, Doug Edwards was the face and voice of CBS on its evening news show. In fact, his critics, then and later, would argue that he never was anything more than that: an announcer masquerading as a journalist, a mere "reader" with no background or training in news. But it was unfair, no matter what his shortcomings, to suggest that Edwards simply jumped into television straight out of an announcer's booth. For although it's true that he had been an announcer at various times during his early radio career, he also had seized every opportunity along the way to establish himself in news.

He had, from the start, a passion for radio. Unlike Murrow, whose first professional interest was education, unlike Collingwood, whose early ambition was the law, and unlike Sevareid, who thought his journalistic destiny would be found in newspaper work, Edwards was a radio freak. As a boy growing up in Alabama, he spent hours glued to his family's crystal set, listening to such early radio stars as commentator Lowell Thomas and indulging in fantasies about his own future. Years later, old family friends would remember that often when they telephoned the Edwards home, young Doug would answer and give them an excited report on the latest news events "just like over the radio."

In 1932, at the tender age of fifteen, he began his career at a station in Troy, Alabama. For the princely sum of $2.50 a week, he did it all: announced the programs, reported the news, played records, even *sang* now and then. Three years later, he was working for a much larger station, WSB in Atlanta, first as an announcer, then as a newscaster. (He was also, by this time, taking journalism courses at the University of

50

Georgia's Atlanta branch.) Reaching out for the big time, he landed a job in 1938 as something called a "Cunningham's News Ace" for WXYZ in Detroit. There he worked with another young man—also a News Ace —named Mike Wallace. Since WXYZ was the source station of several popular radio shows of that time, such as *The Lone Ranger* and *The Green Hornet*, Edwards and Wallace also could be heard as announcers on those programs. (". . . the thundering hoofbeats of the great horse, Silver, the Lone Ranger rides again!")

By 1940, Edwards was back at WSB in Atlanta as the station's news editor, and two years later, following an audition in New York, CBS offered him a job—as an announcer. Since he had gone to a great deal of trouble to break away from announcing and devote his efforts entirely to news, he was hesitant about accepting the offer, even though it meant a big step up to a network. But he was reminded that some of the best newscasters then working for CBS (for example, Robert Trout and John Daly) had started out as announcers, and, encouraged by that, Edwards took the CBS job and moved to New York.

It was the right decision. Because of the war, CBS was beefing up its news operation at home as well as abroad, and within a matter of weeks, Edwards was working as a newscaster under the tutelage of John Daly. But if those first years at CBS brought their share of satisfactions, there were frustrations as well. Edwards was aware that the big reputations were not being made behind microphones in New York, but overseas, where the war was being fought. Yet, whenever he tried to get an assignment as a war correspondent, he was told there were no openings and he would have to wait. Not until 1945 was he able to swing a transfer to London. There he worked briefly with Murrow, but by then it was a case of too little, too late. The war was almost over. He no longer had a chance to become one of "Murrow's boys."

After the war, Edwards stayed on in Europe for a few months. He put in some time as Paris bureau chief, then later went on an extended assignment to the Middle East, which was moving toward a point of crisis over the question of Palestine and the future state of Israel. When he returned to New York in 1946, he was still an obscure reporter, but at least he now had some credentials as a foreign correspondent. One day, not long after his return, a CBS executive named Henry Cassirer asked Edwards if he would mind going on television to be interviewed about the Middle East situation. Mind going on what? Television? Was he serious?

Oh, yes, Cassirer assured him. CBS had a little television news show that was being aired once a week, on Thursday night. Well, well, thought Edwards. Television. Fancy that.

Actually, the first television news broadcast at CBS had occurred a few years before, in the spring of 1941. By the end of that year, the network's New York station was putting on two fifteen-minute TV newscasts a day, Monday through Friday, at 2:30 P.M. and 7:30 P.M. A man named Richard Hubbell was the narrator on these broadcasts, which were basically "chalk talks." Most of the news, naturally, dealt with the war, and Hubbell stood with a pointer in front of a map and talked about what was happening on this front or that front or wherever. He didn't have to be all that precise because reception on the tiny, primitive sets of those days was so poor that viewers—if there *were* any viewers—could barely make out Hubbell, much less the lines on his maps. Yet even then, visual imagination was at work. The day after Pearl Harbor, when war was declared, CBS broadcast the news over television as well as radio. But since the viewers could not see Roosevelt as he delivered his "date of infamy" speech to Congress, to give the story "picture," an American flag was placed in front of the camera and an off-camera fan was turned on it to make it wave. A few weeks later, all commercial television was suspended until after the war.

By 1946, Hubbell was gone, and when Edwards made his television debut, he was interviewed by a man named Milo Boulton. But it was Edwards, more than Boulton, who impressed Cassirer and other CBS executives. Edwards conveyed a very positive "image," although that inspirational Madison Avenue term had not yet begun to enrich the idiom. He brought to television an unassuming manner, a bland but agreeable voice, and what would later be described as "the face of a choirboy." Not long after his first TV appearance, he was asked to take over the weekly television news show, which, in 1947, was expanded to two nights a week. However, he was still primarily a radio newscaster.

Richard Hubbell's two-a-day chalk talks in 1941 had been really nothing more than an idle experiment, an exercise in curiosity. But by 1948, all the networks had decided it was time for television to become seriously involved in broadcast journalism. The first major step in that direction came in the summer of 1948 when the networks committed themselves to television coverage of that year's political conventions.

By later standards, of course, the coverage was extremely static and limited. For the most part, the heavy, immobile cameras were focused exclusively on the podium. The main TV reporter or commentator for CBS was Doug Edwards (the term "anchorman" had not yet been coined), and he worked out of a cramped studio that was dwarfed by the panoply of desks and equipment that made up the extensive radio operation. On occasion, other CBS reporters—notably, Ed Murrow and Quincy Howe—would join in the TV coverage, either to interview prominent politicos or to offer comments of their own. But except for Edwards, their major assignments were in radio. Nor were there that many viewers, at least not in comparison to the vast audiences of later years. There were fewer than half a million sets in the United States in 1948, and since this was well before the days of coast-to-coast television, live coverage was limited to the Northeast section of the country.

Despite all that, television succeeded in making its presence felt in the political arena. During both conventions that year, more and more politicians expressed a desire to be interviewed on camera. They had no idea how many viewers were Out There, but however small the audience, it had to include at least some registered voters. The Convention coverage that year was also the first time that an attempt at TV journalism received serious attention in the press. Reviewing television's performance in the *New York Times*, Jack Gould wrote that "for straight adult reporting, seasoned with humor," the CBS trio of Edwards, Murrow, and Howe "was very much in a class by itself."

After the conventions were over, Edwards went on vacation and was relaxing in Georgia when he received a call from Wells Church, the man in charge of radio news for CBS. Church told him that "the TV people" were planning to put on a news program five nights a week, Monday through Friday, and "they want you to be their guy." The only catch in the deal, Church said, was that if he took on the television assignment, he would have to give up almost all of his radio work. Church said he had to know: What did Edwards think of the idea?

Not much, actually. In the years that followed, it would become part of CBS mythology that while Murrow and the other heavy hitters in radio viewed the onset of television with a mixture of apprehension and disdain, Edwards had the prescience to recognize the great potential of the new medium and what it could do for his career. But that was not the case at all. For one thing, there was the question of money. In addition to their base salaries, which were usually quite modest, newscasters and reporters received a percentage of the advertising revenue every time they appeared on a program that was sponsored. Hence, the more they were on the air, the more money they made. (The fee system had the further advantage, from the company's point of view, of making the reporters accomplices in the policy of airing commercials on news broadcasts. Only a journalist with an exceptionally pure heart was apt to complain about having his newscast interrupted by a sales pitch for toothpaste or deodorant when he personally was getting a piece of the action.) In 1948, Edwards was averaging about $400 a week in commercial fees, which was the bulk of his income. But since it was understood that in the beginning, at least, the television news show would be sustaining—that is, unsponsored—he would lose all that money if he gave up his radio assignments. That problem, however, was resolved when the CBS brass assured him it would make up the difference in salary.

But Edwards's concern went beyond the size of his paycheck. He had worked hard over many years to get where he was in 1948. He realized he would never become a Murrow or even, for that matter, a Bob Trout or an Eric Sevareid, but by this time he was fairly well established in the second echelon of CBS radio newscasters. The highly regarded *World News Roundup* was one of his regular assignments, and he was also featured on a popular midday news program. The way he saw it, to give that up for television made no sense at all. He and his fellow journalists looked upon television with contempt and derision. In their eyes, it was a toy, a carnival that specialized in such garish idiocies as the Roller Derby and phony wrestling. Until now, he had been willing to do the once-a-week and twice-a-week TV broadcasts more or less as a lark, a harmless diversion. His work at the conventions had been more serious in nature, and therefore more worthwhile, yet even then he could not help but notice that when other reporters came into the studio to do a turn on TV, they generally acted as if they were slumming. Clearly, he thought, to become identified with television on a full-time basis could only undermine whatever reputation he had as a respected radio newscaster. So he told Wells Church no.

At this point, Frank Stanton intervened. When Edwards returned from vacation, he was called in for a talk with Stanton, who told him that his fears were groundless, that TV's role in news and public affairs was going to be greater than anyone realized, that in a very short time television—not radio—would be in the forefront of broadcast journalism. (If anyone at CBS was prescient about the future of television news, it was Stanton.) There was one moment in the conversation when Stanton turned to him and said in a tone of sudden intensity, "Doug, I guarantee you, if you do this TV broadcast, you'll soon be as well known as Lowell Thomas."

That was heady stuff, and the fact that it came from the president of CBS himself, and not some intermediary, made it that much more intoxicating. But if television was destined to become such a big deal, Edwards wondered, why him? Why Douglas Edwards? There were, after all, other CBS journalists with much greater reputations. Yes, said Stanton, but some of those people did not have the right kind of chemistry for television. It was an entirely different medium. As for others who might be suitable, they seemed to think a switch from radio to television would be demeaning. They would live to regret that attitude, Stanton added, and so would Edwards if he chose to pass up this opportunity. By the time their conversation was over, Edwards sensed he had no real choice: the television job had become an offer he could not refuse. So in the late summer of 1948, just a few weeks after his thirty-first birthday, he began his new assignment—a fifteen-minute TV newscast five nights a week.

At first it was simply called *CBS TV News.* Two years passed before CBS moved to capitalize on the fact that viewers were responding to Edwards as a news personality, an emerging television star. Not until the fall of 1950 was the name of the broadcast changed to *Douglas Edwards with the News.* By then, the program was being carried across most of the country. With the move to five nights a week, CBS had progressed from a "New York only" local broadcast to the bare beginnings of a network operation. Three other East Coast cities—Boston, Philadelphia, and Washington—carried those first broadcasts in 1948, and as time went on, more and more stations in communities spreading to the West and the South were hooked into the network. Every time a new station was added to the list, Edwards opened the show by welcoming it to the broadcast. It wasn't much of a lead, but as far as CBS was concerned, its rapidly expanding network was a more important story than almost anything that was apt to be in the headlines that day. A major milestone was reached when the West Coast was tied into the network by coaxial cable, and one night in September 1951, Edwards opened with the words: "Good evening everyone, from coast to coast."

For a long time thereafter, that was his standard opening.

Compared to what we now see on the networks, the Edwards show of those early years hardly even qualified as a *television* newscast. Without videotape or communications satellites, there were no film reports on "today's" news from overseas or from distant locations in the United States. There were no television correspondents in the field and no network camera crews to film the stories. CBS did not even begin to develop its own newsfilm operation until the mid-fifties. Prior to that time, it purchased its film pieces from Telenews, which specialized in providing footage for movie-house newsreels. (Fox Movietone provided NBC with a similar service.) Except for wars, floods, and other catastrophes that, because of their duration, retained a certain timeliness, there was little attempt to cover spot news. Instead, Telenews and other newsreel outfits focused their attention on events that were planned in advance or even staged in the hope of attracting pictorial coverage. These early "media events" included sports attractions, beauty contests, dog shows, ribbon cuttings, dam dedications, and the like. Since a little of that stuff went a long way, about 90 percent of a typical Edwards broadcast consisted of Edwards reading the news, or what is known in the trade as "tell" stories.

But if the television newscasts of those days were static and primitive, when judged by later standards there was a constant and unflagging effort to improve them. And at CBS, the person who led that effort, who gave it spirit and drive and creative impulse, was a young man who first came to Edwards's attention during the 1948 political conventions. He had just recently been hired by CBS, and although he didn't appear to be more than college age, the young man had a lot of journalistic savvy. What was far more unusual, he seemed to have an instinctive feel for the needs of television. He kept coming up with one idea after another to make the convention coverage more visual. Edwards was impressed. "Say, what's that kid's name?" he asked at one point. "Hewitt," he was told. "Don Hewitt."

In the years that followed, Don Hewitt would come to be known within the world of CBS as the wunderkind of television news, the man who more than anyone else brought TV journalism out of the Stone Age. (As one of his many protégés, Av Westin, said of him many years later, "Hewitt was the guy who invented the wheel in this business.") But in the summer of 1948, there was little reason to believe that

Hewitt would even remain at CBS very long. An extremely footloose young man, it was not his style to stay in one place for any length of time. Although he was only twenty-five years old (and looked younger), Hewitt by then had already gone through the following jobs: head copyboy at the *New York Herald Tribune* (1942), correspondent for the War Shipping Administration (1943–45), night editor of the Associated Press's Memphis bureau (1945–46), editor of a weekly newspaper in New York's Westchester County (1946–47), and night telephoto editor for ACME News Pictures (1947–48). When his boss at ACME News found out Hewitt was leaving to take a job in television, he snickered and said, "Television? Oh, come on, that's a fad. It'll never last." Hewitt agreed that was probably true, but he was curious enough about the "fad" to give it a try. If it didn't work out, he could always move on to something else. He was accustomed to that, moving on.

So Hewitt joined CBS in the spring of 1948, worked on the convention coverage, and later that summer, when the five-night-a-week newscast began, he was one of several young men who took turns directing the show on a rotating basis. One day in the fall of 1948, Edwards went to Ed Chester, the man in charge of the network's embryonic TV news operation, and said he thought his show would have more stability and more continuity if there was one permanent director. Chester was amenable to the idea: "Which one do you want?" Edwards said his first choice was Hewitt. "Okay," Chester replied, "you've got him." Thus, within a few weeks after the expanded Edwards broadcast had gone on the air, Don Hewitt took over as the show's regular director. His days of restlessly hopping from one job to the next were over. In the new and experimental world of TV journalism, he had found his niche.

Hewitt brought to that world certain qualities that set him apart from most of his colleagues and competitors. Most of the people who were drifting into television news, at least on the editorial side, came from a background in either print journalism or radio, where they were accustomed to thinking in terms of words, not pictures. Hewitt was different. During his brief stay at ACME News Pictures, he had developed a strong visual sense, an ability to see a story in terms of its picture possibilities. That proved to be an excellent apprenticeship for television news, and it gave him a definite edge over the refugees from radio and newspapers.

There was also his family background. Hewitt's father worked as an

advertising man for the Hearst newspapers at a time when that journalism empire was still going strong. Like so many others who made their
living off the Lord of San Simeon, Hewitt's father was rather ambivalent
about being associated with Hearst. With their sleazy sensationalism
and bellicose, jingoistic crusades, the Hearst newspapers fully deserved
their reputation for "yellow journalism." But they had their positive
side as well. In their heyday, Hearst reporters were on a par with the
best in the business, and whatever their excesses and other faults, no
one ever accused the Hearst newspapers of being dull. They bristled
with a hell-for-leather gusto and vitality, and the excitement of the
Hearst world rubbed off on Hewitt while he was growing up. As he once
put it, "While other kids were playing cops and robbers or whatever,
I had fantasies about being a reporter who whips the ass off everyone
to get the story."

This zest for action, for scoops, for *anything* that would "whip the
ass" off the opposition carried over into Hewitt's adult life. One of his
earliest heroes was Hildy Johnson, the sassy and aggressive reporter in
The Front Page, the celebrated Ben Hecht–Charles MacArthur play
about the shenanigans of working, Hearst-style, on a big-city newspaper. During his years at CBS, Hewitt liked to think of himself as an
electronic equivalent of Hildy Johnson. Some of his superiors at CBS
also thought of him that way, and there were times when Hewitt's brash
and exuberant tactics gave them more than a few pangs of discomfort.

Hewitt built his early reputation at CBS as a director, a term that
has a special meaning in television news, not at all the same as the
meaning it has in Hollywood or the theater. In TV news, the director
is responsible for putting a broadcast on the air; he is in charge of the
technical elements that go into a news program, as opposed to its editorial content. The director's domain is the control room, where he is
assisted by several technicians. He is the one who issues the commands,
who decides what camera to "take" for a specific shot, who gives the
"roll cue" for a sequence of film, and so on.

The job of orchestrating the new technology had a certain exotic
appeal during the early years of television. It was a challenge, and no
one met that challenge with more verve and imagination than Hewitt.
In addition to the Edwards show, he directed almost every news broadcast of importance in those days, from the political conventions to *See
It Now.* But beyond that, he brought to the craft of directing a personal

style that can only be described as manic. He rejoiced in the arcane lingo of the new technology ("roll," "super," "track," "lap it"), and he barked the commands with all the élan of a gung-ho platoon sergeant. In his exuberance, he even invented a few terms of his own. One of them, in particular, had a nice, sharp, onomatopoeic ring to it. If, for example, Edwards was reading a story about a tornado in Kansas, a map of the state would appear on the screen. Then, at the moment Edwards named the obscure farming community hardest hit by the storm, Hewitt, in the control room, would holler "Splat!" and a white marker would pop on the map to show the community's precise location.

Hewitt did not direct so much as give a performance. Those who witnessed his antic behavior often lamented the fact that all the viewers ever saw was Edwards soberly reporting the news when the real show was going on in the control room. When things went wrong, as they so often did in those experimental days, Hewitt flew into tantrums, filling the air with marvelously ribald imprecations. Once, overcome by frustration, he jumped up on the console, which housed all the electronic gadgetry, making working conditions a bit unpleasant for the technicians who had to press the appropriate buttons. On another memorable evening, everything went wrong at once. The film wouldn't roll, the sound track wouldn't come up—sheer chaos prevailed. In despair, everyone in the control room looked to the director for guidance. Hewitt, rising to the occasion, slammed his fist into his forehead and shouted the command: "Go to black—while I think!"

But directing was only part of his act. In working on the Edwards broadcast, Hewitt soon became aware of a problem that threatened to impede the development of the program. Many of the technical people on the show had come to CBS from careers in newsreels or documentary films and were not schooled in the mechanics of daily TV journalism. Most of the editorial staff was equally inexperienced. Everyone was learning a new craft, but the real problem, as Hewitt saw it, was that there was a gulf between the two groups, a lack of communication and rapport. Hewitt believed that if the Edwards show was ever going to amount to anything, there had to be more cohesion between the two; the news or editorial side had to relate to what was being done on the production or technical side, and vice versa. In taking steps to bridge the gulf, he eventually assumed control over both the editorial and technical operations. He became, in effect, the man in charge of the entire broadcast, and since this made him something more than a director, he took on the title of producer as well. Indeed, it was mainly to define Hewitt's enlarged role on the Edwards show that the term "producer" came into common usage at CBS News.

His expanded authority gave him more room to maneuver, more of an opportunity to dictate changes aimed at improving the broadcast. Many of his visual innovations in those early years were in the nonfilm area. Since the program was essentially a recitation of tell stories, he strove to illustrate them in various ways, to give them a visual dimension they could not have on radio. Unlike many of the people who, having come into television from newsreels and documentaries, were so engrossed in film that they failed to grasp the value of other visual material, Hewitt was aware that still photos, effectively used, could be just as dramatic as film, and at times even more so. In addition, he created a graphics art department and prodded those who worked in it to come up with charts and maps and imaginative techniques in design and animation to appear on the screen while Edwards read the news.

In the early days, these still photos and graphic displays filled the entire screen, and because they removed the newscaster from view while his off-camera voice proceeded to relate the visual material to the story, they were sometimes called "limbos." A technique was soon developed whereby the graphics could be shown in the background, behind the newscaster, but when they were first tried, they were often very crude in proportion and composition. Hewitt, obsessed with the problem, wrestled with it on his own television set at home. One time, unable to sleep, he got up in the middle of the night and covered various parts of his TV set with brown paper in an effort to determine how large Edwards's head and torso should be in relation to the graphics that appeared behind him. By the time he went to work the next morning, he knew exactly the proportion he wanted.

Nothing pleased Hewitt more over the years than when a big story came along that challenged his imagination in the use of graphics. For example, when the first *Sputnik* was launched in 1957, he felt that it clearly called for "something special." So he constructed a makeshift rig as ingenious as it was simple. First, he took an ordinary globe and attached a motor to it. Then he stretched a wire clothes hanger out in a straight line, fastened one end of the hanger to the bottom of the globe, and on the other end attached a Ping-Pong ball with tiny spikes glued on it to make it look like *Sputnik*. When he turned on the motor, the globe slowly turned, giving the illusion that it was the Ping-Pong ball or satellite that was rotating. A rather clumsy contraption, but it worked. When Edwards used it as an "exhibit" on that evening's broadcast, it greatly helped him explain (to an audience then largely ignorant of space technology) what *Sputnik* was, and what it was doing Up There.

Hewitt was also quick to master the techniques of film, and, in fact, his most important innovation—the double projector system—helped to revolutionize film production in television news. At first, almost all TV news stories were shot on silent film. (The slang term for silent film is "MOS," which stands for "mit out sound.") Once the film was in the shop, a correspondent recorded the "voice-over" narration on an audiotape, and the two elements were combined to form the finished piece. But when the sound camera came into vogue, it was possible for a reporter at the scene of a story to record his sound track on the film as it was being shot. Thus sound and picture could be recorded simultaneously. This method had the advantage of immediacy since the reporter could be viewed at the scene delivering his narration. But it had its limitations as well. Since sound and picture were being recorded on the same film, the camera had to focus on the reporter and his precise location, and the story was basically what is known in the trade as a "stand-upper."

The double projector system changed all that. The breakthrough came when Hewitt discovered that in the editing process, a reel of picture could be run on one projector and a reel of narration (taken from the sound camera) on a second projector. The best elements from each could then be "mixed" to produce the best possible story, in terms of both words and pictures. This led to the practice of shooting film separately on location, concentrating first on silent footage, then later on the reporter's narration—or vice versa. And this, in turn, greatly opened up the mechanics of film reporting, making it more fluid and more flexible. Even viewers who are unaware of the process would have no trouble recognizing its results. Anyone who has taken even a cursory look at television news over the past two decades is familiar with how a basic film story is structured. It begins with a reporter on camera at the scene of the story doing a stand-upper. Then, rather quickly, the film "opens up" to provide pictures of other scenes in the story, while the reporter's words, recorded separately, become a voice-over narration. Finally, toward the end, the reporter appears again to wrap things up with his on-camera "close." Although the method lends itself to far more elaborate variations, that essentially is how the double projector system works.

Like so many other worthwhile innovations, it came about entirely by accident. One day in the early 1950s, Hewitt and his film editors were viewing footage of a speech by Senator Robert Taft. The speech was important, but it was also exceedingly dull as Taft droned on about the swollen federal budget and other perils confronting the Republic. At one point, afflicted by the itch brought on by his typically short attention span, Hewitt wondered out loud if it was at all possible to keep Taft's sound track but illustrate what he was talking about by cutting away to stills or charts or other graphics. (Throughout the history of television news, producers have had an almost morbid antipathy toward "talking heads" in a film report.) Hewitt was told yes, it could be done. Later that same day, while working on something else, it suddenly occurred to Hewitt that if it was possible in such a situation to cut away to stills, then it should also be possible to cut away to film. His film editors and other technicians told him yes, that could also be done. All that was needed was to bring a second projector into the act. Thus was born the double projector system, and in the years ahead, it would become a routine part of film production at CBS News.

In his zeal to improve the show, Hewitt occasionally let his fertile imagination get the better of him. A memorable case in point stemmed from his determination to get Edwards to keep his gaze fixed on the camera during the course of a broadcast. When Edwards read directly from his script, as he was accustomed to doing on radio, he glanced down so often that viewers spent half the time looking at the top of his head. At one point, it was suggested that he memorize the script, but given the deadline crush of a newscast, that was easier said than done. In later years, the problem would be solved by a prompting device mounted on the studio camera and adjusted to roll at a pace consistent with the anchorman's reading speed, but reliable prompting techniques had yet to be developed at that point. As a primitive step in that direction, Hewitt had one of his minions copy the script in big black letters on giant cue cards—one story to a cue card—and then, during the broadcast, another minion held them up in front of Edwards. The eye level was seldom right, however, and since a new card had to be held up for each story, awkward pauses were a common occurrence. Hewitt fretted over this problem, as he fretted over everything about the show that didn't satisfy him. Then, in a flash of inspiration, he came up with the solution.

"Doug, I've got it!" he exclaimed to Edwards one morning. "What you should do is learn *Braille.*" Then all he would have to do would be stare into the camera and read the news—with his fingers.

Edwards had an easygoing nature and was inclined to indulge most of Hewitt's schemes. But this time he drew the line. He would not—not then, not ever—consent to learn Braille.

By the middle 1950s, CBS had taken steps to build up its television news operation. No longer relying on Telenews for its film reports, the network had started to recruit its own TV reporters and camera crews. In addition, there were numerous free-lance cameramen it called on to cover certain stories, and an Assignment Desk had been established to coordinate the expanded coverage. The Assignment Desk was the out-growth of a one-man band named Phil Scheffler. A graduate of the Columbia School of Journalism, Scheffler was a Hewitt protégé; in fact, he was drawn to CBS by a spirited speech Hewitt gave at Columbia on the future of television news. During his first years at the network, Scheffler served as Hewitt's liaison to Telenews, and he also went out every day with a camera crew to cover stories in New York. Later, working with other reporters on what was, by then, the Assignment Desk, he assigned cameramen to cover specific stories. Scheffler and his group kept an index file on all available cameramen around the coun-try, and some of the cards had heavy black lines around the edges to indicate that they were "FFI guys." An FFI guy was a cameraman whose work was so unreliable he was not to be used except in case of Fire, Flood, or Insurrection. The years of feeding off Telenews were soon over, but it would be awhile yet before the network would have its own superior corps of cameramen.

During these years of transition, many of the film pieces for the Edwards show still came in "mit out sound," and when they appeared on the program, Edwards usually provided the voice-over narration. (A major exception to this policy was silent footage from Washington, which was narrated by a young reporter named Neil Strawser, who soon became known as "the voice of Washington.") Film reports from field correspondents at the scene still were a rarity for the simple reason that in the middle 1950s CBS had only just started to hire and train reporters and camera crews to work in television. But even if CBS had had the troops in the field, most film reports had to be flown into New York, and since regular jet service had not yet begun, this meant a delay of at least one day (and sometimes more) in getting them on the air. Network film couriers speeding in from the airport on motorcycles were a frequent sight in Manhattan in those days. Footage of an event was often two or three days old when it appeared on the air, and the words "film just arrived in New York" were usually superimposed on the screen—more or less as an apology. Because delayed film reports could not compete with daily newspapers, there was still a tendency to put mainly "soft" or feature film pieces on the Edwards show, similar to the kind of material that Telenews had provided. The program's film reports were not entirely devoid of serious and timely news, however. Since it was fairly easy to make a "live switch" to Washington every day, the major stories from there were regularly covered on film. But for the most part, the day's important "headline" news was still presented in the form of tell stories, which Edwards, having refused to learn Braille, read from giant cue cards, then later from a less clumsy prompting device.

Since tell stories and voice-overs continued to dominate the Edwards show, much of the burden of filling the fifteen-minute broadcast was shouldered by its editorial staff. Edwards himself had written most of his radio newscasts, but a typical script on his television program was largely put together by the two staff writers assigned to it. In quite a few cases, writing for the Edwards show proved to be a stepping-stone to bigger and better jobs at CBS News. Among those who, at various times over the years, wrote for *Douglas Edwards with the News* were Charles Kuralt, Bill Crawford, Sandy Socolow, and Russ Bensley. Kuralt, of course, later went on to become the popular correspondent of the *On the Road* series, while Crawford, Socolow, and Bensley all became top producers on the Cronkite evening news in the 1960s. But during the best years of the Edwards show, the writer who did the most to make the broadcast work was a woman named Alice Weel.

Weel's special gift was writing to film. Straightforward tell stories were no great problem for anyone who had experience in either radio or print journalism. But taking a piece of silent film and writing a voice-over narration for it, skillfully timing the words to match the pictures, was a new journalistic wrinkle, and Alice Weel had mastered it.

But her talent was just part of her appeal. An effervescent, high-strung woman, Weel endeared herself to her colleagues with her flighty behavior and nervous mannerisms. She chewed on pens and pencils vigorously, and she waged a daily, losing battle with the messy carbon paper on the wire-service printers. By early afternoon, her hands and arms and most of her face were covered with black carbon smudges. Hewitt once threatened to buy her a coal miner's lamp.

Weel always seemed to be pursuing Edwards to fill him in on the latest voice-over she had written. One day, deeply intent on a piece she had just finished, she followed him out of the newsroom and along a corridor, her head down, reading aloud from her script. After they passed through one door and then another, she heard Edwards say, "For God's sake, Alice!" She looked up and discovered she had followed him into the men's room.

Weel also had the mildly eccentric trait of thinking out loud in vague, enigmatic phrases. Others on the Edwards show soon began to make a game out of it; whenever Weel uttered one of her cryptic remarks, everyone tried to figure out what she meant without asking her to explain or elaborate. One morning she came in and said, to no one in particular, "I wonder if the lamas are going to come through the ceiling." That was it; no further clues as to what she was talking about. Hewitt, Edwards, and others puzzled over that one for hours. Tibetan lamas? Peruvian llamas? And what ceiling? Finally they gave up and asked Weel to decipher the comment. It turned out that actor Fernando *Lamas* and his wife, Arlene Dahl, lived in the apartment above her and were in the habit of having such boisterous parties that—well, *that* explained it.

Some of Weel's more frantic moments came during her nightly efforts to get to the studio in time for the broadcast. The CBS News operation in those days was located in the Graybar Building on Lexington Avenue and Forty-second Street. But for a long time, during the 1950s, the Edwards show was broadcast from a studio in Liederkranz Hall on Fifty-ninth Street and Park Avenue. This meant that every night, under the mounting pressure of an inflexible deadline (ready or not, the program went on the air live at precisely 7:30 P.M.), CBS bodies would come flying out of the Graybar Building carrying scripts and graphics and other paraphernalia for the show, and begin to thread their way uptown through the snarled traffic of midtown Manhattan. Some of them hailed cabs, others dashed for the subway, and, on occasion, a few hardy souls sprinted the seventeen blocks to Liederkranz Hall. One evening, having had to make last-minute revisions in her script, Alice Weel was in a cab on her way to the studio just moments before air time. The traffic was even heavier than usual, and when her taxi stopped at a red light next to another cab, she leaned out the window and said to the driver of the second cab, "Excuse me, sir, but could we go ahead, please?"

The driver of the other taxi, a typical New York cabby, growled back, "Come on, lady, what's your hurry?"

In a desperately imploring tone, Weel replied, "We have to make air!"

In later years, those who worked with Alice Weel on the Edwards show would remember her with an amused affection deeply tinged with poignancy. In 1963, she married Homer Bigart, a veteran reporter for the *New York Times*. A widower, Bigart had lost his first wife to cancer, and, tragically, Alice was destined to go through a similar ordeal. While working at the 1968 political conventions Weel became ill, and a few months later she, too, died of cancer.

The atmosphere that prevailed on the old Edwards show—spontaneous, freewheeling, and at times utterly madcap—clearly reflected the spirit and personality of its producer. "I am the original 'Smilin' Jack' of TV journalism," Don Hewitt once said of himself. "I fly by the seat of my pants. I operate by visceral reaction." That was true. Viewing film in a screening room, his reactions were both visceral and colorful. One of his frequent criticisms of a film story was that it was slow in developing, that the lead wasn't "punchy" enough. "How many times do I have to say it?" he would yell. "You've got to get 'em into the fucking tent!" It was a favorite axiom of his that people did not buy television sets to watch the news. Therefore, it was up to them—Hewitt and his staff—to instill the news with enough flair and excitement to get the viewers "into the tent."

Hewitt's enthusiasm for the medium, for the electronic "toy" he was privileged to play with every day, never waned. Even in the late 1970s, after he had been in the business for thirty years, he had a way of making a screening room come alive. "Holy shit, did you see that?" he would holler when a particularly good camera shot popped up on the screen, or, at the other end of the spectrum, "That has to be the worst piece of crap I've ever seen." He also used to say that what made producing the evening news such a challenge was that he had to "get it up" every day. No matter how good the broadcast had been the night before, he had to go in the next day and start all over again.

Hewitt was in many ways more of a showman than anything else, and he worked at playing that role. He seemed intent on cultivating the bouncy, finger-popping style of a Hollywood hipster. Male acquaintances were invariably called "pal," and most of the time it was "honey" to the scores of young women who drifted through CBS over the years. A fairly short and dapper man, in his sartorial taste he also leaned more to a Hollywood look—open collars and the latest in sports coats—than to the Savile Row elegance of a Collingwood or Murrow. When Heywood Hale Broun began reporting for CBS in 1966, he took notice of Hewitt's flashy appearance and the bustling energy that went with it and promptly dubbed him "a smartly dressed ferret."

Unlike more sober journalists, Hewitt richly enjoyed keeping abreast of what was happening in the celebrity world, being *au courant* with the latest in Elizabeth Taylor's love life and so on. He was an inveterate gossip about such matters and a shameless name-dropper. "When I was at Grace Kelly's wedding," he would begin, and then go on to relate an incident that had nothing whatsoever to do with Grace Kelly or Prince Rainier. But it was a nice "intro." It succeeded in getting the listener "into the tent."

As time went on, Hewitt became so adept at pulling the Edwards show together at the last minute that he would wait until late in the day, an hour or so before air time, before preparing a "lineup." ("Lineup" is CBS lingo for the sequence of film stories around which a news broadcast is structured.) During the earlier part of the day, when he was letting things slide, he often immersed himself in poker or in a favorite board game, such as Scrabble. Much of the time his office took on the appearance of a white-collar poolroom, with loose cash and cards strewn all over his desk and the air thick with cigar smoke. If during such times someone ventured into his office with a question about that night's show, it was not uncommon for Hewitt to put him off until "later" because at the moment he was "busy." It was as if it wasn't much fun bringing order out of chaos every night unless he first took pains to create the chaos. Only in that way could he come on as a "Smilin' Jack," who flew by the seat of his pants.

There also were times when, feeling restless, Hewitt went out into the field to help cover a story, and it was on these occasions that he came the closest to fulfilling his Hearstian fantasies of being Hildy Johnson, brash reporter. In 1962, when an American Airlines plane went down in New York's Jamaica Bay, he was among the horde of newsmen who rushed out to the scene of the crash. At the time, there was a tugboat strike in New York, which meant there was no easy way to get out to the site of the wreckage. There was only one tugboat tied up at the dock, which, because of the strike, was "not available." Hewitt made a few inquiries, found out where he could locate the owner of the tug-boat, called him at his home in Connecticut, and, when he learned how much it normally cost to rent the tugboat for a day, offered twice the amount. The owner found that too attractive to resist, and the deal was made. Not long after, Hewitt and his CBS crews were chugging out to the site of the wreckage on the tugboat, while reporters and camera crews from the other networks were left stranded on the dock.

It also was around this time that he came up with what many Hewitt aficionados regard as his most outrageous stunt. One morning while he was sitting in his office, a report came in that there was a "disturbance" at a prison in New Jersey. Suspecting that "disturbance" was an official euphemism for "riot," Hewitt rustled up a film crew and took off for the New Jersey prison, about an hour's ride from New York. For once, journalistic skepticism was unjustified. A disturbance was all it was, and by the time Hewitt and his crew arrived at the prison, it had been quelled.

Hewitt, crestfallen, was not about to return to New York empty-handed. He began badgering the police and prison officials to let him and his crew inside the prison to take a few background, or "place-setting," shots. No, said the authorities. The prisoners were now firmly under control, and the sight of a television camera "and all that commo-tion" might just stir them up again. The same thought, oddly enough, had crossed Hewitt's mind, and so he persisted, couching his demands in lofty paeans about the First Amendment and "the people's right to know."

The prison officials finally relented a bit. They would allow the CBS people into an area from which they would have a partial view of the prison interior and some of the inmates, but only on one condition: neither Hewitt nor anyone else was to say a word to the prisoners. Hewitt agreed to that stipulation, and a short time later, he and his crew were setting up their equipment in the designated area. From that position, they could see about a dozen inmates, who seemed to be mildly curious about the filming procedure, but otherwise they be-trayed no sign of emotion. Hewitt decided something had to be done about that. As soon as everything was set up, he whispered to his cameraman out of the side of his mouth, "Are you rolling?" The cameraman nodded. Then, looking up at the prisoners, Hewitt placed his left hand in the crook of his right arm and thrust his right fist upward, action finger extended, in the classic Sicilian gesture of goodwill or, as it's known in less delicate circles, "Up yours."

The greeting triggered the desired response. The prisoners came alive with catcalls and obscenities and the rattling of bars with tin cups and plates—in short, lots of good footage. The prison officials, who had not seen Hewitt's gesture, now came running over in a fury, demanding to know what had happened. Hewitt, clinging to the letter of the truth, assured them he had kept his end of the bargain: neither he nor anyone in his crew had said a word to the inmates. Hildy Johnson lives!

Edwards himself occasionally went out on a story, and he scored his most spectacular success as a field correspondent in 1956. In July of that year, two ships, steaming through fog and darkness, crashed into each other off the coast of Nantucket. One of them was the *Stockholm,* a Swedish cruise ship, and the other was the Italian liner *Andrea Doria.* On the morning after the collision, Edwards, Hewitt, and a film crew took off for Quonset Naval Station in Rhode Island, which was serving as the "coverage point" for the story. When they arrived, they were disheartened to learn there was no boat or plane available to transport them out to the *Andrea Doria,* which was then still afloat in the North Atlantic. This time Hewitt had nothing in his bag of tricks. But then a naval commander walked up to them with a big smile on his face and said, "Excuse me, aren't you Douglas Edwards?"

The officer, it turned out, was a fan of the broadcast, and a few minutes later he not only offered Edwards and his crew transportation, he gave them a choice between a cutter and an amphibious airplane. They chose the plane, and by a remarkable stroke of luck, Edwards and his party arrived at the collision site just as the *Andrea Doria* was starting to sink. With cameras whirring and Edwards recording an eyewitness narration, the plane continued to circle the ship until the *Andrea Doria* disappeared beneath the waves.

Douglas Edwards with the News began that evening with a shot of Edwards in the plane and then cut to the lengthy footage of the *Andrea Doria* going down. It was one hell of a lead. Aside from clobbering the other networks (which was all Edwards and Hewitt really cared about), it was an early example of the enormous advantage television has over other media in covering a certain kind of news event. Newspapers and magazines could flesh out the story of the disaster in other ways, but in terms of an eyewitness account of the sinking itself, nothing could match the impact of actually seeing, on film, a great ship go to her grave.

As his encounter with the naval commander indicates, Doug Edwards was by this time firmly established as a television celebrity. When his five-night-a-week broadcast first went on the air in 1948, its audience for the entire week was estimated to be about 30,000. By 1956, the weekly figures were well into the millions, and in the years ahead they continued to rise. Even more gratifying to Edwards and Hewitt was the fact that it had become, by this time, the news program with the largest national audience, having surpassed its chief rival, NBC's *Camel News Caravan,* which was anchored by John Cameron Swayze.

Achieving that number one position had not been easy. Although the *Camel News Caravan* lagged behind Edwards in getting started (it first went on the air in February 1949), NBC News in general had moved more quickly than CBS to build up its TV staff and film operation. Largely for this reason, Swayze's show enjoyed a comfortable lead in the ratings during the early 1950s. But as time went on, Edwards began to cut into that lead, and in 1955, he edged ahead of Swayze. Once out in front, the Edwards broadcast was able to maintain its advantage.

Officials at NBC noted this shift of viewers from Swayze to Edwards with growing dismay. It wasn't just a case of losing part of the news audience. That was the least of it, for by this time the networks were beginning to appreciate the "lead-in" value of the evening newscasts. Surveys revealed that it was not uncommon for viewers to stay with one channel—the first one they turned on—through the course of an entire evening. And since many of them began their viewing each night with the news, that was the show that, in Hewitt's phrase, got them "into the tent." Thus the ratings for the newscasts were having no small effect on the rating that truly mattered: the ones for prime-time programs that translated into millions of dollars. Given this situation, it's only natural that NBC would fight back, and it did. It was the opening round of a battle that is still being waged.

5 An Accident of Casting

Douglas Edwards and John Cameron Swayze differed significantly in their on-air personalities. With his soft, serious voice and "choirboy's" face, Edwards came across as personable but in a low-key and thoroughly businesslike way. Swayze, on the other hand, was not so inhibited. With his flashy boutonniere, which soon became his trademark, and his breezy, percolating style of delivery, he was the forerunner of the "happy-hour" approach that would become the vogue on certain local TV newscasts in the 1970s. Like the Edwards show, the *Camel News Caravan* had little to offer in the way of relevant film pieces, but Swayze had his own brisk method of handling the preponderance of tell stories. Toward the end of each broadcast, he would start to bubble with enthusiasm and say, "Now let's go hopscotching the world for headlines!" Then, after zipping through a grab bag of items at a merry pace, he would end the program with a flourish vaguely reminiscent of Porky Pig informing the kiddies that the cartoon is over: "That's the story, folks. Glad we could get together!"

When NBC brought Swayze to New York in 1947, he was forty-one years old and had fifteen years of experience behind him as a radio newscaster, first in Kansas City and later in Los Angeles. But he was a failure in his initial stint as a big-time, network newscaster. His ebullient manner of presentation soon began to grate on his NBC superiors, and after a few months in New York, Swayze was told he was through— through on radio, that is. Television was then making its first, uncertain appearance on the scene, and Swayze was told, more or less as an afterthought, that he was welcome to try his hand at that if he so

71

desired. Since it was the only alternative to outright dismissal, he so desired, but with minimal expectations. Like Edwards, Swayze had no inkling of what was about to befall him.

Banished to the new and experimental medium, John Cameron Swayze became the only NBC newscaster then devoting all his time to television. As a result, he was picked—almost by default—to be the network's TV commentator at the 1948 political conventions. Like Edwards, Swayze did a good job at the conventions, and, having thus redeemed himself in another medium, he was given the *Camel News Caravan* when that program went on the air five nights a week in February 1949. It was not long before millions of viewers became acquainted with the man and his boutonniere.

The carnation in the lapel and the "hopscotching for headlines" may have been corny, but Swayze quickly piled up a huge lead over Edwards in the ratings and went on to enjoy an impressive run as a top TV personality. In those early years, television was not taken all that seriously, even in its newscasts. Swayze was an engaging novelty at a time when television itself was still a novelty. But as attitudes changed, his breezy style began to wear thin. Hence, by 1956, when it became obvious that viewer preference was shifting more and more to CBS and Doug Edwards, NBC's executives quietly decided that the time had come to send Swayze "hopscotching" off their nightly news show.

Throughout the early history of TV journalism, the political conventions served as a showcase for the unveiling of new talent. It was their work at the 1948 conventions that maneuvered both Edwards and Swayze into position to become the pioneers of the evening news at their respective networks. Then, at the 1952 conventions, CBS trotted out a relatively obscure former United Press reporter named Walter Cronkite in the hope that his looks, manner, and all-around ability would strike a responsive chord in the viewers. They did. And four years later, at the 1956 conventions, NBC launched the team that, with Cronkite, would dominate television news for over a decade. When Edwards, like Swayze, finally went out of style, Cronkite for CBS and Chet Huntley and David Brinkley for NBC would enter the field in the most prolonged and spirited ratings battle in the history of TV journalism.

Although they had no national reputations to speak of prior to the 1956 conventions, both Huntley and Brinkley brought to their assignment that summer many years of experience in both radio and television news. Huntley was born in Montana, and from the cattle-and-sheep ranch on which he was raised, he went on to college, where he started out as a premed student. But during his senior year at the University of Washington in Seattle, he worked at odd jobs at a small 100-watt radio station, and that experience was enough to get him hooked on a radio career. He spent the next three years at various stations in the Pacific Northwest, and then in 1937, when he was twenty-five, Huntley landed a job at a station in Los Angeles. It was to be his base of operations for the next eighteen years, most of them with the CBS affiliate there, and the last four—from 1951 to 1955—at the ABC station.

During his years as a top newscaster in Los Angeles, Huntley acquired a reputation as a fearless commentator who took strong stands on McCarthyism and other controversial issues. In 1955, when NBC hired him and brought him to New York, there was talk that he would become that network's answer to Ed Murrow. The political climate of the time was such that some NBC executives were a little nervous about that prospect. But they had nothing to fear. As it turned out, NBC would have it both ways with Huntley: he would become a star of Murrovian magnitude but in a way that was seldom divisive or troublesome. Indeed, in the years that followed, it was Brinkley, far more than Huntley, who made waves with his political commentary.

David Brinkley grew up in North Carolina, and from an early age he aspired to be a writer. By the time he was in high school, his appreciation of the fine points of craft was such that his literary hero was E. B. White, the great *New Yorker* stylist. He began his own writing career as a reporter on his hometown newspaper, the *Wilmington Star-News,* and that was followed by a two-and-a-half-year stint with the United Press. There he wrote for the radio wire, which most of the senior wire-service men eschewed on the grounds that it was beneath them. But Brinkley liked the tight discipline it imposed. More to the point, he felt he had a genuine knack for it, and so in 1943, after a brief hitch in the Army, he went to Washington and offered his services to the networks. His first choice was CBS, which turned him down. He then applied at NBC and was hired.

Brinkley was content, at first, to write copy that others read on the air, but given the economic realities of the business, he soon decided to try to become an on-air "talent." When television started up, he chose to concentrate on that, and, like Swayze and Edwards, he ben-

efited from the fact that the big-name radio newscasters were so scornful of the new medium. By the early 1950s, he had become the counterpart of CBS's Neil Strawser—the "voice of Washington" on the *Camel
News Caravan.* He also did an occasional stand-upper, but prior to 1956,
only the most alert viewers of the Swayze show had any idea who David
Brinkley was. As for Huntley, he still was all but unknown outside the
Los Angeles area. That is how matters stood on the eve of the 1956
conventions when the two men were joined together in electronic
matrimony.

In later years, long after Huntley and Brinkley had gone on to
become the most successful duo in the history of television news, NBC
insiders often would recall, with mirth and wonder, the bizarre way the
original pairing came about. In the words of Reuven Frank, who in 1956
was a top producer at NBC News, it was "a show-business accident—
an accident of casting."

When NBC executives, including Frank, began to discuss how to
cover the 1956 conventions, the memory of what had happened four
years earlier was very much on their minds. At the 1952 conventions,
NBC's main TV commentator had been Bill Henry, a respected newscaster with a solid background in both radio and print journalism.
Henry, in fact, had far more experience as a broadcaster than did his
CBS counterpart, Walter Cronkite. But because of the different ways
the two networks chose to orchestrate their TV coverage in 1952,
Henry was at a severe disadvantage vis-à-vis Cronkite. With Don Hewitt at the controls, and keeping everyone alert with his manic directions,
CBS adroitly structured its coverage around Cronkite, using his presence as the dramatic and editorial focal point. CBS even came up with
a fancy new term to describe its technique. Cronkite, it said, was no
mere "commentator," that old-fashioned radio word. Instead, he should
be known as an "anchorman." In contrast, NBC's coverage was sprawling and amorphous and had no fixed center of identity. Indeed, the
most enduring picture that many NBC viewers took away from the
1952 conventions was of an attractive, insistent woman who kept opening and closing refrigerator doors and asserting, "You can be sure if it's
Westinghouse." People would remember Betty Furness long after they
had forgotten Bill Henry.

It was almost as if NBC had decided, consciously or otherwise, to
treat the conventions as a television spectacle, an extravaganza, a full-

blown media event, whereas CBS viewed them as a running news story that called for a heavy emphasis on reportorial content. The result was that CBS not only won a victory in the ratings, but it suddenly had, in Walter Cronkite, a new star to add to its already impressive stable of prominent journalists. As for NBC, it had four years to get itself in shape for the rematch. But one thing for sure: the NBC people were determined that next time they, too, would have one of those anchorman fellas. Up until 1956, they continued to think in terms of anchor*man*, singular. But the "accident of casting" would change that.

Within the ranks of the NBC management, an intense debate took place over the question of who should anchor the 1956 convention coverage. Most participants agreed that the network should present a new face, someone other than Bill Henry. One group lobbied hard for Huntley, while another faction pushed just as vigorously for Brinkley. The NBC executives remained locked in that stalemate for several weeks until one day, as they were thrashing out the problem for the umpteenth time, it suddenly dawned on them that there was no law preventing them from featuring *two* anchormen. "It was like the light bulb going on over someone's head in the comics," Reuven Frank recalled years later. So that settled it. The new team was born, and by the time the 1956 conventions were over, Chet Huntley and David Brinkley had become household names.

Faced with this dual challenge, CBS did not exactly collapse in terror. With Cronkite in the anchor slot and Murrow and Sevareid paired in another booth to provide occasional commentary, CBS again led in the ratings. (In both 1952 and 1956, ABC finished a distant third, as it would in succeeding convention years up to and including 1976.) But NBC had closed the gap considerably, and, just as important in terms of network morale, it received most of the critical acclaim. The *New York Times,* as usual, was the review that mattered the most. Jack Gould praised the Huntley-Brinkley team for having "injected the much-needed note of humor in commentary" and then added: "The CBS news department needs to cheer up."

Once the conventions were over, NBC was not about to let Huntley and Brinkley slide back out of the limelight. The two new stars were called on to take over NBC's nightly news show, and in October 1956, *The Huntley-Brinkley Report* went on the air. For Swayze, the happy hopscotcher, this marked the end of his career at NBC. Embittered by the decision to relieve him, he left the network soon thereafter. He did resurface for a brief time in the early 1960s as anchorman on ABC's evening news show, but when that comeback failed, he drifted out of the news business, and by the mid-1960s, he had become a Madison Avenue pitchman, Viewers who remembered him from his newscasting days were, at first, mildly startled when a program would break for a commercial and there was John Cameron Swayze extolling the wonders of Timex wristwatches.

Insofar as there was an NBC counterpart of Don Hewitt, it was Reuven Frank. As the first producer of *The Huntley-Brinkley Report,* he guided the show through its difficult, formative years, and by the time he left the broadcast in 1965, it had become the top-rated and, in many ways, the best news program on television. But the first few months of its existence in 1956 and 1957 were a nightmare. One major problem was the set. In his exuberance over the new show, a meddling middle-level executive said the program needed a set that would evoke what he called "a ballet" of the news, and, following his instructions, an NBC designer proceeded to build a set that was big enough to accommodate a lavish production of *Swan Lake.* Among its vivid features were objects shaped like scimitars, which, when viewed on screen, looked like large, ornate pillars; and Frank was soon lamenting that no matter what camera angle he tried, it invariably looked as though "one of those goddamned pillar things was growing out of Huntley's head." (Hewitt, viewing all this from his control room at CBS, gleefully dubbed the NBC set "the Martian Ballroom.") Frank finally persuaded his superiors that the grandiose set should be dismantled, and in its place were constructed, on Frank's request, a couple of "closet sets," as he called them: one closet for Huntley in New York, and another for Brinkley in Washington.

But the scrapping of the Martian Ballroom was hardly enough to relieve the depression that permeated the staff of *The Huntley-Brinkley Report.* In its first year on the air, the broadcast was not only a disappointment but it showed every sign of becoming a full-scale disaster. Not only did it fail to cut into the lead *Douglas Edwards with the News* had built up over Swayze, but it proceeded to slip even farther behind in the ratings. During one thirteen-week stretch, in the summer of 1957, the broadcast was entirely sustaining, which meant it was unable to sell so much as one minute of commercial time. The situation was so bleak that Frank was convinced the program soon would be shelved. And no doubt it would have been if NBC had been successful in its attempt that year to lure Eric Sevareid away from CBS.

Ignoring the show was bad enough, but even worse, a lot of people were making fun of it, especially its close: "Good night, Chet." "Good night, David. And good night for NBC News." That was Reuven Frank's brainstorm, and years later, after it had become accepted as the show's trademark, he would take a rather perverse delight in having dreamed it up. "Supposing you had been the guy who first said 'So's your old man!' or something else that got into the language," he once remarked. "Well, that's what I did. I wrote something that got into the language." In the beginning, however, the tag lines didn't seem to have much of a future, and among those who had no use for Frank's little jingle were the two men who had to utter it every night. "It's corny," protested Brinkley, and, even worse, he added, "it makes us sound like a couple of fags." Frank, his pride of authorship wounded, challenged them to come up with something better. They never did.

Whatever it made them sound like, the show's close helped to underscore Huntley and Brinkley as a team, and eventually viewers began to respond to the chemistry of their interaction. In the late 1950s, David Brinkley was bringing an almost revolutionary new tone to broadcast journalism, a steady dose of wit and irreverence that was a radical, but refreshing, departure from the Murrovian norm. Once, when he was reporting on a rather silly debate over whether the name of Boulder Dam should be changed to Hoover Dam, Brinkley wearily suggested that the way to end the squabble would be to have the former President "change *his* name to Herbert Boulder."

Brinkley's wit flowed from his strong talent as a writer. Over the years, whenever the subject of writing for network news came up, Brinkley's name invariably would be the first one mentioned. Both within and without the industry, he is regarded by many as the best writer ever to grace TV journalism. But since Brinkley's style often hovered on the edge of flippancy and smart-aleckism, it might easily have had a negative effect had it not been balanced by Chet Huntley's solidity—his "plainsman's strength," as one friend called it. Like Cronkite, he projected a sober outlook, a steady, no-nonsense manner. Or as Brinkley once said of his partner in a tone of amused affection, Huntley came across on the air as "relentlessly serious."

In any event, together they began to attract a larger and larger audience, and by the spring of 1958, *The Huntley-Brinkley Report* had progressed to the point where it was able to land a regular sponsor (Texaco, which bought out the entire show). That was the critical turning point; the steady revenue from Texaco enabled Frank to enlarge his budget and improve the program by giving it greater scope. As a result, the upward trend continued, and by the fall of 1958, Huntley and Brinkley had pulled even with the Edwards show. The two broadcasts remained that way, in virtual lockstep, until the summer of 1960 when it was time, once again, for what Murray Kempton has joyously described as "the quadrennial assault on decency and reason."

In his best tone of studied boredom, Brinkley opened one of the early sessions in NBC's coverage of the 1960 conventions with these words: "This is the convention [pause], and there are those who like it." As it turned out, a lot more people liked it on NBC than on CBS. This time, Huntley and Brinkley blew Cronkite and Murrow and the other big CBS guns right out of the arena. Not only did they roll up a huge victory in the ratings, but they received even more critical applause than they did in 1956. This time around, Jack Gould didn't even bother to be polite about it. Huntley and Brinkley, he wrote, "swept away the stuffy, old-fashioned concept of ponderous reportage on the home screen." And in another column, he wrote: "The pontificating commentators of television . . . couldn't withstand the fresh breeze of David Brinkley's wit."

For CBS News, which had become more than a little arrogant in its role as the long-acknowledged leader in broadcast journalism, the rout it sustained at the 1960 conventions was a great humiliation. The far-reaching consequences were even worse. Their victory at the conventions gave Huntley and Brinkley such momentum that they proceeded to open up a commanding lead over Edwards in the evening-news battle for ratings. Indeed, their broadcast became so entrenched as the dominant news show on television that they were able to maintain that supremacy over the next seven years. And in the course of those years, the continued success of Huntley and Brinkley would have a devastating effect on the internal power structure at CBS News. Two presidents of CBS News would be fired, Walter Cronkite would be dumped as convention anchorman in 1964, and later that year, Don Hewitt would lose his job as executive producer of the evening news. For some, the setbacks were temporary; Cronkite was able to regain his old job, and Hewitt also went on to make a big comeback. But Doug Edwards was not so fortunate. Of all the CBS people who were cut up during these years of purge, no one lost more than Edwards because, for him, the career damage was permanent.

By 1960, there were a number of people at CBS who felt that a change on the evening news was long overdue, and when it was over-taken by *The Huntley-Brinkley Report,* that change became impera-tive. Edwards had long been viewed by his detractors as a lightweight, someone who belonged to an earlier era, when television was still in diapers. One handicap was his voice. The importance or appeal of vocal quality in a TV anchorman cannot be overestimated. To cite just some of the more obvious examples: Murrow, Cronkite, Huntley, and Rea-soner all were blessed with strong, resonant voices that helped give any program they anchored a firm tone of authority. Edwards's voice was pleasant enough, but it was rather bland and nonassertive. It wasn't only his voice that was nonassertive. If Edwards was criticized for being merely a "reader," an upgraded announcer, he brought a lot of it on himself. For the most part, he did not become deeply involved in the daily preparation of the broadcast. "You know, Doug," Hewitt would point out, trying to prod Edwards into taking a more active role in his own show, "if people don't like us, they're not going to say that was a lousy Don Hewitt show. They're going to say that was a lousy Douglas Edwards show." But it was no accident that the prevailing view within the world of CBS was that the program was much more Hewitt's crea-tion than Edwards's. Through all these years, it was Hewitt's drive and personality that had dominated the broadcast. Edwards, in effect, had allowed himself to become little more than a reader.

As his ratings declined and the in-house criticism of his work grew more insistent, Edwards became increasingly apprehensive and fell into the habit of taking long lunches, at which he sometimes drank more than he should have. He would almost always be in good shape when it came time for the broadcast, but the CBS News executives who were anxious to replace him claimed to detect slurring and other tell-tale slips in his on-air delivery. It became a sort of vicious cycle. As the ratings continued to slide and the complaints grew louder, the greater Edwards's anxiety; and to relieve that anxiety, the more he drank, giving his critics that much more ammunition.

By 1962, it was decided that a change had to be made, and in March of that year, the network announced that Douglas Edwards, the man who had "pioneered" the evening news at CBS fourteen years earlier, was being taken off that assignment. Starting in April, the broadcast would be anchored by Walter Cronkite.

Cronkite was in his office when he learned of the decision. The next thing he knew, he looked up to see Edwards walking in with a smile on his face, his hand outstretched to offer his congratulations. He said he wanted Cronkite to know that he harbored no ill will toward him, that he had always respected Cronkite and wished him the best of luck on the show. Years later, in recalling the gesture, Cronkite would shake his head and say it was "the classiest damn thing I ever saw."

The move had not taken Edwards by surprise, and when the moment finally came, he was, in a way, almost relieved. But he was not prepared for the *extent* of his fall from eminence. In the months leading up to the switch, Cronkite had been the regular anchorman on two network broadcasts, the *Sunday News Special* and *Eyewitness,* a half-hour program on Friday night that dealt with the week's top story. Edwards had hoped (had even kind of assumed) that he would be given one of the two shows as a gesture to cushion the blow of having lost the flagship, the evening news. But the *Eyewitness* assignment went to Collingwood, the Sunday night broadcast to Sevareid, and Edwards was offered instead the late-night, local newscast, which he accepted without much enthusiasm. He broadcast the local news for the next two years, a job that took him out of the network's mainstream, and he soon slipped to the point where he not only ranked well behind Cronkite and the rest of the old guard, but also behind a wave of younger men who had come along and nailed down the best assignments.

In the years that followed, Edwards's star continued to decline. By the late-1960s his name evoked memories of the past and little else. Almost all of his later work was in radio, although he continued to appear on television as the reader of five-minute newscasts, which went on the air each afternoon. He clung to this sliver of exposure with a grim tenacity. As late as 1977, he would point out, with a kind of stubborn pride, that he had thirty years behind him as a continuous newscaster on network television, a record of longevity unmatched by anyone else in the industry. The fact that for the past decade or so his only TV program had been the five-minute afternoon news strip—basically a "throwaway" time-filler—made it a fairly hollow boast. Nevertheless, it took a certain strength of character to hang on at CBS over the years in such ego-deflating circumstances.

One day in the early 1970s, an NBC News producer was having

lunch with a friend from CBS. Both men had been at their respective networks since the 1950s, and in the course of their conversation they began to reminisce. At one point the NBC man said, "You know, I suppose it's fair to say that neither Swayze nor Edwards was equipped to handle the television thing once it began to get really big. I guess that's why we needed Cronkite and Brinkley and the others to come in and give it some weight. But goddamnit," he said with sudden asperity, "at least your guy had the grace and dignity to stay in the business. What I mean is, he didn't go out and become a fucking watch salesman."

6 Anchorman

When he took over as anchorman on the evening news in the spring of 1962, Walter Cronkite was forty-five years old and a man clearly in his prime. This new phase in his career was soon to elevate him to the point where he would reign over television news as no one before him ever had. But if the best was yet to come, he had already been a working journalist for twenty-five years and had accomplished a great deal, first as a wire-service reporter, then later in television. Like so many other broadcast journalists of his generation (Brinkley, Sevareid, Collingwood, and Howard K. Smith, to name a few), Cronkite was an alumnus of the United Press. But whereas the others put in only brief apprenticeships at UP before moving on to more lucrative jobs, Cronkite spent eleven years with the news agency—and loved just about every minute of it. Even in later years, long after he had achieved his great success at CBS, he would recall his days at the United Press with an affection and nostalgia that put one in mind of Mark Twain writing about his boyhood in Missouri. Appropriately, some of Cronkite's fondest memories were of his first years with the UP in Missouri, the state where he was born and raised.

His paternal ancestors were among the early Dutch settlers who built up communities along the Hudson River in the seventeenth century. (Cronkite comes from solid Teutonic stock, half Dutch and half German.) His forebears remained in upstate New York until the latter half of the nineteenth century, when his grandfather joined the great migration westward and settled in Missouri. An admirer of Leland Stanford, the philanthropist and/or robber baron, Cronkite's grandfa-

ther named his son Walter Leland. The name was passed on to Cronkite, and he, in turn, has passed it on to *his* only son, although to ease
the burden of having to carry the name Walter Leland Cronkite III
through life, he also gave him the nickname "Chip"—as in off the old
block.

Cronkite was born in Saint Joseph, but soon thereafter, his family
moved to Kansas City and then, when he was ten, left Missouri and
moved to Houston. Both his grandfather and his father were dentists,
but Cronkite had no interest in pulling teeth for a living. He wanted
adventure, a line of work that would give him a chance to travel and
see the world. His early ambition was to become a mining engineer
because he felt certain that would take him to exotic places, but his
thoughts soon turned toward journalism. He worked as a part-time
reporter while attending the University of Texas, and by his junior year
he knew he had found his vocation. He quit school to take a full-time
job on the *Houston Press,* and the following year, 1937, he was back in
Kansas City, starting his career with the United Press.

Kansas City was a lively night town in those days. It was also an
important relay point for the United Press and therefore was one of the
largest and busiest UP bureaus in the country except for New York and
Washington. Cronkite was enamored of all of it, the raffish life of the city
as well as the mundane yet fiercely competitive world of the United
Press. He rejoiced in the sweat and drudgery and deadline-every-
minute pressure of wire-service work, and in all phases of that work:
reporting, rewriting, editing, and even wire-filing. Years later, when he
was a big shot at CBS, he often would chuckle and say that he was "the
only young newsman who actually *enjoyed* filing the wire." It is important but tedious work, and most young newsmen assigned to it desperately long for liberation, for a chance to get out on the street and do
some reporting. But Cronkite loved the editorial power that came with
selecting stories from the national wire, then trimming them down and
deciding in what order they should go out on the regional and state
wires. "It was a wonderful feeling," he said. "Here I was, just a kid,
shaping the front pages of the small client newspapers in that part of
the Midwest." A nice irony in that: by the time he was recalling this
experience, his own "electronic front page" had been a major force in
driving many of those small papers out of business.

Cronkite did a lot more than file the wire, however, and by 1942
his UP superiors were so impressed that they sent him to London as a

war correspondent. His first regular beat in London—the U.S. Eighth Air Force—was a tough and often heartbreaking assignment. Every day Cronkite and other reporters went out to the air bases to interview the young fliers when they returned from their missions. The tide in the war had not yet shifted in the Allies' favor, and this was a very rough period; sometimes as many as half of the planes that went out did not come back. But Cronkite handled this assignment with the cool poise and professionalism that later would become so familiar to millions of television viewers. And eventually his work caught the eye of that ever-alert recruiter—Ed Murrow.

The two men met for lunch at the Savile Club, and Murrow was pleased to observe that Cronkite was *not* wearing Argyle socks and that, in all other ways, he seemed to be a sensible and mature young man. Cronkite then was making $67 a week, and when Murrow offered him $125 a week plus commercial fees, he accepted, even though he did not understand radio's fee system and thus had no idea that it would probably triple his salary. He and Murrow shook on the deal, and that seemed to be that.

But Cronkite soon began to have second thoughts. His UP bureau chief, Harrison Salisbury, told him that if he stayed, he would be given a $25-a-week raise. Such spontaneous largess from the notoriously tightfisted United Press was unheard of, and Cronkite was extremely flattered. Even more to the point, he was deeply attached to the UP; to him, the hard, straightforward reporting of wire-service work, with all its emphasis on speed and scooping the opposition, was what journalism was all about. Compared to that, radio seemed vague, gimmicky, and a bit too dependent on frills and showmanship. Cronkite was leery about getting into that world of microphones and sound effects, and so, after thinking it over, he called Murrow and said he had changed his mind: he preferred to stay with the United Press.

Murrow was annoyed; he felt Cronkite had reneged on their agreement. More than that, he was puzzled. He regarded wire-service work as an unrewarding, menial existence, and he simply could not fathom how anyone burdened with that would turn down a chance to become part of the glamorous CBS team of war correspondents. He concluded then and there that while Cronkite was no doubt a first-rate reporter, he was also a man of rather pedestrian values. Having formed that opinion, Murrow never really altered it, even in later years when the two men finally became colleagues at CBS.

From London, Cronkite followed the war as it moved across Europe, and if as a dreamy youth in Houston he had yearned for adventure, he now found it. He went on bombing missions (including one in which he manned a .50-caliber machine gun to help fight off German fighter planes), covered the Allied invasion of Normandy, parachuted into Holland with the 101st Airborne Division, and crash-landed in a glider at Bastogne during the Battle of the Bulge. By the end of the war, he was an important by-line correspondent for the United Press, and in 1946 he was rewarded with a choice assignment—Moscow. But postwar Moscow proved to be a dreary and desolate place, and in addition to the stark living conditions and the UP's parsimony (in response to his request for a new car, his superiors suggested he get a bicycle), Cronkite had to cope with the rising tensions in U.S.-Soviet relations. After two years of Kremlin-watching, he had had enough of Moscow, and he returned to America to discuss future assignments.

By this time, his ardor for the United Press was beginning to cool. He was thirty-one years old, he and his wife, Betsy, were planning to start a family, and although he was making top-scale salary at UP, that only amounted to $125 a week. Yet there was no way that he could buck the wire-service system, and he knew it. Once they had gained some experience, the best reporters usually left the UP for more lucrative jobs somewhere else, and, to replace them, the wire service recruited other bright young men. That was the system. An experienced reporter who was very good and chose to remain at UP did so because wire-service work was in his blood and he was willing to make the financial sacrifice.

That was the decision Cronkite had to face in 1948. If he could have gotten more money, he definitely would have stayed, for he still loved the competitive drive and dash of UP reporting. But he felt he had to think of his future, of the family responsibilities that lay ahead. So he decided to make a change. He went home to Kansas City, and there, through an old friend at radio station KMBC, he more or less created a new job for himself. At a salary of $250 a week, he became Washington correspondent for a string of ten radio stations in Missouri, Kansas, and Nebraska. He still had reservations about radio journalism, with all its reliance on electronic gadgetry, but such qualms now gave way to more pressing financial considerations.

From 1948 to 1950, Cronkite scurried around Washington, rustling up regional stories for his ten radio stations. Most of this work was small potatoes, but he didn't mind. He enjoyed the hustle and bustle of Washington, and besides, he planned to return to Kansas City soon to take over as general manager of KMBC. He had reached the sober conclusion that he would never make much money as a journalist. It was far beyond Walter Cronkite's comprehension that the day would come when he would be paid half a million dollars a year to broadcast the news on television.

When the Korean War broke out in 1950, Murrow, who knew that Cronkite had made the move from print to broadcasting, called him and asked if he'd be interested in going to Korea for CBS. This time there was no doubt in Cronkite's mind; stirred by the old war correspondent's itch, he jumped at the offer. There was a slight complication, however. Faced with a manpower shortage in its Washington bureau, CBS asked Cronkite if he'd be willing to delay his departure and spend his first few weeks on the network's payroll working in Washington. He agreed to that, and as part of his preparation for the overseas assignment, Cronkite began doing the Korean War story every night on WTOP, the CBS television station in Washington. There was no worthwhile film to speak of, so he generally used maps and a blackboard and other graphics to "illustrate" the day's action. In some ways, his nightly presentations resembled Richard Hubbell's 1941 chalk talks on World War II, but Cronkite brought to them two striking qualities: an ability to simplify the copious details of a confusing war, and a sure sense of authority born out of his own experience as a war correspondent. He was so good at it, in fact, that the WTOP people soon asked him to take over the entire evening newscast; and before long, he was also doing network stand-uppers for the Edwards show. In the meantime, Cronkite was growing impatient. When, after several weeks had passed, he finally inquired about the Korean assignment, he was told that the CBS brass had changed its mind: he was doing too good a job "explaining" the war from Washington. "I was madder than hell!" Cronkite later recalled. "I thought I had been sold down the river to a lousy local TV station, and I was ready to quit, right on the spot."

But he didn't. Instead, he continued to report on the Korean War from Washington and to take on other network assignments in both radio and television. In the spring of 1951, he was the reporter on the live TV coverage of General MacArthur's return from Korea after he had been fired by Truman. And on that occasion, Cronkite revealed another gift that would work heavily in his favor: an ability to ad-lib intelligently, to make comments related to the pictures being seen, and to weave in other details that helped explain the overall story.

Among those who came to appreciate Cronkite's talents was Sig Mickelson, who had just recently taken over as head of CBS's small TV news staff. Compared to radio, television news was still a nickel-and-dime operation, but by the fall of 1951, when the coast-to-coast cable was joined, Mickelson knew that his big moment was rapidly approaching. Now that transcontinental telecasts had become a reality, Mickelson believed that 1952 was destined to be a pivotal year in the history of television news. He also believed that the first great test would come that summer at the political conventions, for they would be the first news event of any size and complexity to be telecast live, coast to coast. Furthermore, Mickelson felt that the way to achieve maximum impact at the conventions was for CBS to shape and structure its TV coverage around a central figure, one full-time correspondent. It was he who coined the new word—anchorman—to describe his focal-point concept. Thus, like Reuven Frank with his Huntley-Brinkley tag line, Sig Mickelson invented a term that has become part of the language.

Mickelson's first choice for the assignment was Murrow (naturally) and, after him, either Sevareid or Collingwood. But Murrow and his boys were still wary of television, still disdainful of its propriety as a medium for serious news. Whatever a TV anchorman was supposed to be, none of them wanted to be it. Some CBS people suggested going with Doug Edwards since he had been the main TV reporter during the limited coverage of the 1948 conventions. But Mickelson rejected that. Edwards, he agreed, was doing a good enough job on the evening news, but that was a fairly routine format. The convention role he had in mind called for someone with more weight, a more extensive background in journalism.

The next name to come up was Robert Trout, and in many ways he was the most logical choice of all. Trout had been a top radio commentator at conventions for CBS since 1936, and he had always brought to the assignment a dry humor and a nice, anecdotal style of reporting. Mickelson thought Trout was just great—on radio. But he wasn't sure that Trout's loquacious, often meandering style would be all that suitable for television.

As an alternative, Mickelson proposed Walter Cronkite. It was true, he admitted, that Cronkite was new to the network, new to broadcasting, but he was an experienced and highly respected journalist. Even more important, he had demonstrated an impressive knack for *television* ad-libbing, for talking directly to pictures in a way that was informative yet not intrusive. Mickelson's corporate superiors were a little nervous about Cronkite and continued to lean toward Trout because he had so much more experience as a broadcaster. But since the conventions were Mickelson's pet project, and since he was so sold on Cronkite, they decided to go along with his preference—at least for the first convention. If Cronkite didn't work out, they reasoned, Bob Trout could always be brought in for the second convention.

When Cronkite learned of the decision, he immediately went to work preparing himself for the assignment. Like Mickelson, he believed that those first coast-to-coast conventions had the potential of being a decisive moment in television history, and that this was his big chance. Throughout the spring and early summer of 1952, he sequestered himself in his office for hours on end, studying everything he could find on the candidates, the issues, and all sorts of other convention lore. By the time he went to Chicago, where both conventions were to be held that year, he had so much information stored in his head that he could have ad-libbed through the entire summer if necessary.

On July 7, 1952, Cronkite settled into the new CBS anchor booth as the Republican convention commenced its proceedings, and within hours after the opening gavel, an electric excitement swept through the CBS people assembled in Chicago. The moment was not unlike an opening night on Broadway when a new talent explodes across the footlights for the first time. Before that first day was over, CBS knew it had a winner, and there was no more talk about replacing Cronkite with Robert Trout—at least not *that* year.

The combination of Sig Mickelson's strategy, Don Hewitt's tactical skill as director, and, above all, Walter Cronkite's performance gave CBS a big victory over the other networks at the 1952 conventions. But more than that, it was an enormous breakthrough for television itself. By the time the conventions were over, radio, which had lorded it over television at the 1948 conventions, had come to the end of its reign as the dominant voice in broadcast journalism. As in some massive glacial upheaval, all the weight and influence suddenly had shifted over to television.

Early one morning, as they were nearing the end of their stay in Chicago, Mickelson and Cronkite went for a walk along Michigan Avenue. Mickelson told his anchorman that he had hit it very big, and from now on everything was going to be different. For one thing, he was entitled to a new and much better contract and he must be sure to get himself a good agent. Cronkite, who had been so busy reporting on the conventions that he was only dimly aware of his impact on the TV audience, thought that was silly. He told Mickelson he wouldn't need an agent.

"Oh, yes, you will," said Mickelson.

Cronkite *had* hit it big, but for a long time during the 1950s, CBS seemed intent on building him up into something more (and therefore, less) than a mere journalist. His first showcase broadcast after the 1952 conventions was a Sunday afternoon program called *You Are There,* which went on the air in February 1953. *You Are There* was for Cronkite what *Person to Person* was for Murrow: a show that greatly increased his popularity but did little to enhance his reputation as a journalist. The program was a hokey dramatization of famous historical events, in which Cronkite played a sort of immortal, on-the-scene reporter who went skipping across the centuries with cheerful abandon. One week he would be in Rome for the assassination of Julius Caesar, the next, in Philadelphia for the signing of the Declaration of Independence, then, a few weeks after that, in Moscow for the purge trials of the 1930s, and then back again to antiquity to cover the fall of Troy. The latter broadcast, for example, opened with an exterior shot of Cronkite informing his viewers in an urgent, momentous tone, "We are standing outside the tent of Achilles." Then, as students of Homer across the land blanched in consternation, he gave a thirty-second or so summation of *The Iliad* up to the point where Achilles leaves the battlefield to sulk in his tent. And he wrapped up his "intro" with a customary flourish: "The place: the plains of Ilium outside the great walled city of Troy. The date: 1184 B.C. And—*you* are there."

While *You Are There* was rather shoddy goods, a show-biz exploitation of both history and journalism, it was an extremely popular series in the mid-1950s and, if nothing else, it kept Cronkite's name and face before the public. *You Are There* was eventually succeeded by a documentary series called *Air Power,* and that, in turn, led to *The Twentieth Century,* a much more adult exercise in historical recreation. That program featured Cronkite's narration over actual newsreel and television footage, and he was not obliged to interview actors dressed up to look like Brutus, Thomas Jefferson, or Helen of Troy.

Cronkite proved to be so popular that CBS's next move was to try him out as a TV personality, in the tradition of Arthur Godfrey and Ed Sullivan. By 1954, NBC was already making a big splash with its *Today* show, and CBS decided to challenge it with a similar broadcast of its own, called *The Morning Show*. Cronkite was picked to host the program, and, as CBS's answer to Dave Garroway, his job was to interview celebrities and other guests and to get off a few perky one-liners of his own now and then. (Yes, like all other stand-up comics, Walter Cronkite had his gag writers.) Much of the time, however, he was required to play straight man to an insipid lion puppet named Charlemane.

The shuddering truth is that he wasn't bad. In both his looks and his amiable manner, he bore a striking resemblance to Melvyn Douglas. Indeed, if Cronkite had been truly inclined in that direction, he might have gone on to become a big-name TV personality, more or less in the footsteps of another onetime CBS journalist named John Daly. But the strain of coming on each day with "instant charm" eventually took its toll. He became increasingly uncomfortable in the role of chortling emcee, and after five months on *The Morning Show*, he was replaced by Jack Paar, who made the most of the opportunity. For it was on *The Morning Show* that Paar polished the act that later made him such a big hit on NBC's *Tonight* show.

Fortunately, Cronkite hadn't forsaken his career in journalism. Throughout the 1950s, he had his own regular weekly newscast, the *Sunday News Special*, as well as the highly regarded weekly documentary series, *The Twentieth Century*, and starting in 1959, he was the main correspondent on *Eyewitness*, an assignment that sent him dashing all over the world to report, in depth, on each week's "cover story." In addition to those regular broadcasts, he continued as the CBS anchorman at all political conventions and on election-night coverage.

And, finally, there was space—or *S*pace, as Cronkite would stress it. When the first *Sputnik* went up in 1957, he was quick to grasp, as many others were not, that space exploration was certain to become a big story in the years ahead, especially on television. He was determined to be better prepared for that story than any other TV correspondent, and he spent months studying the deeply complicated subject of astrophysics. As a result, by the time the astronaut program was launched in the early 1960s, he was far more conversant in the language of space technology than any of his colleagues or competitors, and

therefore was able to add that important beat to his reportorial responsibilities. Having given up his earlier flirtations with the show-business
side of television, he was now working exclusively as a journalist. And
by 1961, his stature had grown to the point that, when Murrow left CBS,
he was the one who inherited Murrow's position as the network's premier correspondent. Nevertheless, he did not anticipate being called on
to take over the evening news. For one thing, there was the age factor:
Cronkite was a year older than Edwards, and he had always assumed
that when Edwards stepped down, the network would replace him
with a younger man. For another, Cronkite was so busy flying around
the world on various assignments that he wasn't all that privy to in-
house gossip and the situation on the Edwards show. So the offer, when
it came, took him somewhat by surprise.

He accepted it, although he knew he was moving into a hot seat.
Huntley and Brinkley were then at the height of their prestige and
popularity, and in going up against them at the 1960 conventions,
Cronkite himself had taken quite a beating. But now CBS was dumping
the whole load on him, making him the point man on all major news
fronts in the struggle to overtake NBC. It was going to be a tough job,
but Cronkite relished the challenge. He had always thrived on competition, and besides, whatever the outcome, win or lose, it was a hell of a
lot better than "interviewing" Brutus on the Ides of March or clowning
around with a goofy puppet named Charlemane.

When Cronkite inherited the Edwards show, he also inherited its
producer, Don Hewitt. Hewitt had reacted to Edwards's downfall with
severely mixed emotions. He was deeply fond of Edwards personally,
and, what's more, he felt indebted to him since it was Edwards who had
given his own career such a boost. Yet he also recognized the pressing
need for a change. The show had lost its spark, its competitive fire, and
what it needed, as Hewitt himself said at the time, was "a good, hard
kick in the ass." He was confident that whatever else Cronkite did, he
certainly would give it that. As fate would have it, one of Cronkite's
literary heroes was Walter Burns, the gruff and demanding editor in
The Front Page, which blended in perfectly with Hewitt's vision of
himself as the flamboyant reporter, Hildy Johnson. Working together
on what was now called the *CBS Evening News with Walter Cronkite,*
the two men were able to feed each other's fantasies.

On the practical side, Hewitt was still coming up with fresh ideas to make the show better. One of his major innovations during the early Cronkite years was his "newsroom-studio" concept. Originally, the Edwards show had been broadcast uptown, out of Liederkranz Hall, but in 1955 the broadcast was shifted to a studio in the Grand Central Terminal building, next door to the Graybar Building, where the CBS News operation was centered. It was hoped that the switch would take the frenzy out of the nightly troop movements from newsroom to studio. But that did not prove to be the case.

Unfortunately, the Graybar Building was on the Lexington Avenue side of Grand Central, while the studio was over on the other end, the Vanderbilt Avenue side. This meant that each night, in those last urgent minutes before air time, the *Evening News* staff had to go through a series of complex maneuvers. First, they took an elevator down from the twenty-ninth floor of the Graybar Building and plunged into the congestion of Grand Central Station, elbowing their various props (scripts, graphics, and so on) through the swarms of commuters. (When Cronkite joined this nightly circus, he tried to appear as inconspicuous as possible as he walked briskly, eyes straight ahead, through the crowd. He admitted, however, that there were times when, in the midst of his jostling entourage, he felt rather like "a high-paid comic.") At the other end of the station, the group converged on a rickety freight elevator, which was operated by an elderly grouch—"the nasty guy," Hewitt called him—who seemed to delight in delaying the CBS people who, he knew, were in a terrible hurry. Taking the elevator up one level, they then scurried over a catwalk that extended across the terminal behind a huge billboard, and at the end of the catwalk, they finally reached the studio. To complicate matters still further, the catwalk was adjoined, at one point, by an open locker room where railroad conductors changed into their uniforms. Inevitably it was the mishap-prone Alice Weel who, in one of her frantic dashes to "make air," almost collided with a conductor who was standing there in his long johns.

For years Hewitt had been trying to persuade his superiors to do something about the situation. To avoid that nightly rush, he proposed that a newsroom be constructed that could also serve as a studio. When Cronkite took over the broadcast, he lent his strong support to Hewitt's idea, and finally, in 1963, a newsroom-studio was built on the twenty-ninth floor of the Graybar Building. Its main feature was a large, horseshoe-shaped desk arrangement. In the center of that was Cronkite's anchor slot, and around the rim were the chairs and typewriters of his editor and writers. Installed just a few feet away were wire-service printers, and also nearby was Hewitt's office, where all the production decisions were made. In short, the area served as a working newsroom for Cronkite and his staff during the day, and as air time approached, cameras were wheeled in, transforming it into a studio.

The move to the more compact and efficient newsroom-studio coincided with one of the major events in the evolution of television news: the expansion of the evening news to a half hour. Throughout the early 1960s, the top management at CBS News had been pushing for the enlarged format. But the proposal ran into stiff resistance, particularly from the network's affiliates, which were reluctant to yield the local air time (with its local advertising revenues) that CBS would need for the longer news show. A combination of corporate pressure and cajolery, including financial compensation, eventually brought the affiliates into line, however, and in August 1963, the regular fifteen-minute broadcast was turned over to Harry Reasoner and an auxiliary staff while Cronkite, Hewitt, and their people went into "rehearsal" for the half-hour show. The new era began on the night of September 2 when Cronkite opened with the words: "Good evening from our CBS newsroom in New York on this, the first broadcast of network television's first daily half-hour news program." *The Huntley-Brinkley Report,* its hand forced by CBS, made its switch to a half hour the following week, while ABC, still lagging far behind as the third network, did not follow suit until 1967.

The highlight of that first half-hour broadcast was a conversation with President Kennedy, who, to honor the occasion, had agreed to give Cronkite an exclusive interview at his summer home on Cape Cod. It was one of his last television interviews. Eighty-one days after that first half-hour broadcast, John Kennedy was shot to death in Dallas. So that long and tragic weekend began, and by the time it was over, television news was perceived to have taken on a new dimension, a new maturity. The Kennedy assassination was the biggest news story since World War II; yet if an event of that magnitude had occurred ten or even five years earlier, television would have had neither the technology nor the editorial skills to cope with it the way it was able to that November weekend.

There had been great technological advances during the early 1960s. Videotape had become a routine part of television news operations, which vastly improved the ability of the networks to provide film reports on breaking stories from all over the country. With the advent of videotape, film pieces could be fed over a telephone line into New York and recorded on tape in plenty of time for that night's broadcast. Another major advance came in 1962 when *Telstar,* the first communications satellite, went into orbit. *Telstar,* and the more sophisticated satellites that followed, eliminated the need to fly in all film reports from overseas. Foreign film stories could be transmitted directly via satellite into New York where, again, they could be recorded on videotape in time to be put on the air that night. The combination of videotape and the satellites made it possible for the networks to compete, on film, with newspapers in the coverage of the top news events of any given day. No longer did they have to rely on irrelevant features to fill a newscast, or resort to such lame apologies as "film just arrived in New York."

To take full advantage of the improved technology, the networks made several moves in the early 1960s to bolster their news departments. For example, up until that time, CBS News had domestic bureaus in only three cities—New York, Washington, and Chicago. For film reports from other parts of the country, it relied on free-lance cameramen and/or people from its affiliates. In 1962, CBS News opened up bureaus in Los Angeles, Atlanta, and Dallas and manned them with its own corps of correspondents and camera crews. A similar expansion took place in the overseas bureaus. To coordinate all this heightened activity, the network's news headquarters in New York strengthened its organizational structure. By 1963, the Assignment Desk, which once had consisted of Phil Scheffler and a couple of assistants, had evolved into a bustling, round-the-clock operation that was run by a growling journalist of the old school—another *Front Page* type —named Ralph Paskman. Paskman and the Assignment Desk served as the link between the various bureaus and the New York–based news shows, all of which had enlarged their staffs and responsibilities.

The advances in technology and the heavy increase in manpower were the forces behind the push to a half-hour evening newscast, and that, in turn, was primarily responsible for the great impact television news was to have on the country in the years ahead. More than any other single event, the move to a half hour brought on the new era in journalism, the historic shift from newspapers to television. By the middle 1960s, it was an acknowledged fact that most Americans had come to depend on television as their chief source of news.

The expansion of TV news could not have come at a more opportune time. It almost seems as if history conspired on television's behalf, for just when the networks found themselves capable of taking on a commanding role in journalism, external events played directly into their hands. Throughout the 1960s, from the civil rights movement and the Kennedy assassination at the start of the decade, and on to Vietnam, the antiwar demonstrations, the urban riots, the other assassinations, and the space missions that culminated in the first landing on the moon in 1969, the news was dominated by events that were peculiarly suited for television coverage. The hyperactive 1960s, in short, provided an ideal climate in which TV journalism could flex its new muscles.

As the major stories of the 1960s unfolded, no one was more deeply immersed in reporting them than Walter Cronkite. Yet it almost didn't turn out that way. There were, in fact, several disruptions that rocked CBS in 1964, and for a few tense weeks that year, it looked as if Cronkite were on the verge of losing it all and was about to follow Doug Edwards into the limbo of deposed anchormen. Several forces contributed to the 1964 upheavals, but they were primarily set in motion by the wrath and frustration of one man, the Supreme CBS Being Himself—William S. Paley.

Paley and other CBS executives eventually threw their support behind the move to a half-hour evening newscast in 1963 because they believed it would give the network a big boost in its struggle to overtake NBC in the news ratings. At the time, it was an article of faith at CBS that while NBC had Huntley and Brinkley, CBS's overall team of journalistic talent was superior and that, therefore, the additional resources required for the enlarged format would work to the advantage of CBS. Or as Hewitt once put it to an interviewer from *Variety:* "Huntley and Brinkley may be a pair of aces, but we've got a full house and that beats two aces."

But the pair of aces continued to rake in the chips. Neither the switch from Edwards to Cronkite nor the enlarged half-hour format had enabled CBS to regain the competitive edge in the ratings. What's more, NBC was rubbing it in. Every night, on the orders of NBC president Bob Kintner, *The Huntley-Brinkley Report* ended with an announcer's message that "this program has the largest daily news circulation in the world." Those words cut deeply into the pride of CBS people who for years had taken for granted their supremacy in broadcast journalism. And no one found them more grating, more personally taunting, than Chairman Paley. By 1964, he was determined to light a fire under the CBS news department, and toward that end he was willing to take any number of drastic steps, up to and including the public humiliation of his network's star correspondent.

7 Friendly Fire

Bill Paley had always been intensely proud of the news operation and of the prestige it brought to CBS. There were times, it's true, when he turned on even his best correspondents, as in his altercations with Murrow, Sevareid, and Howard Smith over the question of editorial control. But for every quarrel he had with his star journalists, there were plenty of other times when he used his power to defend and protect CBS News. For Paley often had to contend with executives inside his own shop who viewed the news division in totally negative terms, as a chronic irritant and, even worse, as a constant drain on network profits.

One such incident involved James T. Aubrey when he was riding high as president of the CBS Television Network, a position that placed him third, just behind Paley and Stanton, in the corporate chain of command. The occasion was a 1964 budget meeting in which Aubrey gave a glowing report on the network's profits for the previous year but also remarked that those profits would have been much larger if it had not been for the high cost of news. Other executives at the meeting, confident Aubrey was playing a winning hand, indicated with murmurs and frowns their own dismay over the profligacy of the news division. They misread Paley's mood. When Aubrey finished with his presentation, the Chairman glowered and proceeded to tell him and the others how offended he was by their eagerness to use the news division as a whipping boy. "It should not be forgotten," Paley said, "that news and public affairs helped build CBS and everything we are today."

This sense of heritage meant a great deal to Paley. Throughout his long reign as czar of CBS, he often harked back to the early years when journalism was just about all his struggling network had going for it. That is the main reason why Paley was so infuriated by what was happening in the early 1960s. To fall behind NBC in *news* was to dishonor the very heart of the CBS tradition. It was tantamount in Paley's eyes to a denial of the network's birthright. He was wont to complain during this period that the news department had lost the vision and drive that once had made it the pride of CBS. On such occasions, Paley not only invoked the hallowed name of Murrow, but also those of two other men who, though not nearly as well known to the outside world, had formidable reputations within the company. One day in 1964, he grumbled to an associate that what CBS News needed to get it back on top was "another Ed Klauber or Paul White."

Klauber and White both went to work for CBS in 1930 (just two years after Paley had taken over the infant network), and together they became the founding fathers of broadcast journalism. At the time, radio news had no identity, no guidelines to define it, and if its basic style had been molded by other men, with other values, it might well have taken its cue from the lurid sensationalism of the tabloids and the worst excesses of the Hearst press. The fact that it did not was largely because of Klauber and White, who brought to radio the best traditions of print journalism and imposed those standards on the newscasters they hired to work for CBS. Under their aegis, the early giants of newscasting flourished—such men as H. V. Kaltenborn, Elmer Davis, Robert Trout, and John Daly, all of whom were part of the Klauber-White team at CBS in the years leading up to World War II. Moreover, the standards established by Klauber and White made it possible, or at least easier, for the Murrow group to emerge in precisely the way it did. For while Murrow and his cohorts deserve credit for bringing scope and innovation to radio journalism, they were building on what was already, by then, the start of a worthy tradition.

But if Ed Klauber and Paul White shared a commitment to quality journalism, they were not at all alike in other ways. Klauber was a morose, stiffly formal man who wore pince-nez and, in defiance of the customary casualness of the newsroom, always kept his jacket on and his tie firmly knotted. Prior to joining CBS, he worked as night city editor at the *New York Times*, where his stern manner and exacting demands aroused considerable resentment. But he was a thorough professional, both in his own work and in judging the talent of others, and that's what made him invaluable to Paley in those formative years. He set out to staff CBS with the best (Murrow, Trout, and Davis were among those hired by Klauber), and he saw to it that they performed up to their potential. He continued to make enemies, as he had at the *Times*, but those who benefited from his journalistic prowess had great respect for him.

Paul White was to Klauber what a good quarterback is to a reticent coach: the holler guy, the tactician, the field general with whom the troops more readily identify. A fast-talking, hard-drinking man with a bulldog face, White was yet another journalist who came to CBS from the lean-and-hungry world of the United Press. He brought the competitive spirit of wire-service reporting to the network, and that nicely complemented Klauber's more scholarly or *Times*ian approach. White, in turn, became fascinated with the technology of radio. Throughout World War II, he orchestrated the nightly roundups of shortwave reports from overseas on his "piano," as he was fond of calling the telephone console that hooked his far-flung correspondents into the network. And in sharp contrast to Klauber, he was an easy mixer, a backslapper who richly enjoyed the camaraderie of his fellow journalists. But he loathed playing the company game, kowtowing to superiors, and that was one of the reasons why White—for all his ability—eventually fell out of favor at CBS.

World War II brought an end to the Klauber-White era, and over the next few years a number of men had a hand in running the CBS news department. One of them was Murrow, who for a time after the war was corporate vice-president in charge of news. Taking Murrow away from the microphone and putting him in the executive suite was Paley's idea, and it was a mistake. Murrow had no stomach for administration, especially the dirty work that went with it. (He once complained, "Who am I to be firing people, the Almighty Himself?") In 1947, after eighteen uncomfortable months as an executive, Murrow gave it up and went back on the air, where he belonged.

Others followed in Murrow's path, notably Wells Church, who was so single-minded in his devotion to radio that he failed to grasp the rising importance of television. Even after the historic shift took place in the early 1950s, Church continued to regard television news as a circus act, a gaudy picture show that had nothing to do with serious journalism. As a result, his career at CBS soon lapsed into decline, along with those of other radio diehards. By 1954, the man in overall charge of news and public affairs at CBS was Sig Mickelson, who, in contrast to Church, had placed his bets on television.

A former journalism teacher at the University of Minnesota who later put in six years as news director at WCCO, the CBS affiliate in Minneapolis, Mickelson joined CBS in 1949. His corporate rabbi was Frank Stanton, and within a few months, Stanton asked Mickelson to take on the job of building up the network's minuscule TV news operation, which he did. It was Mickelson who devised the anchorman strategy for the 1952 conventions and who picked Walter Cronkite to execute it, a move that paid off handsomely for both men. Nor was Cronkite the only one to benefit from Mickelson's judgment of journalistic talent. In the middle 1950s, when he was finally given a large enough budget to hire reporters exclusively for television, two of Mickelson's first recruits were Harry Reasoner and Charles Kuralt, who quickly proved to be so good as TV field correspondents that they established standards in that new sphere of broadcast journalism that in many ways were as impressive as the ones set by the Murrow group in radio. In addition to reporters, Mickelson hired producers, writers, and cameramen whose contributions to CBS News would continue long after he himself had left the network.

But if these were executive strengths, Sig Mickelson also had his flaws. One of them was his aloof, professorial manner, his inability to develop a rapport with most of the people who worked for him. And while Mickelson had a shrewd eye for spotting journalistic skills, he was a poor judge of managerial talent. He had his deputies, as many as half a dozen mini-executives who, in theory, were supposed to form a liaison between him and the news staff. But all they were good for, most of them, was drinking long lunches and passing the buck.

It was largely because of this combination—Mickelson's lofty reserve and his ineffectual deputies—that the energetic, strong-willed producers, such as Don Hewitt and Fred Friendly, took on so much authority. They were filling a vacuum. But as the years passed, the lack of executive leadership began to infect the news operation: it settled into a pattern of drift and complacency. For a long time, no one seemed to notice. Then came the 1960 political conventions, when CBS News walked blithely into its Dien Bien Phu.

The CBS people headed into that year's convention coverage with a classic case of hubris: the overweening pride of a team that has never lost, and therefore assumes it never will. Despite all the critical praise accorded to Huntley and Brinkley when they made their debut at the 1956 conventions, CBS, with Cronkite in the anchor slot, led in the ratings, as it had four years earlier. But in 1960, when the first convention ended with Kennedy's nomination in Los Angeles and a sweeping victory for NBC, CBS panicked. Or, to be more precise, Don Hewitt panicked. To counter the Huntley-Brinkley appeal, Hewitt talked Mickelson into pairing Cronkite and Murrow as co-anchormen at the Republican convention in Chicago. In later years, Hewitt would look back on that as "the worst idea I ever had," and with good reason. Cronkite and Murrow did not mesh at all well on the air—two sober-sides reveling in earnestness—and the poor chemistry between them only made Huntley and Brinkley look that much better by comparison. The matchup was further complicated by the fact that there was friction in the Murrow-Cronkite relationship, muted discords that dated back to that time in London when Cronkite told Murrow he would rather stay at the United Press than go to work for CBS.

There was a strong element of elitism in Murrow and his clique. Most of them were well-educated and were drawn more to ideas than to events; they wanted to enlighten as well as inform. And from that vantage point, they viewed Cronkite as something of an outsider. They respected him as a competent, hardworking reporter, but he was not really their kind of journalist. He was still, at heart, a wire-service man, attracted more to facts and scoops than to ideas and analysis. Then, too, the years in London had not rubbed off on Cronkite the way they had on Murrow and his people. He remained an unreconstructed Middle American whose boyish enthusiasm—what one critic has called his "cornball charm"—was not at all in tune with the Murrow group's style. To put it in the context of the 1950s, when they were all working together at CBS, Cronkite more closely resembled the middlebrow, down-to-earth Eisenhower, while the Murrow clique identified itself with the Stevensonian qualities of elegance and erudition.

Cronkite was aware of this condescending attitude and, recognizing it for what it was, resented it. At the same time, he was aware that as a college dropout he did not have the educational background that Murrow and the others did, and he was more than a little sensitive on that subject. Occasionally, he allowed his resentment to surface. Once, at a party with friends, Cronkite stretched out his arms and let his head sag in a parody of Christ on the cross and then intoned, with mock solemnity, the line heard every Friday night on *Person to Person:*

"Good evening, Mr. Murrow." It was a deft put-down, for it poked fun at the pretentious weight that Murrow often tried to bring to a program that was, really, nothing more than a gossipy talk show.

So it was against this uneasy background that Murrow and Cronkite shared the anchor booth at the 1960 Republican convention, where their efforts to establish a good working rapport came across as forced and heavy-handed. Murrow, in particular, was at a disadvantage. Ad-libbing was not one of his strengths, and he was visibly uncomfortable in the open-ended format of convention coverage. The upshot was that CBS fared even worse in the second convention that year.

The 1960 debacle led to a sweeping purge of CBS News personnel. Murrow's departure was voluntary, but there were others who were not given a choice. The first victims were Sig Mickelson's ineffectual deputies—the boozers and buck-passers—most of whom were sacked in the late summer and fall of 1960. Then it was Mickelson's turn. In 1959, when CBS News was formed as a separate division within the corporation, Mickelson had become its first president. Now, in February 1961, he became the first president of CBS News to be fired. He would not be the last.

Mickelson was succeeded by Richard Salant, which represented a sharp break with tradition. The CBS news operation had always been run by men with backgrounds in news, but Salant had never worked as a journalist. The son of a prosperous New York lawyer, he originally set out to follow in his father's footsteps. After his graduation from Harvard Law School in 1938, he worked for five years as a government attorney in Washington, first at the National Labor Relations Board and later at the Justice Department. Then, following Navy service during World War II, he joined the New York law firm of Rosenman, Goldmark, Colin & Kaye. One of the firm's clients was CBS, and by the late 1940s he was handling many of the network's cases. This brought him to the attention of Frank Stanton, who was impressed by Salant's forensic skills and, even more, by his strong belief in the importance of news and public affairs in broadcasting. In 1952, when Stanton asked him to come to work at CBS on a full-time basis, Salant could not have been more pleased. The world of broadcasting intrigued him, and besides, he had become disillusioned with certain aspects of private law practice. But he accepted the CBS offer only on the following condition: that his duties not be confined to legal work. "Next to a disbarred lawyer," he told Stanton, "there's nothing worse than a house lawyer, a *kept* lawyer."

So Salant came aboard in 1952 as a corporate vice-president and general executive, and right from the start he took an avid interest in the news operation. A slight, wiry man with horn-rimmed glasses, he had a rather boyish appearance, and one day, while he was hanging around the newsroom, a radio editor mistook him for a new desk assistant and sent him out for coffee. Not wanting to embarrass the editor, Salant cheerfully carried out the errand. But it wasn't long before the news department people knew precisely who Dick Salant was: an executive who enjoyed a special relationship with the president of CBS; who was, in fact, Frank Stanton's number one troubleshooter. At first, his nosing around the news department in that capacity was resented, but as time went on, reports began to filter down from the executive aeries that Salant was a vigorous champion of news programming in corporate infighting over budgets and air time. By 1961, he had become so closely allied to the interests of the news division that those who were familiar with the inner workings of CBS were not at all surprised when Stanton picked him to replace Mickelson.

Salant himself had not expected it, however, and he was more than a little apprehensive. His main concern was that the news-division people would not accept him because of his lack of journalistic credentials, and he was greatly relieved when that did not prove to be a major problem. He was especially pleased by the reaction of Murrow, who was then on the verge of leaving to take over the USIA job. "You don't need a background in journalism," Murrow assured him. "The main thing is whether or not you love the news, whether you're committed to getting the news on the air."

But Murrow also gave him some bad advice. At the time Salant took over as president of CBS News, the entire Mickelson group had been cleaned out in the 1960 postconvention purge, and he was desperately in need of a good deputy or two. Murrow and others recommended Blair Clark, who had been doing a solid job as newscaster on a highly regarded radio program called *The World Tonight*. (CBS cynics were quick to suggest that the *real* reason Clark was suddenly in such good odor was that he was a Harvard classmate and close friend of the newly elected John F. Kennedy.) Whatever the case, Clark turned out to be a poor executive, not much of an improvement over the hand-wringing losers who had served under Mickelson. His inability to make decisions was so pronounced that his desk seemed to groan under the weight of the backlog piled up on it. It was a most unpromising combination: a new president who, by his own description, was an "on-the-job trainee" and a number two man whose forte was procrastination.

Fortunately for all concerned, Clark had the good sense to appoint as *his* deputy a man named Ernie Leiser, who had spent the previous five years working as a correspondent, mainly in Europe. Leiser soon demonstrated that he was a superior executive: decisive, innovative, and a gifted martinet who thoroughly enjoyed wielding authority. Largely because of his influence, a number of steps were taken in the early 1960s to shake CBS News out of the lethargy that had characterized Mickelson's last years. There was the opening of the new regional news bureaus and the related changes in organizational structure. There was the move to replace Edwards with Cronkite on the evening news, and the decision, in the wake of Howard Smith's departure, to use Eric Sevareid solely as an analyst. A midmorning slot was found for a new program called *Calendar* (which became a showcase for Harry Reasoner), and that, in turn, evolved into the *CBS Morning News,* the first morning show on network television devoted primarily to news, which went on the air in 1963 with Mike Wallace as anchorman. Also in 1963—and most important of all—there was the birth of the half-hour format on the *CBS Evening News with Walter Cronkite.*

Salant and Clark were involved in these decisions, but the driving force behind most of them was Leiser. He was the one who set down the blueprint for the half-hour format. It was his detailed memo that became the chief weapon in the struggle to persuade first the corporate brass and then the affiliates that the move to a half hour on the *Evening News* was an idea whose time had come. Both Salant and Leiser were among those who believed, most fervently, that going to a half hour would not only be a big breakthrough for television news in general but would also be a boon to CBS in its ratings fight with NBC. By the time the two networks expanded their nightly news shows to a half hour in September 1963, Salant was publicly predicting that Huntley and Brinkley would not be able to maintain their lead, that the pressure of the enlarged format would be too much for them. "NBC is a fine organization, but all they've got going for them is a pitcher and a catcher," he crowed. "We've got Walter, an infield, an outfield, and a strong bench."

To this, Brinkley responded with irritation: "If Huntley and I are only a pitcher and catcher, then by that standard, CBS has only a pitcher *or* a catcher. I have no interest in the comments of a CBS lawyer. Mr. Salant is going into an area he knows nothing about."

Over the long run, Salant and Leiser would be vindicated in that conviction. The day would eventually come when Cronkite, backed by a stronger news operation, would surge past Huntley and Brinkley in the ratings. But it would take CBS News four years to do it, and the last thing that Dick Salant had going for him in 1963 was time. By making such a big competitive deal out of the move to a half hour, Salant had escalated the stakes and put the prestige of CBS squarely on the line. The nightly news battle in the new, half-hour format became the subject of a *Newsweek* cover story, and, more than anything else, it was the heightened importance attached to the struggle that brought Paley storming into the picture. Now that the fight for the evening news audience was causing such a fuss, the Chairman wanted results—fast results. And by the end of 1963, when it was clear that the move to a half hour had not ignited a quick and dramatic turnabout in the ratings, Paley was a man on the warpath. In February 1964, Salant completed his third year as president of CBS News, and as far as Bill Paley was concerned, that was long enough: it was time to turn the news division over to someone else.

Frank Stanton did not agree with Paley's dim view of Salant's performance; in his opinion, CBS News had improved in a number of areas over the past three years, and there was no doubt in his mind that this progress would soon be reflected in the ratings. When the criticisms of Salant began to mount, Stanton was quick to defend his protégé. But as time went on, he found himself more and more isolated in that position, and he became increasingly disturbed by the growing hostility of the anti-Salant faction coalescing around Paley. By late February 1964, he was fearful that if the situation continued to deteriorate, Salant would not only lose his job as president of the news division but might also become so tarnished and cut up that it would be difficult to keep him on at CBS in *any* position. So, with great reluctance, Stanton arrived at a decision he found repugnant yet unavoidable: at his insistence, Salant would relinquish the news job and return to a safe and secure haven in the corporate hierarchy.

When Salant learned of the decision, he was shattered. In a tense encounter in Stanton's office, he asked his friend and benefactor if this change had truly been his idea. Stanton looked him straight in the eye and said, "Yes." That was all—no elaboration—and as the two men stared at each other in silence, Salant understood that there was a lot more to it than that. Stanton was purposely avoiding specifics in order to shield Salant from the pressures and unpleasant scenes that had forced him to take this course of action.

The official announcement was a triumph of creative writing, as practiced by the poets of public relations. The "increasing workload at the corporate level" was cited as the reason for Salant's "promotion." In his farewell note to the news division, Salant expressed his thanks to all "you professionals" for the way "you kept an amateur afloat for three years." There was no way of knowing that in just two years the "amateur" would be back again as president of CBS News, and in a much stronger position than before.

Stanton also took the credit (or blame) for picking Salant's successor, even though the choice was more reflective of Paley's wishes than Stanton's. The man Paley decided on was none other than Murrow's old sidekick—Fred W. Friendly. And the fact that the post went to him was a clear indication of just how determined, or desperate, Paley was to breathe new life into CBS News. For Friendly was a gadfly, an unruly individualist who had been a major cause of Bill Paley's recurrent stomachaches back in the *See It Now* years.

To some of his CBS colleagues, he was known as "the Big Moose" and, to others, as "the Brilliant Monster." Both nicknames were appropriate. A huge man physically, Friendly's size was more than matched by his extravagant personality. Impassioned, domineering, and drawn to excess—to the *big* challenge, the *epic* battle—he drove himself and others with a furious energy. Murrow once said that Friendly was the only man he knew who could "take off without warming his motors," and, more significantly, he also described him as "my electric cattle-prod." This apparently was no exaggeration. Some members of the old *See It Now* group have even claimed that if it had not been for the heavy and unremitting pressure applied by Friendly, the McCarthy broadcast and other controversial programs never would have been done—or at least not in the way that they *were* done.

Friendly's contributions had been substantial, and he had every right to regard the Murrow-Friendly team as a full and equal partnership, even though it was Murrow who had the name and reputation. Yet, more often than not, he was extremely awkward in the way he handled the situation. At times he would affect a self-deprecating air that was as cloying as it was unconvincing. Faced with this transparently false modesty, some listeners were left with the impression that what Friendly was *really* saying, beneath the hypocrisy, was that he was the brains and creative force behind the team and that Ed Murrow, bless him, was just another voice and pretty face. Many felt Friendly shamelessly exploited his association with Murrow, and there were indications, from time to time, that Murrow himself was leery of his exuberant producer. (When Salant took over as president of CBS News, Murrow warned him, not entirely in jest, to "watch out for Friendly, he doesn't know a fact.") On the other hand, Murrow had unwavering respect for Friendly's strong points: his technical skills, his fertile, innovative mind, and his ability to stimulate others to share his enthusiasms. For he recognized that these were the qualities that made Friendly a great producer.

As the producer of *See It Now*, Friendly had created the television documentary. Prior to the advent of that program in 1951, it simply did not exist in any coherent form. But by 1958, the year *See It Now* went off the air, the TV documentary had—in Friendly's words—"established a beachhead." Then came *CBS Reports*, the documentary series on which Murrow was denied a regular slot and which Friendly continued to produce after Murrow left the network. In technical terms, *CBS Reports* was a vast improvement over *See It Now*, and Friendly went on to acquire a large reputation of his own. By the early 1960s, he was known not only as the man who, with Murrow, had pioneered the television documentary, but also as the producer who currently was doing more than anyone else to advance the form.

Nor had Friendly lost any of his appetite for controversy. Various pressure groups were annoyed by certain *CBS Reports* programs that were broadcast during the five-year period (1959–63) that Friendly was producer of the series. No less an Eminence than Cardinal Cushing lambasted a *CBS Reports* exposé of police corruption in Boston. Called *Biography of a Bookie Joint*, it was a superb example of "investigative journalism" years before that term came into vulgar usage. In addition, there had been Murrow's last documentary, *Harvest of Shame*, the report on the migrant workers that the powerful farm lobby didn't like; a program called *Murder and the Right to Bear Arms*, which the powerful gun lobby didn't like; and a broadcast entitled *The Business of Health*, which the powerful American Medical Association denounced

as a sinister plea for socialized medicine. While it is true that no single
CBS Reports program caused a furor as great as the one set off by the
See It Now broadcast on McCarthy, it certainly wasn't for lack of trying.

As a producer, Friendly had acquired a reputation within CBS for
excessive behavior, especially in his treatment of those who worked for
him. When he was pleased by an associate producer's effort, he was
nothing if not lavish in his praise. Dissatisfied, he often flew into tantrums and once picked up a table and threw it at the head of a young
assistant. Bill Paley was acutely aware of Friendly's volatile temperament; indeed, he had been witness to a most vivid display of it. At the
time when *See It Now* was being taken off the air, Friendly was summoned to Paley's office to discuss the specific plans for its termination.
While there, he suddenly launched into an emotional appeal for the
program, contending that it was irresponsible of Paley to drop *See It
Now* since that was just about the only worthwhile broadcast CBS had
on its entire schedule. Paley listened to enough of Friendly's harangue
to get his drift and then, with imperious calm, he interrupted him and
said: "Fred, you are speaking beyond your competence." Infuriated,
Friendly turned on his heel to make a grand, dramatic exit, and charged
straight into Paley's private john. It was said that the Chairman dined
out on that one for the next several weeks.

But Paley also recognized that there was a plus side to Friendly's
ardor, that he was a man who, in a favorite phrase of Murrow's (and one
that Friendly himself loved to quote), had plenty of "fire in his belly."
As such, he could be counted on to bring energy, drive, and fierce
commitment to the job of president of CBS News, and those were
precisely the qualities that Paley thought were needed to rouse the
news division out of its prolonged slump. He knew such a move would
be a risk (anything involving Friendly was, by definition, a risk), but he
decided it was one worth taking. That, at least, was the conventional
interpretation of Paley's thinking. But there may well have been more
to it than that.

Those who were close to Paley in those days believe that the sudden upgrading of Friendly was part of a campaign to induce Murrow
to return to CBS. In December 1963, Murrow resigned as USIA director
to recuperate from his bout with cancer, and in the weeks that followed,
there was rising speculation that he would rejoin CBS as soon as his
health improved. Friendly, in particular, was encouraging that speculation. Aware by this time that Salant was in trouble, Friendly had begun

to lobby vigorously for his job, and as part of that effort, he played up the prospect of Murrow's eventual return, a triumphant reunion with his old comrade-in-arms. Indeed, when he was named president of CBS News in early March 1964, Friendly promptly announced that "getting Ed back here is my first order of business."

Nothing would have pleased Bill Paley more. Despite their harsh disagreements during Murrow's last years at the network, he and Paley had remained good friends, and not long after Friendly's promotion, Paley flew out to La Jolla, California, where Murrow was convalescing. In the course of their visit, Paley brought up Friendly's recent appointment. He quite naturally assumed that Murrow approved of the decision to entrust the affairs of CBS News to his former *See It Now* partner. But to Paley's great surprise, Murrow expressed strong reservations about the move. His concern, he told Paley, was that Friendly's restless and explosive temperament would not be compatible with the duties of management. Paley and Murrow also discussed the latter's return to CBS, but only in the most general terms. As a matter of fact, Paley left La Jolla with a very heavy heart, for he was convinced that Murrow was not regaining his health and did not have long to live.

He was right. Murrow's health continued to deteriorate, and in the months ahead there was less and less talk about his resuming his CBS career. He died the following year, and by then, his onetime "electric cattle-prod" was running the network's news operation as it had never been run before.

For most of the people who worked at CBS News, this was their first direct experience with the Brilliant Monster. Of course they were aware of Friendly's reputation. They had heard about his monumental rages and about the extreme lengths to which he would go to get what he wanted out of his people. In fact, at the time of his appointment as president, the key question was whether he would try to bulldoze the news division the way he had bulldozed his documentary units, or whether, now that he had risen to the executive ranks, he would adopt a more decorous approach. The answer to that question was not long in coming.

About three weeks after Friendly took over, there was an earthquake in Alaska, and NBC reporters and camera crews moved so quickly to the scene that *The Huntley-Brinkley Report* was presenting detailed film reports while the *CBS Evening News* was still relying on tell stories rewritten from wire-service accounts. As the extent of NBC's "beat" on the story became apparent, Friendly went into action. He was on the phone day and night to subordinates in New York and in bureaus across the country, demanding to know who had messed up, and why. Then, after the ass-chewings and threats of dismissal, came the lamentations. In loud, theatrical moans, he proclaimed to Don Hewitt and others that the Alaskan earthquake was "my Bay of Pigs."

In his zeal to make certain that nothing like it happened again, Friendly drove everybody very hard over the next few months, and, goaded by his unrelenting lash, the news division entered into a period of overkill, or "bulletin fever," as it came to be known within the shop. For years it had been the policy at CBS and the other networks that if a very dramatic or important story broke, the news department was empowered to interrupt the entertainment schedule with a bulletin. In order to avoid complaints from viewers and advertisers, as well as from affiliates and corporate brass, the news executives were generally careful not to abuse the bulletin privilege. They agreed that the story should be big enough to justify the disruption in programming. But Friendly was not inhibited by such timid concerns, and his policy, in essence, was: When in doubt, put on a bulletin. For example, there was the day that CBS News broke into a soap opera with a bulletin reporting a train derailment in West Virginia. Additional details, which came in later, disclosed that it was a freight train, and that four persons had been slightly injured. It was not always Friendly himself who gave the order for such dubious bulletins, but he created the climate that inspired them; and his various deputies soon learned that in working for Friendly, it was better to err on the side of excess than on the side of caution.

Even so, on one occasion NBC broke several minutes ahead of CBS with a bulletin that President Johnson had been rushed to the hospital. Friendly was furious and gave the Assignment Desk editor a terrible tongue-lashing, telling him, among other things, that he was fired. The young man was reduced to tears, and in that condition he then had to go on the air and read the CBS bulletin. Viewers were startled not so much by the news that Johnson was ill (*that* later turned out to be nothing serious) as by the fact that the disembodied voice giving them this information was that of a man obviously *crying*. But if through his overbearing manner Friendly was making life difficult for others, it's also true that he himself was under a great deal of pressure. His first critical test as president of CBS News came that summer of 1964, at the time of the political conventions. Friendly did not have to be told that his new career as an executive would be made much easier if under his leadership CBS was able to bounce back from its 1960 disaster. So, throughout the spring and early summer, he worked closely with Bill Leonard, who, as head of the CBS News election unit, was directly responsible for the network's convention coverage in 1964.

The first convention that year was the Republican one in San Francisco (Barry Goldwater's moment of glory), and when the CBS team assembled there, Walter Cronkite was in his customary anchor slot. During the gloomy postmortems that followed the 1960 defeat, the prevailing view was not to blame Cronkite, the hero of past convention triumphs. The in-house consensus was that he had done another good job in 1960, but that his performance had been undermined by poor planning and inept leadership on the management level. So in the strategy sessions leading up to the 1964 conventions, there was no serious thought given to replacing Cronkite, especially since he was by this time firmly established as CBS's top correspondent. But Cronkite was not at his best at the 1964 Republican convention—far from it. He had revealed at past conventions an occasional tendency to overplay his talent for ad-libbing, and in San Francisco in 1964 he seemed to be afflicted with a particularly severe case of the verbal runs. Long before the convention was over, CBS's floor correspondents and others were complaining that Cronkite was hogging too much air time and was not switching enough to other reporters when they had information that was more timely and pertinent.

Cronkite himself later admitted that "it was as bad a job as I've ever done." But in his view, Friendly and Leonard had to share a lot of the blame for that. Friendly was in top form, having revved himself up for the convention challenge, and Leonard, under Friendly's influence, had also become rather frantic in his eagerness to excel and motivate others. "The two of them were wild-eyed," Cronkite recalled. "Leonard would come charging into the anchor booth every five minutes with another brainstorm. Now how the hell was I supposed to think and work in that confusion?"

But what really tore it for Cronkite was when Friendly and Leonard put Eric Sevareid in the anchor booth with him. They insisted that he was only there to do commentary, but Cronkite, no stranger to these games, didn't buy that for a minute. He saw it as another first-aid mission, like the maneuver four years earlier when he had had to share the anchor assignment with Murrow. He became sullen and snappish, a mood that adversely affected his on-air performance, and by the time that first convention was over, there were bad feelings all around. Nor were matters helped by the news, which came as no great surprise, that NBC had scored another big victory in the ratings. But the worst was yet to come.

Back in New York, Friendly and Leonard were summoned to a meeting with Paley and Stanton. The two corporate giants wanted to know what had gone wrong: why had CBS taken such a beating—again? Friendly and Leonard offered a variety of excuses, and then, almost as an aside, they made the mistake of saying that Cronkite had probably talked too much. Paley, looking for an opening, seized on that like a fox pouncing on a chicken. Yes, he said, he had noticed that, too. Why did Cronkite talk so much? Paley then said that there would have to be some changes made for the next convention a few weeks hence, and perhaps, he suggested, that should be the major one: a new anchor team to replace Cronkite.

At a later meeting, after talking it over, Friendly and Leonard went back to Paley and Stanton and said they were opposed to such a change. But Paley was insistent. Cronkite should be replaced, he said, and his words and tone now sounded less like a suggestion and more like a command. At one point, he even came up with his own candidates for a new anchor team: Roger Mudd, the young star of the Washington bureau, and Bob Trout, the polished old radio veteran. The combination, Paley contended, had all the right ingredients: youth and age, freshness and experience. By the time that meeting ended, Friendly and Leonard realized that the discussion period was over. They were down to two choices: either accede to Paley's proposal or reject it in such a categorical way that he would either have to yield or get rid of them as well.

The night before the final decision was to be made, three of the news division's top executives—Friendly, Leonard, and Ernie Leiser—gathered at Friendly's home in Riverdale, the fashionable residential enclave in the Bronx. Of this trio, Leiser was the most adamant in arguing that the change must be resisted. It was a matter of principle, he said. Such decisions must be based on professional judgments, journalistic values, and *not* on ratings. And, Leiser contended, despite Cronkite's subpar performance in San Francisco, he was still the best anchorman in the business, or at least the best that CBS had to offer.

It was easy for Leiser to come on strong. He was not directly responsible for the convention coverage, and he had not been involved in the confrontations with Paley and Stanton. But the other two men, and Friendly in particular, were in a more vulnerable position. If he was not overly concerned about losing his job, Friendly was fearful that, in taking a defiant stand now, he might undermine his future. That, really, is what it came down to: Fred Friendly's own ambition. He desperately wanted to please Paley and Stanton and thus strengthen his newly acquired executive status, even if that meant opposing a journalistic judgment he shared with others in the news division.

Leiser left Friendly's home that night convinced that he had persuaded his boss to hold the line in defense of Cronkite. Unfortunately, Leiser did not know his man. When he went to work the next day, he discovered that Friendly had caved in. Indeed, at that very moment, both Friendly and Leonard were en route to California to break the bad news to Cronkite.

Cronkite was on vacation in Southern California, staying at a hotel overlooking Disneyland, which, as he later said, "was the perfect setting for the Mickey Mouse phone call I received." The call was from Friendly, who explained that he and Leonard were flying out that day to "discuss something" with Cronkite. The three men met over drinks in the American Airlines lounge at the Los Angeles airport. Friendly and Leonard were understandably tense, but Cronkite went out of his way to make it easy for them, even going so far as to thank them for taking the trouble to fly out and give him the bad news in person. When Friendly returned to New York, he called Stanton to tell him that the deed was done.

"Good," said Stanton, "the Chairman will be delighted."

In accordance with Paley's "suggestion," Bob Trout and Roger Mudd were assigned to co-anchor CBS's coverage of the 1964 Democratic convention. The selection of Trout, in particular, had ironic overtones that Cronkite was quick to grasp. He had not forgotten that his "overnight success" back in 1952 had been the result of a gamble, a hunch on Sig Mickelson's part that his skills as a journalist and ad-libber would more than compensate for his lack of experience in broadcasting. If Mickelson had not pushed for Cronkite, the anchorman assignment at those first coast-to-coast conventions would have gone to Bob Trout and—who knows?—that opportunity might well have opened the doors to television stardom for him. Now, in August 1964, Trout was at last being given his big chance—and at Cronkite's expense.

At fifty-five, Trout knew this would also be his last chance. A lean, fastidiously groomed man with a thin mustache and a courtly manner, Trout was something of a living legend to his younger colleagues. He had covered every political convention on radio for CBS since 1936, and he was also the man who first tutored Murrow in the techniques of newscasting. Yet, like so many other big names on radio, Trout had trouble making the transition to television. He did anchor the local evening news on WCBS in New York for several years in the late 1950s and early 1960s. But when it came to major assignments on the network level, Trout was generally passed over, at least in part because his swarthy looks were held against him. Don Hewitt, who had so much power to decide who appeared on the network's evening news show during these years, once said that he thought Trout looked like "an Armenian rug merchant." Bill Paley, however, still had a soft spot in his heart for the old radio star from an earlier era, and so, thanks to his intercession, Bob Trout was given a final chance in 1964 to show that he had the stuff to make it big on network television.

It was also a golden opportunity for Roger Mudd, and in his case, timing and luck were the key factors. If Cronkite's ouster had occurred as recently as a year earlier, it's unlikely that Mudd's name would even have come up for consideration. He was regarded as just one of several good correspondents who worked out of the CBS News Washington bureau until the spring of 1964 when his "marathon" coverage of the Senate's civil rights filibuster brought him the kind of exposure and recognition that under normal circumstances would have taken him years to achieve. By the time the civil rights bill was finally passed, Mudd had made a big name for himself, a fact that was not lost on Paley when he decided, a few weeks later, that Cronkite should be replaced.

Thus was born a new electronic species: Mudd-Trout. If it showed itself to be strong enough to thrive in the big pond of a convention, then it would be in a position to take over everything. When the change was announced, Friendly was careful to stress that no thought was being given to knocking Cronkite off the *CBS Evening News*. But nobody, least of all Cronkite, was fooled by that. Obviously, if Mudd-Trout succeeded in taking some of the steam out of Huntley-Brinkley, the pressure would soon begin to build for the new team to co-anchor the

Evening News, and Cronkite would find, as Doug Edwards had found, that few skids are slicker than those greased in network television.

So this was an extremely difficult time for Cronkite, and in the company of close friends he gave vent to his bitter feelings. His anger was directed not so much at Paley (who, after all, lived in the world of ratings and profits) as against the two men whose job it was to protect the interests of the news division. As Cronkite saw it, Friendly and Leonard had been only too willing to sell him out, to let him be the scapegoat for their errors in judgment and frenetic behavior at the San Francisco convention.

But Cronkite was careful not to criticize Friendly, Leonard, or anyone else in his public utterances. At the network's request, he even held a news conference at which he defended the ratings system and the right of CBS to change its anchormen. Still, there were limits to his good-soldier act. He refused to go along with a company PR proposal that he pose next to a television set for an ad that would say: "Even Walter Cronkite Listens to Mudd-Trout." A show of magnanimity was one thing, but he was not about to let himself become an object of ridicule.

The Cronkite news conference was set up because press reaction to the switch had been heavy and negative. Viewer response was also overwhelmingly critical; in one week alone, CBS received 11,000 letters protesting the decision. That was some consolation, but not content with that, Cronkite made a few adroit moves on his own behalf. In late August, when the Democrats assembled in Atlantic City, he was there with his *Evening News* staff, and each night his show originated from the convention site. That enabled him to maintain a high level of visibility, even though he was no longer a part of the network's regular convention team. Also, while in Atlantic City, he indulged in a bit of mischief. When he happened to bump into NBC president Bob Kintner in a hotel elevator, he chortled and said, "Bob, we've been presented with a great moment. Let's make the most of it." A few seconds later, the elevator doors opened, and Cronkite and Kintner stepped out into the crowded lobby arm-in-arm and smiling broadly. In no time at all, the hottest rumor in Atlantic City was about the "great new deal" NBC had offered Cronkite. Actually, Cronkite had received feelers from both NBC and ABC about his future plans, but he was not yet ready to consider a move to another network. For one thing, he was under a tight contractual obligation to CBS, and for another, he had a strong hunch that Mudd-Trout were swimming into troubled waters.

The new anchor team gave a creditable performance at the 1964 Democratic convention. Between them, they kept the rather dull story (the Johnson-Humphrey nominations) moving along. But they didn't really click as a team. They never came close to evincing the kind of easy rapport that characterized the Huntley-Brinkley duo. Most important, from a corporate point of view, they failed to cut into NBC's lead in the ratings; indeed, they didn't even score as well as Cronkite had the previous month in San Francisco. The most painful moment for CBS came when, shortly after his acceptance speech, President Johnson gave a long, spontaneous interview to NBC's Sander Vanocur. Later, as LBJ was leaving the hall, Bill Leonard intercepted him and asked in a beseeching tone, "Will you wave up to Mr. Trout and Mr. Mudd, sir? You've waved to everybody else." The President-of-All-the-People graciously looked up at the CBS anchor booth and waved hello. But for Mudd-Trout, it was already good-bye.

In the weeks that followed, Cronkite was quietly restored to his position of eminence. By the time the November election rolled around, he was back in his customary anchor slot, and, to make his return all the sweeter, CBS News achieved a big comeback. NBC again led in the ratings, but this time its margin was greatly reduced. In retrospect, that 1964 election night would be seen as a turning point: Huntley and Brinkley had crossed their crest, and in the years ahead, they would be eclipsed by Cronkite and CBS.

So Cronkite emerged from his tribulation stronger than ever, and, in a sense, he had Paley to thank for that. Prior to his demotion, neither Cronkite nor anyone else had any idea how vast and loyal his following was. "I never thought it would cause such a clamor," Paley remarked to an associate the day after the change was announced. But if the public protest caught Paley by surprise, he was smart enough to take appropriate heed. When Friendly informed him that he wanted Cronkite to anchor the election-night coverage, the Chairman concurred. And from then on, through all the years that followed, there would be no more corporate meddling with Walter Cronkite.

Friendly also came out of the imbroglio in good shape. He had argued against the switch to Mudd-Trout in his encounters with Paley and Stanton, and subsequent events demonstrated how right he had been. Now that the Cronkite crisis was over, Friendly was free to concentrate on bringing the overall news operation more firmly under his control. Thus, the closing weeks of 1964 were characterized by some rather elaborate choreography on the management level, a series of moves that resulted in another thorough revamping of the power structure within CBS News.

8 Martyrdom and Restoration

For all his energy and exuberance, Friendly had to face the fact that, try as he might, he could not dominate every detail of the entire news operation the way he had dominated every detail of documentary production for *See It Now* and *CBS Reports*. The news division was too big, too diverse, and too sprawling, even for his gargantuan grasp. He needed deputies to whom he could delegate some of his authority. But he was determined not to repeat the mistakes of his predecessors, Sig Mickelson and Dick Salant, both of whom had been victimized by incompetent deputies. Friendly inherited Blair Clark from Salant, but he did not keep him for very long. And by the fall of 1964, he was ready to set up his own executive structure.

What Friendly wanted was two chief deputies of equal rank, each of whom would be given the title of vice-president. One would be in charge of "soft news"—that is, all documentary units and all live coverage of such special events as political conventions. The other would preside over "hard news," meaning the Cronkite show and all other broadcasts that dealt primarily with day-to-day coverage. For his soft-news vice-president, Friendly picked Bill Leonard. He was the logical choice. Having worked as a correspondent and producer on *CBS Reports*, Leonard was no stranger to the world of documentaries, and, more recently, as head of the CBS News election unit, he was familiar with the problems involved in setting up live coverage of conventions and similar events. Moreover, Leonard had a good working relationship with Friendly, which had been strengthened by the support they gave each other that summer during all the turmoil over the Cronkite/-Mudd-Trout affair.

For hard-news vice-president, the logical choice was Ernie Leiser, who, in contrast to the vacillating Blair Clark, had been a real asset to Salant during his term as president. In addition to having demonstrated ability as an executive, Leiser had a solid background in hard news, both as a print journalist and, later, as a CBS News correspondent in Europe. The problem, however, was that Leiser wasn't all that eager to serve as a vice-president under Friendly. Having been elevated to the ranks of management by Salant and Clark, he felt a certain amount of loyalty to those two men, both of whom were ousted from power when Friendly took over. Nor did Leiser care much for Friendly's style of leadership, which he characterized as "all noise and motion." He did not enjoy being constantly on the receiving end of Friendly's fulminations. Finally, he had not been impressed by the way Friendly capitulated to Paley and Stanton on the question of Cronkite's removal. For all Friendly's bluster about the integrity and honor of broadcast journalism, Leiser, having taken his measure up close at a critical moment, was convinced that he was just another ambitious company man.

The job Leiser really coveted was executive producer of the *CBS Evening News.* That's where the action was, and there he would have his own independent power base. Ultimately, he would still be answerable to Friendly, of course, but as producer of the Cronkite show, he would no longer be directly in Friendly's line of fire. In the fall of 1964, Leiser made his move. He had reason to believe that the hard-news vice-presidency was his for the asking but that, deep down, Friendly wanted to appoint somebody else. Playing to that inclination, Leiser informed Friendly that the position he truly wanted, above all others, was executive producer of the *Evening News,* if that could be arranged. It could, but in order to give that job to Leiser, Friendly would first have to take it away from Don Hewitt.

At an earlier time, when the *Evening News* was in a more developmental phase, such a move would have been unthinkable, for Hewitt was regarded as indispensable to the program's growth. By 1964, however, the onetime boy wonder was having his problems. For one thing, the *CBS Evening News* had been trailing *The Huntley-Brinkley Report* for the better part of four years. But the criticisms of Hewitt went beyond the question of ratings. His Hildy Johnson flair for going to extreme and, at times, questionable lengths to get a story was having a disquieting effect on some of his CBS superiors. And they were especially disturbed by an incident that occurred that summer in San Francisco at the time of the Republican convention.

It began at a meeting of news executives from the three networks, the purpose of which was to discuss the sophisticated new computer techniques that were revolutionizing election coverage. As the meeting came to an end, Hewitt spotted a copy of the NBC election handbook on the floor. Acting on impulse as usual, he grabbed it and managed to smuggle it out of the room. Then, accompanied by a few CBS cronies, he repaired to his room in the Fairmont Hotel, where, upon examination, he discovered that the handbook contained nothing more than routine background material on the 1964 election; there were no juicy revelations of NBC's secret plans for convention coverage. It was utterly worthless as an enemy document.

Not long after this discovery, Hewitt had a visitor from NBC, a young man named Scotty Connal, who was in a high state of agitation. He said he was sure that Hewitt had his handbook and that if he didn't get it back, he would lose his job. Since Hewitt had no use for the book, given its contents, he promptly handed it over. Connal, greatly relieved, then smiled and said, in a jocular tone, "I would have thrown you out of that window to get it back." Everyone in the room had a good laugh at that.

But the next day it wasn't so funny, for splashed across the front page of the *San Francisco Chronicle* was a story about Hewitt's "theft" of the handbook. In it, Connal came across as a mighty tough customer who had "threatened" to throw Hewitt out the hotel window before Hewitt, presumably quaking in fear, surrendered the handbook. The story caused a minor fuss, and word soon came down that Frank Stanton and other high-level executives were unhappy with Hewitt for having "embarrassed" CBS. (When he was told about the corporate displeasure, Hewitt was tempted to inquire if Stanton had been similarly embarrassed back in 1948 when his boss, Bill Paley, stole Jack Benny and other stars away from NBC.) It was all very silly, of course—a harmless and childish prank—but it came at a time when more and more people at CBS were starting to think of Hewitt as someone who, although richly talented, was a little too irresponsible for comfort. His hotshot style had been fine back in the 1950s when everything was more innocent, more informal, more open to spontaneous, even playful, innovations. But now, in the 1960s, with Walter Cronkite in the anchor slot, the *CBS Evening News* had become a serious and important program. And according to his critics, Hewitt was too shallow, too flaky, too show-bizzy for his own good and, especially, for the good of the *Evening News.*

Among those embracing that point of view was Friendly. Although he and Hewitt had similar temperaments (it was difficult to say who was more garrulous and hyperactive), they were not at all compatible in their approaches to journalism. As a disciple of Murrow's, Friendly was devoted to the pursuit and clash of serious ideas. Hewitt, on the other hand, had more of a tabloid mentality, a sharper instinct for the kind of story that gets readers or viewers "into the tent."

What's more, their careers had progressed in such a way as to make them natural antagonists. In the early 1950s, Friendly and Hewitt had been the principal pioneers of TV journalism at CBS. Yet because of his association with Murrow and the fact that documentaries then generated far more prestige than hard-news broadcasts, Friendly had earned a much greater reputation. Thus he was unprepared for the subtle change in viewpoint that took place inside CBS in the early 1960s when hard news in general and the Cronkite show in particular had begun to replace the documentary as the *pièce de résistance* of TV journalism. And at CBS everybody knew that the man who had nurtured the *Evening News* to its present level of achievement was not Fred Friendly but Don Hewitt. The notion that Hewitt had contributed more than he had to the growth of television news was one that Friendly, given his ego, found hard to accept.

For these reasons, then, he did not exactly rush to Hewitt's defense when Ernie Leiser proposed to take over the *Evening News.* Friendly sincerely believed that Leiser, whom he regarded as a more "serious" journalist, would bring a stronger, more responsible tone to the Cronkite show. Finally, he liked the idea because it would move Leiser out of the management hierarchy, for, as Leiser had suspected, Friendly really didn't want him to be one of his vice-presidents. So the decision was made: Leiser became executive producer of the *Evening News.* And for his hard-news vice-president, Friendly went outside the company—to a *Newsweek* editor named Gordon Manning.

Hewitt learned about the change in the classic "vote-of-confidence" fashion. Hearing rumors that he was in trouble, he went to see Friendly one morning in December 1964, and was relieved by Friendly's assurance that he had nothing to worry about. Only a few hours later, he was summoned back to Friendly's office, this time to be presented with his head on a plate.

Hewitt was so demoralized that he came close to leaving CBS. Instead, he pulled himself together and spent the next few years producing documentaries, a period he later referred to as "my time in limbo." Then, in 1967, he began to promote an idea he had for applying a magazine format to television news: a biweekly broadcast that would consist of several stories on a wide range of topics, from politics to the arts, from racial strife to scuba diving, from cabbages to kings, from soup to nuts. He even came up with a title for the program. He wanted to call it *60 Minutes.*

It was an idea whose time had come, and *60 Minutes* would do more than any other program of its kind to advance the documentary form that had been Fred Friendly's personal pride and joy. Yet when Hewitt's "magazine" broadcast went on the air in the fall of 1968, Friendly wasn't around to offer his congratulations. A little more than two years earlier—in February 1966—his career at CBS came to an abrupt end in a blaze of martyrdom befitting his flamboyant nature.

One of Friendly's most impressive traits was his enthusiasm, which at times seemed to take on a life-force all its own. Once he became engrossed in a subject or issue, he tore into it with a ferocity that inspired some of his colleagues and intimidated others. Over the years he had been aroused by a number of concerns, and by 1965, almost all his energies were focused on one overriding issue: the war in Vietnam.

That was the year of the first full-scale escalation, the year the Americans took over the war and made it their own. Friendly was one of the first journalists on a high management level to perceive that something was fishy in Vietnam—and Washington. Despite the smug optimism expressed in official statements, the war was not being won and, in all likelihood, was not going to be brought to a swift conclusion. Friendly not only expanded CBS News operations in Vietnam but encouraged the network's correspondents there and in Washington to pursue the story in all its dimensions. When some of his correspondents began filing reports that went against the official line, he vigorously supported them and saw to it that their stories got on the air. That required no small measure of courage on Friendly's part, for by the fall of 1965 he was under mounting pressure to cool it on the war coverage.

Each night when he went on the air in those days, Walter Cronkite could be assured that one of his viewers was President Lyndon Baines

Johnson—if, indeed, "viewer" is not too bland a term to describe the kind of fierce scrutiny that Johnson brought to the network newscasts. In the fall of 1965, as CBS News became tougher and more openly critical in its reporting on the war, LBJ occasionally telephoned his good friend Frank Stanton and blistered his ears with the kind of scalding, scatological abuse that was his specialty. ("Frank, are you trying to fuck me?" "Frank, this is your President, and yesterday your boys shat on the American flag.") Stanton, in turn, relayed Johnson's "concern" to Friendly, strongly implying that the President had a right to be sore, and that maybe CBS had gone too far in some of its war coverage. But Friendly stood firm. No, he told Stanton, it wasn't the reporters who were out of line, it was the government spokesmen, military and civilian; *they* were the ones who were lying to the American people. Frank Stanton did not find these words very comforting. He did not go quite so far as to try to muzzle the news department, but he made no secret of his displeasure with much of the CBS reporting from Vietnam.

It was against this background of rising tensions that, in late January 1966, Senator J. William Fulbright's Foreign Relations Committee commenced hearings on a foreign aid bill, which quickly turned into a public debate on the war in Vietnam. As Secretary of State Dean Rusk and others appeared before the committee, Friendly began to press for live coverage of the hearings. The corporate response to this proposal was not at all enthusiastic, in large part because of the considerable loss of revenue that would result from the cancellation of commercial programming, and also, no doubt, because of a strong disinclination to embroil the network any more deeply in the Vietnam controversy. Still, Friendly was able to extract from his reluctant superiors permission for two days of live coverage. When he requested a third day (to cover the testimony of George Kennan, the former diplomat who had been a chief architect of Truman's foreign policy and who now was a critic of U.S. involvement in Vietnam), the corporate reply was a firm no. Enough was enough. Hence, on the day of Kennan's testimony, NBC broadcast the Fulbright hearings live while CBS resumed its regular schedule, which included, among other light entertainments, a rerun of *I Love Lucy.* Five days later, Friendly resigned in protest.

This was a lofty moment in the life of Fred Friendly. In one press account after another, he was lauded for having sacrificed his career to the cause of the Vietnam hearings and the public's right to view them. Many of Friendly's CBS News colleagues, however, did not look upon his gesture as a gallant stand so much as a characteristic *grand*stand. No one doubted the sincerity of his anger or his commitment to the principle involved, but most of his associates knew (as most of those outside CBS did not) that Friendly's resignation had less to do with the decision against live coverage of the hearings than with the corporate maneuvering that had preceded the decision. Beyond that, some CBS people attributed Friendly's action to his restless desire for a special kind of recognition. In their judgment, he simply could not resist letting the world know that he, at least, had fought on the side of the angels.

One condition on which Friendly had insisted, when he took over as president of CBS News, was that he would have direct and regular access to Paley and Stanton. He did not want to be hobbled by corporate middlemen. Paley and Stanton agreed to the stipulation, but as time went on, both men wished they hadn't. They soon discovered that there was no getting away from Friendly. He was constantly at them, by phone or in person, demanding this, complaining about that, requesting still another meeting to discuss something or other. In the early weeks of 1966, Paley and Stanton saw their chance to give themselves a little insulation, and they took it. The giant CBS corporation was being reorganized into two basic groups—the Broadcast Group and the Columbia Group—and a fast-rising young executive named John Schneider was appointed president of the Broadcast Group. That meant that all of the network's broadcast operations, including news, would now be under his supervision. Henceforth, Friendly was told, Schneider was the man he should contact in all his future dealings with the corporate brass.

The division into two groups had been dictated by CBS's remarkable growth and diversification. By the mid-1960s, the corporation had expanded into several other fields beyond radio and television. Under the aegis of the CBS eye, there now existed a flourishing record company, publishing firms, toy and guitar manufacturers, and even a baseball team—the New York Yankees, which CBS purchased in 1964. Two years later, those acquisitions were herded under the Columbia Group. As head of the Broadcast Group, Schneider reigned over four separate divisions: News, the Television Network, the Radio Network, and the five CBS-owned television stations in New York, Philadelphia, Chicago, Saint Louis, and Los Angeles.

At the age of thirty-nine, Jack Schneider had come a long way in a hurry. He had begun his television career as a time salesman in

Chicago, later moving into administration. For six years, from 1958 to 1964, he was general manager of WCAU-TV, the CBS-owned station in Philadelphia. Then, in 1964, he was brought to New York, and the following year he succeeded the eminent vulgarian, Jim Aubrey, as president of the CBS Television Network. This latest promotion, in 1966, placed him third, just behind Paley and Stanton, in the corporate hierarchy.

Schneider's first major act as president of the Broadcast Group was to reject Friendly's request for live coverage of George Kennan's testimony at the Fulbright hearings. Enraged, Friendly went over Schneider's head. In separate meetings with Paley and Stanton, he railed against the new arrangement that gave Schneider decision-making authority over the news division. In a characteristically vivid mixed metaphor, he referred to Schneider as a "contraceptive" that was blocking his access to top management and thereby threatening the news operation with "emasculation." At one point, in a grim encounter with Stanton, Friendly asserted that if he compromised on the Schneider question, he would "no longer be the man you hired. . . . I won't be Fred Friendly at all, I'll be a flabby mutation." That prospect struck Stanton as being so wildly implausible that he let out a hearty laugh, which broke the tension a bit. But only momentarily. When Friendly threatened to resign if the Schneider "contraceptive" was not removed, Stanton warned him: "Fred, you're painting yourself into a corner."

Friendly must have realized how quixotic his position was. Clearly, Paley and Stanton wanted Schneider to serve as a buffer between themselves and Friendly. And clearly, the decision regarding the Kennan testimony had not been made by Schneider alone. But he made a convenient villain. Because he did not have the public stature of a Paley or Stanton, and because his broadcasting background was in sales and station management, it was easy to depict him as a huckster, a crass philistine interested only in profits, not in the serious, public-affairs side of television.

In fact, Schneider was a bright and well-rounded executive who was far more sympathetic to the interests of the news division than Jim Aubrey had ever been. But that was hardly the impression he conveyed at the time of the Fulbright hearings. His public statements on the subject were distinguished only by their fatuousness. In defending the decision against live coverage, he took the position that housewives, who made up most of the regular daytime audience, weren't interested in the first public debate on the Vietnam War—a war that imperiled members of their own families. Schneider also asserted, presumably with a straight face, that the loss of advertising revenue had not been a factor in the decision, which was palpable nonsense. By making such a claim, he placed himself in the ludicrous position of implying that, since money had not been a consideration, *I Love Lucy* and the other reruns were chosen over the Kennan testimony on the basis of merit. After a few observations like that, even Schneider's most ardent apologists stopped trying to defend him.

In the meantime, Friendly realized he had no choice but to carry out his threat. On the day he resigned, he appeared before a large gathering of CBS News personnel in the main CBS newsroom. It was a highly emotional scene. In his farewell remarks, he urged the assembled throng to keep up the fight to safeguard the honor and tradition of broadcast journalism, and, in turn, he was loudly cheered for his valorous action. It was a classy and dramatic departure, and some of Friendly's more cynical CBS colleagues were convinced that was what mattered to him more than anything else.

Friendly was familiar with the scornful line that had been going around CBS for years, to wit: "Fred Friendly is a man of high principles and low practices." More than once in the past he had allowed his driving ambition to take precedence over his obligations to his fellow journalists. So now, in February 1966, he seized the opportunity to show his colleagues that he was worthy of their esteem. "Sooner or later," he said with chest-swelling pride shortly after his resignation, "somebody had to quit over an issue in this business." Those who were close to Friendly at the time believe he became so enthralled by the prospect of going down in flames over a point of principle that he would have been truly disappointed if Paley and Stanton had relented and given him his way.

A few weeks after his resignation, Friendly began a new career as television consultant to the Ford Foundation, which had become, among other things, the chief benefactor of educational television in America. There the Brilliant Monster threw his prodigious energies into creating a fresh approach to news programming, one that would provide viewers with a clear and dramatic alternative to the commercial networks. The result was the Public Broadcasting Laboratory, or PBL. The program made its debut in the fall of 1967, and, thanks to the Ford Foundation's largesse, it stayed on the air for two years. Although

PBL was the first serious attempt at a multisubject, magazine format on television, it concentrated almost exclusively on large, *meaningful* issues. It wasn't really journalism so much as a series of pompous lectures, and, at times, its tone of moral superiority was insufferable.

Friendly's fingerprints were all over PBL—*Variety* and others referred to it as "Friendlyvision"—and he was largely responsible for the program's holier-than-thou tone. The irony (a rather bitter one for Friendly) was that the commercial networks were quick to adopt the experimental magazine format and make it work. Friendly's pitch for an exciting alternative to conventional documentaries and the regular news shows later found its most sophisticated expression not in PBL but in *60 Minutes* and NBC's *First Tuesday*.

PBL was Fred Friendly's last hurrah. In the years that followed its demise, he lapsed more and more into the role of television dynamo *emeritus*. In addition to his work as consultant to the Ford Foundation, he became the first Edward R. Murrow Professor of Broadcast Journalism at Columbia University, or as Friendly, with his gift for phrasing, put it at the time of his appointment, "I will be a kind of electronic Mr. Chips." His exuberance and his ability to stimulate others made him a popular teacher at Columbia, and, over the years, some of his best students went on to good jobs at the networks, including CBS. But Friendly himself remained on the sidelines, secure in the knowledge that he had made a major contribution to TV journalism, but no doubt wishing, now and again, that he were still in the thick of it.

As time went on, he continued to write articles and issue statements, many of them critical of network journalism, and often, on such occasions, he was primarily identified not by his association with the Ford Foundation or Columbia University but by his past connections with CBS. This tendency irked a number of people at CBS, and no one found it more irritating than Jack Schneider, who had never forgiven Friendly for having made his life so miserable at the time of the Fulbright hearings. In 1974, a full eight years after their public row and Friendly's resignation, Schneider, yielding to a mischievous impulse, had a few hundred business cards printed up and sent a batch of them over to Friendly's office at the Ford Foundation. Inscribed on each card were the words:

Fred W. Friendly
Former President, CBS News

The abruptness of Friendly's resignation put CBS in the position of having to scramble a bit to name a successor. Schneider, in particular, was on the spot. Having played the villain, he now was under pressure to demonstrate his good faith in helping to restore order and morale within the news division. Paley and Stanton purposely stayed in the background. Since the whole dispute with Friendly had been over their decision to give Schneider authority over the news department, it was essential that he be on display as the corporate officer in charge of selecting the next president of CBS News.

The first candidates to come up for consideration were Friendly's two chief deputies, Bill Leonard and Gordon Manning. Leonard, however, was quickly ruled out, primarily because of his close association with Friendly. But Manning was a relative newcomer to CBS, and so, in those first hectic hours after Friendly quit, Schneider turned to him. And Manning turned him down. Having been a vigorous ally of Friendly's in the fight over the Fulbright hearings, Manning felt he should not be the one to benefit from Friendly's resignation.

At this point, the network's two most respected senior correspondents, Walter Cronkite and Eric Sevareid, invited themselves into the decision-making process. Together, they went first to Stanton and then to Schneider to urge that the job be given back to Dick Salant. Salant, they argued, had been a good president who never should have been squeezed out in the first place. Both Schneider and Stanton were delighted by their recommendation. In their private conversations, the two men had discussed the idea of rehabilitating Salant and were already leaning in that direction. All they needed was a slight shove, and now Cronkite and Sevareid had provided that.

Selling the proposal to Salant, however, was not so easy. Although he was bored with his present job as Stanton's special assistant and yearned for a second chance to run the news division, he had been deeply wounded two years earlier when he was muscled aside to make room for Friendly. He did not want to risk a repeat of that humiliation. He knew that many of the people who had pushed for his ouster in 1964 were still around, and, of course, he had Paley to worry about. Salant knew that the Chairman was not one of his fervent admirers. Nevertheless, it was not in him to reject the offer; the job simply meant too much to him.

Eventually, the three men—Salant, Schneider, and Stanton—

agreed on a face-saving stratagem: Salant would be appointed "acting president," and Schneider, in making the announcement, would stress that a permanent successor to Friendly would be named at a later time. That way, if things didn't work out, Salant could relinquish the post with a minimum of damage to his reputation. But a few weeks after he took over, Salant felt secure enough to come out of his acting-president closet and acknowledge that he was Friendly's official successor. More than a decade later, he was still on the job. As a matter of fact, his restoration in February 1966 brought an end to all the disruptions of management and other key personnel that had been a way of life at CBS News ever since the 1960 conventions. With the start of Salant's second term as president, CBS News entered into a period of stability that was to prevail over the next several years.

Working in Salant's favor the second time around was the fact that by 1966, his corporate superiors had grown weary of all the turmoil. That was certainly true of Paley. In 1966, he turned sixty-five, the mandatory age of retirement at CBS. For the Chairman, however, *nothing* was mandatory, and so he stayed on at the helm. But if Paley remained in overall charge of his giant "candy store" (as it was called), he became increasingly less active and, in particular, retreated from direct involvement in the affairs of the news division. He was confident of his own place in history. He knew he could claim, with much justification, that broadcast journalism in general and CBS News in particular might well not have evolved in quite the way they did if in the early years he had not given his enthusiastic support to the likes of Ed Klauber, Paul White, and Ed Murrow and his boys. Yes, those were glorious memories, and Paley was still fiercely proud of CBS News and its fine tradition. But his more recent experiences with the news department had not been happy ones. So, out of weariness and exasperation, Bill Paley withdrew into the corporate shadows. Every now and then, in the years that followed, he would issue an edict or express his concern over something the news division had done. But for the most part, he was content to let Stanton and Schneider keep watch over the news operation.

Frank Stanton was also tired of fighting with the news department, but, more than that, he wanted to make everything as pleasant as possible for his friend and protégé, Dick Salant. Being Stanton's fair-haired boy gave Salant considerable leverage in his dealings with the corporate brass, and he did not hesitate to use it. The two men had their occasional differences, but Salant regarded Stanton as a true friend of the news division, and Stanton, in turn, knew he could rely on Salant not to get carried away and make unreasonable demands, as Friendly had sometimes done.

Nor did Jack Schneider choose to throw his weight around. Having become the target of public criticism with his inane defense of the decision to air *I Love Lucy* instead of the Fulbright hearings, he was determined never to get drawn into that kind of fracas again. As in his dealings with Stanton, Salant did not always get what he wanted from Schneider. But in general, Schneider went out of his way to cooperate, in part because he genuinely liked and respected Salant, as he had not respected Friendly, and in part because he did not want to become embroiled in another public dispute with the news division. Then, too, Schneider was a shrewd company man, and, as such, he was ever mindful of Salant's special relationship with *his* boss, Frank Stanton.

As a news executive, Salant was in many ways ideal: with his connections and corporate savvy, he could play the company game in ways that served to protect and strengthen the news division. Under his supervision, the news operation, which had been given a robust transfusion by Friendly, continued to expand and improve. It was, in fact, during Salant's second term that CBS finally overtook NBC and became, once again, the dominant voice in broadcast journalism.

Even so, Salant had his detractors. Cronkite and Sevareid may have had a high opinion of him, but others at CBS News did not. In particular, those who had been turned on by Friendly's aggressive style thought Salant was dull and aloof by comparison, a corporate smoothie, no doubt, but not a leader in the vigorous Friendly way. The chief complaint against him was that he did not involve himself nearly enough in the day-to-day process of getting the news on the air. One unadmiring producer dubbed him "the Absentee Landlord," and it quickly caught on as an underground term of derision. For his part, Salant believed his function was more that of a publisher than an editor. Since his own background was not in news, he did not think it was up to him to tell the professional journalists under his command how to carry out their assignments. He had plenty of deputies to take care of that, and he delegated a great deal of power to them.

As a result, Bill Leonard and Gordon Manning, the two vice-presidents he inherited from Friendly, now had more of a chance to show their stuff. Working in the shadow of Friendly's domineering presence, neither man had been able to establish his own independent authority. But Salant gave Leonard and Manning free rein to run their respective departments more or less as they chose. Always sensitive about his own lack of credentials, he respected the fact that both men had solid backgrounds in journalism.

For eleven years, from 1946 to 1957, Bill Leonard was the star of an extremely popular radio program called *This Is New York*, which was broadcast six days a week by the CBS-owned station in New York. It started out as an early-morning show on which Leonard, a roving reporter, related offbeat stories he had encountered during a night on the prowl. *This Is New York* was such a big hit that it was pushed up to a later hour, and the format was expanded to include such features as public-service items and reviews of the latest movies and plays. It eventually evolved into a kind of all-purpose information program on life in New York. During these years, Leonard also took on a few spot assignments for CBS (he was a floor reporter at the 1952 and 1956 conventions), and Sig Mickelson made several attempts to bring him into the network on a full-time basis. Some CBS old-timers are convinced that if Leonard had joined the network in those early, formative years, he would have gone on to become a big-name correspondent— on a par, say, with Reasoner or Collingwood, if not quite in the class of Murrow or Cronkite. But he was having too much fun and making too much money as a local big shot, not only on *This Is New York* but also on its various spin-offs, including a TV program called *Eye on New York*. Besides, he figured, there would always be time later on to branch out onto the national stage.

But then, all of a sudden, everything began to go sour. In 1956, when he was forty, Leonard suffered a serious heart attack, which put a severe crimp in his career. No longer able to hustle and chase around the way he did before, he had to give up *This Is New York*, his power base. By the late 1950s, he had lost assignments on other shows as well, and he was doing commercials and other odd jobs to supplement his work in journalism.

It was at this bleak stage in his life that Leonard went to Fred Friendly and asked for a job on *CBS Reports*, which then was just going into operation. He had missed his chance to become a star network correspondent, but he felt that, given his experience, he still had something to offer. Friendly, however, was not so sure. By this time, the word going around was that Leonard was too much of a "New York type" for the network, and that even there, on his own turf, he was rapidly becoming a has-been. But then Friendly remembered that Leonard had been in the Dominican Republic a couple of times in recent years, and that gave him an idea: a story on that country's dictator, Rafael Trujillo. If Leonard thought he could manage that, the assignment was his.

It was asking a great deal. The Trujillo regime did not welcome nosy foreign journalists, especially those who brought television cameras with them. But Leonard had a few contacts in the Dominican Republic, and so he agreed to give the story a try on the condition that he be granted plenty of time to pursue it. He spent the next six months in the Dominican Republic, and eventually, through his contacts, he was able to get an on-camera interview with Trujillo. Not only that, but the interview took place at the dictator's private ranch, where *El Benefactor,* as Trujillo liked to call himself, rode out to greet the CBS crew on a white horse. When he finally returned to New York with the footage, Leonard told Friendly: "Fred, you're going to love this. We've not only got him, but we've got him on horseback."

Trujillo—Portrait of a Dictator was broadcast in the spring of 1960, and, following that impressive debut, Leonard went on to produce and narrate other documentaries for *CBS Reports.* Most of them dealt with various aspects of domestic politics (for example, *Our Election Day Illusions* and *Thunder on the Right*), and that, no doubt, was one reason why he was picked, in early 1962, to run the network's newly formed election unit. The creation of a permanent election unit, responsible for long-range planning, came at a time when computer analysis was still regarded as an exotic and unreliable means of projecting election results. But Bill Leonard helped to change all that. He was among the first to recognize that computers should be used not as a toy or game but as a basic source of information.

Leonard's first test in his new job was the 1962 midterm elections, when he inaugurated the new technique: projecting final results on the basis of computer analysis of votes in certain carefully selected precincts. The public's initial reaction was one of bewilderment and irritation. Many viewers did not think it was cricket of Walter Cronkite to declare that So-and-so had won when only 1 percent of the raw vote had been counted. They were especially disconcerted on those occasions when the actual vote count showed the proclaimed "winner" to be trailing his opponent by several thousand votes. But the computer system that Leonard had gambled on was here to stay, and in time even those who didn't like it had to admit that it was a revolutionary advance in election reporting.

Then came the 1964 conventions and the dumping of Cronkite. Leonard was not proud of the part he played in that affair, and with good reason. He later admitted that if he had been as forceful as Leiser in arguing against the move, Friendly almost surely would have held the line and Paley would have acquiesced. But he had been worried about his own skin. Paley was out for blood, and the thought occurred to Leonard, during those tense discussions in the Chairman's office, that if Cronkite were not made the scapegoat, then somebody else would be. And as the man in charge of the election unit (and therefore the convention coverage), he was a prime alternative. Thus he was not as ardent as he might have been in his defense of Cronkite. Many years later, when one of his young producers made a passing reference to Leonard, Cronkite frowned and quietly confided that he had never been able to "forgive Leonard for the way he sold me out in 1964."

In late 1964, Leonard was appointed vice-president for public affairs, or the soft-news end of the operation. He had come a long way in the past five years, and he owed almost everything to Friendly. Leonard readily acknowledged that debt, but that didn't blind him to Friendly's faults and excesses. "Fred was a great *two-year* president," he once said about his former boss and benefactor. "But I'm afraid if he had lasted much longer, he would have driven everyone crazy. I know for certain that *I* would have wound up a basket case."

Instead, Bill Leonard stayed on as soft-news vice-president over the next decade, and during that time he demonstrated that in his own executive style he was much more like Salant than Friendly. Deliberate, low-key, rather ponderous at times, he also was generous in his delegation of authority to others. It was his policy to stay out of the creative and production process until a project was near completion and ready to be screened. Only then would he view the footage and offer his comments and criticisms. This willingness to give people their head made for a harmonious relationship with the executive producers under his jurisdiction. For by the late 1960s, many production units within CBS News had become semiautonomous domains or fiefdoms, each ruled by its own proud and ambitious lord. They were not unlike feudal barons, and they appreciated the unwritten Magna Carta by which Leonard acknowledged their rights and prerogatives.

At the same time, Leonard was also nicely wired into the corporate hierarchy. He and Frank Stanton had known and liked each other for years, ever since 1945 when on Stanton's advice Leonard applied for the CBS radio job that became *This Is New York*. And he was also on extremely good terms with Jack Schneider, who once said to an associate, "The thing about Bill Leonard is that he's a *broad*caster. His career has been in *broad*casting. The man knows and understands our business." What gave the remark a certain piquancy is not what it said about Leonard, but what it implied about his vice-presidential counterpart, Gordon Manning. His early career had *not* been in broadcasting, and Schneider, who had grown to dislike and distrust Manning, seldom passed up an opportunity to suggest, however obliquely, that he did not understand "our business."

Like Cronkite and so many others, Manning was a "Downholder," a word once frequently used to describe an alumnus of the United Press. The term evolved out of the news agency's stern commitment to parsimony. Those who worked at UP line bureaus received so many orders from their superiors to "downhold" expenses that the word came to symbolize their common plight of being overworked and underpaid. Manning started at the United Press while still a student at Boston University in 1940, and after serving in the Navy during World War II, he returned to UP for a couple of years. Then, in 1948, the heyday of the great mass magazines, he landed a job as a staff writer for *Collier's*. The *Collier's* people were impressed by Manning's industry. He was a fast, competent writer and, even better, he kept coming up with fresh story ideas, an invaluable asset in the highly competitive world of mass magazines. As a result, he eventually became managing editor, a position he held until *Collier's* folded in 1956.

After *Collier's* went under, Manning hooked up with *Newsweek* as features or back-of-the-book editor; then, in 1961, he was promoted to executive editor. He brought to that job all the dash and hustle that had characterized his style at *Collier's*, and *Newsweek* became a better and more exciting magazine. That is what brought him to the attention of Fred Friendly in 1964 when he was considering candidates for hard-news vice-president. Since both he and Leonard, his choice for soft-news vice-president, had spent their entire careers in broadcasting, Friendly felt the other management post should go to an experienced print journalist.

Friendly's admiration of Manning's work at *Newsweek* was from a distance. He did not know Manning personally. But Les Midgley, then one of the top producers at CBS News, had worked briefly with Manning at *Collier's,* and later, when Midgley became managing editor of *Look,* he had a chance to appreciate Manning as a competitor. So when Friendly asked about Manning, Midgley gave him a strong recommendation, as did others, including the publisher of *Newsweek,* Katharine Graham. Thus encouraged, Friendly asked Midgley to sound out Manning himself. The two men met for lunch, and when Midgley broached the subject, Manning responded with enthusiasm, in large part because he was having problems at *Newsweek.* In his zeal to improve the magazine, he was often overbearing and meddlesome in his relations with junior editors, and many of them resented it. By 1964, an anti-Manning faction had formed at *Newsweek.* For that reason, as well as others, he welcomed the opportunity to embark on a new career in broadcast journalism. Following the lunch with Midgley, Manning met with Friendly, and soon thereafter he went to work for CBS News.

During his first few months on the job, Manning had little chance to assert himself the way he had at *Collier's* and *Newsweek.* For one thing, he was working in a new medium; and more than that, it was his first experience with the Brilliant Monster. But in his own restless way, Manning was a kind of half-speed Friendly, and he soon grew to admire his new boss. In fact, by February 1966, his sense of loyalty was so strong that when Friendly resigned from CBS and Jack Schneider, in turn, asked Manning to take over as president of the news division, Manning refused, citing principle.

Schneider was profoundly annoyed by that decision, which he regarded as an act of phony valor. In his view, if Manning was so concerned about the principle involved, he probably had a moral obligation to resign, too. But as long as he was staying at CBS, then his first loyalty, as Schneider saw it, was to the network and to the task of restoring order and morale within the news division. Manning was trying to have it both ways, and Schneider resented it. It was the first sour note in a relationship that would steadily deteriorate over the years until finally, in 1974, Schneider would move to oust Gordon Manning from power at CBS.

But in 1966, neither Schneider nor Manning had any inkling that it would someday come to that. At the time, Manning's position was quite secure, and now that Friendly had been replaced by the more acquiescent Dick Salant, he felt free to be more aggressive in running his own operation. His area of responsibility, like Leonard's, consisted of several semiautonomous domains, but Manning was much less inclined to delegate power to the various producers under his command. In the years that followed, he exercised strong, personal authority over such production units as the *Morning News* and the network's two weekend news shows. But the *CBS Evening News with Walter Cronkite* was another story. That was the broadcast with all the impact and prestige, and yet, in his efforts to assert personal control over it, Manning ran into constant frustration. On paper, at least, he should have had no problem, for officially he outranked Ernie Leiser, the executive producer of the *Evening News*. Unfortunately, it did little good to outrank Ernie Leiser as long as Ernie Leiser declined to behave like a subordinate.

9   Discussing the Lineup with God

During his years of power at CBS News, Ernie Leiser ruled with the severity of a Prussian martinet. There were, in fact, a number of CBS people who, having been exposed to the wrath of both Leiser and Fred Friendly, considered Leiser to be more skilled in the arts of intimidation. Friendly's outbursts were so excessive and so histrionic that the specific point of his displeasure often became lost in all the tumult. Leiser's rages, though less frequent, were far more controlled and coherent, which made him more formidable. His strength emanated from a supreme confidence in his own journalistic judgment and ability, an iron self-assurance made all the more impressive by the fact that his early career had been marked by numerous setbacks and disappointments.

Leiser had earned his journalistic credentials covering the European battlefields of World War II for the Army newspaper *Stars and Stripes,* extremely good duty for a young GI just out of college. Toward the end of the war he was based in Paris, and to supplement his corporal's salary, he began moonlighting for the Paris edition of the *New York Herald-Tribune.* The man responsible for putting this extra change into Leiser's pocket was the *Trib*'s night editor in Paris, a lanky Mormon named Les Midgley, and the two men quickly became friends.

After the war, Leiser hoped to make a name for himself as a foreign correspondent. He worked for a while as a civilian reporter for *Stars and Stripes,* and then, in 1947, he moved on to the Overseas News Agency. Both *Stars and Stripes* and ONA operated on shoestring budgets, and Leiser again turned to moonlighting—free-lance assignments and stringer work—in order to make ends meet. But the big break continued to elude him, and by 1952, he had grown weary of working for peanuts in Europe. He was thirty-one years old with a wife and two children, and his career was going nowhere. It was time, he decided, to give up the "glamorous" life of a foreign correspondent. He returned to the States and took a job as associate editor of a magazine called *United Nations World,* another nickel-and-dime operation. After a few months, he was so bored and unhappy that he was ready to go back to Europe and try his luck at the precarious game of free-lancing on a full-time basis.

Leiser discussed his plight one night over drinks with Charles Collingwood, whom he knew from World War II days, and Collingwood offered to use his influence to get him into CBS. Until then, Leiser had never given any thought to broadcast journalism, but Collingwood assured him that he could make the transition. Collingwood then talked to Sig Mickelson and others, and in the summer of 1953, Leiser went to work for CBS as a writer.

By 1956, he was back in Europe as CBS News correspondent and bureau chief in Bonn. Over the next four years, he specialized in covering stories behind the Iron Curtain, starting with the 1956 uprising in Hungary, where he was arrested by the Russians and kept in jail for three days. Most of his on-air reports from Europe were for radio, and on those occasions when he did send in a film story, it was usually with a voice-over narration. But when he returned to New York in 1960, with the intention of advancing his career as a correspondent, he began doing stand-uppers and other on-camera pieces. This was most unfortunate because Leiser, for all his journalistic ability, was a disaster as a TV correspondent. With his hard, granite face and his horn-rimmed glasses, he was not especially telegenic. His favorite expression was an uneasy glower, and his camera presence was all negative. What's more, he knew it. The more he saw of himself on television, the more he realized that, for him, there would have to be another way.

The other way presented itself in the early months of 1961 when Dick Salant took over as president of CBS News and Blair Clark was appointed general manager. Leiser had a very good relationship with Clark. During his years in Europe, he regularly came up with excellent stories for Clark's radio program, *The World Tonight,* and Clark appreciated it. Now that Clark was second-in-command on the new management team, Leiser saw an opportunity for himself. On his own initiative, he presented Clark with a list of suggestions on how to improve the news operation. This was more than a little presumptuous, and it could easily have backfired. But Clark, who had no executive experience and was nervous about the new management responsibilities that had been thrust upon him, welcomed the unsolicited advice. In fact, he was so impressed that, with Salant's approval, he appointed Leiser assistant general manager of CBS News.

In that position, Ernie Leiser went on to become the strong man of Salant's first term as president. Having failed in his own efforts to become a star television correspondent, he now had the power to determine the fate of other aspirants—and he exercised it. Leiser was the one who pushed the hardest to have Cronkite replace Doug Edwards on the *Evening News*. He also was the one who made the decision to hire a young reporter from Houston named Dan Rather, and who encouraged another Texan, Hughes Rudd, to make the jump from radio writer to TV correspondent. More important, he was the force behind the major executive decisions of those years, including the setting up of new regional bureaus and the expansion of the *Evening News* to a half hour. In his arguments on behalf of the latter, set down in a long and detailed brief he prepared for presentation to the corporate brass and the network's reluctant affiliates, Leiser wrote that "we see it as an entirely new kind of broadcast with a new feeling and a new scope." The new format, he added, would go beyond "the compressed, tabloid treatment" of the fifteen-minute program and present "more news of more kinds, and we will give that news more meaning." Leiser asserted that "we will not only have a front-of-the-book, we will have a back-of-the-book as well."

In practice, however, it didn't quite work out that way. When the half-hour broadcast was launched in September 1963, Don Hewitt remained in overall charge of the *Evening News*, but Leiser's old Paris buddy, Les Midgley, was assigned to the show as back-of-the-book producer. The assumption was that front-page news would occupy about two-thirds of an average broadcast, and that Midgley-developed features would round out the half hour. Instead, the crush of breaking news was such that it quickly filled up the entire half hour, and Midgley soon discovered that he had almost nothing to do. After a few months, he left the broadcast and took on other production assignments for CBS News.

As for Leiser, he was disturbed because the half-hour program was not living up to his vision of it. He believed that some of the secondary "today" stories should be excluded to make room for longer follow-through film pieces. But when he asked Hewitt why the broadcast wasn't presenting more "enterprisers" (a wire-service term for special in-depth stories), Hewitt replied in his best wise-guy manner that "all my enterprise goes into getting the goddamn show on every night." Leiser was not amused. He continued to have a high regard for Hewitt's technical skills, but he began to suspect, as did others, that Hewitt was so wedded to the fifteen-minute format—"the compressed, tabloid treatment" he had created—that he was unable to see that the half-hour program required a different approach. This was one reason why Leiser felt no qualms about promoting himself to Friendly as Hewitt's replacement in the fall of 1964.

There was another reason. Leiser would never have relinquished his managerial post as long as Blair Clark and Dick Salant were his immediate superiors. He got along extremely well with both men, largely because they generally deferred to him on journalistic matters and gave him plenty of room to maneuver. When Salant was replaced by Friendly all that changed, and Leiser discovered, among other things, that he did not like being yelled at. By opting for the *Evening News,* he could put some distance between himself and Friendly, even though it meant forsaking his chance to become hard-news vice-president. At the time, very few people at CBS were aware of how much Leiser disapproved of the way Friendly harassed his deputies. Had they known, they might have been moved to sublime reflections on how the pot, in its zeal to find fault with the kettle, tends to overlook its own tarnished state.

When Ernie Leiser took over as executive producer of the Cronkite show in December 1964, the CBS News operation had just recently moved from the Graybar Building on Lexington Avenue and Forty-second Street to more spacious quarters in a converted milk-bottling plant on West Fifty-seventh Street. In its new home, the *Evening News* area was again set up as a newsroom-studio, featuring a horseshoe-shaped desk arrangement with various slots for Cronkite and his staff writers. While Hewitt was running the show, visitors and other unauthorized personnel frequently wandered into the area to chat or just hang around. That was fine as far as Hewitt was concerned. He enjoyed having people around, especially strangers to the business whom he could dazzle with his manic approach to TV news production. But that was not Leiser's style. One of his first acts as executive producer of the *Evening News* was to have signs nailed up on all doors leading into the newsroom-studio that read: THIS IS A WORKING AREA. NO VISITORS PLEASE. Those words were a warning not only to visitors but to all CBS News personnel: from now on, the prevailing mood in the *Evening News* area would be all business.

As executive producer of the *CBS Evening News with Walter Cronkite*, Leiser, too, was all business. Rigorous, impatient, and often brutally critical, he was interested only in performance, in the job at hand, and the brusque way he issued instructions irritated many of his coworkers. In particular, those who had to deal with him by phone often complained that he barked orders at them and then hung up without even being civil enough to say good-bye. This particular grievance persisted until the day when Sam Zelman, then Los Angeles bureau chief for CBS News, happened to be in Leiser's office while he was on the phone. When the conversation ended, Zelman watched in fascination as Leiser flung the receiver onto the cradle and snapped, "Good-bye"—the "good-bye" coming just a split second too late to be heard on the other end. When Zelman returned to Los Angeles, he happily spread the word that Leiser wasn't such a boor, after all. He was just a little out of sync: a case of the hand being quicker than the voice.

Like all despots, Leiser ruled by fear. A stern-looking man with pewter-gray hair and bushy eyebrows, he exuded such authority that much of the time he did not even have to verbalize his displeasure. His scowl was enough to induce the appropriate cringe, the cower of contrition. Yet Leiser also inspired respect and a kind of surly affection. There was, in fact, a widespread feeling at CBS that he had more going for him intellectually than did most of his colleagues—and there is no doubt that Leiser, a graduate of the University of Chicago during the Robert Hutchins era, was convinced of that.

He also had a reputation for being scrupulously fair. His standards were high, but when somebody's work measured up to them, Leiser let him know it, and in terms as direct and as forceful as those he used in his criticisms. And because of his forbidding manner, a compliment from Leiser usually meant more to the recipient than one from another producer or executive. Nor was he one to play favorites. John Merriman, a writer on the Cronkite show during Leiser's years as executive producer, once said that what impressed him the most about Leiser was that he was "always so generous with his disdain." In suffering through a Leiser reprimand, one could take comfort in the certain knowledge that before the day was out, others would get their turn. Not even his superiors were altogether safe. Fred Friendly discovered that in the summer of 1964 when Leiser all but accused him of being a company whore in the way he acceded to the Cronkite convention switch. And two years later, Gordon Manning would get his.

For the most part, Leiser and Manning had a good working relationship. Leiser admired Manning's aggressive commitment to news, especially in the way it manifested itself in arguments with corporate executives for more air time and larger budgets. As Leiser saw it, Manning also had the executive right to propose ideas and criticize performance, *after the fact.* That was part of his job. It was only when he felt that Manning was trying to encroach on his own *Evening News* turf that Leiser turned sour. There had been enough problems on that score with Friendly. Leiser and Friendly had clashed on several occasions over production decisions involving the Cronkite show, and Leiser had not always prevailed. But that had been Friendly, and even Leiser had had trouble standing up to him. Now, however, Friendly was gone, and Leiser was determined that as long as he was executive producer of the *Evening News,* neither Manning nor any other management type would be allowed to meddle in the day-to-day operation, the specific details that went into shaping each night's broadcast.

Manning, who was similar to Friendly both in temperament and ambition, saw it differently. He viewed Friendly's departure as his chance to dominate, to become the executive titan of CBS News, and in a move to establish personal control over the various hard-news units under his jurisdiction, he began to spend more and more time around the *Evening News* area, as if to insinuate himself into that program's daily decision-making process. Soon Leiser was complaining to Manning in private, and each time Manning assured him he had no intention of intruding on Leiser's authority. Still, he continued to hang around, to hover about, like an eager-beaver Little League father who can't understand why the team's manager doesn't solicit his advice.

Finally, there came a day in the fall of 1966 when Manning happened to be in a screening room viewing a film piece along with Leiser and other members of the *Evening News* staff. When the screening ended, Leiser was about to make his criticisms, as was his custom, but before he had a chance to, Manning began offering *his* comments. That tore it. Leiser turned to Manning and said with quiet fury, "Gordon, I'm tired of asking. Now, for the last time, get the hell out of here, and *stay out!*" An associate producer who witnessed the rebuke said it was followed by a few seconds of "awesome silence, and then, without saying a word, Gordon slithered out."

It was a humiliating moment for Manning. In order to save face, he would have to escalate the incident into a showdown—a test of strength between himself and Leiser—but if he did that, he would be the certain loser. For despite the fact that he was Leiser's titular superior, Leiser held all the high cards. He had been able, through his many years of service as a correspondent and news executive, to build up strong ties with his various superiors, including Manning's immediate boss, Dick Salant. Even in their own relationship, Leiser had a certain psychological edge over Manning; he had been Manning's predecessor and had relinquished that post and the chance to become a vice-president in order to take over the *Evening News.* But the biggest plus he had going for him was his current work as executive producer of the Cronkite show. By 1966, the *CBS Evening News* had improved significantly, and Ernie Leiser deserved much of the credit for that.

Leiser was stronger editorially than Don Hewitt had been. Hewitt's major innovations, from the double projector system to the clever use of graphics, had been in form or production technique. The question he constantly asked was: What can we do to tell the story better? Leiser's passion was for content, the news itself, and his question was: How can we get a better story? While Hewitt thought primarily in terms of film, of visual flair, Leiser concentrated on the word, the meaning. Under his leadership, stories on the *Evening News* became more sharply angled, more deeply probed.

Leiser committed himself and the Cronkite show to the use of frequent enterprisers, six- or seven-minute film reports on recent major news stories, as opposed to film pieces on that day's headline news, which seldom ran more than a minute and a half each. This was a lot of time on a half-hour broadcast, especially since because of commercials and announcements the actual news portion was only twenty-two minutes. More often than not, there was so much going on that Leiser was forced to fill the entire broadcast with breaking news. Still, he squeezed as many enterprisers on as he could, for he believed that they represented an important advance in the evolution of TV journalism, a breaking away from the tabloid treatment of the old fifteen-minute program.

Yet, in another respect, Leiser was unable to translate into reality his 1963 vision of what the half-hour broadcast should be. For all their "new scope," the enterprisers dealt almost exclusively with front-of-the-book stories: war and peace, politics and government, natural disasters and other forms of violence. Except for space and such dramatic breakthroughs as heart transplants, there was little coverage of science or medicine. Except for desegregation and campus unrest, there was no reporting on education. Except for ballyhooed events, such as Woodstock, there was no attempt to explore the revolution in popular music and its relationship to the cultural upheavals of the 1960s. For that matter, all of the arts were either ignored or given short shrift. So, too, were finance, religion, and sports. Even with the enterprisers and the enlarged format, the *Evening News* did not develop the back-of-the-book section that Leiser had prophesied. It still was nothing more than an "electronic front page," as *Time* magazine labeled it in a 1966 cover story on Cronkite and the *Evening News*.

Nevertheless, Leiser had reason to be satisfied with the way things were going. His strong journalistic judgment—along with Cronkite's own talents—had given the show a harder, more assertive tone. And this overall improvement was reflected in the ratings. In the summer of 1965, the *CBS Evening News with Walter Cronkite* edged ahead of *The Huntley-Brinkley Report* for the first time since Huntley and Brinkley opened up their big lead over the Edwards show in the months following the 1960 conventions. But the number one status was short-lived; in the fall of 1965, when the regular-season audience returned, NBC regained the lead, and by a comfortable margin. The same thing happened in 1966: CBS moved in front during the summer months, only to slip back into second place in September. Some NBC people had a rather smug explanation for this seasonal deviation. They contended that their nightly news audience, being brighter and more affluent, spent the summer sailing off Martha's Vineyard or attending music festivals in Europe, while Cronkite's viewers, presumably the dull and the indigent, estivated in front of their television sets because they had nothing better to do. But that theory had to be scrapped in 1967. That year, the Cronkite show once again had its summer surge, but this time it maintained its lead through the fall and winter months. It was the start of CBS's long domination of the evening news ratings; after five years of chasing Huntley and Brinkley, Cronkite finally had passed them, for good.

The summer of 1967 also brought an end to Ernie Leiser's reign as executive producer of the *CBS Evening News.* The period since December 1964, when he took over the show, had been a time of great turbulence, and that summer of 1967 was particularly raucous and eventful. It opened with the Six Day War in the Middle East, which came on top of the war in Vietnam, then raging with more intensity than ever before. And across the domestic landscape that summer there erupted the antiwar protests and riots in the black ghettos of Detroit and other cities. The long hours and constant pressures involved in getting those stories on the air each night eventually took their toll on Leiser, who drove himself as hard as he did others. Even before the summer drew to a close, he went to Dick Salant and, pleading exhaustion, asked to be taken off the *Evening News.* Salant tried to talk him out of it, but Leiser insisted that he needed a change, a less frantic regimen.

Although he wanted off the Cronkite show, Leiser did not want to lose ground in the overall pecking order of CBS News. Therefore, when the question of his successor came up, he was quick to recommend his old Paris pal, Les Midgley. At the time, Midgley himself was one of the more powerful barons within the feudal structure of CBS News. As executive producer of the Special Reports unit, he occupied a key position, one that gave him stature and authority comparable to Leiser's. Thus, if Midgley were to take over the *Evening News,* the way would be clear for Leiser to assume command of Midgley's domain— which is precisely what happened.

Midgley was not all that eager to make the switch, but he went along with it. The fact that the *Evening News* represented a fresh challenge meant almost nothing to him. In his fourth decade of a varied and distinguished career, Les Midgley had long since passed the point of becoming excited over a new assignment.

As a young man starting out in the mid-1930s, Midgley caught the tail end of a journalistic era: that of the itinerant newspaperman. In those days, it was not unusual for a reporter to arrive, unheralded, in a city or town, work on the local paper for a few months, then move on to another community. This was how Midgley chose to learn his craft, and by the time he was twenty-six, he had already worked on six newspapers, drifting from his native Salt Lake City (his grandfather was president of the Mormon church for twenty-five years), to Denver, Louisville, Chicago, and finally New York. There he worked first on the rewrite desk of the *World-Telegram,* and in 1941 he landed a job on the *Herald Tribune.* (He was, in fact, the editor on duty at the *Trib* on December 7, 1941, when the bell rang at Pearl Harbor.) Then, not long after the liberation of Paris in 1944, he was given a choice assignment: to help revive and edit the European edition of the *Herald Tribune.*

Midgley and his *Trib* colleagues did more than simply revive the European edition. They shaped it into such an excellent paper that many Americans visiting postwar Europe considered it to be as good or even better than its New York parent, which was then at the height of its considerable prestige. As night editor, Midgley had a thin staff and welcomed the chance to siphon off some of the work load on moonlight-ers and free-lancers. Most of this extra manpower came from the under-paid staff of the *Stars and Stripes,* a group that included Ernie Leiser. Working on the *Herald Tribune* in postwar Paris was an enriching experience, but in 1949 Midgley returned to New York, to the *Trib's* home base. A year later, the lure of more money as well as a new kind of challenge brought him into the magazine field, first at *Collier's,* where his path briefly crossed Gordon Manning's, and later at *Look,* where he quickly rose to become managing editor.

Then all of a sudden, in early 1954, he was out of a job, and Ernie Leiser, who was now working at CBS, saw a chance to do his former benefactor a favor. He began touting Midgley's talents and vast experi-ence to his superiors, and soon thereafter Midgley joined Leiser at CBS.

He started out as a writer and a year or so later, he became pro-ducer of a Sunday afternoon news broadcast, a post he inherited from Leiser. It was a routine news show anchored by Eric Sevareid, for whose non-TV personality CBS was then going to great lengths to find a suit-able vehicle, but Midgley soon moved into more ambitious areas. In the fall of 1956, he produced an "instant special" on the Hungarian revolt and the Suez invasion. Called *The World in Crisis,* it was one of the first television news programs to deal at length with a major story more or less as it was unfolding. Similar instant specials were aired from time to time over the next three years, and then, in 1959, Midgley began pro-ducing a flurry of them under the title *Eyewitness to History.* The programs proved to be so successful that the decision was made to continue them on a regularly scheduled basis. In the fall of 1960, *Eye-*

witness to History—later shortened to *Eyewitness*—went on the air as a weekly half-hour program, broadcast Friday night in prime time. The executive producer of the new series was Les Midgley.

Eyewitness was in many ways the most advanced television news show of its time. Its production techniques were far more elaborate and sophisticated than those of the *Evening News*, then still in its fifteen-minute format. Yet its programs were also timely and completely oriented toward hard news, which distinguished them from conventional documentaries, most of which took weeks, even months, to produce. Each week, *Eyewitness* devoted its entire half hour to one story. Like the cover story featured in *Time* and *Newsweek*, the focus was usually on the week's top news event, but, again like the newsmagazines, Midgley gave himself a certain flexibility of choice. His preference was for immediacy, for a story that broke late in the week—and the later the better. As a result, the *Eyewitness* staff was often pressed into a lot of spirited last-minute scrambling.

Eyewitness could not have worked in quite the way it did had it not been for the technological improvements of the late 1950s and early 1960s. By taking full advantage of the new technology (especially videotape), Midgley demonstrated that "documentarylike" programs— meaning those that had a certain amount of quality and depth in film reporting—could be put together in a hurry, on a few hours' notice. More than anything else, it was *Eyewitness* that persuaded Ernie Leiser and others that a daily half-hour news show was feasible, and that it could and should be something more than just a longer version of the fifteen-minute "compressed, tabloid treatment."

Yet Midgley himself was not an especially creative producer. His strength was as an editor who knew how to draw out the talents of others. As executive producer of *Eyewitness*, he surrounded himself with the best available writers, field producers, and film editors. The network's top correspondents were also eager to work for *Eyewitness*. (Walter Cronkite, Charles Kuralt, and Charles Collingwood all took turns as the show's anchorman.) Nevertheless, Midgley was the guiding force behind the series, the person responsible for making the ultimate decisions.

Eyewitness had a three-year run as a weekly program, during which time it broadcast "cover stories" on everything from East-West tensions in Berlin *(Danger Along the Wall)* to suicide in Hollywood *(Marilyn Monroe: Why?)*. When it went off the air in the summer of

1963, it was because it had lost its *raison d'être*—in-depth coverage of hard news—to the newly expanded *Evening News.* To help give the Cronkite show that extra dimension, Midgley himself was assigned to the broadcast as back-of-the-book producer. But in the rush of breaking news, the back-of-the-book concept never got off the ground.

The frustration he experienced in that assignment was enough to convince Midgley that there was still a need for instant specials—not on a regularly scheduled basis, perhaps, but periodically, whenever a major story broke that could not get the coverage it deserved on the *Evening News.* He succeeded in selling that idea to Fred Friendly when he took over as president of the news division, and in the spring of 1964 the Special Reports unit went into operation, with Midgley ensconced as its executive producer.

The Special Reports people, most of whom had worked for Midgley on *Eyewitness,* were geared to go into action at the sound of a bulletin. The death of a world-famous personage, a dramatic development in the war in Vietnam, the flaring up of racial strife in Selma, Alabama—and Midgley's staff would commence work on a half-hour special report and have it ready to go on the air in a matter of hours. Then, as time went on, the Special Reports unit began taking on long-range projects as well, thus encroaching on documentary turf that had previously been the private preserve of Friendly and *CBS Reports.* Of these endeavors, the most ambitious was an exhaustive four-hour inquiry into the Warren Commission's report on the Kennedy assassination, which was broadcast over four consecutive nights in June 1967.

Midgley had spent the better part of a year assembling footage and other material for the four programs on the Warren report, and when it finally was aired, he was wrung out. He felt he had earned a rest, and he was looking forward to a few weeks of relaxation. He also had other things on his mind that summer. A widower, he was planning to get married again in August. His bride-to-be was Betty Furness, the one-time Westinghouse lady who had gone on to become President Johnson's special assistant on consumer affairs.

Even before the nuptials, Midgley knew that the wedding gift CBS had picked out for him was the *Evening News.* He would have preferred something more conventional: a diamond-studded watch, perhaps, or an ornate humidor for his expensive cigars. At the age of fifty-two, he did not welcome the prospect of becoming immersed in the ten-hour days and ulcerous pressures of the *Evening News.* Still, he sympathized with Ernie Leiser's need to get off the Cronkite show, and he had a wry appreciation of why Leiser insisted that he be the one to take it over. The proposed switch—a lateral exchange of one power base for another—was an ideal arrangement from Leiser's point of view. At the same time, Dick Salant made it clear that he considered Midgley to be the best man for the job, and that was a judgment Midgley found difficult to dispute.

When Les Midgley assumed command of the *Evening News* in September 1967, he brought to the show a personality and executive style that differed radically from those of his two predecessors. In contrast to Don Hewitt's flair for Hollywood high jinks, Midgley was as restrained and as decorous as a Boston banker. And in contrast to Ernie Leiser's stringent demands and curt manner, he was soft-spoken and serene in temperament. A tall man with a rangy build and closely cropped white hair, Midgley affected a casual sartorial appearance. He frequently wore blue, proletarian-looking shirts, open at the collar. But the casual facade was misleading. Aloof and taciturn, he moved through the bustling world of CBS News with such lofty reserve that he seemed, most of the time, to be oblivious of all the surrounding commotion.

Midgley also differed from his predecessors in the way he chose to exercise power. Unlike both Hewitt and Leiser, he was a firm adherent of the delegation-of-authority approach. He inherited from Leiser a first-rate staff of producers, directors, and writers, all of whom soon discovered that they had a lot more latitude than they had had before. As a matter of fact, they soon learned that Midgley disliked being bothered by unnecessary specifics and details.

For example, one time Midgley wanted to open a broadcast with a certain kind of elaborate camera effect, and he asked his director, Joel Banow, if it could be done. Banow replied that it could, and then launched into a long and technical explanation of how he planned to achieve it. Soon he was not speaking English anymore, but was jabbering on in the arcane mumbo jumbo of the control room. Finally, Midgley had heard enough. Interrupting Banow with a languid wave of his hand, he said, "Look, Joel, I've managed to survive a lot of years in this business without ever knowing what it is you *cinéma vérité* boys do to give me the pictures I want. And I don't *want* to know. All I'm asking is, do we have the capability for this opening shot without making it into a big deal?"

The reaction was vintage Midgley. He constantly told his people, with mild exasperation, that such-and-such a problem was "no big deal." He was interested only in the final result, the end product, and he did not wish to be distracted from his prime concern, which was the daily lineup: deciding what story to lead with, and then choosing the other film pieces to round out the broadcast. Those were the decisions he was getting paid to make; they alone, in his judgment, constituted "a big deal."

John Merriman, who was Cronkite's editor during Midgley's years as executive producer, once was giving a new writer a rundown on the various people who worked on the show and what their specific responsibilities were. When the new man asked what Midgley did, Merriman smiled and said, "Mr. Midgley discusses the lineup with God." Merriman was also fond of saying that Midgley exemplified "the Peter Principle in reverse." He contended that Midgley was "born to be an executive producer," and that it was impossible to imagine him in a less imposing role.

Because he was always so intent on the large picture and so diffident in his dealings with others, Midgley had a tendency to issue instructions in such a vague and tentative manner that he was sometimes misunderstood. There was a clear division between those who were adept at "reading Midgley" and those who were not. One person who prided himself on his ability to read Midgley was Phil Scheffler, who had graduated from his duties on the Assignment Desk to become one of Midgley's top field producers during the *Eyewitness* years. One morning, as he sat in his office lingering over a coffee and Danish, Midgley sauntered by and said, "Phil, I think you should look into this Hong Kong story."

"Good idea," said Scheffler, who knew instantly what story Midgley was referring to, for the *New York Times* that morning had published a lengthy account of the refugees from the Chinese mainland who were streaming into Hong Kong by the thousands. But that's all there was to the conversation, and someone unaccustomed to "Midgleyese" no doubt would have assumed that the remark was merely an overture, a tentative proposal requiring further discussion. But Scheffler knew better. Wolfing down his coffee and Danish, he checked to make sure he had his passport, made a plane reservation, telephoned his wife, picked up a cash advance to cover his expenses—and by that afternoon, he was on his way to Hong Kong. There he found a cable waiting for him from

Midgley, which read: DO WE HAVE A STORY? Scheffler spent the next few hours checking things out, and by nightfall, he not only had cabled Midgley that there was a story in Hong Kong but had also sent along a proposed lineup on how it should be structured. Years later, when he was recounting this experience, Scheffler was asked, "But what if there hadn't been a story?"

"Well," he replied, "I would have treated myself to a very nice dinner—I'm a Chinese food freak—and the next morning, I would have flown back to New York." Then with a smile and a shrug, he uttered the sacred words: "No big deal."

Another favorite expression of Midgley's was "a piece of cake." Each morning when he arrived at CBS his fervent hope was that the day's events would unfold in an orderly fashion so that, by late afternoon, he could look forward to a smooth and relatively easy broadcast, one he could characterize as "a piece of cake." Whereas his predecessors, and Cronkite himself, throve on last-minute frenzy, Midgley did not. Problems he could live without, and the chief criticism of Midgley was that he was overly cautious, that he lacked boldness and energy and competitive fire. Some of the people who worked for him were put off by his world-weary manner, the impression he gave of barely concealed boredom. No matter what happened, in the news or elsewhere, Midgley had a way of suggesting that it was not new or different, but just another variation on an old song, one he had heard many times before. (One day when Ernie Leiser overheard an associate make a passing reference to Paris during the 1940s as a time when he and Midgley were young and inexperienced, Leiser interrupted and said, "Correction. *I* was young and inexperienced. Les Midgley was never young, and certainly never inexperienced.") Midgley paid no attention to his detractors. Impervious and detached, he conveyed at all times a quiet dignity and stature befitting a man who, as John Merriman noted, was to the executive role born.

Yet Midgley was not above fraternizing with the troops. It was not unusual to find him, at the end of a working day, sipping a bourbon on-the-rocks at the bistro situated around the corner from CBS News (named, appropriately, The Slate in honor of the television clientele it served). Midgley was usually content on these occasions to let others do most of the talking, and as a rule, he limited himself to one or two drinks. But one night he went well beyond that limit, and later, while he was driving up the East River Drive toward his home in Westchester

County, he was stopped by the police. The next thing Midgley knew, he was being detained at a nearby Harlem precinct. The situation clearly qualified as "a big deal," and after a frantic phone call to CBS, Midgley was sprung.

And that, to all intents and purposes, was that, except for what happened a few nights later. Dining at an expensive Manhattan restaurant, Midgley left his table to visit the men's room, and there he was addressed in the most familiar way by the attendant, who cheerfully inquired, "Hey, man, don't I know you from somewhere?"

"I don't believe so," Midgley replied, as courteously as possible.

His interlocutor then broke into a broad grin, and said, "Sure, man, now I remember. We were in the slammer together the other night."

Perhaps the best part of that story is that Les Midgley, on the rare occasions he let his hair down, relished telling it on himself.

Under Midgley, the *CBS Evening News* continued to enjoy a great deal of autonomy. Ever since his screening room clash with Leiser, Gordon Manning had given the *Evening News* area a fairly wide berth and, except for an occasional lapse, had ceased trying to inject himself into the show's day-to-day operation. When Midgley took over, he soon demonstrated that he, too—in a much more subtle way—knew how to keep Manning at bay. When he sensed that a particular broadcast was likely to arouse Manning's concern, he often called Dick Salant to discuss it. That way, when Manning called him or sent him a memo, Midgley could say, "Gordon, I've already talked this over with Dick, and he agrees that we don't have a problem here." Manning then either had to drop the subject or contradict his superior, Salant. Of course he also had the option of reprimanding Midgley for going over his head, but there were inhibitions preventing him from taking that course.

As was the case with Leiser, Midgley had certain advantages over Manning, psychological and otherwise. Manning was indebted to him for his support at the time when Friendly was considering candidates for the post of hard-news vice-president. In addition Midgley, like Leiser, had a close relationship with Salant, dating back to Salant's first term as president when *Eyewitness* brought a large measure of prestige to the news division and served as a strong selling point for the leap to a half-hour version of the *Evening News*. Thus Manning discovered that Midgley was, in his own quiet way, as independent as Leiser had been, with the result that he, Manning, continued to be effectively boxed out of direct involvement in the most important broadcast under his juris-diction. This was a great frustration to Manning. Still, he went along with it, not only because it was the prudent thing to do, but also because he was fully confident that, in time, his day would come.

Midgley may not have been as creative as Don Hewitt or as aggres-sive as Ernie Leiser, but under his supervision the Cronkite show pros-pered as it never had before. When he replaced Leiser in September 1967, the broadcast was in the midst of another summer surge, which had moved it ahead of *The Huntley-Brinkley Report* in the ratings. At the time, even most CBS people assumed this was just a seasonal quirk, as it had been the previous two years, and that come autumn, NBC would once again regain the lead. But this time around, the *CBS Eve-ning News* remained in front, and by the following winter, it was evi-dent that, at long last, the Cronkite show had achieved parity, and then some. Over the next three years, CBS maintained a slim lead in the evening news battle, and that is how matters stood in the summer of 1970 when, after fourteen years, the Huntley-Brinkley era came to an end.

Earlier that year, Chet Huntley had announced his decision to retire from broadcasting and return to Montana, where he planned to help develop a recreational complex called Big Sky. He was only fifty-eight, but he did not have much longer to live. He was stricken with the same disease that killed Murrow, and in March 1974, he, too, died of lung cancer.

Huntley's departure in 1970 left NBC News in a state of disarray. *The Huntley-Brinkley Report* was replaced by the *NBC Nightly News,* which featured three correspondents—Brinkley, John Chancellor, and Frank McGee—sharing the co-anchor assignment on a kind of round-robin or "musical chairs" basis. The three-man arrangement was an unwieldy mess, and after a few months, it was dismantled. McGee left the broadcast entirely, switching over to the *Today* show. Then Brink-ley, weary of the daily anchorman grind, relinquished his slot to concen-trate on commentary, a la Eric Sevareid. That left Chancellor, who now became the first sole anchorman on an NBC evening news program since the days of John Cameron Swayze.

John Chancellor brought to that assignment a solid, low-key style that had a settling effect on the *NBC Nightly News.* But in terms of competing with the *CBS Evening News,* it was a case of too little, too late. In the fall of 1970, when NBC was coming on each night with its musical-chairs format, the Cronkite show opened up a huge lead in the ratings. And it never looked back. CBS News would go on to dominate TV journalism in the 1970s just as decisively as it had dominated radio news three decades earlier.

Much of the credit for the CBS resurgence must, of course, go to Cronkite, who by the early 1970s was in a class by himself. But beyond that, NBC News was now paying the price for having relied so long and so heavily on its two superstars, Huntley and Brinkley. Together, they constituted such an overpowering presence—at the conventions, on election nights, and on their evening news show—that NBC's second-line and third-line correspondents were unable to build up the kinds of reputations that their counterparts at CBS managed to acquire in the 1960s. For despite Cronkite's preeminence, other CBS News correspondents—Reasoner, Mudd, Rather, Wallace, Kuralt, et al—were given plenty of chances to flourish during those years.

That is what Dick Salant meant in 1963 when he remarked that, in contrast to NBC's "pitcher and a catcher," his network had, in addition to Cronkite, "an infield, an outfield, and a strong bench." In the years leading up to 1970, as CBS News steadily strengthened its position, its "strong bench" consistently came up with superior coverage on a variety of fronts, from the Mekong Delta to Capitol Hill, and from Saint Peter's Square to the West Wing of the White House.

10 Living-Room War

By 1970, the CBS news operation had grown enormously. In 1959, when CBS News was formed as a separate division within the corporate structure, there were 437 full-time employees on the payroll. A decade later, the figure had swelled to 816. Among newspapers, only the *New York Times* and the *Los Angeles Times* operated on a comparable scale. But if by 1970 there were all those new faces to be found in CBS News bureaus at home and abroad, there were still plenty of old-timers around. Some of the best of them, having exercised the privileges of rank and seniority, were comfortably set up in the major capitals of Europe, cities most of these holdovers from the Murrow generation first encountered in their youth, when trench coats (and the romanticism that went with them) were *de rigueur*. For example, the London bureau continued to be graced by the presence of the Duke of Collingwood, who rejoiced in his title of chief foreign correspondent for CBS News.

During his years in London, Collingwood became more and more British in dress and manner. A sartorial high point of sorts was reached when, on one of his periodic visits to New York, he showed up at CBS sporting a natty Victorian cape, thus adding a Holmesian touch to his overall elegance. Yet for all his Britishisms, Collingwood was actually away from London much of the time on assignment. He went to Athens when the colonels staged their coup there in April 1967, and a few weeks later, he was in Israel reporting on the Six Day War in the Middle East. And throughout the late 1960s, there were numerous trips to Southeast Asia, the most eventful occurring in March 1968, when he became the first American network correspondent to be allowed into North Vietnam.

About a year earlier, Collingwood had written the North Vietnamese embassy in Paris, requesting permission to visit Hanoi. He knew it was a long shot, and when several months went by without a response, he put the matter out of his mind. As a matter of fact, he embarked on a sabbatical in 1968, and in March he was at his vacation retreat in Puerto Vallarta, Mexico, enjoying a winter of sun and relaxation. Then one morning, as he was sitting in his bathrobe on the veranda, sipping from a glass of papaya juice and gazing out at the Pacific, his serenity was disturbed by a call from CBS News in New York informing him that, sabbatical or no, he was due in Hanoi in twenty-four hours.

Collingwood spent a week in Hanoi, conducting interviews, gathering footage, and storing up impressions. Then, following the visit, he put together a one-hour special report on North Vietnam. ("This is the country the United States is fighting: poor, shabby, doctrinaire, but resourceful and still undefeated.") The experience also gave him material for his first novel, *The Defector*. When it was published in 1970, it angered officials in the North Vietnamese government, mainly because Collingwood chose to use real names for some of his characters. "That was vanity on my part," he recalled years later. "But I wanted everyone familiar with the subject to know that *I* knew—by name—the people who were really running things there."

The CBS News correspondent in Paris at this time was another veteran, Peter Kalischer, who for more than twenty years had plied his craft in the Far East. Kalischer first saw Japan in 1945 as an officer in the Counter Intelligence Corps attached to General MacArthur's headquarters. He remained in Tokyo after the war, working as a reporter first for the United Press, then for *Collier's,* and finally, starting in 1957, for CBS News. During his early years with the network, Kalischer roamed the Orient, covering such stories as the fall of South Korea's Syngman Rhee and the brief but heated squabble over the islands of Quemoy and Matsu. By the early 1960s, however, he was spending almost all his time in Saigon, where he reported on the early U.S. involvement in the war and the assassination of Diem. Kalischer's long career in Asia came to an end in 1966, when he was transferred to Paris. He welcomed the move, in large part because he had grown weary of covering the Vietnam War, which he had watched escalate from a few skirmishes into a nightmare. But he soon discovered there was no getting away from it. For in 1968 the Paris peace talks began, and one of his regular beats became the Majestic Hotel, where the deadlocked negotiations dragged on over the next four and a half years.

Collingwood was in London, Kalischer in Paris, and in Rome there was Winston Burdett, who, of all the CBS News old-timers, had the most troubled past. Burdett had been one of "Murrow's boys." As a free-lance reporter working out of Stockholm in 1940, he covered the Nazi invasion of Norway for CBS. And not long thereafter, he joined Murrow's growing staff of war correspondents, reporting on Allied campaigns in North Africa, southern France, and Italy. After the war, Burdett worked in the Washington bureau and later in New York as United Nations correspondent. His career, in other words, was moving briskly along in the right direction until suddenly he became both a victim and an agent of McCarthyism.

In 1955, Burdett testified before the Senate Internal Security subcommittee that he had been a Communist in the late 1930s before he went to work for CBS. Going further, he revealed the names of other journalists who had been party members. In the aftermath of his testimony, both Burdett and CBS were assailed from all sides. From the right came a clamor that "the Communist" be fired, even though Burdett had severed his party ties before joining the network in 1941 and in his Senate appearance had cooperated to the point of blowing the whistle on others. For having done that, he was reviled by the liberal community, especially since as a direct result of his disclosures there were some journalists at the *New York Times* and elsewhere who lost their jobs. In a move to salvage his career and take the heat off everybody, CBS sent Burdett to Rome in 1956. He was told that he would have every opportunity to reestablish himself there, in exile, but with the clear understanding that he had forfeited whatever chance he had of becoming a big-name correspondent in New York or Washington.

Working out of Rome, Burdett covered a wide swath of trouble spots, from Berlin to the Congo, with special attention on the Middle East and the recurring crises there. But his best, most memorable reporting was from within Italy itself. A cultivated and erudite man (at Harvard, he majored in Romance languages and literature), he came up with brilliant pieces on Italian art and history whenever he could find a news peg to hang them on. Even more impressive was his coverage of the Vatican. Having schooled himself in canon law, Burdett brought to his reports on the Vatican II upheavals and related issues a theological sophistication rare in American journalism. Thus, as it turned out, placing Burdett in Italy was inspired casting on the part of CBS. Over the years, a whole new generation of viewers grew up and became ardent admirers of his reporting from Rome, without ever knowing the circumstances that had sent him there in the first place.

A new generation of correspondents was also on the rise. The holdovers from the World War II era may have had the most civilized assignments in London, Paris, and Rome, but they were very much in the twilight of their careers and had to yield ground to younger men when it came to covering the major foreign stories of the 1960s. This was especially true in the case of Vietnam. For although Collingwood and Kalischer had done extensive reporting on the war there, Fred Friendly, that coiner of facile phrases, was right on target when he christened Vietnam "Morley Safer's War."

When Morley Safer went to Vietnam in 1965, the war was at a critical turning point. Until then, it had been essentially a Vietnamese struggle, with Americans operating in the background as "advisers." Now it was swiftly becoming a full-scale American war. At the age of thirty-four, Safer was no stranger to war; a few years earlier, he had covered the Algerian revolution for the Canadian Broadcasting Corporation (CBC). That was a grisly business, but it had been the French and their war. In Vietnam, he would be covering Americans.

A native of Toronto, Safer spent most of his early career with CBC, first as a writer and editor, then later as a correspondent in London. From that base, he covered stories all over Europe, North Africa, and the Middle East. But it was purely a fluke that brought him to the attention of CBS News.

Early in 1964, a disgruntled CBC colleague named Stan Burke, petitioning for a job with an American network, sent CBS News a tape of an end-of-the-year, round-table broadcast on which he appeared with other CBC correspondents—including Safer. The tape was screened by Ernie Leiser, who thought Burke was all right, but he was much more impressed by another correspondent who, on investigation, turned out to be Safer. So, instead of Burke, it was an entirely unsuspecting Morley Safer who received a call from Leiser's deputy, Ralph Paskman, offering him a job with CBS News.

During his first months at CBS, he remained in London, teaming up with Collingwood (whom he quickly grew to admire and, in some ways, emulate) on such stories as the 1964 British elections and, a few weeks later, the death and funeral of Winston Churchill. Then, in the spring of 1965, he received another call from Ralph Paskman, this time asking him if he wanted to go to Vietnam. Safer's initial response was negative; he had paid little attention to the Vietnam War, and he wasn't at all keen about leaving London. But Paskman persisted, assuring Safer that he was talking about a short-term assignment. "Six months at the most," Paskman said. "By then it'll be all over, and we'll be out of there."

Safer's first order of business in Saigon was to get acclimated, a process that included thorough briefings by Peter Kalischer, who in private was a lot more critical of the American role in Vietnam than he revealed in most of his reports. But by early summer, as the war rapidly heated up, Safer was moving out to various combat zones, and in early August he went up to Da Nang, the main staging area for the U.S. Marines, where he learned from some young officers that there was going to be an operation the next day. Even before he had a chance to ask, Safer was invited to go along.

The next morning, as they took off in amphibious carriers, Safer asked a Marine captain if this was to be a search-and-destroy mission. No, he was told, "just destroy." The officer went on to say that their destination was a complex of hamlets called Cam Ne, and that they had orders to "waste" the place, to rip it apart, to level it. When Safer asked why, the captain said they had been getting a lot of fire from the area. According to the local province chief, Cam Ne was a sanctuary for the Vietcong, and therefore should be destroyed.

Advancing toward the village on foot, the Marines encountered no resistance, nothing to indicate the presence of Vietcong. (But there was plenty of fire from the jumpy Marines themselves, with the result that three Americans were wounded in the back, a common occurrence in Vietnam.) Nevertheless, the Marines proceeded to "waste" Cam Ne. Safer watched and his cameraman rolled film as the Marines set fire to the hutches in the village, sending old people and children fleeing in terror. Safer was especially repelled by the casual, almost playful cruelty of some Marines who used cigarette lighters to ignite the thatched roofs. He made certain that his cameraman got pictures of that, and later, when the piece touched off such a furor, that became its identifying mark—the cigarette lighter as weapon. The mission over, Safer wrote a strong and pungent script to go with the film, concluding with this on-camera close:

The day's operation . . . netted these four prisoners. Four old men who could not answer questions put to them in English. Four old men who had no idea what an I.D. card was. Today's operation is the frustration of Vietnam in miniature. There is little doubt that American fire power can win a military victory here. But to a Vietnamese peasant whose home means a lifetime of back-breaking labor, it will take more than presidential promises to convince him that we are on his side.

Yet as tough as the piece was, Safer still had not reported the worst of it. The footage did not include pictures of what happened to some of the villagers who sought refuge in various shelter holes. To get at these people, the Marines either threw grenades down the holes or fired flamethrowers into them.

Safer was no babe in the woods; he had witnessed atrocities in the Algerian war. All the same, he was appalled by what he had seen at Cam Ne. These were not the kinds of actions he associated with Americans. But more than that, it was all so senseless: the unrestrained, haphazard destruction of a peasant village achieved no rational purpose. Safer's main concern after he filed his report was that he had been too soft. He had the uneasy feeling that his script and the film had failed to convey in sufficiently forceful terms what had happened at Cam Ne. He had no need to worry on that score.

Safer's first report on Cam Ne was for a radio broadcast, the *World News Roundup,* which alerted the CBS people in New York to the kind of film to expect from Vietnam. As they awaited its arrival, the tension began to build, and no one felt it more acutely than Fred Friendly, then in the midst of his brief and stormy reign as president of the news division. Friendly himself was shifting ground on the war, adopting an increasingly skeptical view of Johnson's escalation policy. But he had not anticipated anything like this: American Marines burning down Vietnamese huts, killing civilians, leveling a village. He checked back with Safer: Was Morley absolutely sure of his facts? Safer was, and after the film came in and he had screened it, Friendly became even more apprehensive. There was no question of keeping the report off the air —that would have been a journalistic felony—but he knew what the reaction would be, and it was not pleasant to contemplate.

Friendly's dismay was justified. The Cam Ne piece was aired on the *CBS Evening News* on August 5, 1965, and throughout the night, as the show played in various time zones across the country, outraged viewers called in to denounce CBS for portraying American boys that way. In 1965, the prevailing image of the American fighting man was still an idealized one. After all, these young Marines in Vietnam were the sons of GIs who had passed out candy bars to street urchins in Europe, and the grandsons of doughboys who had marched off to the trenches merrily singing "Over There." Most Americans had not yet lost their innocence about Vietnam. Even so, the impact of the piece wasn't all negative. Those who already were opposed to the war (still a small minority in 1965) regarded Safer as a kind of hero for having exposed the ugly realities of the U.S. presence in Vietnam; and others, who were just starting to have doubts about the policy, now became more dubious than ever.

Among those who were quick to grasp the impact and importance of Safer's story was that inveterate viewer of the *Evening News,* Lyndon Johnson. In his rage, the President managed to persuade himself that Safer must be a Communist, and he ordered a secret investigation of the journalist's past. When told that Safer wasn't a Communist at all but just a Canadian, Johnson snorted and said, "Well, I knew he wasn't an American."

In later years, that story would be told around CBS with a great deal of mirth, but there was nothing funny about it at the time. Even Frank Stanton, who was deeply disturbed by the Cam Ne story, had allowed himself to entertain suspicions about Safer. To Friendly and others, he would point out that Safer had been with CBS only a short time and that his background seemed sketchy. Then he would just sort of let the question hang in the air: What do we really know about him? It also bothered Stanton that CBS was all alone on the story, and he asked about that, too: Why weren't the other networks coming up with pieces like Cam Ne? Because, he was told, Safer was a better and more aggressive reporter, just as Ed Murrow had been during World War II and again later at the time of the McCarthy broadcast when, Stanton was reminded, CBS had also been alone.

These were difficult days for Stanton. He was a close friend and admirer of Lyndon Johnson, but by 1965 he had also become the chief patron and protector of the news division, and he richly enjoyed the esteem that went with that role. He did not enjoy finding himself and CBS in a position where they seemed to be attacking the President of the United States and undermining his efforts to win a war. In time, however, Stanton pulled himself together and decided that—whatever his private reservations—he had no choice but to support his news people and just hope to hell that they were right. In January 1966, Frank Stanton appeared before a convention of broadcasting executives and eloquently defended the right of CBS News to report stories like Cam Ne. Some of his associates felt that this was a big psychological breakthrough for Stanton, for in reality he was speaking over the heads of the broadcasters and telling his friend in the White House to stick it in his ear.

During this period, Morley Safer was only dimly aware of how much his name was being bandied about in the most powerful circles of Washington and New York. Friendly and the other news executives absorbed most of the heat themselves and kept Safer insulated from it. He remained in Vietnam, spending most of the next two years there, and he continued to give to his combat coverage a hard, cutting edge. By 1967 he had won numerous awards for his reporting, and in the spring of that year he culminated his tour of duty with a one-hour special called *Morley Safer's Vietnam: A Personal Report.* After that, it was back to London, and then, in late 1970, he went on to a much bigger assignment—as co-star, with Mike Wallace, on *60 Minutes,* a move that elevated him to the anchorman level of correspondents.

But the experience at Cam Ne remained a poignant memory, and even produced a postscript that aroused Safer's disgust all over again. Several years after that August afternoon, while in Vietnam on another assignment, he ran into a reporter from the *Washington Star* who had gone to Cam Ne to do a follow-up story on the destroyed hamlets. He had come across a piece of information that he thought might be of interest to Safer. As Safer had reported, the reason given for the attack that day was that the province chief had fingered Cam Ne as a Vietcong sanctuary. According to the *Star* reporter, the province chief had lied. The truth was that he was angry with the Cam Ne villagers because they had refused to pay their taxes, and he wanted them punished. Of course he did not tell that to the designated punishers—the U.S. Marines—for he was well aware that the avowed purpose of the American presence was to win the hearts and minds of the Vietnamese people.

Morley Safer was not the first reporter in Vietnam to go against the official line. In the early 1960s, a few print journalists—notably David Halberstam of the *New York Times*—aroused the ire of the Kennedy Administration when they dared to write critically of the Diem regime and Washington's support of it. But Safer's piece on Cam Ne had much more visceral impact, in part because of the nature of the story and even more so because of the medium on which it was reported. *Watching* the Marines burn down Vietnamese hutches was somehow worse, more difficult to stomach, than simply reading about it. More than any other single event, Safer's 1965 story ushered in the era of the "living-room war," a phrase first used by critic Michael Arlen to introduce a 1966 article he wrote on television reporting from Vietnam. The Cam Ne report both encouraged and challenged other TV correspondents in Vietnam to sharpen and strengthen their coverage. Understandably, Safer's most direct influence was on his fellow CBS reporters, and of this group, one man in particular stood out. In an essay he wrote several years after his own experience in Vietnam, David Halberstam noted that "by journalistic consensus, the two best television reporters of the war were CBS's Safer and his younger colleague, Jack Laurence."

When he arrived in Vietnam in August 1965 (just a few days after Safer journeyed up to Da Nang, and thence to Cam Ne), Jack Laurence was twenty-six years old and had been with CBS only a few months. Moreover, he had no experience whatsoever in television. He had worked as a radio reporter at a number of stations along the East Coast, and when he was hired by CBS News, in January 1965, it was strictly for radio. His radio reporting over the next few months, in the Dominican Republic and elsewhere, earned him the assignment in Vietnam, but again he was sent there to beef up the network's *radio* coverage of the war. His arrival, however, coincided with that summer's big escalation, and because of the increasingly heavy burden that put on Safer, Laurence was soon called on to do television pieces as well.

So he had that adjustment to make—reporting on camera—and beyond that, there was the war itself. Laurence's views at the time were definitely "hawkish," and he had trouble squaring them with the realities he was now encountering. He was also having his problems with Safer. Safer welcomed the extra help in covering the war, but he was leery of Laurence's limited experience, and therefore was inclined to lord it over his younger colleague and grab all the top stories for himself. Laurence resented this, of course, and the two of them frequently quarreled over assignments and the quality of each other's work. In later years, both men would agree that they probably benefited from this period of mutual antagonism, for in their eagerness to show each other up, they put that much more effort into their reporting. In any event, they eventually ironed out their differences. Safer came to appreciate Laurence's talent and began treating him more like a peer instead of a novice fresh out of journalism school. As for Laurence, he became, in particular, an admirer of Safer's writing, of the way he infused his scripts with a strong point of view without quite violating the reportorial canon of objectivity.

Still, even after they began working in harmony, Safer and Laurence never really became close. They were too dissimilar in temperament and, to a lesser extent, in age. Whereas most of Safer's contacts were to be found among his contemporaries, middle-grade officers in their thirties, Laurence was able to develop a rapport with the young draftees, the foot soldiers—the "grunts," as they called themselves. Laurence's ability to empathize with the semiarticulate yearnings of the grunts gave his reporting an extra dimension, a sensitivity and personal involvement that set it apart from the work of other TV correspondents, including Safer.

But covering the war in such an intimate way also intensified Laurence's own sense of anguish and futility. His worst moment came in the spring of 1966 when his best friend in Vietnam, a twenty-nine-year-old *Look* magazine editor named Sam Castan, was killed while covering some meaningless action. By the time his assignment in Saigon was over, in June 1966, Laurence was having frequent nightmares about the war. Returning to New York, he temporarily abandoned his career in journalism. He left CBS and spent the next few months out of work, and in analysis.

When he told Gordon Manning that he was leaving the network to undergo therapy, Manning seemed sympathetic and assured Laurence that when he was ready to come back, the door would be open. But other comments he made were not notable for their compassion. After Laurence had gone, he was once heard to remark how fortunate it was that "all our war correspondents aren't spooky and shell-shocked." The comment did not go over well with his listeners, who had a sensitive appreciation of what Jack Laurence had gone through in Vietnam.

Six months later, Laurence returned to CBS News, and by the summer of 1967 he was back in Vietnam. He had requested the assignment, and Manning, having concluded, apparently, that he was no longer spooky and shell-shocked, gave his consent. Laurence proceeded to cover some of the worst months of the fighting, including the critical Tet offensive in the early weeks of 1968. As before, his reporting was distinguished by a special feel for the plight of the ground troops, the grunts, and when he returned to the States in the late spring of 1968, he was ready to bring his gift for empathy to the antiwar movement and other aspects of the counterculture. That became his next beat.

Laurence was on the streets of Chicago that summer when police fought with demonstrators during the Democratic convention. That was followed by assignments on various dissident groups, including a long enterpriser on the Black Panthers. Then, during the winter of 1969–1970, he covered the trial of the "Chicago Seven," a boisterous courtroom drama that, in retrospect, would be recognized as the last hurrah of the New Left. Laurence's broadcasting style had always been cool, soft-spoken, understated—and it still was. But now, in his coverage of the Chicago Seven trial, a kind of iron came into his voice, an intensity of feeling that made it clear, however subliminally, that his sympathies were on the side of the defendants.

In February 1971, Jack Laurence's career entered a new phase. When Safer was transferred to New York to work on *60 Minutes,* Laurence began lobbying to replace Safer in London, and, after a few weeks of temporizing, Manning and Salant agreed to the move. Some of Laurence's closest friends at CBS were surprised by his interest in the London job, and they thought that he was making a mistake. Laurence's strength as a correspondent, what gave his work a special identity, was his ability to relate to his own generation of Americans. By going to London, his friends argued, he would lose that identity and become just another foreign correspondent. But Laurence took a different view; the London assignment, he felt, would give him an opportunity to broaden his horizons.

In a sense, both sides turned out to be right. Working out of London, Laurence did cover a wider range of stories. But while his reports from Europe and neighboring trouble spots were generally first-rate, they were also quite conventional, and to that extent, Laurence did lose what had been his special identity. Indeed, as the years passed, he came to be viewed within CBS as someone whose best time had come and gone. Like Bob Dylan, the great troubadour of the 1960s, Laurence continued in the 1970s to sing his songs, but the words and music just weren't the same anymore.

If Morley Safer and Jack Laurence were the best of the CBS News correspondents in Vietnam, there were a dozen or so others who, over the years, made strong contributions to the "living-room war." Some of them, such as Bert Quint, Bruce Dunning, and Bob Simon, remained overseas after they completed their assignments in Vietnam, and worked out of CBS bureaus in Europe and Asia. Others, such as Richard Threlkeld, Bill Plante, and Ike Pappas, returned home and covered beats in California and the Midwest. Every now and then, one of them would catch a hot story (such as the Patty Hearst case, which Threlkeld covered from her abduction through the trial) that assured him prominent slots on the Cronkite show and plenty of recognition.

But most of the time, the field correspondents who worked in outlying bureaus, at home and abroad, encountered frustration and brooded about the way they were being neglected. For in contrast to Vietnam, where they had been in the middle of an important story, there just wasn't enough news in Tokyo or San Francisco or Chicago to warrant inclusion very often in Les Midgley's hallowed lineup. And even when they came up with a fairly good story, they had to fight like hell to get it on the *Evening News.* For even then, and at all times, those far-flung correspondents had to compete against a force of awesome power: the CBS News Washington bureau. Night after night, week after week, and on over the years, the *CBS Evening News with Walter Cronkite* would be dominated by film reports out of Washington, not only because news was being made in the nation's capital, but because most of the network's high-powered correspondents were there to cover it.

11 On the Road and Other Beats

At the head of the class there stood, in all his dignity, "the Gray Eminence." By 1970, Eric Sevareid was fifty-eight and had become even more stately in bearing and grave in temperament. In keeping with his lofty station, he was treated with great deference by others in the Washington bureau and was accorded perquisites that were not available to his younger, less august colleagues, including a private office and his own personal secretary. Yet there was little evidence to suggest that this special status was resented. For the most part, the younger Washington correspondents were the first to agree that Sevareid had earned his privileges.

But some members of the *Evening News* staff in New York were less respectful. There one heard complaints that Sevareid's writing was stuffy and pontifical and that he had become a creature of the Washington Establishment, a defender of the status quo. Although Sevareid was sensitive to this criticism, he sometimes seemed to go out of his way to live up to it.

There was one such occurrence in July 1970, when Sevareid, along with John Chancellor of NBC and Howard K. Smith of ABC, interviewed President Nixon at length in the Oval Office. The Nixon Administration was then under heavy fire (the Cambodian invasion and Kent State had been the big headlines that spring), but the three correspondents spent most of the one-hour broadcast serving up softballs that the President, an old pro at that game, easily turned to his own advantage. The next day, a former *Newsweek* editor named Ed Diamond, who was doing media criticism for the CBS affiliate in Washington, chided the veteran newscasters for their obsequious behavior in the Presidential Presence—and he was especially hard on Sevareid. Diamond's caustic review was, in fact, as severe a roasting as Sevareid had ever received, and later that day word came up from Washington that the Gray Eminence was not feeling well, and therefore would not be doing his commentary that evening. "What's wrong with Eric?" one of the writers on the Cronkite show asked John Merriman in perfect innocence.

"Qualms," Merriman replied with a mischievous smile. "He's suffering from an attack of qualms."

Gathered behind Sevareid in the Washington bureau were more than a dozen other correspondents, at varying stages in their careers. Of them, Roger Mudd, Dan Rather, John Hart, Daniel Schorr, and Marvin Kalb had, by 1970, pulled away from the rest of the pack and established themselves as stars of the Washington operation. This was especially true of Mudd and Rather. Their respective beats—Capitol Hill and the White House—were the most coveted of all the government assignments, and they had been covering them throughout most of the 1960s. By the end of 1970, both Mudd and Rather had also parlayed their Washington reporting into anchorman jobs in New York —Mudd doing the *Evening News* on Saturday, and Rather the Sunday night broadcast.

But so, too, had John Hart. Although not as well known as Mudd and Rather, Hart was coming on fast. For the better part of a year, from March 1969 until the summer of 1970, he had anchored the Washington portion of the *CBS Morning News,* playing second banana to the program's New York anchorman, Joe Benti. Then, in August 1970, Benti left CBS, Hart was brought into New York to replace him, and by the following summer he not only was anchoring his own show but was also filling in regularly for Walter Cronkite on the *CBS Evening News.*

Daniel Schorr never made it to the anchorman level, but even so, he did not suffer from a lack of recognition. He was just about the only CBS News Washington correspondent who regularly covered subjects instead of governmental institutions, such as Congress and the Supreme Court. In the late 1960s and early 1970s, he reported primarily on social issues and environmental concerns, and since Schorr was both thorough and tenacious in his coverage, he usually had a better than even chance of getting his pieces on the air.

Next to the White House and Capitol Hill, Washington's most desirable beat was the State Department, and at CBS News that piece of turf belonged to Marvin Kalb. A specialist in Russian history and culture (which he had studied extensively at a number of schools, including Harvard and Columbia), Kalb reported out of Moscow for CBS in the early 1960s. Then, in 1963, he was transferred to Washington, and by the early 1970s he had become adept at deciphering the nuances and innuendos of another intricate subject: Henry Kissinger. Out of this understanding came a 1974 book on Kissinger, which Kalb coauthored with his brother, Bernard, who was also a correspondent for CBS News. Bernard Kalb had spent most of his first years with the network in the Far East, but by 1970 he, too, was reporting out of the Washington bureau. The prevailing view at CBS was that, of the two Kalbs, Marvin was the superior journalist, and he clearly had the larger reputation— even, apparently, within the Kalb family. That, at least, was how it seemed the day the Foreign Desk in New York received a telephone call from a woman whose first words were: "Hello, this is Marvin Kalb's mother. Can you tell me where my son Bernie is?"

Clustered behind the pacesetters in the Washington bureau was a hustling herd of correspondents who jockeyed with each other for good assignments. Among the old guard, those who had been around since the 1950s or earlier and whose best years were behind them, there was Neil Strawser, the "voice of Washington" back in the days of the Doug Edwards show. By 1970, Strawser (like Edwards himself) was working primarily in radio. Then there was George Herman, who had been White House correspondent in the 1950s and early 1960s. Now, in addition to serving as regular host on the Sunday interview program *Face the Nation,* Herman covered the Supreme Court, although he would relinquish that assignment in 1972 to a younger man, Fred Graham, acquired that year from the *New York Times.* Another veteran was Bob Pierpoint, who had covered the White House during the last months of the Kennedy Administration, but who, in the aftermath of Dallas, lost that beat to Dan Rather, in part because the CBS News management wanted a Texan reporting from Lyndon Johnson's White House. Now, although Johnson was gone, Rather was not, and Pierpoint worked as Rather's backup at the White House, with most of his stories confined to radio.

If Strawser, Herman, and Pierpoint were basically voices from the past, then Bruce Morton and Bob Schieffer belonged to the future. In

1970, Morton's main assignment was still a second-string one: Roger Mudd's backup on Capitol Hill. He had been with the Washington bureau since 1964, and although he was regarded as a gifted writer and reporter, his early career at CBS was thwarted by a general feeling on the part of his superiors that he came across on camera as bookish and overly earnest. But soon Morton began getting better assignments (notably, the Calley court-martial in 1971 and the McGovern campaign the following year), and his performance on those stories apparently assuaged concerns about his looks and manner. For by 1974 he had John Hart's old job—Washington anchorman on the *CBS Morning News*—and he was doing very well at it. As for Schieffer, he was a new man on the staff in 1970, having been hired by CBS News just a few months earlier. At first, he worked mainly in the backwaters, the weekend shows and radio, which were just about the only spots available to him. Then, in the summer of 1970, he suddenly was elevated to a regular beat—the Pentagon—and his reporting from there over the next four years so impressed the CBS management that in 1974 he was picked to succeed Rather at the White House.

Given the circumstances that prevailed in the CBS News Washington bureau—a plethora of correspondents, all absorbed in their own ambitions—career frustrations were inevitable. A case in point was David Schoumacher. In 1970, his situation was similar to Morton's: he had been around since 1963 and hadn't yet been able to break through. His best opportunity had come in 1968 when he was assigned to Eugene McCarthy's insurgent Presidential campaign, and it suddenly caught fire. With such frequent exposure, Schoumacher was sure that he had crossed over into the top echelon and would be working, henceforth, on the Mudd-Rather level. But just like that it ended, almost as abruptly as it did for McCarthy himself. The following year, Schoumacher was back in the pack, scrambling for rail position, and by 1972, tired of being passed over for the top assignments, he left CBS and went to ABC.

Defections such as Schoumacher's were extremely rare. Most of the correspondents in the Washington bureau, even those who had to live on leftovers, preferred to remain with CBS News rather than try their luck elsewhere. They constituted a backup brigade that helped give the bureau depth and stability. To cite just a few names: Nelson Benton, Marya McLaughlin, Barry Serafin, and Hal Walker were CBS News Washington correspondents in 1970, and seven years later they were still there, doing much the same sort of thing. But if they had failed to advance, having reached their plateau in the second echelon of CBS News correspondents, there was certainly no shame in that. They knew that only a small percentage of reporters aspiring to careers in network journalism manage to get even as far as they had gotten.

Moreover, such a competent and eager reserve force did not go unappreciated, least of all by the rival networks. One day in 1971, an NBC News producer, who was based in Washington, remarked to a CBS acquaintance that the people in his shop didn't mind it so much when "our first team gets beat by your first team because your first team is damned good. But what we can't stand is when one of our top guys gets burned by one of your second-line guys. That hurts."

"Happens all the time," the CBS man cheerfully replied.

It didn't happen all the time, but it happened often enough to keep everyone alert, especially members of the CBS News "first team." People like Mudd, Rather, and Schorr really didn't need any extra incentive to hustle, but if they did, the presence in the wings of people like Morton, Schoumacher, and Schieffer would have discouraged them from coasting. More than anything else, it was this spirited internal competition that accounted for the Washington bureau's strength and vitality.

One of the reasons members of the backup brigade were relatively content to settle for second-string status was that there was plenty of action in Washington for everyone. The nation's capital was, without question, the news center of the world, and on any given day as many as twelve or fifteen stories were covered. But unfortunately, there would seldom be room for more than three of them on the *CBS Evening News.* Thus the real competition was focused on getting pieces on the Cronkite show, where they could be seen and appreciated. And the target of these daily efforts was the Washington producer for the *CBS Evening News,* who in the early 1970s was a scrappy, Cagneyesque Irishman from Boston named Ed Fouhy.

Fouhy was the liaison between the Washington correspondents and Les Midgley in New York, and each day, as reports came in from the various assignment points, he went to work on the telephone. He was an aggressive and effective lobbyist who, in his conversations with New York, used the names and reputations of his top correspondents as weapons: "Mudd says the bill will pass this afternoon, and if it does . . . Rather has a tip that Nixon plans to . . . Kalb is convinced that this latest move by Kissinger means . . ." Then, having led off with his big guns, Fouhy would go on to promote other stories: "Morton has . . . Schoumacher is working on . . . Marya just called from the Hill with . . ." Yet he was smart enough not to overdo it. In order to maintain his own credibility with Midgley and the other New York producers, Fouhy himself would downgrade certain Washington stories, and then he usually pinned the blame on New York. ("I did my best, Dan, but Midgley wouldn't buy it.") For the most part, however, he pushed to get as many Washington stories on as possible, and he considered it a triumph—for himself and the bureau—when he succeeded in coaxing four or five film pieces into Midgley's lineup, enough to make it a Washington-dominated broadcast.

To a large extent, it was this daily pressure from high-powered correspondents, as applied through Fouhy, that so often gave the Cronkite show such a heavy Washington tilt—heavier, perhaps, than was warranted, even granting Washington's preeminence as a source of news. It was also extremely easy and relatively inexpensive to bring film reports in from there, and the correspondents in Washington were generally more experienced and therefore more trustworthy—two factors that augured well for the "piece-of-cakeness" that Les Midgley hoped, each day, to achieve. But if the Washington bureau wielded a great deal of clout and influence, the ultimate power was still in New York; and largely for that reason there were a few correspondents who, while conceding that Washington was a livelier news town, preferred being attached to network headquarters.

The CBS News reporters and correspondents based in New York covered the gamut. At the top were the big names, the established anchormen: Walter Cronkite, Harry Reasoner, and Mike Wallace. And at the other end of the scale were those who had just been hired by the network and were still labeled "reporters," a term much less imposing than "correspondent" in the nomenclature of CBS News. These new reporters had to put in a period of apprenticeship on the New York Assignment Desk to acquaint themselves with the overall news operation, and only now and then would they be sent out to cover a story. If they were lucky, they might land an assignment good enough to be aired on the *Morning News* or one of the other broadcasts, but they would have to be extremely fortunate to get a piece on the Cronkite show. For if a story broke in the New York area that was big enough for *that* kind of exposure, it almost certainly would be grabbed by a more seasoned correspondent.

In 1970, three men—Morton Dean, David Culhane, and Bob Schakne—were the workhorses on the New York beat, and they brought to that shared experience diverse backgrounds. Schakne, the veteran, had been with CBS News since 1955, and some of his best reporting had been from Latin America, where he was based in the mid-1960s. Dean had made his reputation as a local reporter for the CBS-owned station in New York (WCBS), where his specialty was state and city politics. He was hired by the network in 1967, as was Culhane, who left his job as London correspondent for the *Baltimore Sun* to join CBS News. Along with their coverage of headline stories, Dean, Culhane, and Schakne were sometimes picked by producers to be the correspondents on various specials and enterprisers. That was one of the fringe benefits that came from working in New York, where the best and most creative producers were located. Nevertheless, in the overall hierarchy they were still in the second echelon of correspondents, on a par, say, with Morton and Schoumacher in Washington or Bill Plante and Ike Pappas in Chicago. But there were two other correspondents working out of New York who had secured positions in the front rank by carving out special niches of their own—Charles Kuralt and Hughes Rudd. Indeed, by 1970 there were some CBS executives on both the news and corporate level who considered Charlie Kuralt in particular to be as valuable a property as any of the "star" correspondents in the network's stable—save for Cronkite himself.

In 1948, when he was fourteen years old and growing up in North Carolina, Kuralt won an American Legion contest for an essay he wrote called "Voice of Democracy." His prize was a trip to Washington, where (along with other contest winners from other parts of the country) he met President Truman. But his biggest thrill came that evening when Edward R. Murrow, one of the judges in the contest, chose *his* essay to read over the CBS radio network. Eight years later, not long after his graduation from the University of North Carolina, Kuralt was working as a reporter for the *Charlotte News* when, once again, he was honored for his writing, this time as recipient of the Ernie Pyle Memorial Award. And once again his achievement was acknowledged by CBS, this time in the form of a letter of congratulations from Sig Mickelson, then in charge of the network's news operation. In his letter, Mickelson also suggested that Kuralt come up to New York to discuss a possible job. Kuralt did not wait to be asked twice; two days later he was in New York, and soon thereafter, in the fall of 1956, he went to work for CBS News as a radio writer.

After a few months on the radio desk, he moved on to television as a writer for the Edwards show, where he learned a great deal about writing to film from Alice Weel. By 1958 he was working as a reporter on the Assignment Desk, and the following year he was promoted to correspondent. Kuralt was climbing very fast, in large part because he had become the apple of Sig Mickelson's eye. Impressed by Kuralt's overall talents—his reporting and on-air presence as well as his writing ability—Mickelson began confiding to associates that in his judgment the young correspondent had the stuff to become "the next Ed Murrow."

To help that prospect along, Mickelson persuaded Les Midgley to feature Kuralt as the star of *Eyewitness* when it became a weekly broadcast in the fall of 1960, a decision that did not sit well with Walter Cronkite. As the chief correspondent on most of the *Eyewitness to History* specials up to that time, Cronkite believed that he had earned the right to be the new show's headliner. But in 1960 he was not yet in a strong enough position to demand that privilege. So Charlie Kuralt, at the age of twenty-six, had a prime-time showcase and might even have been the one to inherit the *Evening News* when the decision was made in 1962 to dump Doug Edwards. The only problem was that Mickelson's enthusiasm for Kuralt was not shared by Jim Aubrey, that slick seller of snake oil who, in 1960, had recently taken over as president of the Television Network.

As a rule, Aubrey would not have concerned himself that much with casting decisions made by the news department, but *Eyewitness* was different. It was broadcast in prime time—that is, big-ratings and big-money time—and that was his domain. In Aubrey's view, Kuralt did not have sufficient star quality. What the show needed, he felt, was someone who had more sex appeal, even, perhaps, a Hollywood actor such as Paul Newman, or, better yet, Keefe Brasselle. But Aubrey knew the news division would never stand for that, and so he and Mickelson reached a compromise. In January 1961, Kuralt was replaced on *Eyewitness* by Walter Cronkite, who, while no actor, was closer to Aubrey's idea of a star.

Kuralt's career now leveled off. He spent the next few years away from New York, first as Latin American correspondent, based in Rio, and later in Los Angeles. His work during this period was still highly respected, but in more conventional, less inflated terms. By the time he returned to New York in 1964, Sig Mickelson was long gone from CBS, and there was no more talk about Kuralt being the new Murrow. Which was just as well, for in his next big move, he would embrace a kind of journalism that was the very antithesis of the controversial, issues-oriented programs that were Murrow's métier.

The idea came to him one night in 1965 when he was flying across the country on assignment. It was an exceptionally clear night, and as Kuralt gazed down at the lights of the small towns, spread out across the otherwise dark landscape, he was struck by a sudden feeling of nostalgia. During his brief stint with the *Charlotte News,* he had written a daily column called "People," which was devoted to offbeat, human-interest stories. Now, as he stared down at the softly illumined towns of America's heartland, so far removed from the centers of national and global crisis that attracted big-time network correspondents, Kuralt realized how much he missed doing the kind of feature stories he had done in Charlotte back in the mid-1950s. Moreover, he thought that a modest dose of such reporting would be good for a network news show, if only as a respite from the nightly clamor of guns, riots, and political bombast.

A few days later, back in New York, Kuralt proposed to the CBS News management that he and a camera crew travel around the country in a leisurely fashion, and whenever they came across something interesting—in a feature rather than news sense—they would stop and do a story on it. Unfortunately, the man at the helm then was Fred Friendly, that implacable foe of the casual and the frivolous, and he told Kuralt, "That's the worst idea I ever heard of." So he dropped the subject and continued covering the news, front-page style. But in 1967, after Friendly had gone, Kuralt brought the idea up again, and this time it received broad support. On the management level, both Dick Salant and Gordon Manning endorsed it, and so, too, did Ernie Leiser, then the executive producer of the Cronkite show. Still, their commitment was tentative and restrained. Kuralt was told that he could spend three months on the project—that was all—and there were a number of CBS people who believed that he would not be able to keep it alive that long.

A camera crew was assigned to Kuralt, and in October 1967 they took off in a newly equipped camper for Vermont and New Hampshire, then at the height of their annual spectacle—the fall foliage. A few days later, on the *Evening News*, Walter Cronkite introduced the "autumn leaves" piece and identified it as "the first of a series of special reports, which we're calling 'On the Road with Charles Kuralt.' " On the screen appeared pictures of the brilliant New England landscape, and over the sound track came Kuralt's strong and genial voice: "It is death that causes this blinding show of color, but it is a fierce and flaming death. To drive along a Vermont country road in this season is to be dazzled by the shower of lemon and scarlet and gold that washes across your windshield."

Other features followed, and the three-month time limit was soon forgotten. Kuralt's *On the Road* series went on to enjoy a long and happy life, and over the years it gave birth to several prime-time specials and garnered every major award available to practitioners of TV journalism. Yet in certain respects, that first piece—a hymn to Mother Nature—was not truly typical. For Kuralt was far more of a humanist than a pantheist, and the subjects of his most memorable reports were people, especially those who, in one way or another, were quietly resisting the inroads and pressures of modern civilization. They included a ninety-year-old hermit who had been living alone in a cabin in the Yukon wilderness for the past fifty years; another nonagenarian in North Carolina who made bricks on a mule-powered mud mill; an Iowa farmer who built his own boat, all by himself, then packed up his family and sailed away from it all; still another old man in Virginia who planted and maintained a garden alongside a highway for the scenic pleasure of passing motorists. On other occasions, the focus was on group activities: gandy dancers working on railroad tracks in Mississippi; "worm-grunting" in Sopchoppy, Florida; "tubin' " on Wisconsin's Apple River (which featured Kuralt himself floating on an inner tube); or even something as simple as youngsters playing on a tree swing in California.

In strictly professional terms, the *On the Road* stories worked as well as they did because of Kuralt's superior skills as a reporter and writer. But their appeal was greatly heightened by the personal qualities he brought to them. With his plump, slouchy build, his cherubic face, and his deep voice that seemed always to be on the verge of a hearty chortle, Kuralt came across as a big, friendly bear of a man. Which he was. Although he had spent almost all his adult life in New York and other large cities, he still had the down-home, "just-folks" personality of a good ol' boy from rural North Carolina. Given these traits, he was able to endow his pieces with a neighborly warmth, even a kind of love that, quite often, was as touching or as sentimental (depending on one's point of view) as a Norman Rockwell painting.

Viewers lapped it up. Month after month, year after year, the letters of thanks and appreciation poured into Kuralt's New York office. At a time when television screens were filled with grim pictures of Vietnam and all kinds of domestic turmoil, Kuralt emerged as that journalistic rarity, a bearer of happy tidings, a herald of *good* news. His special value to CBS was never more evident than during the Nixon-Agnew years when the networks were accused of dwelling excessively on *bad* news. At one point during this difficult period, a distressed Gordon Manning exclaimed to a luncheon companion, "Thank God for Kuralt." This sense of gratitude permeated the executive reaches of CBS.

Journalists being what they are, however, there were some subversives within CBS News who found fault, in a mild and affectionate way, with Kuralt's *On the Road* stories. From time to time these detractors suggested, not altogether facetiously, that a kind of "truth squad" should tail Kuralt around to do follow-up stories on his quaint and rustic subjects. CBS viewers might then learn that these lovable old codgers also had less attractive qualities, such as, perhaps, an unwillingness to bathe as often as they should, or a tendency to drool at the dinner table. Furthermore, Kuralt's cynical colleagues were agreed on who should head such a mission. For if there was one correspondent at CBS News who, by temperament and inclination, was equipped to find the vinegar in Kuralt's syrup, the sour in Charlie's sweet, it was Hughes Rudd.

If Kuralt put one in mind of Norman Rockwell, then Hughes Rudd was a spiritual descendant of Hogarth. Whereas Kuralt was sanguine and full of goodwill, words like "sardonic" and "cantankerous" must be used to describe Rudd. Or as he himself liked to put it, he often felt as "mean as a Gila monster." He would then usually explain, in his rasping Texas drawl, that the reason Gila monsters are so mean is that they don't defecate, thus leaving his listeners to ponder the possibility that the only thing standing between Rudd and a cheerful disposition was a good laxative.

Rudd was yet another CBS News correspondent who, as a young man, spent the early 1940s touring Europe. But he did not go through World War II as a journalist; he was an artillery-spotter pilot who, for his efforts, received a Purple Heart and other medals. His journalism career began in the years after the war when he worked as a reporter for the *Kansas City Star.* Other jobs at other newspapers followed, including a brief stretch in Wyoming as editor of something called the *Rock Springs Daily Rocket and Sunday Miner.*

From time to time during the 1950s, Rudd left the news game to concentrate on trying to make his mark as a "serious" writer. He spent three years at Stanford on a creative-writing fellowship, another year at a writer's colony in Taos, New Mexico, and soon his articles and short stories were appearing in journals ranging in taste from the *Paris Review* to the *Saturday Evening Post.* (A collection of them was published in 1966 under the title *My Escape from the CIA and Other Improbable Events.)* At one point, he also worked as a *baby* photographer. The mind boggles at what that must have been like, both for Rudd and the sundry cherubs who were trundled into his presence. By the late 1950s, he was back in Kansas City, working as a writer and editor of industrial films, a job he loved on payday but loathed the rest of the time. So one day he called his old friend Walter Cronkite, whom he had known from his earlier years in Kansas City, and asked if there was any chance of hooking on at CBS. Cronkite spoke to the right people, and in 1959 Hughes Rudd went to work for CBS News as a radio writer.

On the radio desk, Rudd quickly fell into the habit of grumbling about the quality of the network's television reporting, and Ernie Leiser, who had a hunch that Rudd's gruff and aggressive manner just might play well on camera, urged him to get off his fanny and give it a try himself. Thus goaded, Rudd began his career as an on-air correspondent. In 1962, when the new regional bureaus were opened, he went to Atlanta, and for the next two years he covered the major civil rights stories breaking all over the South. From Atlanta he moved on to Chicago, and thence to Moscow where, in 1965, he suffered his first heart attack. The following year, while on assignment in Paris, he was hit by a second attack. Transferred back to New York in 1968, he went to Chicago that summer to help cover the Democratic convention. And there he had a third heart attack.

Rudd was now forty-seven and concerned not only about the state of his health but also about the way his career was going. Working out of New York (a city he detested), he found he was bored most of the time. He had grown weary of chasing headlines, conventional news stories, and was eager to try something different. He was, after all, a gifted, distinctive writer, and he believed his talents could be put to better use on feature stories, but Charlie Kuralt had beat him to the punch, at least as far as the *Evening News* was concerned. Still, Rudd chose to mine that lode, even though it meant his reports would be relegated most of the time to the secondary news programs. So he established a working relationship with various field producers on these shows, and by the early 1970s he was doing the kinds of stories he wanted to do, mainly for the weekend broadcasts and the *Morning News.*

Some of Rudd's best pieces during this period were, naturally enough, crotchety put-downs. For example, he came up with a charmingly derisive story on dog shows and the sort of people who breed animals for public display, and once while he was filming an on-camera report in front of a tacky outdoor exhibit, a woman came flouncing up and thanked him for doing an "art appreciation" story on the assembled schlock. "Madam," Rudd growled in his amiable way, "if you weren't such a bubblehead, you'd realize that is the last thing I'm doing." The woman blinked a couple of times, and then informed Rudd with haughty indignation, "I'm not a bubblehead. I'm an art major."

On another occasion, he attracted the attention of fellow diners at a posh New Orleans restaurant when he admonished a petrified waiter, "Goddamnit, I ordered Chablis. I don't know what this is, but it isn't Chablis. Chablis tastes as pure as virgin piss."

Rudd's behavior on the road often made life difficult for his field producers. A vigorous drinker in spite of the state of his health, the more he drank the more irascible and abusive he generally became, and there was alway a risk that he might get into a nasty quarrel with someone who, in turn, might decide to write an irate letter to CBS. Nevertheless, many field producers welcomed the chance to work with Rudd, in part because they admired his talent but even more so because, despite all the abuse and aggravation, they truly enjoyed his company. Even when in his cups and snarling, he was a superb raconteur, a genuinely funny man whose bilious nature gave his humor that much more of a cutting edge.

Numerous CBS viewers appeared to enjoy his company as well. Hughes Rudd was their favorite grouch, a journalistic curmudgeon whose reports were regarded by many as a refreshing antidote to the customary blandness of television news. By 1973, even his superiors were aware that Rudd's surly, downbeat approach was striking responsive chords Out There. Accordingly, that spring, when the decision was made to revamp the *Morning News* and replace John Hart with a male-female duo, he was picked to co-anchor the broadcast with Sally Quinn, a feature reporter for the *Washington Post.* Quinn proved to be a disastrous choice, but after she left the show and CBS, Rudd stayed on as the *Morning News* anchorman, and made a success of it. His natural crankiness was, if anything, even more appealing at that hour. Looking at the sour expression on Rudd's droopy, basset hound face and listening to his gruff, gravelly voice, many viewers felt an overwhelming sense of "Right, pal; me, too."

So Rudd's gamble paid off. By eschewing the *Evening News* firing line and concentrating, instead, on developing feature stories for the secondary news shows, he was able to revive his languishing career and vault into the front rank of CBS News correspondents. It was a calculated risk that most of his colleagues would not have been willing to take, for the prevailing view all down the line was that steady exposure on the *CBS Evening News* was by far the most promising road to prominence. Bill Plante once summed up this attitude as well as anyone. When he was told that one of his reports from Vietnam had been "passed" by the Cronkite show but had been given a big play on the *Morning News,* he shrugged. "If it ain't on Cronkite," Plante said, "it ain't on the air."

12 Off-Camera Cadre

There was never any evidence to support John Merriman's engaging assertion that Les Midgley discussed the daily lineup with God. But as executive producer of the *CBS Evening News,* he did consult with other mortals. One of them was Walter Cronkite who, in addition to anchoring the program, carried the title of managing editor to underscore his journalistic authority. Much of the time, however, Cronkite, pressed by other duties, was unable to give the lineup his full attention. So the main burden of decision fell on Midgley and his two principal deputies, Sandy Socolow and Russ Bensley.

Socolow and Bensley shared the title of producer, and they both exerted a great deal of influence on the broadcast. Socolow, in particular, was the driving force behind the Cronkite show, the man who kept all the engines running and who, night after night, invigorated the program with his own blend of dash and muscle. It was also recognized within CBS that Socolow's importance to the broadcast derived in large part from his special relationship with Walter Cronkite. Cronkite was on cordial terms with just about everyone at CBS News, but he generally maintained a certain distance and was inclined to be strictly professional, even perfunctory, in his dealings within the shop. This was not the case with Socolow, however. He and Cronkite were close personal friends, and had been for years.

They became acquainted back in 1956, shortly after Socolow went to work for CBS News. Six years earlier, he had graduated from the City College of New York (CCNY) on the very day the Korean War broke out, an event that dictated the course of his life over the next few years.

Drafted, he spent most of his Army hitch in Japan (except for a few unpleasant side trips to Korea), and when his tour of duty was over, he landed a job in the Tokyo bureau of the International News Service. He reported on the Asian scene for INS until 1956, when he returned to New York on an extended vacation. By then, Socolow was tired of both the Far East and INS, and through contacts he had at CBS, he was able to arrange an interview with one of Sig Mickelson's deputies. He was hired as a writer, and one of his first assignments was to write for a midday television news show. The newscaster on the program was Walter Cronkite. It wasn't much of a show, basically a time-filler between soap operas and the like, but Cronkite, having recently moved away from the hokum of *You Are There* and his brief stint as emcee on *The Morning Show,* was striving to clarify his television identity as a journalist. Hence, he was eager to take on every news assignment that was offered to him. At the time, most of the best writers and editors were still wedded to radio. Except for a few choice enclaves, such as *See It Now* and the Hewitt-Edwards evening news operation, the level of journalistic competence on the television side was low, and the people Cronkite had to work with were, as a rule, so unprofessional that encountering Socolow was a most pleasant surprise. Here was a kindred spirit, a fellow wire-service man who had worked in the trenches and had been through the grit and pressure of deadline reporting. Like Cronkite, Socolow approached the news in a straightforward, no-nonsense manner, and he wrote copy the way Cronkite did: tight, clear, accurate, with no frills and no stylistic embellishments. In working with Socolow day in and day out, Cronkite grew quite fond of his young writer. Socolow himself had a vague sense of this, but full awareness came in the fall of 1957 when, at the age of twenty-nine, he suffered a heart attack. While he was recuperating in the hospital, only a few people took the trouble to visit him. Walter Cronkite was one of them.

Socolow made a strong recovery from his heart attack, and in 1958 he was picked to replace Charlie Kuralt as a writer on the Edwards show. Cronkite was more than a little miffed by this move. Yet he was hardly in a position to complain; writing for Douglas Edwards was then a much better job, in terms of both money and status, than anything Cronkite had to offer. But *Eyewitness* reunited them. When Cronkite took over as the star of that weekly broadcast, Socolow was assigned to work with him as writer and editor. During the next several months they were together constantly, traveling to all parts of the world in pursuit of weekly "cover stories," and their friendship deepened.

In 1962, Cronkite succeeded Edwards on the evening news, and Socolow, having received a CBS fellowship, took a few months off to study at Columbia University. Following his return to the network in the spring of 1963, he was upgraded to producer and assigned to the new half-hour *Evening News*. His primary value was as a liaison between the executive producer and Cronkite, and when Ernie Leiser assumed the post, he used Socolow adroitly for that purpose. Indeed, Socolow's presence helped to temper the occasional frictions in the Leiser-Cronkite relationship that, for the most part, grew out of Leiser's insistence on the frequent inclusion of long enterprisers. Cronkite approved of the enterprisers in theory, but on any given day, when a hard decision had to be made as to whether to feature one in that night's broadcast, he often took the position that it would be too time-consuming and that too many breaking stories would have to be shelved to make room for it. That, at any rate, was always his stated objection, but Leiser (and others) believed another reason involved personal arithmetic: the more air time devoted to film reports, the less time for Cronkite's on-camera tell stories. Leiser, in fact, once privately complained to an associate that if Cronkite had his way, there would be no film stories at all from other correspondents but "just an entire half hour of Walter reading the news." Whatever the case, on those occasions when Leiser anticipated trouble over a particular lineup, he usually dispatched Socolow to Cronkite's office to smooth the feathers and absorb the flak. When he wasn't engaged in these diplomatic duties, Socolow schooled himself in all aspects of TV news production and, over the years, steadily built up confidence in his own ability to run the broadcast. By 1967, when Leiser began making noises about leaving the show, Socolow believed that he had earned the right to succeed him.

Les Midgley got the job instead, and Socolow was unhappy about that. He soon discovered, however, that in working for Midgley he had much more of a chance to assert himself and impose his own will and ideas on the broadcast. Midgley had no interest in the specifics, the routine details, and he was more than willing to delegate all that to Socolow. Socolow, a man of restless temperament, welcomed the extra action and readily became Midgley's detail man, his nuts-and-bolts man, and often, when a correspondent or field producer had to be reprimanded, his hatchet man.

On a typical day, Socolow arrived at the office a little after 9:00 A.M.

and checked with the Traffic Desk to find out what film shipments had come in during the night and what others were due later that day. Then he picked up the latest information from the Assignment Desk and from the national and foreign editors, both of whom were based in New York. From all this preliminary data, he put together an "outlook," a rundown of what was happening (or would be happening) at home and abroad, and what seemed to him to be the best story possibilities to pursue. The outlook, copies of which were distributed to Midgley, Cronkite, and other members of the *Evening News* staff, was a kind of "morning line," and as the day moved along, many candidates would be scratched and breaking news would bring fresh entries into the field.

Much of the necessary pruning was done in a late-morning conference call with bureau managers around the country. Midgley himself took part in that, but most of the time, through the course of the day, it was Socolow who kept in touch with the bureaus and with correspondents and field producers on assignment at various story locations. As he relayed the steady stream of updated information to Midgley, he generally made a point of including his own assessment of the fluctuating news developments. In this way, he exerted a strong and direct influence on the daily lineup. When Midgley sat down each afternoon to make it out, Socolow's preferences were uppermost in his mind, and, more often than not, he agreed with them.

The lineup defined that day's course of action, and Socolow now shifted his attention to pulling all the elements together. Through his production supervisor, he ordered the telephone lines and "loops" needed to bring film reports in from domestic locations; and if the lineup included one or more foreign stories that had to be transmitted by satellite, he also "ordered a bird." In the meantime, he conferred with correspondents and producers whose stories had made the lineup, informing them how long their reports should run and finding out when they would be ready to feed their film into New York. That taken care of, it was then primarily a matter of sitting back, with fingers crossed, and waiting for all the pieces to fall into place. But even then, there was always the chance that a late bulletin—a jury verdict, an airplane hijacking, an assassination attempt—might force the production staff to dash off a new lineup and issue new instructions to everyone.

Those were the moments that brought out the best in Sandy Socolow; or if not the best, then certainly the most. Unlike Midgley, he welcomed the chaos of late-breaking stories. No "piece-of-cake" yearnings for him. A robust, sturdily built man, Socolow met the pressure with a ferocious élan, his bursts of energy Fred Friendlian in their intensity. To see him in action, bounding about the newsroom-studio, shouting commands, slamming down phones, and, in general, whipping himself and others up into a lather, it was difficult to believe that just a few years earlier he had been hospitalized with a heart attack.

In spite of their sharp differences in temperament, Midgley and Socolow had a good working relationship—at least on the surface. Since there were any number of correspondents and producers who found Midgley's style of phrasing vague and cryptic, they came to rely on Socolow's interpretations. If he told them that a story they were working on was likely to make the lineup, it invariably did; similarly, if Socolow's response was negative, that usually turned out to be Midgley's reaction as well. Still, there were times when Midgley crossed him up and chose to go off on another tangent entirely. These occasions served to remind Socolow that for all his delegated authority he was still a subordinate, and, more than ever, this was a situation he found frustrating. From time to time he would gripe to friends that here he was, doing all the work—the hard, day-to-day, gritty stuff—while Midgley continued to receive all the credit, not to mention a much larger salary.

In the fall of 1970, Midgley began his fourth year as executive producer of the Cronkite show, and Socolow's patience was wearing thin. But by then there were definite signs that Midgley was growing weary of the grind (even though Socolow stoked most of the fires, Midgley still had to put in ten-hour days and, of course, the daily pressure of decision was ultimately his) and that he was fast approaching the point of demanding, as Leiser had before him, a less strenuous regimen. And Sandy Socolow was supremely confident that when that day came he would realize his ambition and be promoted to executive producer of the *CBS Evening News with Walter Cronkite.*

Most of the time the Cronkite show included at least one film report that did not deal directly with an event occurring that day. There even were days when the flow of breaking news was so stagnant that as many as three or four stories would be drawn from "the bank" of film pieces already in the house. When that happened, it represented a triumph of sorts for Russ Bensley, who was the producer in charge of the bank and all other facets of the *Evening News* film operation. It was a job for which he was peculiarly suited. For if Socolow's strength was breaking news, then Russ Bensley's forte was film.

Unlike Socolow, who cut his teeth as a wire-service reporter, Bensley was a child of television. A native of Chicago, he enrolled in Northwestern University's Medill School of Journalism with the intention of preparing for a newspaper career. But he became intrigued by the "gimmickry" of electronic journalism, and in the spring of 1951, even before he graduated, he went to work for WBBM, the CBS-owned station in Chicago. Over the next nine years, Bensley acquired experience in just about every phase of radio and television news: writing, directing, producing, and, from time to time, on-air reporting. In the process he helped to pioneer TV journalism at WBBM, and in 1960 CBS News brought him into New York as a writer.

During his first two years there, Bensley wrote for a number of news programs, eventually moving up to the Doug Edwards show. He was hoping to go on from there to the Assignment Desk and thus be in a position to do some on-air reporting. But Ernie Leiser told him that he was not the on-camera type—and he may well have been right. Bensley greeted the world with a scholarly face and a serious, soft-spoken manner. Those who worked closely with him soon came to appreciate his dry, penetrating wit, but it's doubtful that it would have enhanced his on-air appeal, for his humor was often *so* dry, so elusive and subtle, that it went over the heads of casual listeners. So instead of trying to become a correspondent, Bensley chose to focus his efforts on the production end. He worked for a few months as a director and producer on *Eyewitness,* and then, in early 1964, he joined Socolow as a producer on the newly expanded *Evening News.*

As the producer in charge of the broadcast's film operation, Bensley was told by Leiser that he should concentrate on developing enterprisers and other more ambitious film pieces. Leiser knew he was entrusting his pet project to a capable man, but at the time he did not yet fully appreciate just *how* capable Bensley was. Filming and editing a breaking news story, the kind that would run two minutes or less on the *Evening News,* was a fairly routine procedure. There were deadline pressures to cope with, but in terms of craft, such film reports were comparable to the conventional format and style of a front-page news story. Enterprisers were different. The television equivalent of newspaper features or magazine articles, they required a special touch: a feel for shaping and pacing, and knowing where to use narration to maximum effect and where to let the pictures and "natural sound" speak for themselves. Bensley, having developed over the years a strong visual sense, soon demonstrated that he had that touch. Indeed, he was the one who put together the *On the Road* pieces (from the footage and narration that Kuralt sent in), and Kuralt himself was often generous in his praise of Bensley's contribution to the success of his series.

As soon as he was satisfied that an enterpriser or feature was ready for broadcast, Bensley arranged to have it screened by the executive producer. Midgley was generally supportive, and if he liked a piece, he would see to it that it got on the air—eventually. The problem, as always, was when and how to make room for it, and in the daily battles for air time—for spots in Midgley's lineup—Bensley and Socolow were natural adversaries. And in arguing, day after day, for more hard news and less of what he called "artsy-craftsy stuff" in the lineup, Socolow was not only voicing his own predilections but was also reflecting the bias of his close friend and colleague, Walter Cronkite. That gave Socolow's position considerable weight. But Bensley also had his allies; and although even in aggregate they could not match the authority of Cronkite, they did have the advantage of numbers. For by 1970 Bensley was presiding over a seven-man staff of associate or field producers, all of whom shared a vested interest in getting enterprisers and similar film reports on the air.

Field producers were a relatively new wrinkle on the Cronkite show, but they came out of an honored tradition at CBS News. Throughout the 1950s and early 1960s, they were an essential part of documentary production—and in some cases, the *most* essential part. To cite just one of many examples: the person who deserved the most credit for *Harvest of Shame,* the celebrated *CBS Reports* story on migrant workers, was not Fred Friendly and certainly not Ed Murrow (who actually entered the project very late in the game), but a field producer named David Lowe. Lowe spent the better part of a year living in migrant camps, and, more than anything else, it was his diligence and compassion that made *Harvest of Shame* such a superb program. Nor was it just documentaries that relied heavily on the work of field producers. To a great extent, the unsung heroes of *Eyewitness* during its years of glory were the show's field producers, especially John Sharnik, Phil Scheffler, and Bernie Birnbaum. They were the ones who, with camera crews in tow, did most of the hard work for each week's cover story.

But during these years, field producers were not an integral part of the *Evening News* operation. Their emergence in the mid-1960s epitomized the evolution of the *Evening News* into a new and more complex format. For it was primarily the advent of enterprisers that made field producers a necessity. The longer, in-depth reports naturally required more time to develop, and it was decided, as it had been in the documentary sphere several years earlier, that high-salaried correspondents could not be spared for such laborious, detailed legwork. Instead, field producers spent several days (even weeks) pursuing the story and laying the groundwork. Then, at a propitious moment, a correspondent would be flown to the scene for a day or two of concentrated interviews so that the finished piece would be graced by his face and voice—as well as, in some cases, his narrative style.

It was also not uncommon for field producers to work with correspondents on more routine assignments. Some correspondents simply preferred having a producer around, partly for company and partly to act as a buffer between them and their bosses in New York. In other cases, a producer might be assigned to a correspondent because the latter's professional competence was limited to reporting and writing, and when it came to the mechanics of transmission and other production details, he needed help. Finally, there were the free spirits and the recalcitrants to whom field producers were assigned, in part, as chaperones. There were, however, some field producers who could hardly act as chaperones—a case in point being Stanhope Gould. Gould had been an associate producer on the Cronkite show since 1964, longer than any of his 1970 colleagues, and he was generally regarded as the most talented member of Russ Bensley's team. He certainly was the most flamboyant.

Gould was an improbable combination of Harvard and hippie. On the one hand, he was the son of a prosperous Chicago lawyer who had gone to the best private schools (prior to Harvard) and who was conversant in a wide range of conventionally cultural subjects, from Balanchine choreography to modern art. On the other, he lived in a Greenwich Village "pad," preferred to "rap" in the jazz/rock argot of that milieu, was heavily "into" pot, and in numerous other ways had immersed himself in the counterculture of the 1960s. Gould served his apprenticeship in TV journalism at WBBM in Chicago, where his path briefly crossed Russ Bensley's. Bensley moved on to New York, and Gould soon followed. By 1964, Ernie Leiser was hearing a lot of good things about Gould, and when he asked Bensley for an assessment,

Bensley told him that everyone he knew at WBBM thought Gould was "brilliant." That summer, Gould was brought into New York as an associate producer and assigned to work with Bensley on the *CBS Evening News*.

Gould may have been brilliant, but he was also headstrong and politically committed in ways that often made his superiors nervous. He joined CBS News at a time when the civil rights movement was just starting to veer toward the stridency of "black power" rhetoric and urban rioting. On college campuses the SDS and other New Left groups were making their first moves to mobilize protest against the war in Vietnam. Gould zeroed in on these phenomena and made them his special beat. He produced a series of stories on draft resistance that included the first detailed look—in any medium—at the growing number of deserters living in Canada. On the racial front, he put together a five-part series on the discrimination practices employed by the building trade unions. And during the winter of 1969–1970, when the Chicago Seven trial brought all the radical movements of the decade to a point of convergence—and climax—Gould produced the day-to-day coverage of that for the Cronkite show.

The correspondent he worked with on many of these assignments was Jack Laurence, whose own counterculture sympathies were strengthened by his association with Gould. But while Laurence took some pains to maintain at least the appearance of objectivity, Gould made no effort to conceal the fact that he personally identified with most of the voices raised in protest during these years. Although they deplored his ideological motives, Gould's superiors could not fault his work. The stories he chose to focus on were important to an understanding of the currents then sweeping across the American scene, and, what's more, he developed them very well. Even those CBS people who viewed him as a discreditable radical and hippie grudgingly conceded that as a field producer Gould had few peers.

To go along with his politics, Gould cultivated a "flower child" appearance. He let his hair grow to shoulder length, and he complemented that with a rather villainous-looking beard and mustache. The flowing hairstyle certainly helped him gain entry into the more esoteric counterculture circles, but Gould (who was nothing if not resourceful) also had among his accoutrements a "straight" wig, which he sometimes donned when he had to interview FBI agents and other Establishment types.

Gould was a divorcé, yet even there his situation was fairly exotic. Other CBS News producers and correspondents had former wives living in Westchester County or New Jersey or back in the Midwest somewhere, but Gould's "ex" was making the scene in Marrakesh, Morocco. In the meantime, stories about his own exploits, personal and professional, enlivened many a bull session at CBS News. There were times, in fact, when Gould himself did the enlivening, for he was keenly aware that he had become something of a cult figure within the shop, and he often went out of his way to nourish his "Peck's Bad Boy" reputation.

One morning, for example, he came into the producer section of the *Evening News* area and proceeded to divert his colleagues with an account of a "mind-blowing triple-header" (as he called it) that he had experienced the night before. It had involved getting very high on pot, then listening, through earphones, to Beethoven's Ninth Symphony while a lady friend pleasured him in a manner in which he liked to be pleasured. Gould's description of his attempt to climax his own efforts with the climax of the *Ode to Joy* choral was quite graphic. What's more, he related the blow-by-blow account in a loud and clear voice that carried over a span of several desks, and at one point, a secretary on the Cronkite show, a prim Catholic girl who had just recently emerged from the sheltered upbringing of a parochial education, stood up and angrily stalked out. Gould interrupted his narrative and asked in mock bewilderment, "What's the matter with her?"

Sam Roberts, a fellow associate producer, was quick to reply. "I don't know, Stanhope," he said with a straight face. "Maybe she doesn't like Beethoven."

In between field assignments, Gould and the other associate producers attached to the Cronkite show worked each day on various in-house chores. By 1970, the crush of film material coming in each day from news locations around the world was such that Russ Bensley could not hope to screen and edit it all himself. So every morning, while Socolow was preparing his outlook, Bensley typed up a "Who Does What" list, assigning producers and film editors to work on specific pieces. In the daily process of transforming raw footage into tightly structured reports, producers always worked hand in hand with film editors; and in some instances it was the film editor, not the producer, who furnished the creative touch. Not everyone on Bensley's team had Bensley's gift for cutting and shaping film—not by a long shot.

Given a choice, Gould and most of the other associate producers preferred being away from New York, pursuing and developing their own film stories. This, however, was not the case with Ron Bonn, who ranked next to Gould in seniority and was, perhaps, Gould's equal in all-around ability. Bonn had taken on his share of field assignments, but in contrast to Gould, who had no desire to advance any farther in the hierarchy, Bonn had his sights set on moving up to a producer's post on the Socolow-Bensley level. And he believed that working closely with Bensley on a day-to-day basis was the best way to strengthen his in-house position and put himself in line for such a promotion.

Bonn had been working on the Cronkite show since 1963, first as a writer and then, starting in 1966, as an associate producer. What helped make him such an asset to the broadcast was his aptitude for highly technical, science-oriented stories. Ever since an early sampling of aeronautical engineering at the Drexel Institute of Technology, Bonn had kept up a lively interest in subjects most journalists, with their conventional liberal arts backgrounds, regarded as branches of the occult. One of his first big assignments after becoming an associate producer was to put together a three-part enterpriser on the controversy simmering over the Pentagon's new antimissile missile—and everyone agreed that Ron Bonn was the only one of Bensley's crew equipped to make any sense out of that. He was also well versed in space technology, which put him in excellent odor with Walter Cronkite.

Bonn was inclined to take himself and his work very seriously, so much so that a fellow producer described him as suffering from "an excess of earnestness." He was, in all his attributes, the antithesis of Stanhope Gould: impeccably square in appearance and manner, with a life-style strictly that of a "breakfast-eating, Brooks Brothers type." That was, of course, his privilege. But while Gould and his idiosyncrasies seldom infringed on the lives and work of the other associate producers, Bonn was often in a position to impose his personality on his colleagues.

By 1970, Bonn had become Bensley's regular backup, taking over his duties when he was on vacation or on another assignment. These brief interludes of authority usually brought out the worst in Bonn: a priggish, fussbudgety style of command that was part shop foreman and part headmaster. It soon reached the point where the other associate producers on the Cronkite show would bristle and groan whenever they learned that Bensley was going to be off for a few days. But Bonn was largely oblivious of the negative effect he had on his temporary subordinates. He was aware of periodic grousing but was inclined to dismiss it as sour grapes, maintaining that he was, after all, a genuinely nice guy, and everybody knew it. In truth, Bonn *was* a nice guy most of the time, but he never understood how much he ceased to be one when he was given a chance to exercise authority. As a result, he was obliged to learn the hard way. In 1971, when producer positions suddenly did open up on the Socolow-Bensley level, Bonn was passed over for promotion—and solely because of what Bensley sometimes described, in private, as "Ron's unfortunate people problem."

One co-worker who frequently found himself torn between a desire to offer Bonn some friendly advice and a less charitable urge to "punch his smug, fucking face in" was Paul Soroka. Soroka came to CBS News from the *Wall Street Journal* in 1964, and after the usual writer's apprenticeship, he joined the Cronkite show as an associate producer in 1967. His mercurial attitude toward Bonn was all too characteristic of Soroka, who was of Russian extraction and was very Russian in temperament. A man who sensed deviousness at every turn, he had a way of imbuing even a simple morning greeting with sinister, conspiratorial undertones. As Stanhope Gould once said, "A brief encounter with Paul at the drinking fountain is enough to make me wary of opening my desk drawer for fear of being bitten by an asp."

But if Soroka's colleagues and superiors were not always sure how to react to his sly glances and innuendos, they responded favorably to his work. They were especially impressed by a two-part enterpriser he produced in 1969 on the problems of aging, and by a three-part series he put together the following year on the then-emerging Women's Liberation movement. (Not yet emerging at CBS News, however; in addition to a male field producer, the correspondent on the Women's Lib story was David Culhane.)

Gould, Bonn, and Soroka were the "heavyweights" on Bensley's seven-man team during the late 1960s and early 1970s, and their presence generally overshadowed the other members of the staff. But the difference between them and their fellow associate producers was not so great that they could afford to relax. They were constantly aware of being challenged. As was the case with the hustling correspondents in the Washington bureau, Bensley's troops engaged in a spirited competition with each other—a competition that Soroka once characterized as "almost sexual in its intensity."

In their various ways, Les Midgley, Sandy Socolow, and Russ Bensley and his crew—not to mention the correspondents, field producers, and camera crews scattered around the world—were all preoccupied with just one aspect of the Cronkite show: the picture portion, the film reports. But only about two-thirds of a typical *Evening News* program was given over to film pieces. The rest of the broadcast was taken up with Cronkite's on-camera copy—tell stories and lead-ins to the film reports. And the group responsible for preparing that material was Cronkite's editorial staff, which consisted of one editor and three writers.

During the first four years of the half-hour show, Cronkite's editor was a bald, round-faced man named Ed Bliss, who brought to the job a wealth of experience. He had been with CBS since the early days of World War II, and for several years during the 1950s he wrote the news portion of Ed Murrow's nightly radio program. (Murrow also included in his evening newscast a commentary, which was usually written by another colleague, Raymond Swing.) Largely because of his Murrow assignment, Bliss remained in radio long after others had shifted over to television, but his worth was recognized on both sides of the electronic fence. Thus, in 1963, when he evinced an interest in becoming editor of the new half-hour *Evening News,* Cronkite grabbed him.

Bliss was an able and conscientious editor, but more impressive in many ways was his gentle spirit, his kindly, even sweet disposition— qualities seldom found in journalists, especially editors. He did not let his benevolent nature compromise his professional standards, but when he had to criticize slovenly work, he always did so more in sorrow than in anger. With young people in particular, he was unfailingly patient and supportive. Many of his colleagues thought Bliss had the makings of an excellent teacher. That idea also appealed to Bliss himself; so much so that in 1968, at the age of fifty-five, he left CBS News to begin a new career as a professor of journalism at American University. He had only one flaw as a teacher: as his best friend at CBS put it, "Imagine what a shock it will be for those kids when they get out in the real world and discover how awful the rest of us are compared to Ed Bliss."

That comment was made by John Merriman, who, like Bliss, had been around CBS since World War II days. Eleven years younger than Bliss, Merriman looked up to him as his mentor, but Bliss, with characteristic modesty, always protested that he had learned as much from Merriman over the years as Merriman had learned from him. Again like

Bliss, Merriman was a radio diehard and did not switch over to television until the 1960s. He became a writer for the *CBS Evening News* in 1966, and two years later he succeeded Bliss as Cronkite's editor.

As an editor, Merriman was, if anything, even more painstaking than Bliss. He, too, had a generous nature (*most* of the time) and a strong penchant for pedagogy, but he was far more volatile in temperament and caustic in his criticisms. In working with Bliss, writers hated to make mistakes because they caused him such visible grief. Merriman, on the other hand, saw to it that the errant writer suffered as well.

He had a special talent for spotting and ridiculing clichés. In looking over a piece of copy, he might comment to the writer, "Well, I see you've moved the 'dire straits' again. Last week you had them in Vietnam and now they're back in the Middle East. Pretty shifty." At other times, Merriman's remarks took the form of a query. "Tell me," he would ask a writer, "this 'stinging rebuke' of yours—strikes the victim in the back of the neck, does it? It must raise a terrible welt. Do you treat it with some kind of salve, or what?" He was also concerned about the "giant palls" that kept settling over troubled cities from Berlin to Buenos Aires. "That's what's causing all the air pollution," he once complained. "Forget about the smog. Let's get rid of the 'giant palls.' "

Merriman spent the morning and early afternoon of a typical day going through wire-service copy, setting aside the top stories and making notes on what specific angles should be stressed. He also kept an eye out for offbeat feature items that struck his fancy, for Merriman not only had a rich sense of humor, he had that rarer gift: a sense of the absurd and the eccentric. (One day, for example, when he came across a UPI story about a man in Scotland who had choked to death on a clove of garlic he kept clenched in his teeth every night to ward off vampires, Merriman pointed out, as only he would, that the garlic had fulfilled its intended purpose: there was no evidence that the victim had been bothered in any way by vampires.)

The busy part of Merriman's day began around midafternoon when Midgley made out the lineup. With that to guide him, Merriman then conferred with the three writers on the show, assigning various tell stories and lead-ins, and deciding how many seconds to allot each item, always a vital consideration given the nightly time squeeze. (A tell story seldom ran as long as a minute; twenty to thirty seconds was the usual length. Lead-ins averaged about fifteen seconds.) As soon as he and the writers had reached agreement on all assignments, Merriman typed up an editorial lineup, which rounded out the bill of fare, filling in the spaces between the film reports set down in Midgley's lineup.

Along with being a good editor in the conventional sense, Merriman had a knack for recognizing what stories were apt to arouse Cronkite's particular interest on any given day. Although he was not especially close to him socially, as Socolow was, he had developed over the years an excellent feel for Cronkite's professional tastes and peculiarities. From time to time he assigned an item to a writer who protested that it really wasn't worth including in the broadcast. "*You* may not think so," Merriman would say, "but Walter will want it. Just wait and see." And invariably, Cronkite wanted it. Cronkite had long since learned to trust Merriman's news judgment and, beyond that, to respect his conscience and devotion to principle. For Merriman was just about the only person at CBS News who did not hesitate to take Cronkite to task if he thought he was wrong about something. Others might defer and acquiesce, but Cronkite knew from experience that he could count on Merriman to raise objections—in the loudest and most forceful language—if he felt they were warranted.

One of their more memorable scraps occurred in 1967 when Merriman was still just a writer on the show. The heavyweight champion of the world had recently announced that he considered Cassius Clay a "slave name" and that he wished henceforth to be called by his Black Muslim name, Muhammad Ali. The initial reaction of the sportswriting establishment was to ignore his request, but Merriman complied, and when he wrote a story about the champion's latest squabble with the draft board, he identified him as Muhammad Ali. Cronkite's response was not only to change the copy to "Cassius Clay," but to chide Merriman for being taken in by what he characterized as a publicity ploy to evade the draft. Merriman, incensed, speculated on how wonderful it must be to be a big and important TV anchorman and play God by telling black athletes how uppity they were for wanting to change their names. That was for openers; from that promising start, the exchange escalated into a real row.

The quarrel ended with Cronkite pulling rank, reminding Merriman in blunt terms that it was his show and he was the boss. When the show went on the air, Merriman sat in a chair just a few feet from Cronkite (but well outside of camera range) and glowered at him with fierce disapproval. Cronkite must have felt the moral censure behind Merriman's glare, for when the moment of truth came, he looked at the prompter and the words "Cassius Clay," drew in a deep breath, and intoned, "Heavyweight champion Muhammad Ali today . . ."

Each of the three writers on the Cronkite show had his special sphere of operation. One concentrated on foreign news, a second on national developments (primarily Washington stories and domestic politics), and the third on an area categorized as "all else." The all-else writer was responsible for a potpourri of subjects deemed, somewhat arbitrarily, to be outside the province of either the foreign or national writer. They included space, economics, the arts, ecology, plane crashes, hurricanes and other natural disasters, as well as man-bites-dog stories.

The regular foreign and national writers in 1970 were, respectively, John Sumner and Charlie West, who shared a common regional and professional background. Both were former Associated Press reporters from North Carolina who had worked their way up from AP bureaus in the South to important desk jobs in New York. Sumner was a top rewrite man on the AP's foreign desk in 1962 when he moved over to CBS and a writer's job on the *Evening News,* just a few weeks after Cronkite replaced Edwards as the show's anchorman. West, who had worked with Sumner in the AP's Charlotte bureau, later followed him to New York, where he became one of the main rewrite men on the national desk. After Sumner went to work for CBS News, he began touting West to Cronkite and others, and eventually, in 1966, West joined his fellow Tarheel as a writer on the *Evening News.*

As a couple of wire-service pros, Sumner and West were writers in the Cronkite mold. Their desk experience in the AP's New York office had equipped them to write fast under pressure, with clarity and accuracy. "The story writes itself!" a frenzied Socolow loved to shout to Cronkite's staff writers whenever one of them was forced, by a last-minute bulletin, to prepare a new lead for the broadcast and have it ready for Cronkite to read on the air in the next thirty seconds. Stories did not write themselves, of course, but Sumner, and especially West, had a way of making it seem as though they did.

In contrast to the stable presence of Sumner and West, a number of writers passed through the all-else slot during these years. One of them was John Merriman, for that was the post he occupied during his stint as a writer on the show; and although he did a creditable job, he was, by his own admission, a better editor than writer. The all-else slot was in some ways more demanding than the other two. Since the writer assigned to it had to cope with a grab bag of unrelated stories, from lunar landings to wage-price controls, versatility was almost as vital a prerequisite as speed and accuracy. Merriman and some of the other all-else writers had their moments, but in terms of sheer writing talent, the best of the lot was a man named John Mosedale.

Mosedale acquired his early experience as a writer and editor for the North American Newspaper Alliance back in the 1950s, and later, during his first years at CBS, he worked primarily in sports. But he did take on news assignments from time to time, and the job he did at the 1968 political conventions so impressed Socolow and others that in early 1969 he was brought on to the Cronkite show as the all-else writer. Mosedale was more erratic than Sumner and West, lacking, at times, their dogged thoroughness, but he was also more of a stylist. A man of exuberant, rollicking humor, he sometimes injected droll touches into his copy—touches Cronkite appreciated, even though, given his sober and stately on-camera persona, he did not always do them justice on the air.

The combination of Merriman as editor and Sumner, West, and Mosedale as writers was recognized as the strongest editorial staff yet to be assembled on the Cronkite show. As a matter of fact, the level of competence in almost every aspect of the *Evening News* operation was higher than ever by 1970, the year in which it all came together for the *CBS Evening News with Walter Cronkite.* Thanks in no small part to the breakup of the Huntley-Brinkley team, it was the year that the Cronkite show opened up such a commanding lead in the ratings that its reign over the nightly news field would continue, unimperiled, for years to come. The various supporting players, from the correspondents in the field to the producers and writers working on the inside, all helped, in varying degrees, to bring CBS News to this point of supremacy. But they were, after all, merely that—supporting players whose names appeared below the title—and such were the dynamics of television news that the heaviest burden each night had to be borne by the star, the solar center around whom all this vigorous activity revolved. This basic truth was fully appreciated within CBS News, where the prevailing view in 1970 could be summed up in a paraphrase of Browning: "Walter's in his anchor chair—all's right with the world."

13 Uncle Walter

He had become, by this time, an institution. There now existed millions of young adults who could not remember a time when Walter Cronkite's electronic presence had not been a part of their lives, his crinkly smile and military drumroll voice as familiar to them as the faces and voices of relatives they had known since childhood. The road he traveled to get where he was had not been all that smooth. When he first emerged as a television star back in the 1950s, all the stature belonged to Murrow and his group, and later, even after he had succeeded Murrow as CBS's premier journalist, he did so poorly in the early competition with Huntley and Brinkley that he came perilously close to being shunted aside permanently, as Douglas Edwards had been. But by 1970, all the bumps were behind him, and he towered over TV journalism as no one before him ever had.

It was especially appropriate that the term "anchorman" had been coined to describe the role Cronkite first assumed at the 1952 political conventions. As the term became ingrained in the vocabulary of television news, Cronkite was perceived as its embodiment; indeed, anchormen in Sweden came to be known as "Cronkiters." In his own country, Cronkite's place in the American consciousness was such that in the early 1970s the Oliver Quayle polling organization decided to use his name as a benchmark against which to measure the level of public trust in potential presidential candidates. When the poll was taken in the spring of 1972, he decisively led all contenders, including the then-untarnished President Nixon. Even though the Watergate scandal had not yet erupted, the best Nixon could manage was a tie for fourth.

All this was very heady wine for the ego, and there were times when Cronkite allowed a sense of self-importance to get the best of him. When John Hart, then anchorman on the *Morning News,* went to see Cronkite to solicit his support for a fellowship project, Cronkite was cordial and sympathetic, but he was also wary. He told Hart that he had to be careful how he used "the name." ("That's exactly how he said it," an awed Hart later told a *Morning News* associate. "Not 'my' name, but *the* name!")

Yet such lapses into pomposity were not truly characteristic. There is no doubt that Cronkite rejoiced in his eminence and all the perquisites that came with it, but he was not one to put on elitist airs as, for example, members of the Murrow clique were wont to do. Much of the time, in fact, he came across as aggressively *un*sophisticated. "Go, baby, go!" he hollered at the moment of blast-off in July 1969 when *Apollo 11* was launched on its historic flight to the moon. Still, Cronkite was careful not to overdo it. What made his emotional outbursts so engaging (and effective) was that they contrasted so sharply with his customary demeanor of controlled, unflappable cool.

All the same, it was his transparent enthusiasm for people and events that accounted for much of Cronkite's appeal. By 1970, he had met and interviewed just about every famous person in the world worth meeting and interviewing, and yet he had not become jaded. Viewers seemed to sense this, to sense that even though Cronkite was constantly rubbing elbows with all kinds of celebrities, he did not quite think of himself as a celebrity. Instead, he conveyed to Middle Americans the impression that he was still, somehow, one of them: a hardworking, unassuming guy from Saint Joe, Missouri, who had been lucky enough to get into a racket that brought him into contact with all these fascinating people.

That impression also helps explain why he had a reputation within the trade as a "soft" interviewer. Given his passion for thoroughness, Cronkite almost always went into an interview well prepared, but he was inclined to shy away from the tough questions, the combative exchanges. The most notorious and least justifiable example was his interview with Chicago's Mayor Daley at the 1968 Democratic convention. This was at a time when the strong-arm tactics of Daley's security people at the convention hall had outraged just about everyone in the press corps, including Cronkite. Just the night before, in fact, CBS News floor correspondent Dan Rather had been slugged by one of Daley's goons. Cronkite's on-air response to that was to say, with eyes ablaze and in a voice shaking with rage, "It looks like we've got a bunch of thugs in here." He then added, "If this sort of thing continues, it makes us, in our anger, want to just turn off our cameras and pack up our microphones and our typewriters and get the devil out of this town and leave the Democrats to their agony."

It was the first and only time in his long career that Cronkite displayed such undisguised wrath on the air, and the next day, when he obtained an exclusive interview with Daley, most of his CBS colleagues anticipated, with considerable relish, a sharp and spirited confrontation. Instead, he took an excessively deferential approach, and Cronkite was roundly criticized for his performance. He subsequently agreed that "it was a very bad interview." But, in partial defense, he explained that he did not "trust myself" to get into a pointed debate with Daley because, as he put it, "I was deeply involved emotionally and I was seeking desperately to maintain my objectivity." Yet in its overall tone, the Daley encounter did not differ significantly from other interviews Cronkite has conducted over the years; what made him so vulnerable to criticism on that occasion was the fact that the circumstances were so much more volatile than they were, say, for his lofty discourse with Britain's Prince Philip or his long, postpresidential ramble with LBJ down at the ranch.

In truth, unlike some other CBS News correspondents—notably, Mike Wallace, Dan Rather, and Roger Mudd, three hitters who generally gave the impression that they regarded television interviews as a verbal branch of the martial arts—Cronkite had no real instinct for the jugular. It was as if he had a built-in aversion to using the enormous power of his television presence to cause anyone embarrassment or discomfort, as if to do so would have been, somehow, not quite cricket. And the evidence suggests that this quality, a kind of old-fashioned sense of fair play, was also a large part of his appeal. As Martin Mayer wrote in his book *About Television:* "Cronkite's strength with the American people . . . rests on the near-universal perception that he is what another culture calls a *Mensch.*"

But if millions of viewers saw Cronkite as a reassuring, sympathetic figure—everybody's "Uncle Walter"—many of them were still curious about the man behind the image. Anyone who worked for CBS News during those years soon became accustomed to being asked by friends, relatives, and even chance acquaintances: "What's Walter Cronkite really like?"

For most CBS News people, even those who were a part of the *Evening News* operation, it was not an easy question to answer, and there was a tendency to fall back on the easy banality—that what you see is what there is. Others, less guarded, would reveal that this was not entirely true, that there were plenty of times when the off-camera Cronkite bore little resemblance to Uncle Walter. But the deviations they had in mind were largely superficial (flashes of temper here, touches of vanity there), for with the exception of Sandy Socolow and one or two others, Cronkite's co-workers did not really know him, and did not feel close to him. Some of this, no doubt, could be attributed to the simple fact that he was who he was (the aura of Cronkite's stature was a palpable reality at CBS News), but it was also in keeping with his own temperament.

He did not encourage intimacy. In a profession known for its camaraderie and casualness, he was basically detached and impersonal in his day-to-day relationships. He was not stuffy, exactly; as a matter of fact, he had a certain zest for ribaldry and frequently made a point of passing on the latest joke he had heard. But even on these occasions, when Cronkite was engaging in levity with his writers or producers, some of them often had the uneasy feeling that he was still holding back, still maintaining an arm's-length distance between himself and them. And invariably, after they had shared a laugh, he was the one to break the mood, to move abruptly on to more serious matters. In short, most of his colleagues found Cronkite to be formally pleasant rather than friendly. Courteous and agreeable, yes; warm and outgoing, no.

In a 1970 interview with Oriana Fallaci, Cronkite acknowledged that "I do not have the gift of openness. I am overcautious to the point that people think of me as kind of remote . . . of being too slow at friendship. Which certainly is not intentional. I would like nothing better than being an Irish bar drunk, making friends with everybody." When the interview appeared in *Look* magazine, that last line, in particular, touched off some spirited snickering at CBS News. For within the shop, even those who were not on intimate terms with Cronkite knew that unlike so many journalists, in both print and broadcasting, he was in no danger of becoming a drunk, Irish or otherwise. He took a drink now and then, but he rarely if ever overindulged, and he did not look kindly on those who did—especially during working hours. Over the years various members of his *Evening News* staff were heavy drinkers. Cronkite tolerated that up to a point, but if he became convinced that drinking was having an adverse effect on someone's work, he quickly moved to have him replaced. During one concentrated period in the early 1970s, three of the broadcast's most talented producers and writers were banished from the show for good, and in all three cases the sauce had been their undoing. Such dismissals were entirely justified, for by the early 1970s Cronkite simply could not afford to have on his staff any writer or producer who, for whatever reason, did not perform up to snuff, for he had come to rely on those people more than ever before.

In the numerous interviews he gave over the years, Cronkite often made a point of stressing that he was usually in his office each morning by ten o'clock, which was true. The implication, however, was that he thus was deeply involved in the daylong preparations for each evening's broadcast, which was not true; or, to be more precise, it was, by 1970, no longer true. There had been a time, back in the early and middle 1960s, when Cronkite had assumed a more active and visible role in the daily decision-making process, from the selection of film pieces for the lineup to the assigning of tell stories for his on-camera script. But by 1970 it was his custom to spend most of the day, until an hour or so before air time, holed up in his private office, insulated from most of the tumult. It was not a question of shirking. His unparalleled success had in no way diminished his diligence; he was still as hard and as persevering a worker as anyone in the business, and there were many nights when, following the broadcast, he would return to his office and spend another hour or two poring over material for some future assignment. The problem was that he was now being pulled in so many directions at once. In addition to the *Evening News,* there were the ever-recurring elections, space shots, and various prime-time specials to anchor, all of which required study and preparation. Then, too, there were speeches and other outside commitments constantly pressing in on him, eating up still more of his time. Cronkite was a classic overachiever, and therefore was determined to be at the center of all the action, which meant that several hours of an average day had to be devoted to other matters besides the *Evening News.*

The reason Cronkite was able to regard this as a satisfactory arrangement was that he had complete confidence in the people who had evolved into leadership positions on the *Evening News* staff. He and Les

Midgley had a harmonious, if somewhat formal, relationship. Even more reassuring was the presence and increased importance of Socolow, his confidant and surrogate. Socolow was in and out of Cronkite's office several times throughout the day, which was how Cronkite generally kept abreast of breaking stories and other developments. If he could no longer screen film pieces himself or talk on the phone to other correspondents on assignment, Socolow was there, in the screening rooms and on the phones, and Cronkite knew he could depend on Socolow to give him an accurate and thorough assessment of any and all situations.

Yet even though he had relinquished most of his personal involvement in the routine, day-to-day details, Cronkite continued to exercise authority over the broadcast in other ways. In his capacity as managing editor (a title he clung to with tenacity, as though to give it up would, in some inscrutable way, deprive him of journalistic legitimacy), he occasionally proposed future assignments, especially those of a more ambitious nature. For example, it was at his insistence that the *Evening News* aired a series of enterprisers on environmental problems in the early 1970s. Just as he had been prescient about the space age in the late 1950s, so now, a decade later, he anticipated the ecology movement, and it was his pep talks to producers Russ Bensley and Ron Bonn that set in motion the various reports on the perils of air and water pollution.

The stories were produced under the overall title of *Can the World Be Saved?*, and to give the series visual identification, the graphics department came up with a display showing the earth being squeezed by a giant human hand. The display became known around the *Evening News* area as "the handjob," and whenever a decision was made to include an environmental piece in the lineup, one of the technical people would holler, "Order up the handjob" or "We need the handjob." Cronkite suffered through this recurring indignity in silence for several weeks, but one day, finally, he inquired wearily if it wasn't possible to call the display something else. The problem, he disclosed, was that the last few times it had come on the screen while he was on the air, the word "handjob" automatically flashed through his mind, and his thoughts began drifting off into areas that had nothing to do with ecology or his responsibilities as the doyen of television journalists.

It was not until late afternoon, between five and five-thirty, that Cronkite usually emerged from his office, leaving behind the speech drafts, the telephone messages, and the reams of research material piled on his desk. Settling into his anchor slot at the huge, horseshoe-shaped desk, surrounded by John Merriman and his three writers, he assumed command. It was a measure of Cronkite's trust in Socolow, Merriman, and the other members of the staff that he felt he could wait until that late in the day to join in the action. With air time scarcely more than an hour away, the basic decisions regarding film and script had been made; the emphasis was now on pulling the complex elements of the broadcast together in terms of time, and then delivering the goods. It was a hazardous, tension-producing process that required, each day, a kind of miracle of cohesion. Cronkite relied on his producers and the various technical people to see to it that the film portion of the broadcast was in proper shape. All his efforts were focused on his on-camera script, and it was during this harried period that Walter Cronkite—the on-air *Mensch*—gave a worthy imitation of Walter Burns, the growling, fist-pounding editor in *The Front Page*.

Although sequestered in his office most of the day, Cronkite was always well wired into the day's news, and, in going through the script, he peppered his writers with pertinent queries. From time to time, he threw copy back at them with precise, staccato instructions on how to improve it. This put extra pressure on the editorial staff at a time when it had to cope with other last-minute developments, such as late-breaking stories or changes in the lineup, and Merriman and the writers often resented it. From their point of view, life would have been a lot easier if Cronkite were less demanding and meticulous; or if that was not possible, they felt he should get into the mix earlier in the day and start kicking ass then. Cronkite himself throve on the pressure, and he seemed to think that everyone else shared his exhilaration for performing under the gun. Clearly, many of his co-workers did not, but if some of them thought he was irresponsibly tardy in taking on his editorial duties each day, none of them questioned his editorial acumen. His grasp of the news, its details and nuances, was truly impressive, and it was a daily challenge for the editorial staff to keep up with him.

Nevertheless, he had his blind spots, especially in the area of art and culture. When he came out of his office one day in the fall of 1967, he was greeted with the news that Woody Guthrie had died. Cronkite's response to that was: "Who's Woody Guthrie?" His ignorance in the field of letters was revealed in his treatment of Edmund Wilson's death in 1972. That was kissed off in a 15-second tell story, in which the only book cited was *Memoirs of Hecate County,* thus giving the erroneous impression that that fictional romp (not at all typical of Wilson's métier) was the most significant work of a long, distinguished, and enormously influential literary career.

Still, Cronkite was, on balance, a solid "front-page" editor who, in addition to his generally strong news sense, was also adept at cutting stories. This talent, in particular, often impressed new writers assigned to the show. Never having worked with Cronkite before, they were inclined to think of him primarily as a broadcaster, an anchorman—that is, until he began trimming the fat off their copy. One young writer was so struck by his ability with a pencil that he made a point one day of saying to Merriman that he had no idea Cronkite was such a good editor. Amused by the new man's tone of astonishment (Cronkite was, after all, in his fourth decade as a working journalist), Merriman replied with mock solemnity, "I'm glad you've noticed, but please, don't tell Walter. We've got him convinced that he's just another pretty face."

He was, of course, never that, but for all his protestations about being strictly a newsman, Cronkite was responsible for many of the show-business touches that went into his nightly "performance." The silly tag line he dreamed up ("And that's the way it is") was an obvious attempt to compete with the equally fatuous "Good night, Chet, Good night, David" close that Reuven Frank conceived for Huntley and Brinkley, and both sign-offs were theatrical flourishes that had nothing to do with journalism. Dick Salant once said that "if I were a tyrannical boss, I would forbid Walter to end the *Evening News* that way." His objection was not so much to the line's corniness as to its grossly misleading implication that viewers had just been informed of all the news there was to report.

Cronkite also had an actor's keen sense of how to use a prop effectively. For years it had been his habit at the end of the broadcast, when the credits appeared on the screen over his lingering presence, to lean back in his chair and fiddle with his pipe, as though he were about to light up and relax. He did not have to be told that the pipe, that time-honored symbol of serene sagacity, helped reinforce his "Uncle Walter" image.

The disparity between Cronkite's on-camera personality and the demanding editor who barked orders at his staff was never more evident than during the broadcast itself. The editing and rewriting process continued right up until air time, and often beyond. It was not uncommon for copy to be revised and updated even after Cronkite had said "Good evening" and had begun to move crisply through the day's lead stories. He was always careful to conceal from viewers the stress and displeasure he sometimes felt over the way things were going. But when the program went into a commercial or a film piece and he was momentarily off camera, he often complained, sometimes with desk-thumping emphasis and angry scowls, about the way such-and-such had been handled. Then, when he received the cue to go back on camera, the genial expression immediately returned, and in his customary tone of calm authority, he picked up the thread of the broadcast.

Because of Cronkite's ability to turn "Uncle Walter" on at a moment's notice, viewers almost never saw his competitive fury, which was, perhaps, his most striking professional trait. He never allowed himself to let up. Even after he had secured his position at the pinnacle of his profession, the competitive fires still raged. He expected his *Evening News* program to be, night after night, the best in its field, and when somebody's work did not measure up to his exacting standards, he did not hesitate to raise hell. Both his show and the *NBC Nightly News* were broadcast live to some communities at 6:30 P.M., Eastern time, while the taped versions went out to New York and other large cities at 7:00 P.M. That meant the rival networks were able to monitor each other's broadcast with considerable scrutiny, and Cronkite, in particular, availed himself of that opportunity. When Southern California was hit by an earthquake in February 1971, NBC's coverage of the disaster was vastly superior, both in terms of pictures and all-around reporting. After watching the NBC version alone in his office, Cronkite stormed into Les Midgley's office, where most of the show's producers were gathered. They, too, had been watching the *NBC Nightly News* and were, therefore, wearing long faces. Cronkite proceeded to say a great deal, but it was his first words that brought the group snapping to attention: "I think someone should be fired." Sure enough, not long after, the Los Angeles bureau chief for CBS News was removed from that post. When Walter Cronkite suggested that someone should be fired, the chances were very good that someone *would* be fired.

Cronkite's relations with the news staff were correct and strictly professional. He seldom went out for lunch, and when he did he invariably dined with VIPs, either from within or without the network. Nor, except on extremely rare occasions, did he join the tipplers who assembled at The Slate each night to indulge in postmortems and other pursuits. The one notable departure from this general pattern was his annual Christmas party. Every year Cronkite threw a sumptuous bash at his East Side brownstone for members of the *Evening News* staff and their wives or husbands, many of whom looked forward to it as the social event of the Yule season, if only because they welcomed the chance to behold, once again, Walter Cronkite's famous striptease.

Year in and year out, Cronkite's parody of a burlesque queen doing her number was the highlight of his party. He did not disrobe, nothing so vulgar as that. Instead, he did it all with napkins and tablecloths and lewd grins and highly suggestive movements. It was a very funny routine, and most of his guests responded with whoops of laughter, especially those who were catching the act for the first time. One year an associate producer was attending his first Cronkite Christmas party. When, toward the end of the evening, the host began going through his bumps and grinds, the new producer's wife managed to stop giggling long enough to whisper to her husband, "I had no idea Walter Cronkite was such fun. Why didn't you tell me?"

"Because I didn't *know!*" he replied.

For all his success as the star of the *CBS Evening News,* that show's format, with its rigid time structure, did not play to Cronkite's chief strength as an anchorman. He was still at his best during the coverage of live events, such as political conventions and space shots, for as Sig Mickelson recognized back in the early 1950s, it was Cronkite's ability to ad-lib with clarity and intelligence that made him so effective on television. Not that it was all off the cuff; Cronkite always had a team of writers and researchers working with him on live assignments, but the flow of the broadcast on such occasions was dictated not by written material but by the events themselves as they unfolded on the convention floor or out on the launchpad. Cronkite himself had a clear understanding of the skill required in anchoring live coverage, and, what's more, he saw that as one area in which broadcast journalists had developed their own craft. "The anchorman has a tremendous load," he once told an interviewer. "Memory to be called on. Knowledge to be called on. A set of events to be kept in perspective . . . It's true that most of what we do is an extension of written journalism. But not standing up at a riot or a convention and explaining it while it happens. That sort of 'spontaneous journalism' is *new*."

Still, there were times when he overdid it, and a few of his colleagues bitched about his being an "air hog." Eric Sevareid became so incensed with Cronkite for the way "he kept cutting me off" at the 1968 Republican convention that he stalked off the set and threatened to take the next plane back to Washington. Terrified by this prospect, various news executives and producers took turns stroking Sevareid's ego and giving assurances that henceforth neither Cronkite nor anyone else would be allowed to interrupt the Gray Eminence when he was in the midst of an exegesis.

Ironically, this internal flare-up occurred just a few months after Cronkite, breaking with his own code of conduct, had edged onto Sevareid's turf of on-air commentary and personal opinion. For years he had prided himself on his objectivity, and yet in February 1968 Walter Cronkite made the decision to cross over the line into advocacy journalism. What induced him to take this drastic step (drastic for him, at any rate) was the war in Vietnam and his own sense of complicity in the early justification of it.

Like so many Americans of his generation who as young men had been involved in World War II, Cronkite was conditioned to believe in the intrinsic morality and high purpose of U.S. foreign policy. He not only accepted the Cold War rhetoric, he had also been an exponent of it in documentaries on American air power in the 1950s. Thus, as the United States gradually slid into the Vietnam quagmire, Cronkite supported the increased military commitment. At the time of the big buildup in 1965, Cronkite decided to take a firsthand look at the situation, and his reports from Vietnam that summer reflected the optimism of the senior commanders, who were, after all, men of his own generation. He identified with them and trusted them in ways he did not identify with or trust the younger reporters in Vietnam, whose cynicism about the U.S. presence there greatly irritated him. So Cronkite's reports from Vietnam in 1965 echoed the smug assurances of the American mission that it was pursuing the right course of action and would soon have Communist aggression under control.

But over the next two years, as the war continued to escalate and casualties mounted, Cronkite watched on his own news show the increasingly skeptical and critical reports out of Vietnam, reports that challenged his pat assumptions just as they challenged those of millions of viewers across the country. Gradually, his own doubts about the war began to form. In the summer of 1967, he decided to review his famous interview with John Kennedy, conducted four years earlier to inaugurate the half-hour news show, and to rebroadcast the part in which Kennedy had warned against just the kind of full-scale involvement in Vietnam that had taken place since his death. Then came January 1968 and the Tet offensive. More than any other single event, that nationwide uprising by the Vietcong made a mockery of Washington's repeated assertions that the war was being won and that the Communists in Vietnam were on the verge of defeat. As the bleak film reports on the Tet offensive came into New York, a profoundly disturbed Walter Cronkite decided the time had come for him to make another trip to Vietnam.

Accompanied by Ernie Leiser, who had hired on as his field producer, Cronkite flew to Saigon, a city no longer insulated from the war. A few days earlier, the U.S. Embassy in Saigon had been occupied for six hours by Vietcong guerrillas, and enemy forces were still lurking in and around the capital. Again, as in 1965, Cronkite found the senior commanders unwavering in their jut-jawed optimism. The way General William Westmoreland explained it, the Tet assault was actually a great and dramatic victory for the Americans. But this time Cronkite was determined to take a closer look for himself.

The heaviest fighting was then taking place in the north, around Khe Sanh, and there was some talk about Cronkite and his crew going up there. But the military people would not give their okay to that: too risky. The Tet offensive was enough of a public-relations problem; the last thing they needed was for something to happen to Walter Cronkite. Instead, he and Leiser and the rest of his entourage were flown to the old citadel city of Hue. Just the day before, Westmoreland had told Cronkite that the Marines had Hue under control, but when he and his group arrived there, they found the Marines engaged in a ferocious battle to recapture the city. It was a deeply revealing moment for Cronkite. There, in Hue, he saw a microcosm of the Vietnam conflict; there was the reality of the war as opposed to the official version of it. Cronkite's CBS colleagues were impressed and more than a little alarmed by the way he went charging headlong into the street fighting. It was almost as if he wanted to be absolutely certain that what he saw in Hue was truly happening.

On his last night in Vietnam, Cronkite had dinner with a group of correspondents in Saigon, and, clearly distressed, he asked over and

over again: How could it have happened? What in the name of God
went wrong? The other reporters, some of whom had been covering
the war since the early 1960s, did not mince words. They replied that
the whole sorry mess had been wrong from the start, and deceptions
had been employed at every step along the way to cover up that original mistake.

Flying back to New York, Cronkite was in a subdued, introspective
mood. Ernie Leiser sensed that a slow, hard anger was building up
inside him. Years later, Leiser would recall, "I think Walter must have
felt that he had been had, and he got mad because he felt that this was
an inexcusable and, maybe, a criminal deceit by the federal government."

Even so, he was still reluctant to speak out. Cronkite had built his
formidable reputation on the solid rock of impartiality, and to forsake
that stance, even temporarily, was tantamount in his view to a violation
of principle. Moreover, he was acutely aware of the risks involved in
becoming engulfed in controversy. Yet he also agreed with Leiser and
others who argued that this was one instance in which traditional objectivity was probably the more misleading, the more dishonest position.
So even though he still had serious reservations and continued to ago-
nize over whether he had the right to use his power this way, Cronkite
made the leap into the alien sphere of advocacy journalism.

For the first time since he had taken over as anchorman on the *CBS
Evening News,* he used that show as a forum for his own commentary.
Portions of four successive broadcasts in late February and early March
of 1968 were devoted to reports on different aspects of the Vietnam
tragedy, and each night Cronkite included personal remarks critical of
just about everything, from the much-heralded pacification program,
aimed at winning the "hearts and minds" of the Vietnamese people, to
the overall military strategy. The central message running through all
his observations was that the war was not being won, and that the influx
of still more American troops would not succeed in turning it around.
In addition to his comments on the *Evening News,* Cronkite anchored
a prime-time special report on Vietnam, concluding that broadcast with
the following words:

> We have been too often disappointed by the optimism of the Ameri-
> can leaders, both in Vietnam and Washington, to have faith any longer in
> the silver linings they find in the darkest clouds. . . . For it seems now more

certain than ever that the bloody experience of Vietnam is to end in a stalemate. . . . To say that we are closer to victory today is to believe, in the face of the evidence, the optimists who have been wrong in the past. . . . It is increasingly clear to this reporter that the only rational way out then will be to negotiate, not as victors, but as an honorable people who lived up to their pledge to defend democracy, and did the best they could.

Cronkite's criticism of the war was cautious, measured, and, all things considered, quite mild. He did not align himself with the militant antiwar groups, the raucous protesters. Instead, he reached out to his natural constituency: the moderates, the nondoctrinaire. Until then, the majority of Americans in the political mainstream had been willing to go along with the Johnson Administration's war policies. But Cronkite sensed that the mood across the country was shifting, and that, in speaking out the way he did, he was reflecting that shift even as he was helping to guide it.

One viewer who was quick to grasp the importance of his editorial remarks was that shrewd political analyst, Lyndon Johnson. After watching the broadcasts, LBJ began confiding to aides that the jig was up: if he had lost Walter Cronkite, then he had lost the country, lost his consensus. It's true that other forces were bearing down on him by then (notably the insurgent candidacies of Eugene McCarthy and Robert Kennedy within his own party), but people who were close to Johnson at the time were convinced that Cronkite's critical reporting helped to push him toward his decision not to run for reelection. Thus, for all his qualifications and tone of restraint, Cronkite's antiwar stand had plenty of impact and was a definite milestone. Looking back on the broadcasts several years later, David Halberstam wrote: "It was the first time in American history that a war had been declared over by a commentator."

The Tet offensive and Johnson's abdication were merely the first shock waves that crashed against the American consciousness in 1968, a year that, even before it was over, would be regarded by many as the most turbulent and tragic since World War II. And from beginning to end, Walter Cronkite was in the thick of it all. Four days after LBJ announced that he would not seek reelection, Martin Luther King was assassinated, and a few weeks later (and less than five years after Dallas), Bobby Kennedy met the same fate. Cronkite anchored most of the live coverage of those two desolate stories, from the first bulletins through the funeral eulogies, and again, as in 1963, he struck an admirable balance between sorrow and reassurance.

And so it went, on through the stormy Democratic convention in Chicago, the fall campaign and Nixon's hairbreadth victory over Humphrey. The 1968 election night marked the fifth time, dating back to 1952, that Cronkite had anchored CBS's coverage of the presidential returns, but never before had the race been so close and the task so arduous. By the time CBS News wrapped up its coverage, Cronkite had been on the air nearly seventeen hours. That kind of staying power was another attribute that set him apart from most of his colleagues and competitors. Co-workers often talked about his "iron pants" and likened him to a boxer who can carry his strength into the late rounds and finish off his opponent then. But if Cronkite demonstrated his iron pants during the all-night reporting of the 1968 election returns, he surpassed that performance the following summer at the time of the *Apollo 11* flight to the moon. On the day of the historic landing, he was on the air for an uninterrupted stretch of eighteen hours; then, after taking a six-hour snooze, he returned to the anchor slot for another nine-hour stint. But that was his story, and nothing so trivial as fatigue could have prevented him from being at the center of it, from blast-off to splashdown.

Throughout the 1960s, space was one of the few major stories that did not make people wince. It was a positive, upbeat series of achievements, a continuous celebration of America's technical know-how and spirit of adventure in meeting the challenge of a new frontier. And through it all, from the first Mercury suborbital flights, on through the Gemini phase, and then to the Apollo missions, Walter Cronkite was the chief celebrant. More than any other journalist, he was identified in the public mind with the space program. Because of his unabashed enthusiasm and the ease with which he handled the arcane terminology, he was affectionately dubbed "the Other Astronaut."

His constant identification with a "good" news story helped Cronkite build up his reservoir of trust and goodwill. But more than that, he sincerely believed that the moon landing in 1969 was the epic event of the age, and this sense of epochal excitement was shared by millions of viewers. Not since the weekend of the first Kennedy assassination six years earlier had so many Americans sat, transfixed, in front of their television sets. When the lunar module touched down on the surface of the moon, Cronkite wiped his brow and, in a soft, reverential voice, confessed to his audience that he had nothing to say. There was a moment: Walter Cronkite with nothing to say. Viewers could readily appreciate that. Many of them had not been all that comfortable with the other Cronkite, the one who had spoken out against the war—just as Cronkite himself had not been comfortable in that role. But now, with man's first landing on the moon, everything was "A-okay" again.

Thus, as the 1960s drew to a close, Walter Cronkite was at the apex of his own prime time. He had become the acknowledged giant of his profession, and, having reached that peak, he had no intention of yielding an inch. As 1970 began, he was still only fifty-three, and, given his robust constitution, he was looking forward to another full decade of action. This was good news for Cronkite and good news for CBS, but it was not necessarily good news for some of his colleagues—notably Harry Reasoner.

By the late 1960s, Reasoner was firmly established as Cronkite's regular backup, the correspondent who invariably took over the *Evening News* anchor slot when Cronkite was on vacation or on an assignment away from New York. He was, in fact, such an excellent replacement that CBS News executives were fond of boasting that in Harry Reasoner they had a number two man good enough to be number one at any other network. As subsequent events would prove, that claim was not altogether farfetched.

14 Wild about Harry

It has long been part of the romantic lore of American journalism that lurking inside just about every newspaperman is an aspiring novelist yearning to break free. One of Harry Reasoner's claims to distinction is that he reversed the fantasy: he wrote and published a novel in 1946, when he was twenty-three, and went on from there to a successful career in journalism. Some of Reasoner's co-workers over the years found this aspect of his past a trifle disconcerting. It reminded them a little of the old Bob Newhart routine in which Lincoln, confused about the sequence of events in his early career, goes around telling people that he first practiced law and *then* became a railsplitter.

The novel, entitled *Tell Me About Women,* is a fast-paced, bitter-sweet story of young love set against the intrusive background of World War II, and like most first novels written at a tender age, it is transparently autobiographical. The first-person narrator, just out of college, works as a cub reporter on a newspaper in Minneapolis until he's inducted into the Army, which precisely conforms to the external facts of Reasoner's own life during this period. One of the most autobiographical passages in the book is also one of the most poignant. It comes in the midst of a moody reminiscence:

> I remembered my mother, the first and only woman I ever slept with in an innocent love and trust, and how she died, wanting to die, wanting to get the hell out of the world, sorry only because I was young and afraid and vulnerable. I remembered my father, the big dark man with the laughing eyes and lines under them, the tireless energy, the lust for life.

214

> I remembered the breathless bright morning on a northern lake when the
> support gave way and he fell, down to the rocks, with me running and
> people screaming. He was calm as he fell. I saw his eyes and they were just
> disgusted. "Oh, damn!" he said.

Reasoner was twelve when his mother died of cancer, and he had just
turned sixteen when he witnessed his father's fatal accident.

But if his adolescence was shadowed by loss and sorrow, he was able
to take comfort in memories of a happy childhood. He was born and
raised in a small town in northern Iowa, where both his parents were
schoolteachers. In 1935, the year before his mother died, the family
moved to Minneapolis, where his father, having left teaching, embarked on a new career as a small-time impresario who organized and
sold assembly programs to schools throughout the upper Midwest.
Growing up in Iowa and Minnesota imbued Reasoner with a strong and
enduring sense of regional pride. He was, in fact, a spirited chauvinist
about the Midwest and he often made sweeping claims on behalf of the
region, such as his contention that the Midwest was the true home of
democracy because it was never tainted by slavery or by the more
subtle form of class elitism that flourished in New England. Reasoner
never tired of pointing out that he grew up in an atmosphere relatively
free of racism and anti-Semitism, although he did concede that such a
blissful state could probably be attributed to the fact that there were
no blacks or Jews living in his hometown.

"All right, then, goddamnit," a mildly exasperated Southern friend
once asked him, "who *did* you discriminate against?"

"Well, we did have Catholics," Reasoner replied, repressing a
smile. His friend was quick to laugh, however, for he appreciated the
piquancy of that remark. He knew that Reasoner's wife was Catholic
and that his seven children had been raised Catholic, even though
Reasoner himself remained a member of what he liked to call "the one,
true holy and apostolic faith—the Episcopal Church."

Like Cronkite, Reasoner was a college dropout who left school to
work on a newspaper. But while he didn't stay at the University of
Minnesota long enough to pick up a diploma, he was unusually fortunate in the contacts he made there. He took a journalism course from
a young teacher named Sig Mickelson, who would figure most prominently in his future career. At the time, however, Reasoner had a much
closer relationship with another professor named Mitchell Charnley,

who took an avid personal interest in his writing talent and urged him to develop it. One of his fellow students was Max Shulman, who later used the Minnesota campus as a setting in his comic novels. Another was Tom Heggen, who, like Reasoner, would soon go off to war and then celebrate his return to civilian life by publishing his first novel, *Mister Roberts.*

Tell Me About Women was a far cry from being a success on the *Mister Roberts* scale. Although it received favorable critical attention, Reasoner had serious doubts about whether novel-writing was really his bag, after all, and in later years he would dismiss *Tell Me About Women* as "third-rate Irwin Shaw." He eventually decided to chuck the Muse and concentrate on journalism. He went back to work for the *Minneapolis Times,* the paper he had started out on before going into the Army, and he stayed with the *Times* until 1948, when it folded.

From then until 1954, Reasoner moved around from job to job: two years as a public-relations man for Northwest Airlines, a year as a radio writer at WCCO (the CBS affiliate in Minneapolis), and three years in the Philippines with the United States Information Agency. He took the USIA job more or less as a lark, having been drawn to it in part by a desire to get away from the harsh Minnesota winters. (Regional chauvinist or no, there were limits.) But government salaries being as rigid as they were, there was no financial future in the USIA—at least not for a man in the process of siring a large family. He left the agency in 1954, and on his way back to Minneapolis, he stopped off in New York to say hello to his former journalism teacher, Sig Mickelson, who by then was running the CBS news department. When Reasoner inquired about a possible job, Mickelson advised him to get some experience in television.

So Reasoner did. Returning to Minneapolis, he landed a job as news director of a small TV station, KEYD, which kept him busy for the next two years. At the end of that time, Mickelson, who had been keeping tabs on Reasoner's progress through his Minneapolis contacts, came through with a CBS offer: a position on the New York Assignment Desk. The job was a fairly modest one, and so was the salary: $156 a week. This posed a real dilemma for Reasoner, since he was making nearly twice that much as a news director. Given all the mouths he had to feed (four children by then, with three more yet to come), he felt he had no choice but to turn the CBS offer down. But his wife, Kay, insisted that he take the job. It was a big opportunity, she said, and if he let it slip by, he might drift into his forties miserable and resentful and "blaming us." Better to starve in New York than have to live with that, she said.

So, at the age of thirty-three, Harry Reasoner took his family East to start a new life. They would not starve.

Sig Mickelson would eventually be fired as president of CBS News on the grounds that under his uninspired and indecisive leadership the news division had lost the initiative—and the ratings—to NBC. Yet even those who helped bring about his ouster in 1961 agreed that during his tenure Mickelson made several key decisions that had a profoundly beneficial effect on the future of the news operation. One, obviously, was the heavy pitch he made, in the face of corporate resistance, to go with newcomer Walter Cronkite as the anchorman at the 1952 political conventions. The other, in 1956, was hiring Harry Reasoner and Charlie Kuralt, and his subsequent decision to make full use of their talents in the embryonic craft of film reporting. In the middle and late 1950s, CBS News was putting together its first corps of television field correspondents, and there were several young reporters who were part of that pioneering effort. The best of them—the ones who set the standards—were Reasoner and Kuralt.

Reasoner certainly did not envision such a pivotal role for himself when he reported for work on the CBS News Assignment Desk in July 1956. The Assignment Desk was expanding by then, but compared to the bustling nerve center it would later become, its responsibilities were still quite limited. Its chief function was to assign cameramen to cover major stories. But every now and then, someone on the Assignment Desk would be sent out on a story, and on those occasions he was known as a "reporter-contact," a term that dated back to the newsreel years when it described a low-level assistant who carried out mundane chores for the cameraman, such as helping him set up his tripod or asking story subjects how they pronounced their names.

In the middle and late 1950s at CBS, reporter-contacts gradually began to take on more responsibility, often serving, in effect, as modest field producers. Even so, they were not supposed to appear in the reports themselves, either as interviewers or narrators. But as time went on, reporter-contacts—Reasoner and Kuralt among them—were encouraged to inject more of themselves into the stories they covered, and in the process they learned how to write to film and how to orchestrate other aspects of television reporting as well. Since this was a new experience for most of them, their early efforts were characterized by an understandable timidity, a reliance on certain visual clichés to ease them through an assignment. Reasoner, for instance, liked to tease Kuralt about his habit of opening stories with a shot of an outdoor café (to establish, presumably, a man-in-the-street presence), and Kuralt countered that he didn't think much of Reasoner's tendency to begin *his* pieces in the local barbershop, interviewing a customer in mid-haircut. Other reporters, on being assigned to a civil rights story, could not resist the temptation of opening with a shot of the community's Civil War statue, be it Union or Confederate.

Don Hewitt was the lord and master of the reporter-contacts, schooling them in the intricacies of shooting picture and narration separately, the technique that formed the basis of his double projector system. More to the point, perhaps, he was the one who decided whether their work was good enough to be aired on the Doug Edwards evening news show. Knowing that their fate as CBS News television reporters lay almost entirely in Hewitt's hands, the new men often went to great lengths to win his approval. For example, Reasoner was assigned to cover Nikita Khrushchev's tour of the United States in 1959, and, goaded by Hewitt, he finagled his way past a tight security cordon to get a brief but exclusive on-camera interview with the Soviet premier. Later, when a State Department friend admonished him, pointing out that he could have gotten in serious trouble for pulling a stunt like that, Reasoner simply chuckled and said, "You don't understand. I'm more afraid of Don Hewitt than I am of the Secret Service."

A few months before Khrushchev's visit, Reasoner had been named a correspondent. It was quite an honor, for he was the first reporter from the TV Assignment Desk to be given that title. Soon thereafter, Kuralt was also promoted to correspondent, and the day of the announcement, Reasoner offered his congratulations, telling his younger colleague, "I'm sure there's room enough for both of us." Before long, however, he was not so sure. For by 1960 it was Kuralt, not Reasoner, who had become the darling of the new breed. Sig Mickelson was touting him as "the next Ed Murrow" and was pushing him for one choice assignment after another, culminating in his being picked over Cronkite himself to anchor *Eyewitness.*

Up until then, Reasoner had assumed that of all the new reporters/-correspondents, he stood the best chance of eventually moving up to the anchorman level. But now he had a clear sense of having been passed over, and he saw that, ominously, as the start of a pattern. Much of Reasoner's irritation was fueled by the fact that Kuralt, in 1960, was only twenty-six, whereas he was thirty-seven. All of a sudden Reasoner felt caught in an age squeeze between the established senior correspondents (Cronkite, Sevareid, Collingwood, et al), who were still in their forties, and the wave-of-the-future generation, represented by Kuralt and God knows how many other bright young hustlers.

Oddly enough, it was radio and not television that brought Reasoner out of the doldrums. Bored and discouraged by the television assignments he was getting, he began writing and broadcasting radio news on a regular daily basis. In March 1961, Jack Gould of the *New York Times* wrote a review in which he said that the two best things currently coming out of CBS News were *Eyewitness* on television and Harry Reasoner's radio newscasts. He praised Reasoner's ability "to take the curse off the lifeless wire service prose of hourly newscasts" and noted that he did not hesitate to use "a touch of his own dry humor where circumstances warrant."

A few days after the review appeared, Blair Clark, who had just taken over as Dick Salant's chief deputy, called Reasoner in and told him about a new midmorning television show CBS News was planning to put on that fall called *Calendar*. Clark and Salant wanted Reasoner to co-host it with a Broadway actress named Mary Fickett.

Calendar had a fairly brief life span, remaining on the air only two years, but Reasoner and others who worked on the show always looked back on it as a highlight in their respective careers. In talking about the broadcast in later years, *Calendar* alumni often characterized it as "a literate *Today* show," and while that smacked of snobbish overstatement (*Today* itself being more literate than most programs of its kind), *Calendar* went out of its way to be more liter*ary* in tone, which gave it a quality seldom found on commercial television. The show's format was similar to that of *Today*, but the *Calendar* people were often inventive, even inspired, in the diversions they conceived for the program. For example, to observe the first day of spring in 1962, the staff came up with a Robert Frost poem praising winter, and another by A. E. Housman celebrating spring. On the show that morning, Reasoner, "defending winter," read the Frost poem, then Mary Fickett countered with Housman and spring. *That* was certainly a departure from routine television fare.

Another time, Reasoner decided to enlighten his viewers with a discussion of a truly bad novel written by an esteemed author. Several candidates were proposed, and the list was eventually narrowed down to a choice between Hemingway's *Across the River and into the Trees* and James Gould Cozzens's *By Love Possessed.* Reasoner conceded that *By Love Possessed* was "more pretentious," but he insisted that *Across the River* was the more fitting example because it was so vastly inferior to Hemingway's best work.

Reasoner and Fickett had a harmonious working relationship, but it did not extend beyond the life of *Calendar* itself, whereas another alliance that began on that show was destined to be far more enduring —the one between Reasoner and writer Andy Rooney. Rooney was just one of several good writers assigned to *Calendar.* Also on the staff were John Mosedale and Ron Bonn (both of whom went on to write for Cronkite on the *CBS Evening News*) and John Sack, who, after leaving CBS, won acclaim as the author of *M,* one of the best books written about the tragic involvement in Vietnam. But Rooney was the senior man, the one with the experience and television savvy.

He had been associated with CBS since 1949, when he was hired as a writer for Arthur Godfrey, and over the next twelve years he took on numerous assignments in both the news and show-business spheres of radio and television. (Amused by the mutual wariness, bordering on paranoia, that defined relations between those two worlds-within-a-world, Rooney once compared them to two men forced to sleep in the same bed who dare not touch each other for fear of giving rise to the wrong impression.) When he was given the *Calendar* job in 1961, he telephoned Reasoner, whom he had never met, and suggested that they have lunch and get acquainted. Reasoner brushed him off, saying they would have plenty of opportunity to get acquainted in working together on the show. It was an inauspicious beginning of a partnership that, over the years, would prove to be as fruitful as any ever forged within CBS News.

As the top writer on *Calendar,* Rooney's dry, understated style, heavily sprinkled with irony, blended in perfectly with Reasoner's own writing and broadcasting personality. A strong and creative rapport quickly built up between them, and after *Calendar* went off the air, they continued to collaborate. Throughout the 1960s, Rooney wrote and produced a number of television specials for Reasoner, which were described as "essays" and which dealt with subjects that were so commonplace—so insistently *un*eventful—that they came across as original and offbeat. One self-styled essay was on "doors," another on "chairs," and still another, *An Essay on Women,* which began on this intrepid note: "This broadcast was prepared by men, and makes no claim to being fair. Prejudice has saved us a great deal of time in preparation."

Over the years, Rooney acquired a solid reputation of his own, in large part because Reasoner, secure in his own skills as a writer, did not feel threatened by Rooney's talent and generously praised him in one public forum after another.

Calendar was taken off the air in the late summer of 1963 to make room for a more orthodox news program, the *CBS Morning News,* featuring Mike Wallace as anchorman. At the time, Wallace had just recently joined CBS News, and Reasoner knew him only by his reputation as an abrasive and often crass interviewer of celebrities, someone who trafficked in the more tawdry spheres of television. Losing *Calendar* was bad enough, but to be replaced by a Mike Wallace struck Reasoner as unseemly and degrading, rather like discovering that your wife has left you for an actor.

All the same, he had little to complain about, for in terms of advancing his career, *Calendar* had more than served its purpose. Not long after he began co-hosting that program, he was called on one night to substitute for Doug Edwards on the *Evening News,* and by the spring of 1962, when Cronkite replaced Edwards, Reasoner and Charles Collingwood shared the assignment of Cronkite's regular backup. They did not share it for long. In the summer of 1963, Reasoner alone was assigned to anchor the *Evening News* every night for a month while Cronkite and other members of the "first team" were rehearsing for the debut of the new half-hour broadcast.

By this time, Reasoner was also ensconced as anchorman on a Sunday night news show, having replaced Eric Sevareid in that slot in March 1963. So in the span of just two years, 1961 to 1963, it all came together for Harry Reasoner. In terms of anchorman status, he had not only eclipsed his onetime nemesis, Charlie Kuralt (who in 1963 was working as a field correspondent in Los Angeles, *his* career now having stalled somewhat), but had also edged past Sevareid and Collingwood, the two most formidable holdovers from the Murrow Era. And in the years ahead, Reasoner would steadily strengthen his position as the number two man in the hierarchy of CBS News correspondents.

Even so, he soon became restless. None of his assignments required the kind of day-to-day involvement he had thrived on during the *Calendar* years. Eager for more action and exposure, he readily acceded to Fred Friendly's suggestion that he move to Washington in 1965 to take over the White House beat. But that proved to be a disappointment. Reasoner was bored by the company-town atmosphere in Washington, and he found the White House assignment especially tedious: nothing more than a routine succession of handouts and briefings. He returned to New York in the summer of 1966, more restless than ever.

Then, at some point in 1967, Don Hewitt began talking about his scheme for producing a new, prime-time "magazine-style" program, with Reasoner as its star. Reasoner was flattered, but he didn't place much hope in the project's ever becoming a reality. It was no secret that Hewitt had fallen out of favor with the network brass, which was one reason why he had lost his job as executive producer of the *Evening News*. Reasoner was sorry about that; he liked Hewitt personally and had not forgotten all that Hewitt had done for him in the early years when he first ventured off the Assignment Desk to cover stories in the field. So whenever Hewitt brought the subject up, Reasoner refrained from telling him he thought he was pursuing a pipe dream.

The years since 1964, when Fred Friendly took the Cronkite show away from him and reassigned him to documentaries, had not been easy for Hewitt. Having been at the center of action and power for so long, he had a great deal of trouble adjusting to the far less strenuous world of documentary production. He retained many of his baronial perquisites (a plush office, the title of executive producer, and so on), but he no longer had a domain to rule or numerous minions to command. He was determined to get it all back, one way or another. Aware that his flamboyant behavior had made some CBS executives leery of him, Hewitt kept his excesses and enthusiasms in reasonable check, and during the middle 1960s he diligently applied his talents to the documentary field. But in the process, he discovered that he didn't care much for the documentary form. He felt that very few stories or subjects warranted the full-scale treatment of an hour-long broadcast in prime time. As an avid student of popular culture, he believed that the secret behind the success of *Life* (and other magazines that catered to a mass audience) lay in its variety, a shrewd mixture of serious subjects, briefly treated, and feature stories on show business and other less weighty matters. If that formula worked for *Life*, then, he reasoned, it had great potential for television, the ultimate mass medium. Out of these vague stirrings evolved Hewitt's conception of *60 Minutes:* a "magazine-style" television program with a multisubject format.

Hewitt had no trouble selling the idea to his immediate boss, Bill Leonard. Leonard was eager to develop something original, and the prospect of putting on a new and innovative public-affairs program, one that would reflect credit on his tenure as soft-news vice-president, greatly appealed to him. Dick Salant, however, was much less receptive to the proposal. He argued that such a program would encroach on both documentaries and the hard-news operation, and that would lead, inevitably, to all kinds of intramural squabbling over territorial rights and privileges. Salant preferred to keep everything neatly compartmentalized. But Hewitt and Leonard persisted, and they eventually won Salant over. Once committed, Salant fought hard to enlist the support of his corporate superiors, who had the final say in granting air time and approving the budget for such a program. After four years of being denied access to the heavy action, Don Hewitt had the dice again and was ready to roll.

From the beginning, *60 Minutes* was conceived with Harry Reasoner in mind. Hewitt believed that of all the CBS News correspondents only Reasoner had the experience and catholicity to handle the broad range of subjects he envisioned for the broadcast. Reasoner's background as a hard-news reporter gave him authority in that area, and the work he had done on *Calendar* and the Andy Rooney specials demonstrated his touch for softer feature material. But as Hewitt and Leonard discussed the project in more detail, they came to the conclusion that the multisubject format would benefit from a dual on-camera presence, especially if the second man had a style that clearly contrasted with Reasoner's. Various candidates were considered and rejected, and eventually Hewitt and Leonard settled on Mike Wallace.

Reasoner would have preferred doing a solo, but he was not opposed to working with Wallace, who was no longer anchoring the *Morning News* and was therefore available for the new show. The two men had gotten to know each other, and Reasoner had come to appreciate Wallace's journalistic skills, even though he still considered him to be a bit of an on-air ruffian in his browbeating approach to interviews. Yet he was shrewd enough to realize that this quality in Wallace could work to his, Reasoner's, advantage. Wallace, he was certain, would be assigned to most of the tough and ugly stories, the ones that were apt to cause the network grief and distress, thereby leaving Reasoner free to work the sunny side of the street. Sticking Wallace with the "black hat," the villain's role, while he took on most of the charming, "nice-guy" stories, was the kind of casting that Reasoner found most congenial.

The "first edition" of *60 Minutes*, aired in September 1968, featured a story on the Nixon-Humphrey presidential campaign, a piece on "Cops" (then very much in the news because of the police riot at that year's Democratic convention), and a look at aesthetic sensibility, entitled "Why Man Creates." Thus, the multisubject format was established, and all subsequent programs offered a similar blend of hard news and soft, front-page stories and back-of-the-book features, with most of the latter going to Reasoner. The new broadcast was a critical success, and the sincerest flattery came from NBC. A few months after *60 Minutes* went on the air, the rival network introduced its own magazine-style news program, *First Tuesday.*

But the ratings were another story. During its first years on the air, *60 Minutes* did not attract a large audience, at least not by prime-time standards. It was broadcast opposite *Marcus Welby, M.D.*, then one of the most popular shows on television, and if ratings alone had been the criterion, *60 Minutes* would not have survived. But Salant and Leonard were able to keep the corporate hounds at bay with the persuasive argument that *60 Minutes* was bringing more prestige to CBS than any prime-time news program since the Murrow Era. Acknowledging that, the network's senior management grudgingly went along with the news division's wishes, but *60 Minutes* led a precarious life during those early years. In the meantime, Hewitt and his cohorts proceeded to win Emmys and other awards with impressive regularity, thereby reinforcing the prestige argument.

There were several reasons why *60 Minutes* worked as well as it did. For one thing, Hewitt staffed the show with some of the best field producers in the CBS News organization and consistently employed top camera crews—even, at times, going outside the company to hire outstanding free-lance cameramen. On the executive level, Salant and Leonard lobbied vigorously to procure the lavish budgets Hewitt required to pursue and develop difficult stories. And there was, of course, Hewitt himself. Rejuvenated by his release from limbo, he brought to the broadcast all the flair for production techniques that, a decade earlier, had made him the wunderkind of television news at CBS. To cite just one of many examples, the show's "ticking stopwatch" motif was a Hewitt inspiration. But Hewitt and others at CBS believed that *60 Minutes'* greatest asset was Harry Reasoner. Without taking anything away from Wallace, whose contribution to the program was considerable, the prevailing view within the shop was that Reasoner's droll and literate style gave the show its distinctive tone and accounted for much of its sophistication. During those early years, it was difficult to think of *60 Minutes* without him, and yet the program's towering success—in popular as well as critical terms—was destined to come later, in the mid-1970s, long after Reasoner had left both it and CBS News.

In choosing to build *60 Minutes* around Reasoner's presence and talent, Don Hewitt was reflecting an attitude that, by the late 1960s, had taken root in the minds of many people at CBS News. Reasoner had acquired a sizable faction of devotees, unabashed fans who contended he was the best correspondent on the CBS payroll, especially when it came to anchoring a news show. Reasoner's admirers conceded that Cronkite, given his thoroughness of preparation, his skill as an ad-libber, and his "iron pants," had no peer in anchoring live coverage. But they argued that Reasoner was more effective on the tightly structured news programs, in large part because he was a more gifted writer than Cronkite. That was his strength, and out of it evolved his broadcasting style: an appealing combination of urbanity and Midwestern common sense. Blessed with a natural wit, Reasoner went out of his way to embellish any program he anchored with striking touches of wry humor. In this respect, he was the CBS counterpart of David Brinkley.

Reasoner was just as wry off camera and, again like Brinkley, his barbs often cut to the heart of a situation. At one point in 1970, it looked as if correspondent Jack Laurence and producer Stanhope Gould, both known to be outspoken critics of the U.S. involvement in Vietnam, were about to receive visas to visit Hanoi. One day, encountering Laurence in the newsroom, Reasoner admonished his younger colleague, "If you do go to Hanoi, Jack, remember one thing. We have a strict company policy which states that correspondents are not allowed to accept awards from foreign governments for meritorious reporting." Laurence's response was a wan smile, for although he knew Reasoner was kidding, he was very sensitive to even a facetious suggestion that his coverage of Vietnam and antiwar groups at home had compromised his journalistic integrity.

Like Cronkite, Reasoner relied on staff writers to prepare the straight-news portion of a show he anchored, but a Reasoner newscast was almost always highlighted by an "end piece," which he wrote himself. More often than not, his end pieces were wry commentaries on aspects of the news that struck him as pompous or silly. Politicians and overly earnest reform movements, such as Women's Lib and certain causes espoused by Ralph Nader, were among his favorite targets. He also addressed himself to such nonheadline subjects as the idiosyncrasies of cats, the difficulty of dieting, the intake of liquor during the Christmas holidays, and democracy as practiced in the Reasoner household ("Of course we vote on everything. Each child has one vote, their mother has eight votes, and I have seventeen"). At other times, he used the end-piece time slot for obituary tributes to people he admired, such as Ernie Kovacs and John O'Hara, and on those occasions he allowed the more contemplative side of his nature to surface. When Kovacs was killed in an auto accident in 1962, Reasoner left his viewers with this thought:

> Somebody dies in an unprepared hurry and you are touched with a dozen quick and recent memories: the sweetness of last evening, the uselessness of a mean word or an undone promise. It could be you, with all those untidy memories of recent days never to be straightened out. There's a shiver in the sunlight, touching the warmth of life that you've been reminded you hold only for a moment.

Reasoner's most imaginative end pieces were aired on his own television program, the *CBS Sunday News.* Those he wrote for the *Evening News,* when he was filling in for Cronkite, were generally more restrained and conventional. But the Sunday show was his domain, and there he felt free to follow his more adventurous instincts, wherever they might lead him. There was, for instance, a lazy Sunday afternoon in the summer of 1970 when Reasoner was so amused by a baseball game argument over a close play at the plate, which featured a histrionic player dropping to his knees and pounding the turf in a paroxysm of rage and anguish, that he decided to end that night's broadcast with footage of it. The voice-over copy he wrote to go with the film was studded with quotations from the Book of Job ("My bowels boiled, and rested not. . . . I cry unto thee, and thou dost not hear me"). Reasoner's co-workers on the Sunday show agreed that he was probably the only anchorman in the business who had the effrontery to use the afflictions of Job as comic counterpoint.

A spirit of camaraderie pervaded the Sunday news operation, and Reasoner himself set the tone with his relaxed and affable manner. During the hours leading up to air time, he kept up a lively, irreverent patter that was often so entertaining that it compensated for having to work on Sunday. Once the broadcast was over, the Sunday news staff repaired to P. J. Moriarty's, Reasoner's favorite East Side bistro, where he always bought the first round of drinks and led the conversation over a wide range of subjects. On certain topics, such as sports and literature, he had passionate likes and dislikes, and one sure way to incur his displeasure was to break into a discussion of baseball—a game he was daffy about—to offer an observation on horse racing, a pastime that, to his way of thinking, appealed only to the demented and the depraved. Or, if the subject happened to be F. Scott Fitzgerald or *The New Yorker* style of the Thurber-White years, Reasoner would level a scornful glance at anyone who dared to suggest that Norman Mailer was worth reading. Yet even those who occasionally chafed under his arbitrary ground rules regarded Reasoner as a genial companion, and all hands reveled in those Sunday night bull sessions. Because Reasoner encouraged his *Sunday News* colleagues to think of him as a friend, they felt a strong sense of loyalty to him. He was *their* anchorman, and they were among his most ardent admirers.

Reasoner also had close ties with the members of Walter Cronkite's editorial staff. He and the show's editor, John Merriman, had known and liked each other since the early 1960s, when they worked together on radio, and John Mosedale had been a favorite since the days when he wrote for Reasoner on *Calendar.* But his closest friend on the *Evening News* staff was another writer, Charlie West. He and Reasoner shared an almost religious enthusiasm for the cuisine at a French restaurant called Le Biarritz, near the CBS Broadcast Center, and they fell into the habit of having lunch there together on an average of three times a week. Over the years, the two men became so attuned to each other's moods that when one of them was preoccupied they would dine in silence for ten minutes or so, their friendship, by then, being so firmly rooted that it didn't require the lubricant of constant chatter.

The other members of Cronkite's editorial team were not so enamored of Le Biarritz that they cared to lunch there that often, but from time to time Reasoner and West were joined by Merriman, Mosedale, and the show's third writer, John Sumner, in varying combinations. It was perhaps an indication of Reasoner's sense of values that his most intimate friends at CBS were writers, not fellow correspondents or producers or, God forbid, executives. For even though he had become a big-name broadcaster, a star anchorman, he considered himself to be, first and foremost, a writer.

Occasionally, Cronkite betrayed a certain resentment toward Reasoner's constant socializing with *his* editorial staff. He liked and respected Reasoner well enough, but his competitive antennae were so sensitive that he could not help but view him as a rival, the one CBS News correspondent who, conceivably, loomed as a threat to his premier position. One day in 1969, Cronkite complained to Les Midgley about the frequency with which West and the others had lunch with Reasoner. Midgley did not regard that as a "big deal," it having nothing to do with the lineup or getting the broadcast on the air, and so he responded, with a world-weary shrug, "Look, Walter, I'm sure if you asked them, those guys would be delighted to have lunch with you." Cronkite's only reply was to frown and walk away. That was not what he had in mind.

Whenever Reasoner sat in for Cronkite on the *Evening News,* his casual, convivial personality tended to infect the entire operation. This was especially evident in the conduct of Merriman. Although a man of high spirits, given to puckish flights of humor, he usually kept a fairly tight rein on his mirth when Cronkite was on duty. But when Reasoner was anchoring the show, Merriman felt encouraged—even challenged —to take things less seriously. Like Merriman, Reasoner was a connoisseur of journalistic clichés. Indeed, back in the early 1960s, when they worked together on radio, the two of them dreamed up an all-star football team composed of hackneyed phrases, which included a Scandinavian tackle named "Bodes Ill" and, at fullback, a Sherpa tribesman named "Mounting Tension." Over the years, the game took on many elaborate forms, and another favorite category was "double redundancies." They would rejoice over a wire-service story from Houston, say, that identified someone as a "rich Texas oilman" ("oilman" in that context, needing no such qualifying adjective) or pounce with glee on a story out of Dublin referring to a disturbance that had taken place in a "crowded Catholic pub." They were also ever on the alert for what they called "damning-with-faint-praise superlatives," a group that included such lines as "Singapore, the cleanest city in Asia" and "Ecuador's finest playwright." There were even times when they got into arguments over which cliché was truly the tritest. One day, for example, Reasoner contended that the most successful realtor in America had to be "some guy named Posh" since almost every community he had read about lately was identified as a "posh suburb." Merriman's rejoinder was to assert that while Posh was probably cleaning up in Westchester County, a hustler named Sprawling still had a lock on the market in Southern California.

And so it went for Harry Reasoner during the years leading up to 1970. He not only loved his work, but he richly enjoyed the company of the people with whom he worked. More than most of his colleagues, he seemed inextricably wedded to CBS News, where he had arrived at a high point of professional satisfaction. Therefore, when Dick Salant and others contended that in Harry Reasoner they had a number two man good enough to be number one at any other network, he had a gracious way of returning the compliment. For his part, Reasoner was fond of saying, he would rather be number two at CBS News than number one anywhere else. But the day was fast approaching when he would change his mind about that.

15 The Trouble with Harry

Even during the years when Reasoner was riding high at CBS, everything was not altogether sweetness and light. For one thing, there were some people at the network who were not all that wild about Harry; and for another, he was not nearly so content in the role of Cronkite's backup as he pretended to be in his public utterances on the subject. In truth, he lusted after Cronkite's post and all the trappings that went with it. Yet Reasoner was enough of a realist to know that given Cronkite's towering stature and sturdy constitution he was likely to remain in Cronkite's shadow for many years to come. And that only whetted his sense of frustration, for included in the coterie of CBS people who regarded Reasoner as the best anchorman in the business was Reasoner himself.

Not that he was blind to Cronkite's strengths; on the contrary, he was often generous in his assessment of them. Yet he also believed that in certain vital areas his own skills were superior. He was certainly conscious of being a better writer, and he seldom passed up an opportunity to drive that point home. There were times, in fact, when Reasoner's sportive assaults on journalistic clichés were directed not only at the impersonal wire-service copy but also at Cronkite's own broadcasting style. Cronkite, having learned his craft in the inelegant sweatshops of the United Press, often revealed a weakness for pedestrian phrasing, and Reasoner, in his impish way, considered that fair game. Every now and then, he regaled his *Sunday News* colleagues with deft parodies of Cronkite's on-air delivery and syntax. Mimicking Cronkite's sonorous voice and crisp cadence, he spouted lines like "the strife-torn

230

island of Cyprus" and "the oil-rich sheikdom of Kuwait."

Most of Reasoner's co-workers on the Sunday show found these spoofs diverting enough. But others, having little sympathy for the obvious resentment that triggered them, were not so amused. There were some who felt that he was, at times, just a little too glib and frivolous, both for his own good and the good of his broadcast. By the late 1960s he was sharing the weekend spotlight with a Saturday evening news program anchored by Roger Mudd. Mudd's producer, Paul Greenberg, was one of Reasoner's few outspoken critics, and he soon began referring, in a sneering tone, to the "country-club atmosphere" of the *Sunday News*. It was a phrase he often used in conversations with Gordon Manning, who had jurisdiction over both weekend broadcasts, and Manning, in turn, adopted it as his favorite term of derision.

Manning had a built-in bias in favor of the Saturday news show. It had been his creation, and he had personally picked Mudd to anchor it and Greenberg to produce it. Thus, in executive sessions with Dick Salant and others, he was often lavish in his praise of both Mudd and Greenberg, and frequently found fault with Hal Haley, the producer of Reasoner's Sunday show, although he generally refrained from criticizing Reasoner himself. Even so, Manning's bias had certain disquieting implications for Reasoner. For it meant that just as Cronkite, on occasion, felt mildly threatened by Reasoner, so Reasoner had to look over *his* shoulder to keep a wary eye on Mudd. Indeed, by 1970 there were definite signs that Manning was leaning toward Mudd as his choice to become Cronkite's eventual successor. Moreover, there existed a minority faction at the network that heartily approved of Manning's manipulations on Mudd's behalf. According to this group, the serious, hardworking Mudd was more in keeping with the CBS News tradition of professional sobriety that had been established by such worthies as Murrow, Sevareid, and Cronkite himself.

Reasoner was not totally unaware of his in-house critics. There were times when he had to face the unpleasant realization that his high opinion of himself was not shared by everyone at CBS. One such moment had occurred in 1968 when he discovered, much to his consternation, that he was being denied a major role in the television coverage of that year's national election.

The policy at all the networks was to put their biggest names on display at the conventions and on election nights; and in keeping with that policy, Reasoner had been prominently involved in CBS's political reporting since his emergence as a star correspondent in the early 1960s. Accordingly, he was among those given top billing in CBS's coverage of the 1966 midterm election returns. Cronkite was in his customary anchor chair, and assigned to posts around the perimeter of the election-night set that year were Eric Sevareid, Mike Wallace, Roger Mudd, and Harry Reasoner. Cronkite, Sevareid, Wallace, and Mudd all acquitted themselves well on that occasion—but Reasoner did not. He was simply not prepared. He had neglected to study the reams of research material put together by the election staff, and as a result, his on-air performance was halting and inadequate. That did not come as a surprise to Reasoner's critics, for in addition to finding him overly glib and cavalier in manner, they felt he was indolent.

In point of fact, Reasoner did not have much stomach for home-work, whatever the assignment, and he was the first to admit that this was a flaw in his professional makeup, especially in comparison to a workhorse like Cronkite. But he was also quick to suggest that his strong points—his writing skill and broadcasting style—more than made up for his defects as a drudge. What's more, he had a reputation for being able to wing it as well as anyone in the business. On the night of the 1966 midterm elections, however, Reasoner's ability to wing it failed him. He did not have command of his subject, and this time, for once, it showed.

Bill Leonard, the executive in charge of election coverage, was livid. He seemed to regard Reasoner's performance almost as a personal affront, a violation of trust. By failing to prepare himself, Reasoner had said, in effect, that he really didn't give a damn, and Leonard was not about to tolerate that. To let Reasoner get away with his nonchalant, slipshod effort would not be fair to the other correspondents, like Wallace and Mudd, who had worked hard. Nor would it be fair to those waiting in the wings, like Dan Rather, who, with his solid coverage of the Johnson White House, had earned a chance to play on the election-night first team. So, after discussing the situation with Salant and others, Leonard made the decision: the next time around, in 1968, Reasoner would be replaced.

Reasoner did not learn of the decision until just a few weeks before the 1968 election, and now it was his turn to be livid. He protested to Leonard that it was "asinine," as well as unfair, to judge him solely on the job he had done in 1966. After all, he had proved his worth as a political correspondent on numerous other occasions. Reasoner conceded that he was not as diligent as Cronkite and others, especially when it came to memorizing the obscure little facts of a political campaign. But, he argued, if that sort of trivia was deemed so important, then a couple of researchers could be assigned to his desk on election night to remind him that a candidate running for Congress in such-and-such a district was a defrocked priest, while in another the incumbent was being challenged by a used-car salesman who claimed to be a direct descendant of John and Priscilla Alden. In the meantime, he could bring to the coverage other attributes worthy of consideration. If he was good enough to be Cronkite's regular substitute on the *Evening News* and good enough to co-star on *60 Minutes* (the latter decision having been endorsed by Leonard himself), then he was certainly good enough to be featured in the television coverage of election returns. In other words, the "star system," which had become such an integral part of TV journalism, all but demanded his presence on a broadcast that the network traditionally regarded as an important showcase in terms of both ratings and prestige. But Leonard was adamant. He agreed that Reasoner was a big star, and said he expected great things from him on *60 Minutes.* He contended, however, that the qualities that made Reasoner an excellent choice for that show did not necessarily entitle him to a central role in the election-night coverage.

Reasoner never really forgave Leonard for treating him like an errant schoolboy. As far as he was concerned, Leonard had acted out of childish pique. But he viewed Leonard's reprisal as an aberration, an isolated incident that had no real bearing on his overall status at the network. Indeed, compared to all the nice things that were happening to him during this period, being deprived of a television slot on one election night struck Reasoner as a trivial setback. Nor was he unduly concerned about the way the news division's other vice-president, Gordon Manning, was energetically promoting the career of Roger Mudd, more or less at his expense. Hence, full disillusionment did not hit him until the summer of 1970, when his contract with the network came up for renewal.

The contract had covered an unusually long period—seven years —and under its terms, which included escalation clauses and commercial fees, Reasoner was earning, by 1970, a little more than $100,000 a year. In 1963, when it was negotiated, he had only recently moved into the front rank of television correspondents; since then, he had strengthened his position considerably, and he believed he was entitled to a substantial raise. Like most big-name correspondents, Reasoner employed an agent to handle his financial affairs. He was represented by Ralph Mann of International Creative Management, and in opening the new contract talks, Mann told CBS News that Reasoner wanted enough of a pay hike to put his income over the $150,000-a-year mark.

The salary demand obviously had little to do with financial need, but it had everything to do with ego and status. The inflated salaries of television correspondents are recognized within the industry as a measure of their rank in relation to each other, and Reasoner understood that. He knew that Cronkite was making over $250,000 a year. And he also knew that some of CBS's other star correspondents, such as Mudd and Wallace, were on the verge of joining him in the land of six-figure salaries—if, indeed, they were not already there. Reasoner wanted to close some of the gap between himself and Cronkite and, at the same time, propel his income well beyond the reach of those who, by 1970, were starting to press in on him.

But the management of CBS News declined to cooperate. Through its chief negotiator, business affairs director Don Hamilton, the word was passed to Ralph Mann that while CBS was willing to give Reasoner a modest raise, the figure Mann suggested was far in excess of what the network had in mind. CBS contended that Reasoner was already receiving a generous salary. Mann assumed that this was merely the usual opening gambit, but as time passed, CBS adhered to its original position, and Reasoner's mood gradually shifted from irritation to concern to outright anger. By offering him only a token raise, CBS News was saying, in effect, that there was little or no difference between his worth to the network and that of correspondents on the next echelon—and that was exactly what Harry Reasoner did not want to hear. For the most part, during this difficult period, he kept his bitter feelings to himself. But some of his friends at CBS had heard through the grapevine that Reasoner's contract negotiations were not going well, and one day, over lunch at Le Biarritz, one of them asked him how he felt about it. Glowering, Reasoner replied in a voice filled with wrath, "I find it offensive and insulting, and if you don't mind, I'd rather not talk about it!"

In the fall of 1970, with the negotiations still locked in stalemate, Mann proposed to Reasoner that they make overtures to another network—specifically, ABC. He pointed out that ABC might be willing to offer Reasoner the one job not available to him at CBS: anchorman on the *Evening News*. If they could negotiate on that level, Mann said, it would really loosen the purse strings. But he cautioned Reasoner to think it over before giving him an answer. Unlike some agents, Mann considered it unethical to play one network off against another. He wanted Reasoner to understand that if they entered into talks with ABC, they would have to negotiate in good faith.

Until then, Reasoner had never given much thought to working for another network. Like many of his colleagues, he felt an intense identification with CBS News. He was proud of its tradition, and he believed that he, personally, had the kind of class and style that discerning viewers recognized as being characteristic of CBS News. It would not be easy to forsake that for ABC's news department, which was notoriously lacking in class and tradition. Moreover, he was aware of the risk involved in Mann's proposal. If ABC responded in a negative manner, the word would surely get back to the management at CBS, which would weaken his bargaining position there.

Nevertheless, Reasoner felt it was a risk worth taking. He was now forty-seven, and if he was ever to make a bold and dramatic move, now was the time. Then, too, for all his loyalty to CBS News, he was weary of playing Anthony Eden to Walter Cronkite's Churchill. Assuming Cronkite remained in his anchor chair until the mandatory retirement age of sixty-five (and from all indications, he intended to do just that), Reasoner would then be fifty-eight—too old, probably, to take over the number one post. As he told a reporter a few weeks later, after he had made the jump to ABC, "I took this job because Walter Cronkite was showing no inclination toward stepping in front of a speeding truck."

After it was all over and they had lost Reasoner, various CBS executives would try to blame it all on that. Years later, Dick Salant still claimed that he had done everything he could to keep Reasoner, but that the opportunity to be an anchorman on a network evening news show was the one offer CBS could not match. It was an explanation that took the CBS News management off the hook, of course, but it was grossly misleading. The fact is that before Reasoner gave his agent the green light to open negotiations with ABC, he let it be known around CBS that he was thinking of offering his services elsewhere. He hoped that the threat of his going to another network would induce CBS News to reconsider its position. For even at that late date, Reasoner was willing to kiss and make up. All he wanted, really, was some significant stride toward meeting his salary demands. In other words, the desire to have his own evening news anchor slot did not surface in his bargaining strategy until *after* he became convinced that CBS didn't really care whether he stayed or left. Then, and only then, did he authorize Ralph Mann to establish contact with ABC.

The timing could not have been more fortuitous. In recent years, the ABC News people, tired of being scorned as the dregs, the universally pitied "third network," had been taking steps to upgrade their operation. The process dated back to 1967 when, nearly four years after the other two networks, ABC finally expanded its evening news program to a half hour. But the results, for the most part, had been discouraging, and by 1970, Elmer Lower, then president of ABC News, was convinced that what his shop most urgently needed was an anchorman who had what Lower called "box-office value." Accordingly, he commissioned an audience-research survey to find out how viewers across the country rated the big-name correspondents. As Lower had anticipated, the survey revealed that Cronkite was, far and away, America's favorite; he was surprised to discover, however, that ranking next to "Uncle Walter" in viewer preference was not NBC's David Brinkley or John Chancellor, or ABC's own senior anchorman, Howard K. Smith —but Harry Reasoner.

Neither Reasoner nor Mann was aware of this audience survey when they plotted their strategy. Hence, Mann was mildly startled by the enthusiastic reception accorded him when, in October 1970, he telephoned ABC and said that his client, Harry Reasoner, was looking for a job. Negotiations moved swiftly and smoothly, and a few days later, the ABC News people came up with an offer. They wanted Reasoner to co-anchor their evening news show with Howard K. Smith, and for that they were willing to give him a $1-million contract spread over five years—or $200,000 a year. Since this was far more than Reasoner had hoped, in his wildest dreams, to pry out of CBS, it did not take much prodding to get him to accept. Indeed, he spent the next few days practically wallowing in vindication.

Yet even in the midst of his elation, Reasoner was still puzzled and hurt by the way he had been treated by CBS. On the day he formally agreed to join ABC News, he purposely stayed away from the CBS Broadcast Center on West Fifty-seventh Street, where the news operation was located. Instead, he paid a visit to Jack Schneider's office in the corporate headquarters across town. Many of Reasoner's news-division colleagues regarded Schneider as a superficial, sales-oriented executive who was more interested in profits than in quality programming. But Reasoner had a warm relationship with the youthful president of the CBS Broadcast Group. ("Sure he's a slick operator," he once said in defense of Schneider, "but he's my kind of slick.") Schneider was visibly upset when he heard what Reasoner had done, and, professing to be unfamiliar with the details of the recent contract dispute, he asked to be filled in. Then, after listening to Reasoner's embittered version of the negotiations, Schneider shook his head and said, "Well, Harry, it sounds to me like we blew it."

Three days later, when Reasoner's move to ABC News was publicly announced, Walter Cronkite ended the *CBS Evening News* with these words: "My colleague, Harry Reasoner, is about to become my competitor. After a long and distinguished career here at CBS News, Harry is leaving to become co-anchorman of the *ABC Evening News.* We regret to see him go, and we wish him well—though not *too* well, of course." Reasoner, watching the broadcast at home, was quite touched. He and Cronkite had never been close, either socially or professionally, and he thought that, in bidding him farewell, Cronkite had struck just the right grace note. Reasoner was somewhat less touched, however, the following day when he learned that the send-off Cronkite read on the air had been written, in its entirety, by his good friend Charlie West.

Jack Schneider was right: CBS had blown it. The problem had not really been indifference (although that was how it looked to Reasoner) so much as arrogance. Salant and his fellow executives had been aware that Reasoner was unhappy and was dropping hints about negotiating with another network, but the evidence suggests that they did not take the threat seriously. They seemed to be confident that if push came to shove, Reasoner would not be able to bring himself to leave CBS News. It was an article of faith at CBS that except for rare and special cases, such as Murrow's decision to accept a challenging government post, correspondents of Harry Reasoner's stature were simply too immersed in the pride and tradition of CBS News to make the break. Having made the mistake of taking Reasoner for granted, Salant and his associates were stunned by his defection to ABC.

Below the management level, Reasoner's many friends among the working stiffs were outraged. But fortunately, for their psychic well-being, they had a plethora of villains on whom to vent their spleen.

Some focused their wrath on Gordon Manning; others, closer to the mark, blamed Bill Leonard for poisoning the well. A few choice epithets were also directed at Salant and his "absentee-landlord" style of leadership; had Salant been a journalist, it was said, he would have had a finer appreciation of Reasoner's talent. Still others shrewdly contended that the strings had been pulled from the corporate level, and in refusing to give Reasoner the raise he wanted, Salant and his budget people simply followed orders that had come down to them from On High. But on one point, all hands agreed: in letting a correspondent of Reasoner's ability and reputation slip away, CBS had done more to bolster the *ABC Evening News* than anything ABC had ever been able to do on its own.

The bolstering was long overdue. Since the dawn of television news two decades earlier, ABC had been the Harold Stassen of network journalism: not only a perennial loser, but a laughingstock to boot. Even when it hired good people and tried to use them effectively, nothing seemed to work. For example, in the 1950s, ABC's first television nightly news show had been anchored by another highly regarded CBS alumnus, John Daly. In Daly, ABC had an anchorman who, in terms of both experience and ability, had a lot more going for him than either Douglas Edwards or John Cameron Swayze. But he never caught on the way Edwards and Swayze did, in part because he drifted more and more away from news into the show-business side of television. (Viewers in the 1950s came to know Daly not so much as a journalist, but as the moderator of the enormously popular panel program *What's My Line?*) Daly's career as anchorman on the *ABC Evening News* came to an end in 1960, and over the next eight years no less than four correspondents passed through that slot. One of them was Swayze, in his last fling at journalism, and the other three were something less than household names: Ron Cochran, Peter Jennings, and Bob Young. In fairness, they all had to operate under a severe handicap, for during most of these years, the *ABC Evening News* remained locked into the fifteen-minute "compressed, tabloid" format of the 1950s. Even after the broadcast finally moved out of the dark ages in 1967, it was still in an almost hopeless position. For by then the great majority of viewers across the country had committed their allegiance to either Cronkite or Huntley-Brinkley.

In 1969, ABC made another major move to give its evening news show more weight and quality. Switching to a two-man anchor, it paired Howard K. Smith, who had been languishing in semiretirement, with

Frank Reynolds, who had impressed the ABC brass with his reporting from the Johnson White House. Smith and Reynolds were, without question, an improvement over the lackluster parade that preceded them, but they never really clicked as a team. The problem, basically, was that both men had an aggressive, even abrasive broadcasting style. But now, in 1970, by hiring Harry Reasoner to replace Reynolds, the ABC people felt they finally had the right guns in place, and they were ready to do battle.

Actually, Reasoner and Smith did not exactly jell as a team, either, but at least they presented an interesting contrast. Smith had adopted, over the years, the views and manner of a conservative curmudgeon, which meant that Reasoner once again had a "heavy" to play off of, and as an antidote to Smith's often bellicose commentaries, he brought to the broadcast his own special brand of wry. Reasoner was aware that his new employers were counting on him to lure millions of new viewers over to the *ABC Evening News,* and, his aversion to work notwithstanding, he made a diligent effort to justify that faith. The results were dramatically impressive.

In the weeks before Reasoner joined ABC, the comparative ratings of the nightly news shows were as follows: CBS was averaging a 31 percent share of the audience, NBC 28, and ABC a measly 15 percent. Less than three years later, in the spring of 1973, CBS and Cronkite had slipped to an average share of 27, NBC and John Chancellor to 25, while the Reasoner-Smith duo at ABC had shot up to 22. ABC was still third, but for the first time in the history of TV journalism, its evening news program had become competitive; indeed, there were some weeks when ABC and NBC practically ran a dead heat. What's more, these figures translated into millions of dollars: an increase of one share point over the course of a year was worth roughly $1 million in additional advertising revenue. So by 1973, exultant ABC executives were chortling that the $200,000 a year they were paying Reasoner was shaping up as one of the best bargains since Peter Minuit euchred Manhattan Island away from the Indians.

Reasoner had a clear appreciation of what he had accomplished, and he was looking forward to 1975 when his contract would expire, for he intended to hit ABC for a big raise. Nor was that all. No longer being number two was an improvement, but he was still just one of two, and so he also planned to propose, in the strongest possible terms, that Howard Smith be relegated to the secondary role of analyst, à la Sevareid, and that he be made sole anchorman on the *ABC Evening News.*

When he reported for work at ABC News in the late fall of 1970, Reasoner joined a contingent of former CBS News people who were already there. To begin with, there was Howard K. Smith himself. And beyond the new anchor team, many of the most important off-camera positions were occupied by CBS alumni, a group that included: Elmer Lower, president of the news division and the man who hired Reasoner; Av Westin, executive producer of the *ABC Evening News;* one of the show's other top producers, David Buksbaum; and the program's graphics artist, Ben Blank, whose innovative headline slides (or "light boxes," as they were sometimes called) opened the broadcast each night. Moreover, they were soon joined by still others. Such CBS News veterans as Ernie Leiser and Andy Rooney followed Reasoner over to ABC in the early 1970s, though they did not remain there. By the mid-1970s, Leiser, Rooney, and Buksbaum had returned to CBS.

Reasoner also kept in close touch with most of his other CBS friends and maintained many of his old social habits. One day, not long after Reasoner had gone over to ABC, Les Midgley sauntered into Le Biarritz and was confronted by a familiar sight: Reasoner seated at a large table surrounded by the entire editorial staff of the Cronkite show. As he glided past their table, Midgley made a sweeping gesture and said in a languourous voice, "You can have all of them, Harry."

Reasoner's sense of attachment to his former colleagues was so strong that there were even times when he used his end-piece slot on the *ABC Evening News* to extol their work. When Andy Rooney returned to CBS News in 1973, following his brief stint at ABC, it was to launch a new career. After more than two decades of writing award-winning scripts for others, he was being given a chance to go in front of the cameras himself and broadcast his own highly stylized "essays." For his first major venture as an on-air performer at CBS, Rooney put together an hour-long special called *In Praise of New York City,* and on the night the program was to be aired, Reasoner, acknowledging that he was committing an act of heresy, urged his ABC audience to switch over to CBS and watch the show. It was, no doubt, a measure of Reasoner's secure position that he was able to get away with such unorthodox behavior. He was, by then, in such good odor at ABC that his superiors were willing to indulge his periodic whims, even when they were directed against the network's own prime-time programming schedule.

On another occasion, when John Mosedale, another comrade from the *Calendar* years, wrote and published a book on the 1927 New York Yankees, Reasoner gave it a plug on the *ABC Evening News*. But his most poignant on-air tribute to a member of the old gang came in the late summer of 1974, when John Merriman was killed in a plane crash. After describing Merriman as "the editor and in many ways the conscience of the *CBS Evening News*," Reasoner went on to tell his ABC viewers:

> Even at his death I have to remember him with smiles, because we always had a couple of language projects going that made us laugh. We kept track of journalistic clichés. He would call me and say: "The wires say that a giant pall has settled over Washington. Did you fellows get pictures? Oh well, I suppose under the pall it was too dark for pictures." Or he would call back and say: "Do you suppose that's the same giant pall that covered Paris when de Gaulle died?" We'll miss those calls, and the trouble is more sloppy writing may go unnoticed in this craft without John around.
>
> John was fifty, too young to die, especially when you like good food and good language and good sports as much as he did. . . . He had only one fault in my view—an inexplicable fondness for horse racing. Nobody's perfect.
>
> I have tried to be very careful in writing this piece, because I have the strong feeling that if some sloppy cliché crept in, John would know about it, wherever he is, and he would object strongly. Just the same, his friends do feel there is a sort of giant pall over the day.

There were many other words and deeds no less indicative of the affection that continued to bind Reasoner to his former colleagues. In some respects, it was as if he had never left CBS at all.

16 Marathon Man

Harry Reasoner had worn so many top hats at CBS News that even before he had a chance to clean out his desk, in the fall of 1970, a concerted move was under way to pick his various successors. One of the hats—the anchor slot on the Sunday night news show—was bestowed on Dan Rather. As with Roger Mudd, who spent the week in Washington reporting from Capitol Hill and then flew up to New York on Saturday to anchor his weekend broadcast, Rather's new assignment would not interfere with his regular White House beat, which, by 1970, was rapidly becoming a focal point of controversy. Having honed his reportorial skills during the turbulent years of Lyndon Johnson's Presidency, Rather was now bringing a great deal of muscle and insight to his coverage of Richard Nixon's White House. This did not exactly endear him to Nixon and his disciples, but Rather's CBS superiors appreciated his work, and the Sunday anchor job was his reward.

Moving up to the anchorman level also put Rather on the road toward big money. The immediate salary hike was not all that substantial: an increase from $43,000 to $49,000 with escalation clauses calling for modest raises each succeeding year. But the sharp rise in status that the anchorman assignment helped bring about was such that four years later, when the time came to negotiate a new contract, Rather's income soared to over $100,000 a year.

The question of who should succeed Reasoner on *60 Minutes* was not so easily resolved. A chief strength of that program had been the chemistry in the Reasoner-Wallace relationship—a kind of cheerful antagonism that produced an oddly appealing tension. The decision was

242

primarily up to Don Hewitt and Bill Leonard, with Dick Salant having final approval, and all three men agreed that the correspondent whose style and varied background most closely resembled Reasoner's was Charlie Kuralt. Like Reasoner, Kuralt had paid his dues as a hard-news reporter; and he had also demonstrated, in his *On the Road* pieces, a fine touch for softer feature material. But despite the importunings of Hewitt, Leonard, and Salant, Kuralt said he wasn't interested. He had just embarked on his fourth year of doing *On the Road* stories, and his devotion to that assignment was, if anything, stronger than ever. As far as Kuralt was concerned, he had the best, if not the most lucrative, job in television news. Moreover, he was vigorously supported in his preference by Gordon Manning, who felt that the *CBS Evening News,* which was under *his* jurisdiction, could ill afford to lose Kuralt's *On the Road* series. So Hewitt and Leonard considered other candidates, and after numerous discussions, a call was put through to Morley Safer in London.

On the surface, Safer seemed to be an unlikely choice. His reporting from Vietnam had stamped him as a hard-hitter, very much in the Mike Wallace style, and there were many who believed that, in pairing Safer with Wallace, *60 Minutes* would lose the delicate balance in tone that Reasoner and Wallace had achieved. Hewitt took a different view. He had noticed that since Safer had been working out of London, he had become more polished, almost urbane, in his on-camera persona, a subtle transformation Hewitt correctly attributed to the not-so-subtle influence of Charles Collingwood. For all his preoccupation with visual technique, Hewitt was also a perceptive judge of writing talent, and he had felt for some time that all the furor caused by Safer's aggressive reporting from Vietnam had obscured the fact that he was a first-rate writer.

Hewitt was right on both counts. When, in the late fall of 1970, Safer arrived in New York to commence his new career, there were, in some of his Britishisms, traces of Collingwood's elegant manner, and a few members of the *60 Minutes* staff were put off a bit. Some of the secretaries used to snicker at the fussbudgety way he insisted on having his tea every afternoon at four o'clock. But the on-air effect was quite positive. Safer quickly demonstrated that he could handle the diversified format of *60 Minutes* as effectively as he had covered the war in Vietnam. And his writing ability proved to be a valuable asset to the show. What's more, now that Wallace no longer had to play the foil to Reasoner, he adopted a more versatile style. On stories that did not lend themselves to his customary truculence, he relaxed and allowed the more genial side of his nature to surface. The new combination worked well. Hewitt was so pleased that, by the fall of 1971, when *60 Minutes* was moved into a new Sunday evening time slot, he was even contending that Morley Safer was a better writer than Reasoner. That smacked of fulsome praise indeed, especially to those who remembered how often Hewitt had proclaimed, in years past, that of all the correspondents at all the networks, Harry Reasoner had no peer as a writer.

In divvying up all the territory Reasoner had vacated, the most valuable piece of turf, in terms of strategic position for the future, was the backup role on the *CBS Evening News*. At the time, there seemed little doubt as to who would get that assignment. The sense of certainty was, in fact, so pervasive that in the days following the announcement of Reasoner's departure, total strangers came up to Roger Mudd and congratulated him on his good fortune. For with Reasoner out of the way, just about everyone, both within and without the industry, assumed that Mudd would be given the job that, by definition, would put him in line to become Walter Cronkite's eventual successor. It was a measure of how far Mudd had come in the nine years he had worked at CBS News.

Yet those who knew Mudd well were aware that he was more than a little ambivalent about his profession and the *kind* of success it had brought him. For unlike most of his colleagues, he had not gone into journalism with the intention of making it his life's work. His first job as a reporter was supposed to have been a way station en route to his real goal: a Ph.D. in American history and, after that, a career as a scholar. It was understandable that Roger Mudd would have been drawn to the subject of history, if only because his own family tree was so deeply rooted in the struggles and passions of America's past.

Mudd's paternal ancestors were among the group of seventeenth-century English Catholics who, having failed to cultivate a martyr's taste for persecution, had followed their coreligionist, Lord Baltimore, to his New World colony of Maryland, where "popery" was at least tolerated, if not encouraged. One of the descendants of those original settlers was Samuel Mudd, the doctor who treated John Wilkes Booth's broken leg following his escape from Ford's Theater. For his ministrations, Dr. Mudd was vilified and imprisoned on trumped-up charges that he had been a coconspirator in the plot to assassinate Lincoln.

(More than a century later, his grandson and other members of the Mudd clan were still seeking redress, through legal action and other means.) Roger Mudd was a collateral rather than direct descendant of the unfortunate Dr. Mudd, but whenever he was asked about the familial connection, he invariably pointed out that "all the Maryland Mudds were related in one way or another."

Mudd was born and raised in Washington, where his father worked for the federal government as a cartographer. His name was John Dominic Kostka Mudd, and he signed all his maps "K. Mudd." In later years, when his son was working as a reporter, he sometimes ran into map buffs who would ask him if he was related to K. Mudd. On those occasions, he did not have to shake the whole family tree, as he sometimes felt obliged to do when pressed to elaborate on his link with the doctor who aided John Wilkes Booth. To all queries about K. Mudd, he could simply reply, "Yes, he's my father."

The first college Mudd attended was Washington and Lee, where, in addition to majoring in history, he acted in campus productions and lettered in rowing. Then, following his graduation in 1950, he went to the University of North Carolina and began work on his master's. Having grown up in Washington during the New Deal era, he felt an affinity to that subject, and, in particular, he was fascinated by the role certain intellectuals—the celebrated "Brain Trust"—had played in those early Roosevelt years. For his master's thesis, he concentrated on the basically hostile press reaction to the influence of FDR's Brain Trust. Ideally, the next step would have been Yale and work toward his Ph.D. Mudd was attracted to Yale because a history professor there, Ralph Henry Gabriel, was a renowned authority on the Roosevelt years, and he wanted to study under him. But unfortunately, he had run out of money.

In an effort to build up a nest egg, Mudd taught for a year at a private boys' school in Georgia, then spent another year working as a research assistant on Capitol Hill, that being his first, superficial exposure to the inner workings of Congress. He still had his sights set on Yale, but he had not been able to save as much as he had hoped, and he was growing more and more restless. Then one day it dawned on him: since it was his intention, in his Ph.D. work, to delve more deeply into the adversary relationship between the press and government, he could do himself a favor by using this interlude to engage in a little empirical research. Borrowing his father's car, he drove around Virginia looking for a newspaper job and eventually found one at the *Richmond News Leader*. A few months later, he switched over to the paper's radio station, WRNL. Mudd's favorite professor at Washington and Lee had once told him that with his strong, assertive voice, he was a "natural" for radio. Now, three years later, Mudd was determined to prove that his old professor was right.

He enjoyed working at WRNL a lot more than he thought he would, and, as time went on, the Ph.D. dream began to fade. Finally, yet still with some reluctance, Mudd gave it up altogether and reconciled himself to the fact that he had wandered, inadvertently, into a career in journalism. That being the case, he decided to seek a larger challenge, beyond Richmond. Accordingly, he began applying for jobs in Washington, and in 1956 he was hired by the CBS affiliate there, WTOP—the same station where, six years earlier, a new employee named Walter Cronkite had impressed his superiors with his chalk talks on the Korean War.

Mudd worked at WTOP over the next five years, and by 1961 he was the station's top reporter. Among those who had been observing his work with growing admiration was Howard K. Smith, then Washington bureau chief for CBS News as well as the network's premier Washington correspondent. By the spring of 1961, Smith had seen enough of Mudd to conclude that the time had come to have a talk with WTOP's talented young reporter. An interview was arranged, and soon thereafter, Roger Mudd went to work in the Washington bureau of CBS News.

One of his first assignments at the network was a history major's delight. In July 1961, a Civil War centennial group staged a reenactment of the First Battle of Bull Run, in which the Federal troops were routed, and Mudd was sent to the Virginia site near Washington to cover it. Surrounded by the sights and sounds of battle, 1861 vintage, he captured the spirit of the occasion and concluded his report with these words: "This is Roger Mudd of CBS News in full retreat toward Washington."

Mudd continued to bring this kind of aplomb to his assignments, including his coverage of Congress, which became his regular beat in 1962. He had spent a great deal of time on Capitol Hill during his years at WTOP, and therefore was no stranger to the stately rituals and labyrinthine procedures of the House and Senate. Still, there were times when the solid self-assurance he displayed on the air was deceptive. In the late summer of 1963, Martin Luther King and an estimated 200,000 other Americans—black and white—converged on Washington to bear witness to the need for new civil rights legislation. Several CBS News reporters were assigned to cover various aspects of the demonstration, but as the network's Congressional correspondent, Mudd was picked to anchor the live coverage of the story. It was an important and dramatic event—the biggest assignment of Mudd's career up to that time—and on the day of the huge rally, he was so tense with anxiety that at one point he secluded himself behind some boxwood trees near the Lincoln Memorial and threw up.

But there was no sign of agitation in his reporting that day. When the rally ended, he coolly noted that despite the upbeat mood of the demonstrators, their demands were not likely to be approved by Congress because the necessary votes simply were not there. What Mudd could not envision that August evening was that John Kennedy's assassination a few weeks later would give renewed and, as it turned out, decisive impetus to the civil rights legislation he had proposed. Nor did Mudd have any way of knowing that when the fight over passage of the 1964 civil rights bill entered its critical phase several months hence, he, in an odd way, would be a principal beneficiary of that legislative struggle.

It was Fred Friendly who came up with the idea that was destined to have such a profound impact on Roger Mudd's career. By March 1964, the most comprehensive civil rights bill since Reconstruction had been passed by the House and was ready to go to the floor of the Senate for debate and an eventual vote. In an effort to thwart passage of the bill, its Southern opponents had marshaled their forces for a filibuster that was almost certain to last several weeks, perhaps even months. In contemplating that prospect, Friendly, who had just taken over as president of the news division, had one of his more ingenious brainstorms. He wanted Mudd to provide saturation coverage of the Senate debate, an assignment that would put him on every major CBS News radio and television broadcast every day as long as the filibuster lasted. Mudd's initial reaction to the proposal was negative; to him, it sounded like a "stunt," comparable to flagpole-sitting. Nevertheless, there were compelling factors that he could not afford to overlook. For one thing, given the network's fee system—extra money for each on-air report—his salary would skyrocket during the period of the debate. And in terms of his future, the constant exposure could be worth far more.

The Senate debate began in late March and lasted until the middle of June. During that time, Mudd broadcast an average of five television and seven radio reports a day. By the time cloture was finally imposed and the bill was passed, he had delivered 867 reports on the debate. What's more, the daily scramble for fresh angles to justify all those updates had forced him to probe more deeply into the *modus operandi* of the Senate than he ever had before, and he came away from the experience with a less romantic view of that august institution. He learned a great deal about human vanity during this period, for even some of the most respected members of the Senate sought him out to be interviewed or favorably mentioned in his reports. He also discovered how ill-informed most of the senators were on the issues, and how much they relied on their staffs to do their homework for them.

Mudd's marathon performance that spring was, without question, the dramatic turning point in his career. Prior to 1964, he was obscurely perceived as just one of many young television correspondents who reported out of Washington. But the "stunt" Friendly dreamed up made a strong impression on viewers and critics alike. Several articles were written about the "Iron Man of the Airwaves," as Mudd was described in one of them. Since television cameras were not allowed inside the Senate chamber, Mudd broadcast all his reports from the steps of the Capitol, and in the early weeks of the debate, when the weather was inclement, he was usually seen peering out from beneath an umbrella. He soon began receiving hundreds of letters from viewers, many of whom expressed concern about the effect all that exposure to the elements might have on his health. The tone of some of the letters was quite indifferent to the civil rights debate itself, but God forbid that Roger Mudd should catch a cold. He had become a star. But there is such a thing as pushing a new star *too* fast—and that was the mistake CBS now made with Mudd.

It was a period of turmoil at CBS News, the year when Bill Paley was wielding the ax in his effort to shake the news division out of its second-place rut. And after NBC scored another big victory over CBS at the Republican convention that summer, it was Paley who proposed Bob Trout and Roger Mudd as an anchor team to replace Cronkite at the Democratic convention. Mudd was summoned to New York, where he was told of the new arrangement. It was a high honor for a correspondent of his age (thirty-six) who had been with the network only three years, and Mudd appreciated that. But he was also apprehensive. He thought the move smacked of panic, and he had the uneasy feeling that he and Trout were being thrown into a desperate situation.

He was right, of course. The chief effect of the Mudd-Trout experiment was to reinforce Cronkite's position at CBS News. For Trout, such an opportunity would never come again. The 1964 co-anchorman assignment represented his last hope of becoming the kind of headliner in network television that he had been in radio. Trout did keep his hand in for a while longer, but by the late 1960s he was living in semiretirement in Spain. Thus, his last years at CBS were spent in almost total eclipse, a rather melancholy fade-out for the man who had once tutored Ed Murrow and had helped shape the early standards of broadcast journalism.

Nor did Mudd emerge from the affair entirely unscathed. He returned to the ranks of supporting players with the distinct feeling that some of Cronkite's New York loyalists were taking their revenge out on him, as if *he* had been to blame for what had happened. Mudd sensed that he was being put on short rations, that some of his stories from Capitol Hill were being passed over by Cronkite's *Evening News* staff for the precise purpose of limiting his exposure, thereby teaching him a lesson. It was another advance in the continuing education of Roger Mudd, an experience that left him wary of the CBS News management and the Machiavellian power games played in New York.

Mudd was eventually able to work his way back into good favor. He knew for certain that his period of penance was over when, in the fall of 1965, Gordon Manning came to him with another tempting proposal. Manning had been given permission to expand the *CBS Evening News* to six days a week, and he wanted Mudd to anchor the new Saturday night broadcast. This time, Mudd's reaction was all positive. He readily welcomed a chance to anchor a major, regularly scheduled television show, a privilege then enjoyed by only three CBS News correspondents: Cronkite, Mike Wallace on the *Morning News,* and Harry Reasoner on his Sunday night broadcast.

Having sewed up Mudd, Manning turned his attention to the question of who should produce the new program. Mudd recommended Washington producer Bill Crawford; like most of the correspondents in the Washington bureau, he placed a very high value on Crawford's ability. Indeed, among producers at CBS News during the 1960s, Crawford was something of a cult figure in Washington in much the same way that the flamboyant Stanhope Gould was in New York. But there were certain circumstances involving Crawford's background that, from Gordon Manning's point of view, made him an unacceptable choice.

He was the son of the distinguished journalist Kenneth Crawford, who had written the "TRB" column in *The New Republic* in the 1940s and, in more recent years, had been a columnist for *Newsweek*. With his jet-black hair, his sharp features, and his trim, Faulknerian mustache, Bill Crawford bore a strong resemblance to his father. He also inherited much of Ken Crawford's intellectual prowess—as well as some of his arrogance.

Joining CBS in 1954, Crawford received his early training in television news in New York as a writer on the old Doug Edwards show, and by the late 1950s, he had moved up to a middle-level management position. These were the last years of Sig Mickelson's tenure as president of CBS News. It ended with the 1960 convention disaster, when NBC and Huntley-Brinkley dumped all over CBS, and the subsequent purge of Mickelson and his deputies. By the time all the smoke had cleared, there were only two members of the Mickelson management team who had survived: Crawford and Ralph Paskman, who by then was in overall charge of the Assignment Desk. During the last few months of Mickelson's reign and the early weeks of Dick Salant's first term as president, Crawford and Paskman were the field commanders of the entire CBS News television operation. Since Crawford was only thirty-two, eight years younger than Paskman, some of his friends started to speculate on how long it would be before he took over as president of the news division. But Bill Crawford was riding a roller coaster that, having reached its crest, was about to plunge in the other direction.

His troubles began in the summer of 1961 when Ernie Leiser was appointed assistant general manager of CBS News. Leiser set out, through asperity and intimidation, to bring everyone under his command to heel, but Crawford refused to cower. He did not hesitate to let Leiser know how much he resented his overbearing methods, even telling him at one point that "ruling by fear is no way to cover up your own shortcomings." For his part, Leiser felt that Crawford was not only scandalously lacking in obeisance, but also that his work left much to be desired. Having lost his management position in the shuffle that had put Leiser in charge of TV news, Crawford was now producing a Saturday afternoon show and various specials. Unfortunately, he bungled a couple of assignments, and that gave Leiser all the ammunition he needed. He proceeded to harass Crawford with taunts and threats of dismissal until finally, in 1963, he shipped him off to Washington, a transfer Crawford welcomed if only because it put some distance between himself and Leiser. And no one was more amused than Crawford when, one year later, Leiser fled his executive post to get away from the verbal abuse Fred Friendly was inflicting on *him*. Those who live by the sword . . .

In Washington, Crawford had no trouble salvaging his career. The Washington bureau was sorely in need of good producers, and Crawford, whatever his failings in New York, had both talent and a solid background in television news, still a rare combination in the early 1960s. Beyond that, he had studied at the feet of "the Maestro," as he was fond of describing Don Hewitt, and thus was able to pass on valuable tips to new correspondents who were in the process of learning the CBS system of television reporting. That, more than anything else, was what endeared him to Roger Mudd, Dan Rather, and other members of the Bill Crawford fan club.

But Washington was not New York, where Leiser's influence was still very strong. He continued to regard Crawford as arrogant and intractable, an opinion he passed on to Gordon Manning when he took over as hard-news vice-president in late 1964. That was all Manning needed to hear, for in truth, he had his own reasons for being leery of Crawford.

For the most part, Manning's three-year record as executive editor of *Newsweek* (1961–64) had been commendable, but toward the end of his stay there, things began to go sour. He had a mania for writing memos to propose story ideas so obvious that they were insulting. In addition, his zealous pep talks and the seemingly capricious way he played favorites antagonized some of his subordinate editors, and by 1964 they were openly complaining about his methods. That was one reason—perhaps the main reason—why he jumped at the chance to go to CBS. Understandably, Manning wanted his new CBS colleagues to know as little as possible about his problems at *Newsweek,* and the son of *Newsweek*'s veteran columnist Ken Crawford was apt to be familiar with those problems. Therefore, he was not someone Manning cared to promote to an important new post in New York, where all the gossip lines fed directly into the CBS power structure—and Leiser's low estimation of Crawford gave him just the excuse he needed.

With Crawford eliminated from consideration, the most likely candidate to produce the new Saturday version of the *Evening News* became Hal Haley, who had a kind of territorial claim to the job. Since 1963, Haley had been producing Harry Reasoner's Sunday night broadcast and a more modest Saturday afternoon news show that had been anchored by a number of correspondents over the years. Like Crawford, Haley joined CBS in 1954 and served the usual apprenticeship, writing for various news programs, both radio and television. And among those who admired Haley's work was none other than Ernie Leiser, who once commented that Haley's news judgment was almost as good as his own, the highest possible praise anyone could hope to receive from Leiser. It was Leiser, in fact, who made Haley a producer and put him in charge of the weekend news broadcasts.

Gordon Manning, however, was not all that sold on Haley. He thought the weekend shows were competent but pedestrian. He was also influenced by office scuttlebutt that portrayed Haley as being too nice a guy, someone whose amiable disposition resulted in his running a lax ship. That was a canard. Haley, it's true, did have a friendly, outgoing nature, but it did not extend to the toleration of slipshod work. Nevertheless, Manning was not convinced of that and finally decided on a compromise arrangement: Haley would stay on as producer of Reasoner's Sunday broadcast, but would lose his Saturday assignment now that the afternoon program was to be replaced by the far more ambitious evening show. And for the job of producing that, Manning reached into the bowels of the *Morning News* operation and came up with associate producer Paul Greenberg.

The choice was so unlikely that it bordered on the bizarre. Greenberg had been with the network only a year, after having been fired at ABC, not exactly a recommendation to inspire confidence. Furthermore, except for his co-workers on the *Morning News*, hardly anyone at CBS knew him or anything about him. But from Manning's point of view, the fact that Greenberg was new to the network and had not built up powerful associations and loyalties within the shop was not a liability at all. Manning had large plans for the new Saturday edition of the *CBS Evening News,* and he was determined to wield direct personal control over its development. It suited his purpose, therefore, to have the show produced by someone who was exclusively his man. Manning could also take comfort in the fact that Greenberg had no familial connection with the *Newsweek* phase of his career, as Crawford did. Nor did he have Haley's alleged weakness for excessive civility. For although Paul Greenberg had certain personality defects, no one ever accused him, then or later, of being too nice a guy.

A native New Yorker, Greenberg was the son of a doctor and a nephew of the eminent criminal lawyer Emile Zola Berman. But he had no desire to follow in either of those footsteps. Instead, he took an early interest in journalism, and, after graduating from the University of Michigan, he began his professional career at a small station in Pittsburgh, WIIC, working there from 1957 until 1961, when he landed a job in New York at ABC News. One of Greenberg's first assignments at ABC was to produce Howard Cosell's radio show, an experience that provided him with a rich treasury of Cosell stories that he relished telling in later years, mimicking Cosell's bombastic style with malicious accuracy.

After a few months on radio, Greenberg switched over to television, where he worked on everything from documentaries to local news programs, and at the end of two years, he had established himself as one of the best young producers at ABC News. Then, in the fall of 1963, he became embroiled in a quarrel with his superior, Jesse Zousmer, that was so bitter, so destructive, that it put him squarely on the road toward eventual dismissal. Zousmer had just recently joined ABC News, bringing with him an impressive set of credentials from his many years at CBS. He had been Ed Murrow's chief radio writer in the 1940s and later was coproducer of Murrow's highly successful television show, *Person to Person*. That background gave Zousmer a reservoir of strength that Greenberg, his subordinate and a relative newcomer to network journalism, could not match when the two men turned on each other in November 1963.

Their clash grew out of a monumental blunder, the kind of snafu that only served to underscore ABC's reputation as a feckless news organization. Two days after the Kennedy assassination, Greenberg, working in Dallas as a field producer, was in charge of the two camera crews assigned to cover the transfer of Lee Harvey Oswald from the city jail to the more secure county prison. He had his remote trucks staked out at both sites, but shortly before the transfer was to take place, he received a call from Zousmer demanding that one of the camera crews cover a church service. Greenberg did not want to relinquish either of his trucks, but since Zousmer was his boss, he had no real choice in the matter. So he released the crew assigned to the city jail, figuring he could pick up coverage of the story when Oswald arrived at the county prison. Of course, Lee Harvey Oswald never completed that journey. Jack Ruby greeted him in the basement of the Dallas city jail with a fatal bullet through the stomach, an encounter that NBC broadcast live, and that CBS, its cameras also having recorded the scene, presented to its viewers on videotape a few moments later. Thus, throughout that long day of continuous coverage, as NBC and CBS aired periodic "replays" of Oswald's murder, ABC had to make do with nonfilm accounts of the story.

During the inevitable postmortems, Zousmer and Greenberg blamed each other for the foul-up, and the exchange of accusations and insults became downright brutal. From that point on, the two men were avowed enemies. In particular, Greenberg, whose disdainful attitude toward certain colleagues and superiors would later cause him trouble at CBS, made no secret of his contempt for Jesse Zousmer. Zousmer put up with Greenberg's insolence for about a year while he steadily strengthened his own position at ABC News, and then, in the fall of 1964, summarily fired him. A few weeks later, Greenberg, licking his wounds, found refuge at CBS as a writer on Mike Wallace's *Morning News* show.

Paul Greenberg had a high regard for his ability as a writer, but that opinion was not shared by some of his new co-workers on the *CBS Morning News,* nor were they shy about letting him know how they felt. On one occasion, when he was away from his desk, a note was taped on his typewriter that read: "This machine writes only clichés." Greenberg's real talent, as well as the bulk of his experience, lay in production, working with film, and thus his value to the *Morning News* rose considerably after he became one of the show's associate producers in the spring of 1965. But the overnight hours—"the lobster trick," as it's known in the trade—were killing him, and after working on the *Morning News* for a year, Greenberg went to Gordon Manning and requested another assignment. He seemed to imply that if his request were not granted, he couldn't stay on at CBS News—at least that's how it sounded to Manning.

"Don't try and threaten me!" Manning scolded.

Greenberg, exasperated, responded in kind: "Goddamnit, Gordon,

I'm not trying to threaten you. I just can't live with these hours any-more. I'm not asking for a promotion. I'll take anything, the worst job you've got, as long as it's in the daytime and I can sleep at night."

On leaving Manning's office, Greenberg berated himself for having lost his temper. He hoped that he hadn't talked his way onto another shit list, for the last thing he needed was the kind of trouble that had plagued him at ABC. In point of fact, the opposite was the case. Man-ning had already taken appreciative notice of Greenberg's work on the *Morning News,* and now, quickly recovering from his initial reaction of annoyance, he decided he rather liked the fire and spunk in Green-berg's manner. The more Manning thought about Greenberg, the more his name suggested itself as a suitable alternative to Bill Crawford or Hal Haley. As a result, the "anything" Greenberg was willing to settle for turned out to be producer of the new Saturday broadcast.

He wound up his tour of duty on the *Morning News* on a note of macabre irony. In January 1966, his former *bête noire,* Jesse Zousmer, was killed in a plane crash, and Greenberg was assigned to put together his film obituary. It was, in a way, an act of exorcism, a cathartic release from his past, and a few days later he began his new career as producer of the *CBS Evening News with Roger Mudd.*

Just about everyone at CBS News was surprised by Manning's deci-sion to entrust the new Saturday show to a comparative newcomer and unknown. But because the expansion of the *Evening News* to six nights a week was in itself viewed as a minor development, a token advance, it hardly seemed to matter much who produced the Saturday program. At the time, no one could foresee how powerful the Manning-Green-berg alliance was to become in the years ahead. With Manning serving as his godfather, promoting his cause at every turn, Greenberg would quickly build his modest weekend base into an empire, and go on from there to become, in 1972, executive producer of the Cronkite show. As for Manning, by using Greenberg as his principal instrument, he would realize his long-frustrated goal of exerting personal influence over that broadcast, the flagship in his hard-news flotilla.

17 Weekend Update

The most urgent task that confronted Greenberg in his new assignment as producer of the Saturday show was winning the allegiance of Roger Mudd. Mudd was stunned by Manning's decision. He scarcely knew Greenberg, and he had no idea whether he was any good or not. Once again, he was struck by the dubious logic that seemed to govern the actions of the CBS management in New York, and he was starting to have second thoughts about his own commitment to the new broadcast.

Mudd made a special trip to New York to discuss the situation with Manning. After the meeting, Greenberg offered to drive him to the airport for his shuttle flight back to Washington. It would give them a chance, he said, to thrash things out in private. On the ride out to LaGuardia, Mudd told Greenberg that his personal choice for the job had been Bill Crawford, and that he frankly had reservations about Manning's decision. Greenberg, who knew how to turn on the charm when it suited his purpose, chuckled and said he wasn't sure Manning himself knew what he was doing. The ice broken, the two men began to talk about the new show. Because they couldn't expect the kind of news flow on Saturday that the Cronkite people were accustomed to dealing with, Greenberg proposed structuring the program to meet that reality. By making an aggressive effort to build the Saturday show around long features on sports and other back-of-the-book subjects, they could give the broadcast its own special tone and identity. Mudd heartily approved of that "casual approach," as he called it, even though he had a reputation for being a stickler for hard news. By the time they reached the airport, they were chattering away in cordial agreement, and on his flight back to Washington, Mudd was in a much better frame of mind. That initial conversation, in fact, formed the basis of his future relationship with Greenberg. Preoccupied for the most part with his daily duties in Washington as Capitol Hill correspondent, Mudd gave Greenberg free rein to develop the Saturday news along the lines they had discussed, and over the years he became, next to Manning, Paul Greenberg's biggest booster.

Right from the start, Greenberg believed that the new show should have a regular sports feature. For one thing, he himself was a sports nut, but beyond that, he felt that sports, an area the networks generally ignored in their evening news broadcasts, was a natural for a Saturday night program. At the same time, he wanted something different and offbeat, a clear departure from the bland cheerleading of most television sports coverage. He discussed the idea with Manning, who said he doubted that any of the correspondents currently on the CBS News payroll had the qualities Greenberg was looking for. Manning proposed that they go outside the company—to a friend of his named Heywood Hale Broun.

"Woody" Broun was then, in 1966, a forty-seven-year-old actor whose career was going nowhere. As a young man, he had set out in pursuit of what he conceived to be his genetic destiny, and had worked as a sportswriter on *PM* and other newspapers. But the constricting pressure of being the son of the great Heywood Broun was too much for him. He quit journalism in 1949, and over the next seventeen years, a period marked by generous stretches of unemployment, Broun acted in a number of marginal roles—heavies, best friends, attendant lords, and the like—in sundry plays and films of modest repute. He also had a mordant way of complaining to friends that people talked too much about the Oedipus complex and didn't give enough attention to the Laertes complex: the Odyssean burden of having to live up to a legendary father. And among those who sympathized with Broun's situation was Gordon Manning. He and Broun belonged to the same private club, the Coffee House, and they often had lunch together. Manning had a hunch that Broun's dual experience as a sportswriter and actor could be put to positive use on television, so he urged his friend to audition for the new sports reporter's job on the Saturday news. More or less as a lark, Broun decided to take Manning up on his offer.

Woody Broun passed the audition and was a featured player on the maiden broadcast of the Saturday night news in February 1966. For his debut as a TV journalist, he eschewed the seasonal headline sports, basketball and hockey, and reported instead on a dog show at Madison Square Garden. In the months and years ahead, viewers would become accustomed to such deviations. For although Broun thoroughly covered baseball, football, and the other conventional sports, he was usually at his best reporting on such quirky pastimes as ice fishing, wrist wrestling, Indian rodeos, crawfish racing, and the Italian game of boccie.

Broun also brought to his "sports essays," as he labeled them, a literacy and erudition rarely seen in sports journalism outside the columns of Red Smith. He once dismissed an event as having about as much appeal as "an Ibsen festival in Las Vegas." And his report on one of the Super Bowls was adorned by allusions to Charles Dickens, George Meredith, and Alexandre Dumas *père*. Some critics charged that Broun overdid it, that his ornate, metaphor-laden style was too rich, especially for the thin blood of television. (Roger Mudd once likened Broun's pieces to baked Alaska: "delicious but, at times, a little too filling.") Still, his idiosyncratic essays, enhanced somewhat by the gaudy, multicolored sport coats he wore on the air, attracted a large and devoted following over the years, and they clearly helped to give the Saturday show what Paul Greenberg wanted: a tone and identity all its own.

In the meantime, the legend of Heywood Broun *père* continued to shadow his son. One day in 1971, a fan came up to him and effusively predicted that at the rate he was going, he would soon be as famous as his father. Broun's ample, drooping mustache seemed to sag even more than usual as he rather curtly replied, "Thank you, sir, but I hope you realize that when my father was my age, he had been dead two years."

Broun's sports reports were merely the first step. As time went on, Greenberg began flooding the Saturday broadcast with features on other back-of-the-book subjects, from country music to California wine. By the late 1960s, the show had become a regular outlet for Hughes Rudd's cranky studies of human foibles as he traveled the back roads in search of the warts on Charlie Kuralt's sunny landscape. Greenberg also made effective use of other correspondents, such as David Culhane and Bill Plante, who had demonstrated a flair for the kind of offbeat stories he wanted. Thus the Saturday edition of the *CBS Evening News* gradually established its casual format. By 1970, there were some occasions when over half the program—in terms of air time—was devoted to features that had nothing to do with the news of the day.

Greenberg could have gone in another direction. He could have built the show around hard-news features that dealt primarily with "important," front-of-the-book subjects. He chose not to, however, largely because he felt weekend viewers deserved a respite from all the stark-reality stuff. The danger was that light features, lacking the timely appeal of hard news to sustain them, required more than routine skill in the cutting and shaping process. Fortunately, that was Paul Greenberg's strength. Like Don Hewitt and Russ Bensley, he was a child of television, and, like them, he had an unusually fine touch for film, for blending picture and narration to maximum effect.

Greenberg was also able to sweet-talk Manning into giving him a budget to hire associate producers, which was a big help. For example, much of the credit for the success of Broun's weekly sports reports belonged to his field producer, Bud Lamoreaux. When Broun went to work for CBS, he didn't know a thing about television production; nor was it a subject that aroused his intellectual curiosity. Hence, he relied entirely on Lamoreaux to handle that end, to orchestrate the coverage and see to it that the pictures harmonized with the narration—not an easy task when dealing with Broun's self-indulgent flourishes. "We work together like a good double-play combination," Broun once said, "except that Bud is the one who has to execute the difficult pivots. All I do is flip the ball to him."

Lamoreaux was a graduate of the CBS mail room, where he had started his career in 1958. Eight years later, he was working as a sports-writer in the syndication department, a dreary backwater operation, when Greenberg picked him for the job of Broun's field producer. For more than a year, Lamoreaux was Greenberg's only extra hand, and he worked exclusively on Broun's sports pieces. Then, in the fall of 1967, Greenberg received permission to take on another associate producer, and this time he hired a young woman named Joan Snyder.

Snyder was yet another refugee from the United Press, or UPI as it had become by her day. It was her particular misfortune, however, to have been condemned, at a tender age, to the UPI bureau in Newark, a baptism of squalor that she likened to incarceration on Devil's Island. Compared to that, writing for Mike Wallace on the *CBS Morning News* was bliss, which is what she was doing in 1964 when Paul Greenberg joined the show. Snyder was, in fact, one of the pranksters who had taped the note about his addiction to clichés on Greenberg's typewriter.

Nevertheless, Greenberg had a high estimation of her ability, and three years later he made her the second field producer on the Saturday news team. It proved to be an excellent choice. Joan Snyder shared Greenberg's enthusiasm for back-of-the-book subjects, and she was adept at developing them into film stories. Her particular passion was country music, and at one point, during the early 1970s, she practically commuted from Nashville, the scene of some of her best work.

Other associate producers followed; the big expansion occurring in 1970 when the *CBS Evening News* was extended to seven nights a week, with Mudd anchoring and Greenberg producing both the Saturday and Sunday editions. Greenberg was upgraded to executive producer, and with his increased budget he quickly put together a staff of field producers worthy of comparison with the one Russ Bensley had assembled on the Cronkite show. But his first two recruits, Bud Lamoreaux and Joan Snyder, continued to set the pace, and the newer members of the team soon discovered how difficult it was to measure up to their level of achievement.

They were also discovering how difficult it was to work for Paul Greenberg. A brooding, complicated man with a mercurial temperament, Greenberg played favorites, nursed grudges, and initiated bitter quarrels. He had a gift for obscene invective that most Marine drill instructors would have been hard-pressed to match, and in bringing to task people who worked for him, he often resorted to harsh attacks on their intelligence, their looks, or anything else that might serve to humiliate them. As a result, no one at CBS News during those years was more roundly despised. In defending Greenberg, his apologists usually chose to talk about his considerable talent rather than his caustic personality.

He was involved in a number of bruising scraps over the years, but the most memorable—in terms of what it revealed about his spiteful nature—was his falling-out with Hughes Rudd. Greenberg was rather short and balding, and, quite sensitive on both counts, he took to wearing sporty hats, which served the dual purpose of covering his bare pate and adding an inch or two to his height. In February 1971, he and Rudd were among those invited to a gala birthday party for Roger Mudd, which was held at the Tio Pepe, a popular Washington restaurant. When Greenberg showed up wearing a Russian-style winter hat, Rudd couldn't resist teasing him, in his grouchy way. Frowning at the hat, Rudd said: "Surely, you're not going to wear *that* into the restaurant."

That tore it. Rudd had committed the heinous sin of embarrassing Greenberg in front of Roger Mudd's fancy Washington friends. Spoiling for retribution, Greenberg waited for a propitious moment, and several weeks later, when Rudd called him to complain about his rejection of a story he had done, Greenberg flew into a tirade—a clearly calculated rage—and informed Rudd that he was through doing pieces for the *CBS Evening News with Roger Mudd*. Rudd did not learn until sometime later that the real reason for Greenberg's wrath was not his piece or his phone call about it, but the critical remark he had made about the hat Greenberg wore to Mudd's birthday party.

Greenberg was able to get away with such arbitrary and boorish behavior because just about everyone at CBS knew that he was Gordon Manning's fair-haired boy. During his first months as producer of the Saturday news, Greenberg had gone out of his way to butter up Manning. But as time passed and he came to realize how high he stood in Manning's eyes, he became more assertive and rebellious, like a pampered child who knows he can talk back to his parents with impunity. Whereas other producers were obliged to treat Manning with extreme deference or suffer unpleasant consequences, Greenberg could subject him to a certain amount of scorn—and get away with it. Indeed, the more brash and insolent he became, the more Manning seemed to delight in his tough, ass-kicking style. The fact that Greenberg was rapidly acquiring powerful enemies throughout the world of CBS News did not appear to bother Manning in the slightest. By the early 1970s, unsympathetic observers of their complex and fascinating relationship were privately suggesting, not altogether in jest, that Manning would be well advised to read Mary Shelley's famous novel. Baron Frankenstein, they noted, thought he had created a good thing, too.

In some respects, Manning *had* created a good thing. Thanks primarily to Greenberg, the weekend editions of the *CBS Evening News* were an unqualified success, clearly reflecting favorably on Manning's judgment. He had taken a big chance on Greenberg, the ABC castoff, and Greenberg had delivered, in spades. More to the point, perhaps, Greenberg remained entirely dependent on Manning. Manning had made him, and Manning had the absolute power to break him, should he ever veer seriously out of line. Thus Greenberg, for all his back talk, was still utterly loyal to Manning, his patron and protector. And that, from Gordon Manning's point of view, made for a most satisfactory arrangement.

Manning was also pleased with the way Roger Mudd was working out. When the Saturday show went on the air in 1966, Mudd joined a highly select group of veterans. The anchormen on the network's other three major news programs—Cronkite, Reasoner, and Wallace—all had years of experience behind them. But Mudd did not, and it showed. He frequently came across as uptight and unsure of himself. Whenever something went wrong, technically or otherwise, and the situation called for a sudden ad-lib, the kind of impromptu patter that Cronkite and Reasoner were so good at, Mudd's solution, more often than not, was to glare at the camera in sullen silence, as if to say, "Don't look at *me*, goddamnit. This isn't *my* fault." As time went on, however, he developed more poise, and by the early 1970s, he had polished up his act considerably.

Mudd's relationship with Greenberg also went well. Like Manning, he thoroughly approved of all that Greenberg had done to make the weekend *Evening News* a success, and since it was Mudd's show (at least as far as the viewing public was concerned), he felt a personal sense of gratitude. In turn, Greenberg was generally on his best behavior in his dealings with Mudd. He almost always went along with Mudd's wishes regarding the hard-news portion of the broadcast, while Mudd deferred to Greenberg's judgment in matters relating to the longer feature reports. Still, the two had their occasional differences. For example, Mudd was sore as hell when he learned that Hughes Rudd had been banished from the program, in part because Rudd was a close friend, but also because he thought Rudd's features were one of the show's brightest assets. Yet even though Rudd appealed to him for help, Mudd made only a token effort to persuade Greenberg to change his mind. He knew how obstinate Greenberg could be when he had his back up. And Mudd also knew that, when it came right down to it, he did not have the power to overrule his producer.

In all the years they worked together, they had only one serious quarrel. It occurred in the summer of 1970 when Greenberg decided to include on a Saturday evening broadcast a film report from Cambodia by correspondent Don Webster. The story dealt with the extreme danger Webster and other journalists had to contend with in covering that phase of the war. In fact, several reporters, including CBS newsmen George Syvertsen and Gerald Miller, had recently been killed in Cambodia. But Mudd felt that Webster's report was self-serving and unseemly. He strongly believed that correspondents did not have the right to use network air time to dwell on their personal hardships. Covering a war, after all, was not supposed to be a picnic. Greenberg disagreed. He thought Webster's piece was relevant and well worth using, and he was adamant about it. Tempers rose, and soon he and Mudd were shouting at each other in front of the entire weekend news staff. As their argument grew more rancorous, it occurred to Mudd that his only recourse was to go over Greenberg's head to Manning. But knowing how Manning doted on Greenberg, he had no stomach for that kind of showdown. So Mudd backed down, and Don Webster's story went on the air. It was an impressive display of Paul Greenberg's muscle.

But the angry confrontation had no lasting ill effects on their relationship. Those who knew both Mudd and Greenberg well were frankly surprised that they didn't clash more often, for they were both strong-willed and egocentric. Yet they were prudent enough to realize that the success of the weekend *Evening News* depended, to a large extent, on their ability to get along with each other.

There was a lot more at stake than just the weekend news. Mudd and Greenberg were aware that they both figured prominently in Manning's future plans. By 1971, Manning was taking preliminary steps to maneuver Greenberg into the job of executive producer of the Cronkite show, and Mudd, everyone knew, was Manning's choice to become Cronkite's eventual successor. Manning, in fact, regarded them as a team, *his* team, and he was advancing their careers almost in tandem. Hence, like political candidates running on the same ticket, Mudd and Greenberg were locked into a position of mutual support.

Some of Mudd's co-workers found him as difficult to deal with in his way as Greenberg was in his. Mudd did not go in for personal attacks and obscene tirades—his sensibilities were too refined for that—but he could, on occasion, be extremely arrogant. He had a clear appreciation of himself as being well-educated and a credit to his profession, and he was often scornful of colleagues who, in his judgment, fell far short of his intelligence and ability. A New York producer who worked closely with Mudd over the years once offered this observation: "Roger rubs a lot of people the wrong way because he automatically assumes that he's a lot brighter than the rest of us mere mortals. That's what can happen to somebody who spends so much of his time hanging around Congress, talking to politicians," he said, laughing. Then in a more thoughtful tone, the producer added: "Actually, Sevareid suffers from the same delusion. Working in Washington, where journalists are taken much too seriously, gives these guys an inflated sense of their own worth."

But if Mudd was viewed by some as a Washington provincial, all hands agreed that he excelled in that milieu. His coverage of Capitol Hill was consistently first-rate—so good, in fact, that it almost measured up to his estimation of it—and there was a solid faction within the shop that regarded him as the network's best political reporter. Whether pursuing candidates out on the campaign trail or collaring delegates on the convention floor, he invariably was in top form. Mudd brought to both his Congressional beat and his political reporting a sophisticated understanding of the issues and a vigorous skepticism that at times bordered on the supercilious. He was an aggressive interviewer, as numerous senators and convention delegates learned to their discomfort, and his combative manner was enhanced by his formidable physical presence. A tall, big-boned man with a voice like a bowling alley, he usually towered over his interviewees and often seemed to shout them into submission. Even when his questions weren't especially hard or penetrating, the visual effect was one of intimidation.

As an anchorman, Mudd was tense and demanding. Yet when he was away from his work and relaxing, he could be quite charming, even jovial, and Washington hostesses constantly requested the pleasure of his company. Much of Mudd's social eminence stemmed from the fact that he and his wife, Emma Jeanne (whom he called "E.J."), were close to the Kennedys. That association dated back to the 1950s, when Mudd was covering the Senate for WTOP and Robert Kennedy was counsel for the Senate Rackets Committee's investigation of corruption in the labor unions. Their friendship ripened during the New Frontier years, and by the middle 1960s, the Mudds were among the select group that frequently attended parties at the Kennedys' Hickory Hill home in Virginia.

In 1968, when Bobby Kennedy launched his insurgent drive for the Democratic Presidential nomination, Mudd was assigned to cover the campaign. He had requested the assignment, and in taking it on, he was confident that his personal bias would not interfere with his integrity as a reporter. That proved to be the case. Mudd's coverage of Kennedy's march through the primaries that spring was scrupulously fair, and there were times, in fact, when he seemed to be leaning over backward to make it so. On such occasions, when he peppered Kennedy with tough and penetrating questions, the senator may well have wondered if it was really to his advantage to have his "friend" on the campaign trail, reporting for CBS News.

That trail led eventually to California in June, and Kennedy's impressive victory in that state's primary. CBS's live coverage that night was highlighted by Mudd's one-on-one interview with Kennedy. It was the first time since the start of the campaign that the two men had relaxed enough to allow the warmth they felt toward each other to surface in a public forum. As a result, viewers saw a side of Bobby Kennedy that sharply contradicted the image of the cold and ruthless political infighter that had plagued him over the years. They also saw an appealing side of Mudd that was seldom in evidence on the TV screen. It was one of the last interviews Kennedy gave.

Later that night, when the assassin struck, Mudd instinctively decided that his obligation as a friend took precedence over his duty as a journalist. When the shots rang out in the ballroom of the Ambassador Hotel in Los Angeles, and pandemonium ensued, Mudd's first move was *not* to go after the story. Instead, he sought out Ethel Kennedy, and, clutching her hand, he guided her through the mob to the spot where Bobby Kennedy lay dying. Six years later, at a Washington luncheon honoring her husband's memory, Ethel Kennedy would recall that night. Describing Mudd as "a man of courage," she went on to say, "It was Roger who led me through the crowd so that Bobby and I could say good-bye to each other." Then, after a pause to allow the moment of emotion to pass, she added, "So I'll always love him for that. Thank you, Roger."

The feeling was mutual. Unlike so many others who were drawn to the Kennedys first by the glamour of Camelot and later by the promise of Restoration centering on Bobby's Presidential aspirations, the Mudds did not drift away after the assassination. As a matter of fact, their friendship with Ethel Kennedy grew even stronger in the years following her husband's death.

Mudd thoroughly enjoyed hobnobbing with the Kennedys and the other social perquisites that, he knew, were an outgrowth of his position as a rising star in TV journalism. Yet in other respects, he was not at all comfortable with the "fishbowl" aspect of being an on-air correspondent and anchorman—a "talent," to use the trade term that he (and others) found demeaning. He hated to be pestered by strangers and was often rude to autograph-seekers and the like. Mudd's co-workers had little sympathy for this petulant attitude toward his celebrity status. Some of them were quick to suggest that if he truly preferred anonymity to being a household name, he could always chuck television and get a job as an editorial writer. No one had forced him to become an on-camera performer and accept a star's salary.

But in all fairness, there was more to Mudd's attitude than simple hypocrisy. His uneasiness over the star system was part of a larger dissatisfaction with the entire show-biz side of TV journalism. To friends he often complained about the superficiality of most television news shows and the personal frustration he usually experienced whenever he tried to inject more insight and depth into his on-air reports. For years he remained circumspect, confining his criticisms to private conversations. But in December 1970 he suddenly went public—and promptly threw his career into a tailspin.

The shot was fired from the campus of his alma mater, Washington and Lee. Invited to speak there, Mudd delivered a sharp attack on the shortcomings of broadcast journalism, saying at one point, "The inherent limitations of our media make it a powerful means of communication, but also a crude one which tends to strike at the emotions rather than the intellect." He then went on to deplore the "dangerous and increasing concentration on action which is usually violent and bloody rather than on thought; on happenings rather than issues; on shock rather than explanation; on personalization rather than ideas."

It was a thoughtful as well as a provocative speech. The issues Mudd raised were entirely legitimate and, in truth, his concerns were shared by many of his colleagues. But the speech could not have come at a worse time. A little more than a year earlier, Spiro Agnew had launched his assault on the networks, and while his motive was clearly unscrupulous—an attempt to thwart television's critical coverage of the Nixon Administration's policies in Vietnam and elsewhere—Agnew had touched on some of the same points Mudd now raised. Hence, on a superficial level, Mudd seemed to be reciting a variation on Agnew's theme, and that struck his superiors as the lowest form of betrayal. Some of them thought his speech was even more treacherous than Ed Murrow's 1958 diatribe against "decadence" and "escapism." In the midst of the Nixon-Agnew barrage, the last thing television needed was to be taken to task by one of its own, no matter how constructive his intent.

The timing of the speech also could not have been worse from the standpoint of Roger Mudd's own career. Harry Reasoner had just moved to ABC, and all speculation pointed to Mudd's inheriting Reasoner's job as Cronkite's regular backup on the *Evening News,* with all that implied. A public attack on TV journalism was hardly conducive to achieving that end, and even some of Mudd's friends wondered if he had fallen victim to a kind of death wish. Mudd's own view was that the criticisms he made were valid, and that he had no idea his speech would get him in trouble. Such faith in the permissiveness of his CBS bosses was touching but ingenuous, and it indicated that the former history scholar still had a lot to learn about the real world.

Two days after the speech, Mudd received an angry note from the president of CBS News, Dick Salant, who rebuked him for "biting the hand that feeds you." And a few days after that, he was summoned to New York to attend a luncheon meeting of news executives and top-level producers, who took turns working him over. To his credit, Paul Greenberg stood up for Mudd, arguing that his speech had merit and should not be confused with Agnew's broadsides, but he was the only one to do so. After that grilling, Mudd was driven, in Salant's limousine, across town to "Black Rock," the industry's favorite sobriquet for the CBS corporate headquarters in the heart of midtown Manhattan. (So called because of the building's dark and austere granite facade, and also because the machinations that went on *inside* the building reminded many of the ominous mood conveyed in the Spencer Tracy film *Bad Day at Black Rock.*) Roger Mudd's day at Black Rock was certainly not a good one. He received a severe chewing out from a senior executive named Richard Jencks, who, at the time, ranked just below the Paley-Stanton-Schneider triumvirate in the corporate hierarchy.

In reprimanding Mudd, Jencks clearly spoke for Schneider, if not necessarily for Paley and Stanton (who, in keeping with the above-the-battle stance they had recently adopted, did not become directly involved in the Mudd affair). As it happened, Schneider had been leery of Mudd even before the Washington and Lee speech. He respected Mudd's talent, but he resented his arrogance. In his mind, Mudd had aligned himself with the news division "purists" who viewed the corporate world of CBS—the world of commercials and profits and *The Beverly Hillbillies*—with Pecksniffian disdain. And now Mudd had made the mistake of fouling his own nest in public. From Jack Schneider's point of view, the timing of the Washington and Lee speech was perfect. He had been telling Salant and Manning that they were pushing Mudd too fast, that given Mudd's arrogant attitude, he didn't deserve to become entrenched as Cronkite's regular replacement. And now Mudd, through his own folly, had given Schneider sufficient cause to block that move.

Schneider quietly passed the word down through the news division's chain of command, and a few weeks after the speech, Washington bureau chief Bill Small took Mudd out to lunch and gave him the message: Because of the speech, Mudd could forget about filling in for Cronkite on the *Evening News,* at least for the time being. He would continue in his present assignments, and through them he would have ample opportunity to work his way back into the company's good graces. But in the meantime, Small warned, he'd better learn to keep his mouth shut.

The chastisement of Roger Mudd was carried out with the utmost discretion. Even within the confines of CBS, only a few people knew he had been put on ice. Thus, most of his co-workers were quite surprised in the summer of 1971 when Walter Cronkite went on his first extended vacation since Reasoner's departure the previous autumn, and the assignment of anchoring the *Evening News* in Cronkite's absence was given not to Mudd but to John Hart.

Compared to Mudd, Hart was a new face, a correspondent who, since joining CBS News in 1965, had spent most of his time covering stories in the field, at home and abroad. For the past year, however, he had been anchoring the *Morning News,* and the refreshing, conversational style he brought to that dreary grind had impressed Dick Salant and other executives. Hart was the latest in a long line of people who had been thrown into the early-morning slot to compete against NBC's formidable institution, the *Today* show. He was already discovering, as his predecessors had discovered, what a futile and frustrating task that was. But in the summer of 1971, John Hart could hardly complain about an assignment that, in just a few months, had propelled him into Walter Cronkite's anchor chair on the *CBS Evening News.*

18 Morning Blues

When Hart took over as anchorman on the *Morning News* in 1970, the *Today* show had been lording it over CBS for nearly two decades. Like *See It Now*, it was born in the mists of the early 1950s, when television itself was still a toddler. But unlike Murrow's great showcase and other pioneering broadcasts of that era, *Today* demonstrated remarkable staying power. It not only survived those experimental years, it went on to become even more popular in the 1960s and 1970s. Yet when *Today* made its debut in January 1952, its future did not look at all promising. One reviewer called it "a comedy of errors," and another dismissed it as "a hodgepodge." The program, in fact, was almost scrapped after its first thirteen weeks on the air, and it continued to struggle without sponsors and without much of an audience until the arrival of a chimpanzee named J. Fred Muggs. Muggs was a big hit, and from that point on, *Today* never looked back. By the 1970s, the show's "hodgepodge" of news headlines, weather, interviews, and feature film reports had become so ingrained in the nation's consciousness that it was all but impossible to conceive of early-morning television without it.

Working in *Today*'s favor over the years was the stability of its on-air talent, especially during its first two decades. The original host, Dave Garroway, stayed with the show nine years, until 1961. After John Chancellor tried it for a year, during which he annoyed the NBC brass with his refusal to do commercials, Hugh Downs hosted the program from 1962 to 1971. Since then, the turnover has been more rapid. Frank McGee served as host until his death in 1974. Then came Jim Hartz and

Barbara Walters (she had been appearing on the broadcast since 1964 but was upgraded to co-host in 1974, the only woman to be given that rank), and since 1976, *Today*'s headliner has been Tom Brokaw. But connoisseurs of *Today* tend to agree that the show's real "star" over the years has been its variegated format, precisely the feature that turned some critics off back in 1952.

CBS made its first stab at competing with *Today* for the breakfast audience in March 1954, when *The Morning Show*, with Walter Cronkite as host, went on the air. But Cronkite and his sidekick—Charlemane, the lion puppet—were no match for Dave Garroway and his chimp, and, after a few months, Jack Paar took over. Paar hosted *The Morning Show* for a year, and was replaced by Dick Van Dyke, who also lasted only a few months. Obviously, in all three cases, the failure to make the show a worthy rival of *Today* did not stem from its hosts' inaptitude for the medium; Cronkite, Paar, and Van Dyke all became, in other milieux, three of the biggest stars on television.

In February 1956, CBS gave the program a new name, *Good Morning*, and trotted out still another personality, Will Rogers, Jr., to host it. Rogers did not fare any better than his three predecessors, and he also had the misfortune to be involved in one of the most ludicrous mishaps ever to occur on network television. In the summer of 1956, *Good Morning* originated from Chicago during the week of the Democratic convention. At one point, some genius decided that since Rogers was a cowboy (or, more accurately, the son of a famous cowboy-humorist), he should open the show each morning by riding a horse up Michigan Avenue to the entrance of the Conrad Hilton Hotel, jockey his way into the lobby, then dismount with a flourish and commence his duties as host. The first day, everything went fine until Rogers and his steed arrived at the hotel entrance. There the horse balked, and when Rogers nervously applied the spurs, the wretched beast began to defecate. While this indelicate business was being transmitted to breakfast viewers across the land, correspondent Ned Calmer, waiting in a nearby studio to broadcast the news portion of the program, turned to his writer, Sandy Socolow, and exclaimed, "Good God, what a fuckup—and on national television!" Just seconds before Calmer spoke, however, the show's director, understandably in paroxysms, had cut away from the horse to the studio, and Calmer's lively comment went out over the air. The size and apathy of the show's audience can be gauged by the fact that the incident provoked almost no viewer reaction. A few months later, *Good Morning* quietly expired as CBS gave up trying to compete with *Today* on its own terms. By the late 1950s, the network's major offering in the early-morning time period was a kiddie show called *Captain Kangaroo.*

CBS's next experiment with a *Today*-type format came in 1961 when *Calendar,* featuring Harry Reasoner and Mary Fickett, was inserted into the morning schedule. But in order to avoid a head-on confrontation with the NBC powerhouse, *Calendar* was broadcast at 10:00 A.M., Eastern time, one hour after *Today* went off the air, which was in accordance with one of the sacred precepts of TV programming: if you can't lick them, stay out of their time slot. *Calendar* built up a solid audience of its own and served to elevate Reasoner into the front rank of television correspondents. But in the summer of 1963, it was replaced by the *CBS Morning News,* anchored by Mike Wallace, who was then at a critical point of transition in his personal and professional life. Wallace had joined CBS News a few months earlier in an effort to get away from the kind of work he had been doing in recent years. While Cronkite, Murrow, and other broadcast journalists had dabbled in the show-biz side of television during the 1950s, Wallace had practically wallowed in schlock. In the process, he had made a great deal of money, but he had also lost much of his self-respect. Now, at the age of forty-five, he was determined to get it back.

Myron Leon Wallace was born and raised in the Boston suburb of Brookline, in a neighborhood that also spawned such contemporaries as Leonard Bernstein, David Susskind, and John F. Kennedy. From Brookline, he went to the University of Michigan with the intention of becoming an English teacher. But following his graduation in 1939, he drifted into radio work at station WXYZ in Detroit. His duties there ranged from writing and broadcasting the news to being the announcer on such popular entertainment programs as *The Lone Ranger* and *The Green Hornet,* a potpourri of assignments he shared with another young newsman-announcer named Douglas Edwards. After service in the Navy during World War II, Wallace settled down in Chicago, working as a reporter at WMAQ. Then he met and married actress Buff Cobb, the granddaughter of humorist Irvin S. Cobb, and that put him on a path that led him away from journalism. He and his new wife began doing a midnight radio show from a Chicago nightclub, and in 1951, CBS brought them to New York to co-host a daytime television gabfest called *Mike and Buff.*

Wallace's marriage to Buff Cobb (his second) ended in divorce in

1955, which also terminated the *Mike and Buff* show. But by this time, he was trying his hand at just about every game in town. In 1954, he had made his debut as a Broadway actor, appearing in a comedy called *Reclining Figure.* And after that closed, he became the emcee on an NBC quiz show, *The Big Surprise.* Then, in the fall of 1956, Wallace began hosting a television interview show called *Night Beat.* That program quickly transformed Wallace into a figure of considerable notoriety who came to be known by such endearments as "Mike Malice" and "the Grand Inquisitor."

Talk shows built around interviews with celebrities had been going on since the early days of television, and, determined to avoid controversy at all costs, they consisted almost entirely of puff and patter. Even the best of them, such as Murrow's *Person to Person,* suffered from an excessive blandness. Mike Wallace was anything but bland. On both *Night Beat,* broadcast locally in New York, and its network successor on ABC, *The Mike Wallace Interview,* he subjected his guests to a third degree that frequently had them squirming and stammering. He told Grace Metalious, the author of *Peyton Place,* that he thought her book was "basic and carnal." He asked social butterfly Elsa Maxwell why she had never married. (Her reply: "Quite frankly, I was never interested in sex. I was never interested for one minute, ever.") And he asked Mr. John, a New York milliner, why the fashion world attracted so many homosexuals. (His reply: "That's not worth talking about.")

The punch Wallace put into his questions was heightened by his feisty manner and his pockmarked, prizefighter's face. He looked as tough as he talked. All in all, his sledgehammer interrogations were such a departure from the vapid pleasantries of most TV interviews that he became the talk of the industry. The talk soon turned sour, however, as Wallace discovered what Murrow and Friendly were discovering at CBS with *See It Now:* namely, that network executives would allow controversy on the air only as long as it didn't offend. Abusing guests was all right because they, in a sense, asked for it by consenting to go on the show. Indeed, some of them did seem to get a masochistic kick out of being worked over by Wallace. But a few of his "victims" used the forum to fire off some hard shots of their own. When Wallace interviewed mobster Mickey Cohen, who promptly libeled the Los Angeles police chief and members of his department, the cops responded with a damage suit. ABC had to make a public apology on the air. In addition, some of the same critics who had praised Wallace for his boldness and candor when he first went on the attack now began to accuse him of sensationalism. His ratings began to drop, the show lost its sponsor, and in the summer of 1958, ABC took it off the air. When Wallace's contract with the network ran out a few months later, it was not renewed.

Over the next four years, he moved through a variety of television roles, as if searching for his proper identity. In 1959, he took another fling at "straight" journalism, appearing as a headliner on a local nightly newscast in New York. But that lasted only a few months, and soon he was back in the TV personality parade, doing the unctuous charm bit on a conventional, all-smiles-and-gush talk show called *PM* and occasionally sitting in on game shows. By the early 1960s, the bulk of his income came from the commercials he did for Parliament cigarettes. Wallace knew he was working the dregs, and he was not at all happy about it, for beneath his various TV faces he was an intelligent, even sensitive man who longed to be taken seriously. But the money he made from all this carnival work (his annual haul was deep into six figures) was too strong a lure to resist. Besides, as he often said to friends, he had the future of his kids to consider.

Wallace had two sons from his first marriage to the former Norma Kaphan, Buff Cobb's predecessor. By the early 1960s, he was happily married to his third wife, the former Lorraine Perigord, who also had two children from a previous marriage, and his first wife, Norma, had recently married Bill Leonard, who was on his way to becoming a vice-president at CBS News—and Wallace's future boss. But the small (and complicated) world these two television families shared suddenly turned desolate in the summer of 1962 when Wallace's eldest son, Peter, fell to his death while on a camping trip in the mountains of Greece.

Peter's death had a devastating effect on Wallace, not only in the usual sense but also in terms of the direction his professional life had taken. Peter was just nineteen when he died, and he had expressed journalistic aspirations of his own; in fact, he had worked as a desk assistant for CBS News at the 1960 political conventions. Wallace had encouraged his son's interest in journalism, telling him it was both a stimulating and honorable profession. That, he knew, was a lot more than he could say for what he was doing with his own life. In the period of mourning following Peter's death, Wallace had several long and searching talks with himself. His huge income notwithstanding, did he really want to continue hustling viewers into buying Parliaments and laughing it up on talk and game shows? The answer, he decided, was no. He had started out working in news, and now, if it wasn't too late, he was determined to get back on that track, no matter how great the financial sacrifice.

It almost was too late. A few weeks after his son's death, Wallace wrote to the presidents of the three network news divisions, requesting a job as a correspondent. Their responses were negative, chillingly so. Wallace's early roots may have been in journalism, but he was now perceived entirely in terms of his more recent past. As far as Dick Salant and his counterparts were concerned, Wallace was damaged goods; they wanted no part of him. After a long and depressing winter of rejection in New York, he decided, in March 1963, to accept an offer as anchorman on a local news show at KTLA in Los Angeles. In the meantime, to underscore the new leaf he was turning over, Wallace told the Parliament people that he was willing to buy up his commercials to keep them off the air. When Salant heard about that, he had a change of heart. If Wallace was willing to go that far, then, Salant concluded, his desire for redemption must be more than a passing fancy. In what he later described as "one of the best decisions I ever made," Salant called Wallace and told him to forget about Los Angeles. He had a job for him at CBS News in New York.

The next question to be faced was what to do with this forty-five-year-old television celebrity who had made his reputation outside the province of conventional journalism. His first weeks as a CBS News correspondent were an awkward time for Wallace as he took on a few modest assignments and tried not to appear too conspicuous. Then, in the spring of 1963, the decision was made to replace *Calendar* with a harder, more orthodox morning news program, and Salant, influenced by the fact that Wallace had been a big star, if not exactly a star journalist, picked him to anchor the new show.

That decision aroused a great deal of resentment within the shop. As the host on *Calendar,* Harry Reasoner certainly did not view the change as an improvement. He regarded Wallace as a brash interloper, and he made no attempt to conceal his hostility. "Harry used to look at me," a laughing Wallace said many years later, "like I was a strand of hair in his soup." Nor was Reasoner alone in that respect. "Oh, we were all quite contemptuous," recalled Joan Snyder, who was one of the writers on those first editions of the *Morning News.* "Why on earth, we wondered, had this sleazy Madison Avenue pitchman been chosen to anchor a CBS News broadcast? As long as we were going camp, I would have preferred Johnny, the Philip Morris bellhop."

But Snyder and her colleagues soon changed their minds about Wallace. They discovered that while he was just a so-so writer, he was an excellent editor, both in terms of his news judgment and his handling of copy, and, like Cronkite, he was not at all shy about tossing stories back to his writers for revision. His favorite epithet for copy that displeased him was "baby shit." The writers assigned to the *Morning News* came to dread that indignity, and to avoid having it leveled at them, they began putting more care into their work.

As an anchorman, Wallace struck an admirable balance between the abrasive style of his *Night Beat* interviews and the genial manner he had displayed on *PM* and the *Mike and Buff* show. Viewer response was most encouraging. The *CBS Morning News* went on the air in September 1963 (the same day the Cronkite show moved into its half-hour format), and in just a few weeks it was attracting a larger audience than *Calendar* ever had. As the show grew steadily stronger and more popular, Wallace began to relax and rejoice in his success. The period of uncertainty was over; his new career as a full-time journalist was working out even better than he had hoped. Years later, Wallace would remember with great clarity the day he knew for certain that he had made the grade and was accepted by his CBS News colleagues as one of their own. It was in the spring of 1964 and Wallace was standing in the newsroom when Harry Reasoner came up to him, stuck out his hand, and said, "Look, this is silly. I can't stay sore at a guy who's doing as good a job as you're doing. Let's be friends."

Mike Wallace *was* doing a good job on the *Morning News*. But so, too, was the show's executive producer, Av Westin. In fact, many CBS people believed it was Westin, even more than Wallace, who was responsible for its success. Westin had been around CBS since 1948. He started out as a desk assistant while still a student at New York University, and eventually he worked his way up to become first a director and then a producer. Like so many of the young men who came into the CBS news department during the early years of television, he was a Don Hewitt protégé.

By the early 1960s, Westin was working as a field producer in London, and in the spring of 1963, he received a memo from Dick

Salant. It was a general memo that Salant sent to producers throughout the news division informing them of the two major programming changes in the works—the expansion of the *Evening News* to a half hour and the switch from *Calendar* to the *Morning News*—and asking for their suggestions on how to meet that dual challenge. During his years in London, Westin had been making an informal study of the BBC's news programs, and he had been impressed, in particular, by their background reports and their clever use of feature material. He wrote about his observations in some detail in his reply to Salant's memo, and Salant, in turn, was so impressed that he brought Westin back to New York and appointed him executive producer of the *Morning News*.

Instead of emulating NBC's *Today* format, as *The Morning Show* and *Calendar* had done, the *Morning News* turned it inside out. Whereas *Today* and its imitators concentrated on personalities and interviews, with news headlines serving as periodic bridges, the Wallace-Westin show put the emphasis on news. Still, the broadcast usually included at least one live interview every day, thus taking advantage of Wallace's acknowledged forte—with or without the brass knuckles. Also, in deference to its midmorning time slot, there was a heavy slant toward news that was deemed to be of particular interest to women. For example, the show dealt quite candidly with sexual subjects: birth control, venereal disease, menopause, and other delicate matters. Viewed from the vantage point of the X-rated mid-1970s, the topics aired on the *CBS Morning News* a decade earlier would be dismissed as child's play. But at the time, some of its forays into then-taboo areas were rather daring, especially for television. In the words of Washington producer Bill Crawford, it was "the only news show on the tube that was in constant danger of being hauled into court on charges of appealing to prurient interests."

The morale on the *Morning News* during the Wallace-Westin years was uncommonly high, which was all the more remarkable in light of the early-to-bed, early-to-rise hours the staff had to keep. Av Westin deserved most, if not all, of the credit for that. Like his mentor, Hewitt, he was a man of boundless enthusiasm, and it rubbed off on his associates. He eagerly schooled newcomers whose journalistic backgrounds were in print in the techniques of TV production, encouraging them to be creative and take chances. Under Westin's tutelage, Joan Snyder and Paul Soroka learned the craft of field producing that they would later ply so skillfully on the *CBS Evening News*.

Like *Calendar*, the *Morning News* benefited enormously from being broadcast at 10:00 A.M., where its half-hour format was safely beyond the range of *Today*'s big guns. But in August 1965, the program was shifted to a 7:00 A.M. time slot. The drastic change was ordered by the corporate brass, and it was prompted by the favorite vice of network executives—greed. Even though the *Morning News* had built up a strong and loyal audience, CBS could make more money by airing *I Love Lucy* and other reruns in that time period; so that, naturally, was what it chose to do. Fred Friendly, then president of the news division, argued against the move, but to no avail. His clash with Jack Schneider over that switch was, in fact, a prelude to their bitter quarrel over live coverage of the Senate hearings on Vietnam, which precipitated Friendly's resignation a few months later.

With the shift to the 7:00 A.M. air time, where it couldn't possibly compete against the more established and more elaborate two-hour *Today* show, the *Morning News* lost just about everything it had carefully cultivated over the past two years: its audience, its identity, and its morale. And it also lost the two men who had done the most to shape its character—Av Westin and Mike Wallace.

Westin's departure from the *Morning News* coincided with the move to a new time slot. He did not necessarily want to abandon the broadcast in its hour of transition, but Friendly told him it was time to branch out and start producing documentaries and special reports. Friendly strongly intimated that he had big plans for Westin, although neither man had any inkling then that those plans would involve leaving CBS. Yet that is what happened. When Friendly resigned in February 1966 and assumed his new post as television consultant to the Ford Foundation, he induced Westin to become executive producer of the Public Broadcasting Laboratory, the experimental program that, as Friendly envisioned it, would revolutionize TV journalism. PBL was a disaster, but fortunately Westin emerged from the experience with minimal damage to his reputation, and in the spring of 1969 he returned to commercial television as executive producer of the *ABC Evening News*.

The hiring of Westin was one of several steps ABC was then taking to upgrade its evening news show, and Westin himself proceeded to make significant contributions to that effort. It was, for example, at his instigation that Howard K. Smith was summoned out of semiretirement and paired with Frank Reynolds as the broadcast's anchor team. Then, with the arrival of Harry Reasoner in 1970, came the big push. The combination of Westin's talents as a producer and the new on-air team of Reasoner and Smith generated a dramatic surge in the ratings, and for the first time in the history of TV journalism, ABC's evening news program became competitive.

In 1973, Westin was rewarded with a big promotion. Moving up to the management level, he became vice-president in charge of documentaries. But in the meantime, the news show he and Mike Wallace inaugurated at CBS a decade earlier had fallen on hard times. Following the shift to the earlier time slot, the *Morning News* sank into a dismal rut—and there it floundered.

Wallace continued to anchor the broadcast during its first year in the 7:00 A.M. time period, but he couldn't stand the new hours. It was bad enough reporting for work every day at 6:00 or 7:00 in the morning, as he had done under the old schedule, but now he had to get up in the middle of the night. Moreover, with Westin gone, the program no longer had the same spark and vitality. So, in the summer of 1966, Wallace decided to call it quits. He gave up anchoring the *Morning News* to try his luck as a field correspondent. Once again, he took a pecuniary step backward, for in making the move he was depriving himself of a prime source of income: the sizable commercial fees he received as a five-day-a-week anchorman. But he wanted to get out in the field and do some reporting.

Wallace joined the ranks of general-assignment correspondents just at the time that Richard Nixon was reemerging from the political shadows. Nixon's energetic campaigning on behalf of Republican candidates in the 1966 midterm election was the start of his remarkable comeback that, two years later, won him the Presidency. Wallace, who was something of a Comeback Kid himself, covered Nixon's efforts in that campaign and picked him up again the following year when his Presidential drive began in earnest. He stayed with the Nixon story through all the primaries and up to his nomination in the summer of 1968. Had Wallace continued on that beat through the fall campaign, he almost surely would have become CBS News's chief White House correspondent during the Nixon years. But that was also the summer that Don Hewitt, then in the process of making *his* big comeback, was putting together *60 Minutes*, and when Hewitt and Bill Leonard offered him the job of co-starring with Harry Reasoner on that broadcast, Wallace readily accepted.

Nixon and his people were sorry to see Wallace leave their campaign. His reputation as a hitter notwithstanding, they felt that his coverage up to then had been eminently fair, much more so than that of many other journalists. On the last night of the 1968 Republican convention, when Wallace told Nixon he was leaving the assignment to begin working on "this new feature program," Nixon looked at him as though he had lost his mind. "I'd call that a big mistake," the future President said. "We're going to win this thing, Mike, and when we get to the White House, we're going to take some great trips." At the time, that struck Wallace as an odd, rather frivolous inducement, but in fact, he did miss out on the historic visit to China and other Presidential junkets—including Nixon's ultimate "trip" through the looking glass known as Watergate.

Going to *60 Minutes* was no mistake, however, even though that program did not start out as the marvelous showcase for Wallace that it later became. The show was conceived with Reasoner in mind, and during its first two years on the air, it was subtly structured to take full advantage of his writing talent and casual broadcasting style. Wallace was generally assigned to the routine stuff, the hard-news stories, while Reasoner concentrated on the lighter features that gave *60 Minutes* its distinctive tone. The two correspondents had become friends by this time, but there remained an underlying tension in their relationship. They both were expert needlers, and their off-camera dealings with each other were frequently spiced by jocular insults. On one occasion, when Wallace taunted his co-star with a fan letter he had received expressing a preference for his work over Reasoner's, Reasoner haughtily insisted it had been written by "your hair colorist." (This was something of a sore point with Reasoner, for although Wallace was five years older, his black hair and trim figure gave him a more youthful appearance than the prematurely gray, stockily built Reasoner.) Every now and then, their good-natured baiting spilled over into their on-air work, and when that happened, the show took on an appealing edge, a lively touch of friction.

But all that came to an end when Reasoner left CBS in 1970 and Morley Safer inherited his slot on *60 Minutes.* Following that move, the complexion of the broadcast soon changed as it began to reflect Wallace's more muscular style. It became harder in tone, more investigative in subject matter; and while, in keeping with its diversified format, it continued to air soft features, Wallace and Safer now divided those assignments. Thus, in the post-Reasoner years, Wallace, now very much the senior man, became the dominant presence on *60 Minutes*. And as the program steadily grew in prestige and popularity, Wallace's own reputation grew with it. He was still viewed as a tough customer, regarded by many as the most aggressive interviewer in all of TV journalism, but his image was now entirely respectable.

By the mid-1970s, Wallace ranked among CBS News correspondents on a level just below Cronkite, and were it not for his age (he is just a year and a half younger than Cronkite), he would no doubt have become a leading candidate for the post of Cronkite's successor. The change in his status did not go unnoticed. Several newspaper and magazine articles were written about "The Mellowing of Mike Malice" (as one of them was titled), and younger readers must have perused them with the fascination of discovery. For by then, there were millions of viewers who were well acquainted with Mike Wallace, the star of *60 Minutes,* but who had no memory at all of the "Mike Malice" phase of his career.

In the meantime, he was taking paternal pride in the career of his son, Chris, who, by the mid-1970s, was working as a reporter at the local NBC station in New York. And, as had been his habit for years, Wallace continued to wear black much of the time. It was always understated —usually nothing more than a tie or a sweater—and most of his colleagues scarcely noticed it or, if they did, attached no particular significance to it. Only those who were very close to Wallace were aware that it represented a private memorial to his other son, Peter, whose death in 1962 prompted him to reexamine the values that governed his own professional life.

Wallace's successor as anchorman on the *Morning News* was a newcomer named Joseph Benti, who was recruited for that post by none other than Wallace himself. A native of Brooklyn, Benti picked up his early broadcasting experience in the Midwest, taught journalism for a year at the University of Iowa, and in 1963 moved on to Los Angeles, where he became political editor at the CBS-owned station, KNXT. When Wallace went out to the West Coast on an assignment in the summer of 1966, he met Benti, observed his work, and, following his return to New York, informed Gordon Manning that Benti had the stuff to become a top correspondent at CBS News. He suggested, in fact, that Benti be hired as his replacement. Manning checked him out, agreed with Wallace's high estimation of him, and, in August 1966, Benti was brought to New York to anchor the *Morning News*. He was only thirty-four, and just like that, Joe Benti had made the jump from a middle-level position at a local station to network anchorman.

But as a recruiter, Wallace was no Ed Murrow. Benti came in with a chip on his shoulder, and by the time he left CBS News four years later, his superiors were as disenchanted with him as he was with them. Money was at the bottom of his unhappy start. His original contract was negotiated by a New York agent, and when all the papers were signed, Benti discovered that even with commercial fees he would be making less as an anchorman than he had made at KNXT and (as he later found out) less than several of the network's field correspondents. He was able to persuade his new bosses that his contract should be renegotiated, and it was, but the experience left an unpleasant aftertaste, a sense of having been played for a sucker.

Benti did have one very good year at the network, but, significantly enough, it had little to do with the *Morning News*. In the early-morning hours of June 5, 1968, when Robert Kennedy was shot in Los Angeles, he was the only CBS News correspondent of any worth who was in a position to anchor the live coverage of that story: the eyewitness accounts of the shooting, the arrest of Sirhan Sirhan, and the vigil at the hospital where doctors struggled in vain to save Kennedy's life. It was one time when being awake and on the job at 3:00 A.M. worked to Benti's advantage. He was later joined in the anchor slot by Cronkite, but Benti stayed on the air for twelve straight hours that day and, in the process, displayed his own brand of poise under pressure and iron-pants durability. He went on from that impressive performance to the political conventions, where he was one of the floor correspondents, and on election night that fall, he joined Cronkite, Sevareid, Wallace, Mudd, and Rather in the big spotlight. Thus, as 1968 drew to a close, Joe Benti had the look of a winner.

The Benti buildup was given another apparent boost in March 1969 when the *Morning News* was expanded to a one-hour format, a move that was trumpeted as a fresh and forceful challenge to the *Today* show. (*Time* magazine called it "Duel at Daybreak" in an article on Benti that spring.) But the longer program proved to be no more competitive than its half-hour predecessor, and as time went on, Benti became increasingly discouraged and sullen. The combination of deplorable hours, terrible ratings, and a listless staff soon drained all the enthusiasm he had brought to his job, and he eventually came to regard it more as an onerous duty than a golden opportunity. Beyond that, he was sore at Gordon Manning, who, he felt, had welshed on his promise to give the program's new one-hour format a full-scale promotion. In the meantime, Manning and others at CBS News had soured on Benti and were now blaming him for the torpor and tedium that pervaded the *Morning News* operation, both on air and off.

The denouement came in the summer of 1970. Thoroughly fed up with the *Morning News,* Benti requested another assignment—specifically, the post of Moscow correspondent—and Manning, who was just as eager to make a change, promptly agreed to the transfer. But the deal fell through when Soviet authorities, in one of their periodic harassments, closed down the CBS News bureau in Moscow. Manning then asked Benti what his next choice was, and Benti replied, with heavy sarcasm, that the only other job he was interested in was Cronkite's. If he couldn't become Moscow correspondent or anchorman on the *Evening News,* Benti went on to say, then he would just as soon leave CBS News. Manning feigned regret about that, but he was privately delighted. He had reached the conclusion by this time that hiring Benti—and, in particular, starting him out on the anchorman level— had been a big mistake. So, before Benti had a chance to change his mind, Gordon Manning sent out invitations to his going-away party.

Benti was not on his best behavior at the party Manning threw for him at his home in Connecticut. When he arrived, he glanced up at a huge banner Manning had put up identifying him as the anchorman on the *CBS Morning News,* and bitterly remarked that "this is the most publicity I've had since I began doing the show four years ago." He then proceeded to get quite drunk and offensive. At one point, he insulted the wife of a *Morning News* producer, telling her that she needed to lose some weight. When members of the *Morning News* staff presented him with a transoceanic radio, Benti waved it away, saying he didn't want a radio, goddamnit, he wanted a camera. Soon thereafter, the guest of honor, having worn out his welcome, headed for his car with Manning in hot pursuit, clutching the unwanted gift and shouting after him, "Joe, you forgot your radio." Then, in a more beseeching tone, "But Joe, what about the radio?"

Benti spent the next few months in Europe, getting the *Morning News* out of his system, and then returned to Los Angeles, where he worked for a time at the ABC-owned station, KABC. By the mid-1970s, he was back at KNXT, where Mike Wallace had discovered him, and was anchoring its evening news show. Meanwhile, at CBS News in New York, Joe Benti was soon forgotten. His impact on viewers and colleagues alike had been negligible. Like the perpetrator of a perfect crime, he had left no fingerprints.

One of the few bright spots on the *Morning News* during the Benti years was the reporting out of Washington by John Hart. When the broadcast was expanded to an hour in March 1969, Hart was assigned to the show as its regular Washington correspondent—a kind of anchorman, junior grade. His handling of the Washington news every morning was distinguished by smooth writing and an appealing, low-key broadcasting style. Indeed, some insiders believed that Hart's work on the *Morning News* helped to undermine Benti's reputation; that the more CBS executives saw of Hart on the program, the more they became convinced that he, not Benti, was the one with the talent. Therefore, no one was surprised when, following Benti's sudden departure, Hart inherited his anchor slot on the *Morning News*.

A native of Oregon, Hart was the son of a Baptist minister, and one of his first radio jobs (while a college student in Minneapolis) was reading religious poetry to the accompaniment of organ music. Like Benti, Hart served his broadcasting apprenticeship in the Midwest before moving on to KNXT in Los Angeles. In 1964, he left Los Angeles to become Washington bureau manager and national correspondent for the five CBS-owned television stations, an assignment that brought him to the attention of Fred Friendly, then running the show at CBS News. In August 1965, Hart was hired as a network correspondent.

His first assignment was in the South. Hart worked out of Atlanta for more than a year and followed that up with a six-month reportorial tour in Vietnam. By 1968, he was back in Washington, covering politics. There he scored a major coup when he broke the story on Robert Kennedy's decision to run for President, and he went on to assist Roger Mudd in the coverage of Kennedy's primary campaign as it moved across the country to its tragic end in California. Other political assignments followed, and in March 1969, he began anchoring the Washington portion of the *CBS Morning News*. When Benti cut himself adrift in 1970, Hart jumped at the chance to succeed him.

Hart brought to his new assignment a very positive attitude, an energy and élan that was a welcome change from the surly defeatism that had characterized Benti's last few months on the *Morning News*.

He came in early every day and worked closely with his producers and editorial staff, often going out of his way to let them know how much he appreciated their contributions to the broadcast. As a result, staff morale, which had been such a problem in recent years, soared to its highest level since the Wallace-Westin days.

Still, the transition was not entirely painless. The people most deeply affected by the change in anchormen were the show's writers, most of whom had a difficult time adjusting to Hart's predilections. Hart himself was a facile writer, with such a passion for clarity and simplicity that his copy read, at times, like the famous Dick-and-Jane children's primer. He was, at first, so dissatisfied with his writers (who had grown lazy under Benti) that he usually wound up writing or rewriting most of his script himself. But he handled these revisions with such grace and affability that his writers, instead of taking umbrage, strove all the harder to give him what he wanted. The only writer on the program whose work consistently pleased Hart was a bearded veteran named Ray Gandolf. Once, when another member of the editorial staff asked him what the secret was, Gandolf, suddenly looking very mysterious, replied, "I hear him talking in my head; I hear his rhythms as I write."

Hart's limpid writing style was perfectly tailored to the low-key, informal persona he assumed on the air. To underscore his relaxed approach, he even began doing the broadcast in shirt-sleeves and an open collar, a casual innovation that lasted until word came down through channels that it offended Bill Paley's sense of propriety. (Paley, who was known to suffer from insomnia, was an habitual viewer of the *Morning News,* which was one reason—some insiders insisted it was the *only* reason—the program stayed on the air. The sardonic motto around the *Morning News* area was "We do this show for an audience of one.") Hart may have overdone it a bit with his shirt-sleeves, but for the most part he scored points with his easygoing, conversational style. The show's ratings were still about as dismal as ever, but his superiors were not inclined to blame him for that. Besides, ratings weren't the only criterion, and the prevailing view within the shop was that Hart's fresh approach had enlivened the *Morning News* considerably. Even so, few people realized just how high his stock had risen until the summer of 1971 when, with Harry Reasoner gone and Roger Mudd in purgatory because of his Washington and Lee speech, Hart was assigned to anchor the *Evening News* during the month of August while Cronkite was on vacation.

It was not a definitive commitment on the part of the CBS management. Hart understood that even if he did an outstanding job on the *Evening News,* he was not to assume that he had inherited Reasoner's role as Cronkite's regular replacement. As a matter of fact, Jack Schneider and others were opposed to having that prerogative devolve on any one correspondent. What Schneider found most irritating about Reasoner's move to ABC was the way CBS had groomed a major star only to lose him to another network; he did not want to see that happen again. So it was decided to spread the backup action on the *Evening News* around among two or three correspondents. That, it was felt, would prevent any one of them—Mudd, Hart, or whoever—from attaining the stature and bargaining position Reasoner had built up over the years. Still, the opportunity bestowed on John Hart in the summer of 1971 was fraught with promise. He was only thirty-nine (four years younger than Mudd), and if he performed well in the *Evening News* showcase, he was certain to be called on to anchor the broadcast again, and again, and in time he would become a leading contender for the post of Cronkite's successor.

But Hart made the mistake of abusing the privilege. Instead of using the month-long assignment to ingratiate himself and demonstrate his worth as a substitute for Cronkite, he seemed to view it as an opportunity to show Cronkite up. He set out, from his first day in the anchor slot, to reshape the *Evening News* to fit his style, rather than the other way around. He rewrote almost every piece of copy that crossed his desk, thereby letting the program's regular writers know that while their work might be acceptable to Cronkite, it did not measure up to his standards. In other ways as well, he evinced disdain for what he called "traditional" newscasting, which, he contended, had been overly influenced by "stodgy" wire-service prose. Whatever his intent might have been, such remarks were interpreted as slaps at the traditionalist and former wire-service reporter who normally occupied that anchor chair.

On the surface, at least, Hart's presumptions were tolerated with equanimity, thanks in part to his own cheerful personality. He had a disarming way of pulling rank and throwing his weight around without being obnoxious about it, which helped mollify the situation. But beneath the surface, there was plenty of resentment. The main reason it was held in check was that Hart wasn't taken all that seriously. After all, he was the one on trial, and in his strenuous attempts to draw a sharp contrast between his *modus operandi* and Cronkite's, he was only hurting himself. As one of the show's associate producers put it that summer, "The man's obviously on an ego trip, so let him have his fun. He won't be back. He may be good, but he's not *that* good."

When Hart's one-month stint came to an end, he wound up his last broadcast with the announcement that Cronkite would be back from vacation the next day. He then smiled and said, "I *was* John Hart." The words were prophetic. He was not blackballed; as a matter of fact, Hart anchored the *Evening News* a few times after that, but only in a pinch when other correspondents were unavailable. For all his talent and charm, he was now regarded as an overeager meddler who had interfered too much with the intrinsic rhythm and ethos of the *Evening News* operation. Members of the staff who felt a strong sense of loyalty to Cronkite were especially wary of Hart. All things being equal, they preferred having a substitute anchorman who was more appreciative of the fact that, even when absent, Walter Cronkite was the sun around whom their snug and powerful world revolved. So from the standpoint of the show's producers, Hart had been more trouble than he was worth, and they quietly passed that message up to the management level, where it was heeded.

As a result, that summer of 1971 turned out to be the high-water mark of John Hart's career at CBS News. He had come a long way in a hurry, but his course was now headed in the opposite direction. The decline was gradual, at first almost imperceptible. Indeed, he went on to have another big year in 1972. He was on the first team of floor correspondents at that summer's conventions and was one of the headliners on the network's election-night coverage. He also received permission to apply for a visa to North Vietnam. When it was granted in September 1972, he flew to Hanoi, becoming the first CBS News correspondent to go to North Vietnam since Charles Collingwood's visit in 1968. Hart's reports from Hanoi that fall were prominently featured on the Cronkite show as well as on his own *Morning News* program.

For there was still the *Morning News*—his power base, such as it was—but by the end of 1972, Hart had lost much of his enthusiasm for that assignment. The lethal combination of vile hours and feeble ratings was wearing him down, just as it had worn down his two predecessors, Wallace and Benti. He had not yet become disgruntled enough to give up the program, but as it turned out, that decision was made for him. A few weeks after Hart returned from Hanoi, Salant and Manning called him in and suggested it was time for him to start planning for his future beyond the *Morning News*. The meeting was entirely cordial, unsullied by even the slightest hint of reproach. Both Salant and Manning emphasized that they were thinking only of Hart's best interests, and they assured him that he still had a great career ahead of him at CBS News. Hart was not opposed to the change, and, in fact, the more he thought about it, the more he agreed that it was probably the right step to take. But as he later said to a *Morning News* associate, "I would have preferred it if leaving the show had been *my* idea, not theirs."

So in the summer of 1973, the *CBS Morning News* was given yet another new face—or, on this occasion, faces. Chosen to replace Hart was the male-female anchor team of Hughes Rudd and Sally Quinn, while Hart himself began doing Sevareid-like commentaries on the show. The opportunity to play the sage, to revel in analysis, had its own rewards in terms of ego gratification, but it was still the *Morning News*, the broadcast with "an audience of one," give or take a million or so other viewers. In addition, he anchored several documentaries and special reports over the next few months, which were also worthwhile assignments, but they didn't get him on the air very often. Thus, without a daily anchor base or a glamorous beat, Hart began to fade more and more into the background. There was only so much room at the top, and by the end of 1974, he did not need a visitation from the Ghost of Christmas Present to tell him what was happening. Thoroughly frustrated, he entered into negotiations with NBC News.

Hart went to work for that network in February 1975, and he became, in essence, the NBC counterpart of Roger Mudd: Capitol Hill correspondent, weekend anchorman, and occasional substitute for John Chancellor on the *Nightly News*. Like Harry Reasoner five years earlier, he discovered that he could parlay his CBS credentials into a better job at another network. In the final analysis, the assessment of him back in the summer of 1971, when he was filling in for Cronkite on the *Evening News*, seemed to reflect the opinion of the CBS management: John Hart was good, but he wasn't *that* good.

19 "Don't Let the Bastards Scare You"

Even during the period when Roger Mudd was quietly doing penance for the blasphemies uttered in his Washington and Lee speech, his name was invariably the first to be mentioned whenever the question of Cronkite's successor came up. For example, at a private affiliates meeting in 1972, Dick Salant was pressed by queries about the future of the *CBS Evening News*—will there be life after Cronkite?—and he indiscreetly told the gathering that if Cronkite were hit by a truck tomorrow, the post would go to Mudd. When the remark was leaked to the trade press, Salant was furious ("I'll murder the son of a bitch who told *Variety*," he fumed), and almost immediately, he began to back away from such a strong endorsement. As time went on, he even adopted the ploy of applying twists to his earlier statement, telling one outside reporter in 1973 that he couldn't guarantee what would happen "if Cronkite were hit by a ship instead of a truck." Some insiders dismissed such remarks as executive caginess, managerial reluctance to make a premature commitment. But others were not so sure. For by 1973, there were signs that Salant and other CBS executives were giving increasingly serious consideration to another correspondent. By then, the challenger to be reckoned with was not John Hart, whose moment had come and gone, but Mudd's Washington colleague and *former* friend—Dan Rather.

The early 1970s were, for Dan Rather, both the best of times and the worst of times. Through his aggressive coverage of the Nixon White House, he had become a star, but he had also become a divisive and controversial figure, more in the style of Murrow than in the anchor-

288

man tradition of Cronkite and Reasoner. He was playing it hot in a cool medium, and there were many who felt he was in danger of burning himself out, as Murrow had done. Rather himself had a clear understanding of the volatile situation he was in. He knew that the heat he generated with his reports from the Nixon White House could as easily break him as make him. Indeed, given the problems he was having with some of his CBS superiors during these years, there were dark moments when he privately agreed with those who predicted that his own career would not survive the Nixon whirlwind. But for the most part, he welcomed the pressure. Intensely ambitious, Rather had come up the hard way, and now that he had made it this far, he wasn't about to start pulling his punches. Besides, he was by nature a gambler, and he had a strong hunch that if he did survive this difficult period in his own way and on his own terms, he would come out ahead.

Struggling and taking risks to get ahead (by leaps and bounds, if possible) had been a way of life for Dan Rather ever since his early years in Texas. He did not start out with the comfortable, middle-class advantages that helped ease the course for other big-name television journalists. Rather came from working people, country people, which over the years has been a source of both strength and insecurity. He grew up on the outskirts of Houston, where his father worked on an oil pipeline gang, digging ditches. "Rags" Rather was a gruff, no-nonsense type who used to tell his son that if he wanted to stay out of trouble in life, he had to learn "to keep your nose down and your ass up." It was honest, well-meaning advice—a sort of pipeliner's credo—but Rather, by the time he was an adolescent, had begun to dream beyond the oil fields of East Texas.

His mother encouraged the dreams. She was determined that he go to college, even though no one on either side of his family had ever done so before. She cashed in a couple of $25 U.S. Savings Bonds to enroll him in Sam Houston State Teachers College in nearby Huntsville, and that was it as far as family financing was concerned. From that point on, Rather had to come up with the necessary funds himself. He had played football in high school, and so he set out to win a football scholarship. It was a quixotic hope, for Rather lacked both the size and the speed for college football. When the bad news came, he left the coach's office with tears streaming down his face. He had pinned all his hopes on the scholarship.

But help was quick to come from another source. Rather had already set his sights on a career in journalism, and in the brief time he had been at Sam Houston State, he had grown close to a journalism teacher named Hugh Cunningham. Cunningham saw in Rather a raw talent, a large potential, and he now made Rather's future his personal concern, finding him jobs and loaning him money to keep him in college. More than that, he meticulously nurtured him in the skills of reporting and writing.

From Cunningham, Rather learned not only craft but also about the kind of character it takes to be a superior journalist. At one point, when he and his classmates were studying the career of Elmer Davis, whose moral courage was as formidable as his talent, the professor asked them, "For the working reporter, what's the most important thing Elmer Davis ever said?"

After a few seconds of silence, Cunningham gave them the answer, one Dan Rather would never forget: "Don't let the bastards scare you."

One of the jobs Cunningham lined up for Rather was at a small radio station in Huntsville. It was not only his chief source of income while in college, it also proved to be a useful, trial-and-error learning experience. Then, following his graduation in 1953 and a brief hitch in the Marines, he returned to Houston, where he worked for a few months on the *Houston Chronicle,* soon shifting over to the paper's radio station, KTRH. After five years there, he moved into television, and by 1961, he was news director and anchorman at the CBS affiliate in Houston, KHOU.

Throughout his career, Rather would have the good fortune, on several occasions, to be in the right place at the right time—with the reportorial strengths to take full advantage of each situation. The first time a big story fell in his lap was in September 1961, when a hurricane named Carla slammed into the Texas coast. For three days, while the storm was at its peak, Rather and his KHOU camera crew were marooned on Galveston Island. His live coverage from there, which included pictures of the hurricane itself (eye and all), beat the hell out of the opposition and was monitored by CBS News in New York. During those three days, Rather, until then a nonentity outside of Houston, made a big hit with the network brass. As Walter Cronkite later put it, "We were impressed by his calm and physical courage. He was ass-deep in water moccasins."

Among those who admired the job Rather did on the hurricane

story was Ernie Leiser, then in charge of beefing up the network's television news operation. Accordingly, Leiser reached out for Rather, and in early 1962, he went to work for CBS News, starting as a New York–based correspondent with the understanding that he would stay there only about six months, just long enough, Leiser told him, "to get the feel of our system, how we do things."

Rather had his problems in New York. He had not been outside Texas that much, and in numerous ways he was still quite green—and more than a little uptight about that. Once, Leiser's chief deputy, Ralph Paskman, invited him to dinner at his home in Westchester County. Rather accepted, then later remembered that his wife, Jean, was planning to fly up to New York that weekend. (Since he was going to be there only a few months, he hadn't moved his family from Houston.) Paskman had a gruff, intimidating manner, and Rather, who felt cowed in his presence, did not want to complicate the arrangements. So he chose not to tell him that his wife was going to be in town that weekend, and when the night came, he parked her in a Manhattan hotel and went off to dinner at Paskman's house, alone. Jean Rather was not amused.

After a little more than a month in New York, Rather, restless and unhappy, went to Leiser and pleaded for an assignment in the field. His request came just at the time CBS News was preparing to open up two new bureaus in the South, in Atlanta and Dallas, and Leiser decided that Rather's talents could be put to better use on his native soil. So, in the spring of 1962, he returned to Texas to set up and run the new bureau in Dallas. His counterpart in Atlanta was Hughes Rudd, and between them they were responsible for coverage of all the major stories in the Old Confederacy, not exactly a pleasant assignment in those days.

The civil rights movement was in full eruption across the South, and the networks were giving it a big play. It was, in fact, a pivotal moment in the history of TV journalism. For the first time, television had the technology and other resources to compete, on film, with newspapers on a day-to-day basis, and the civil rights movement was the first important and sustaining story to come under the new microscope. On the network level, the coverage of the region's racial problems was often critical, and many Southerners, long accustomed to the constraints of local press accounts, didn't like it. Throughout the Gulf states, angry defenders of the status quo began referring to the three networks as the "African Broadcasting Company," the "Colored Broadcasting

System," and the "Negro Broadcasting Company."

The fact that Rather and Rudd were Texans helped assuage some of the hostility they aroused as correspondents for one of the "Yankee" networks. Still, they often had a rough and ugly time of it as they covered the violent upheavals of that difficult period, from the riots at the University of Mississippi when James Meredith was enrolled as its first black student to Sheriff "Bull" Connor's police-dogs-and-fire-hose treatment of demonstrators in Birmingham, Alabama. Rudd was older, more experienced, and a more gifted writer than Rather. But Rather had more drive and stamina, and he generally outhustled Rudd, beating him to the scenes of major stories and working harder to come up with fresh angles. As a hard-news reporter, Rather was soon running circles around Rudd, and Rudd resented it. As a matter of fact, he continued to harbor a grudge for a long time afterward; later, during the Nixon years, Rudd sometimes made sneering remarks about how Rather's soaring reputation far exceeded his journalistic worth. Those who were familiar with the early 1960s background, when they shared the Dixie beat, were inclined to attribute such put-downs to Rudd's own wounded pride, which had been trampled in the vintage where the sour grapes are stored.

Part of Rudd's problem was that the numerous acts of cruelty then being committed in the name of racial segregation filled him with such revulsion that he had no reportorial appetite for the civil rights story. Rather was just as offended by some of the things he witnessed, but being younger, fresher, and, above all, acutely conscious that this was his first major test as a network correspondent, he made a more determined effort to suppress his personal feelings and concentrate all his energies on the journalistic job that had to be done. At the same time, both men were legitimately concerned about the one-sided picture of the South being presented on national television during this troubled period. The many decent white Southerners who were more moderate in their racial views were largely ignored for the simple reason that they chose to avoid the conflict and remain in the background. By the spring of 1963, Rudd was so fed up with the overall situation that, at his request, he was transferred to Chicago. CBS News then decided to consolidate the Atlanta and Dallas operations into one bureau, which Rather relocated in New Orleans. He left Dallas in the summer of that year, only to return a few months later to join in the coverage of President Kennedy's visit to Texas.

November 22, 1963, was, in career terms, the most important day in Dan Rather's life. His swift and accurate reporting on the Kennedy assassination and its aftermath that weekend transformed him from a regional journalist into a national correspondent. A few days after the assassination, he received a call from Ernie Leiser informing him that he was being transferred to Washington to cover the White House. He had just turned thirty-two, and he was being promoted over the heads of several more experienced correspondents who were then working in the Washington bureau. In assigning him to the White House beat, Leiser and Dick Salant were also influenced by the fact that the new President was Lyndon Baines Johnson from Johnson City, Texas. As a New York producer said at the time, Rather was given the post because CBS News wanted to have someone there who could understand "chili talk."

The Dan Rather who covered the first year of LBJ's Presidency bore little resemblance to the self-assured and incisive correspondent whose reports from the White House a few years later would make such a strong impression on viewers of the *CBS Evening News*. When he took on the job in early 1964, he did not know Washington at all, and, despite the chili-talk connection, he did not know Johnson and his people very well, either. On top of that, he had to cope with the problem of Bob Pierpoint, the man he had replaced as White House correspondent, who was understandably bitter about having been taken off the beat. To his many friends within the CBS bureau and among the White House press corps, Pierpoint portrayed Rather as an undeserving upstart who had been given the assignment only because he was from Texas and was Ernie Leiser's pet protégé. That aggravated what, even under the best of circumstances, would have been a difficult transition, and Rather floundered about a great deal during his first few months as a White House correspondent. Still, he felt he was making steady if undramatic progress and was therefore stunned and dismayed when, following Johnson's landslide victory in the fall of 1964, he learned that CBS News wanted to send him to London.

Fred Friendly had recently taken over as president of the news division, and the move was his decision, prompted in large part by his desire to assign Harry Reasoner to the White House. Reasoner, by then, had staked out his position as the network's number two correspondent, but he was not getting enough regular exposure. Covering the White

House would rectify that. In addition, Friendly thought that Rather was still a little too provincial and thus would benefit from the broadening experience of an overseas assignment. Rather protested the move, but Friendly's mind was made up.

Rather's overseas tour did prove to be an enriching experience. It gave him an opportunity to work with (and learn from) some of the top veterans from the Murrow Era—Charles Collingwood, Alexander Kendrick, Winston Burdett, and Peter Kalischer—and he made the most of it. His reportorial ability was beyond reproach—he had, by then, conclusively demonstrated that—but in other ways he was still a bit rough around the edges. Collingwood, in particular, helped him polish up his act, giving him tips on the kind of style and elegance that, in the Murrow canon, ranked close to Godliness. Collingwood would tell him, in his patrician way, that any hooligan can cover a fire or riot, but that a well-rounded journalist should also be able to comport himself with savoir faire in a drawing room or art gallery. Rather, ever conscious of his deficiencies in background and education, welcomed the guidance and took it to heart.

He was also seeing quite a bit of the world. From London, he was sent off to cover stories in Greece and India and other trouble spots. Then, in the fall of 1965, he requested and was granted a transfer to Saigon. Rather spent the next several months in Vietnam, and by the summer of 1966, the war was starting to consume him, just as it was consuming Kalischer, Morley Safer, Jack Laurence, and almost every other reporter who came into direct contact with that dreadful abuse of American power and resources. Indeed, Vietnam might well have become the central experience of his professional life during these years, the arena in which he would make his reputation; but in the summer of 1966, Harry Reasoner left Washington to return to New York, and Rather was brought home and reassigned to the White House. This time, he dug in and established such a strong foothold that, in the years ahead, two Presidents would be driven out of office before his next departure from that post.

Not long after Rather's return to Washington, Lyndon Johnson, who was recuperating from a minor operation on his vocal cords, summoned the three network White House correspondents—Rather, Ray Scherer of NBC, and Frank Reynolds of ABC—to his hospital room for an impromptu interview. Actually, it was a ruse. It was Scherer's birthday, and since he was regarded by Johnson and his people as a sympathizer, a friendly correspondent, the President wanted to express his personal gratitude. A birthday cake was wheeled in, and Johnson presented Scherer with a gift, a pair of pajamas. Later, as the three reporters were leaving, LBJ signaled Rather to wait. Then, in a sly yet paternal voice, Johnson said, "Son, you stay in Sunday school and keep your nose clean and maybe someday you'll get a pair of pajamas, too."

Rather never got his pajamas. He was, by this time, far more sure of his ground than he had been in 1964. Vietnam had become the overriding issue of Johnson's Presidency, and, having recently been there, Rather felt he had a perspective on that story that gave him an edge over most other White House correspondents. His reporting took on more muscle, more authority, and became increasingly critical, thus reflecting the rising wave of dissent that was starting to close in on the Johnson White House.

Johnson did not appreciate it. After viewing Rather's reports on the *CBS Evening News,* he sometimes telephoned him, and invariably his first words would be: "Are you trying to fuck me?" One did not have to be a native of the Lone Star State to understand that kind of chili talk. At other times, LBJ tried to exploit the Texas connection, commenting once, "Goddamnit, Dan, *you,* of all people, should understand what I'm trying to do." He then followed that up with the accusation that Rather had betrayed his roots and was "reading the *New York Times* too much."

Rather certainly did not enjoy being on the receiving end of Johnson's fulminations, but at least LBJ dealt with him out front, man-to-man. Once a tirade was over, that was usually that—until the next time. As he would soon discover, the group that followed Johnson into the White House preferred to operate in more insidious ways. Indeed, the time would come when Rather would look back on his raucous but open clashes with the Wild Bull of the Pedernales with twinges of nostalgia.

For several months during 1968, after Johnson announced that he would not be a candidate for reelection, Rather assumed that his days at the White House were also drawing to an end. The unofficial policy at CBS News was to change White House correspondents every time a new President took office. And in all likelihood, Rather would have been replaced by Mike Wallace had he chosen to continue covering Nixon's 1968 campaign instead of leaving that assignment to co-star on *60 Minutes.* But with Wallace out of the picture, there was no clear-cut alternative to Rather following Nixon's victory that fall. So he was told that the job was still his if he wanted it.

Rather did want it, but not because he had any inkling of what the next few years would be like. Quite the contrary; the last two years of Johnson's Presidency had been so stormy and acrimonious that he told Washington bureau chief Bill Small that he was looking forward to covering the White House "when things are a little more tranquil." Things *were* tranquil, at first, but by the fall of 1969, with the war in Vietnam still raging, the protest movement that had helped drive Johnson out of office flared up again. Press accounts—including reports by Rather from his White House beat—began to reflect the growing impatience with Nixon's piecemeal efforts to "wind down" the war. The Nixon people did not like this treatment any more than the Johnson people had, but instead of confronting individual reporters in private, as Johnson had done, they launched a robust and full-scale attack on the press.

This tactic had been predicted, in an oblique way, by Senator Eugene McCarthy two years earlier. At the start of his insurgent candidacy for the 1968 Democratic Presidential nomination, itself an outgrowth of the antiwar movement, McCarthy said that he knew he was embarking on a hazardous course. He pointed out that human nature probably had not changed much since ancient times when Persian generals killed the messengers who brought them bad news. McCarthy, who had an oddly playful penchant for martyrdom, had himself in mind, but the *real* messenger during these years was the press, both print and electronic. So, in the fall of 1969, the Nixon Administration set out to "kill the messenger" by arousing public mistrust of its integrity and even, in some cases, its patriotism.

The principal target, in speeches by Spiro Agnew and others, was television, the medium with the most powerful impact and a mass, nationwide audience. The antitelevision assault was brilliantly orchestrated by Bob Haldeman, Nixon's chief of staff and media expert, and it struck a responsive chord. At the end of a jarring and turbulent decade, which also just happened to be the first decade of daily, saturation television coverage, many Americans had grown so weary of the unrelenting clamor of "bad news" on the tube that they were willing, when prompted, to regard the messenger as the villain. The poison injected into the body politic at the time was, in fact, so potent that it continued to fester over the next several years. Even after the Watergate investigations revealed, in appalling detail, that it was the policy-makers in Washington—and not the journalists at home and abroad—who had been the true masters of deceit, many Americans still harbored suspicions about the press in general and the networks in particular.

While the Nixon forces labored to discredit all three networks, they focused their attack on CBS. It not only had the largest audience, it was also the network with the strongest news tradition. Hence, the Nixon strategists agreed, if CBS could be brought to heel, the other networks would follow suit. And as part of their campaign to bend CBS News to their will, to reduce it to a propaganda arm of the Nixon White House, Haldeman and his cohorts made a clumsy attempt to run Dan Rather off his beat.

The hit man on this particular mission was Haldeman's onetime college classmate and current White House sidekick, John Ehrlichman. On a visit to New York in the spring of 1971, after an interview by John Hart on the *CBS Morning News,* Ehrlichman had breakfast at the Plaza Hotel with Hart and Dick Salant. In the course of their conversation, Ehrlichman told Salant that "Rather has been jobbing us" and proposed that he be reassigned to a new bureau in Austin, Texas, or better yet, given a year's vacation. Salant immediately recognized, even if Ehrlich-man did not, just how gauche a tactic this was. Under the circum-stances, the surest way to keep Rather at the White House was for someone like Ehrlichman to press for his removal. If he had backed up his complaint with hard evidence of factual errors Rather had commit-ted in his coverage, then Salant would have been obliged to take him seriously. But Ehrlichman did not offer such evidence, and so Salant laughed him off. To embarrass him further, he later leaked details of their conversation to the outside press.

One newspaper account of the breakfast meeting subsequently appeared in Washington, where it was read, with more than routine interest, by Dan Rather. He did not find Ehrlichman's proposal all that funny. He was not concerned about his job, especially after he talked to Salant, who assured him he had no need to worry. But he demanded an appointment with Ehrlichman, who told him, in a memorable en-counter in Ehrlichman's office, that he welcomed the opportunity "to say to your face what I said to your boss."

"Oh, I appreciate that," said Rather, "but what I don't appreciate is what you tried to do."

Ehrlichman shrugged that off, then said, "I don't know whether it's just sloppiness or your letting your true feelings come through, but the net effect is that you're negative. You have negative leads on bad stories."

"What's a bad story?" asked Rather, bristling.

"A story that's dead-ass wrong," Ehrlichman replied. "And you're wrong ninety percent of the time."

"Then you have nothing to worry about," Rather assured him. "Any reporter who is wrong ninety percent of the time can't last." But when he asked for specifics, Ehrlichman became vague and began talking about "tone" and "attitude."

While this engaging colloquy was in progress, the door opened and in walked Haldeman, the advertising man, the media guru, who offered a few general observations about television reporting and impressed Rather with his knowledge of the craft. Then he said, "What concerns me is that you are inaccurate and unfair, but your style is very positive. You sound like you know what you're talking about. People believe you."

"Yeah," echoed Ehrlichman, "people believe you, and they shouldn't."

Rather, by this time, was finally starting to see a little humor in the situation. With a smile that he hoped did not look too triumphant, he said, "Well, I hope they do, and maybe now we are getting down to the root of it. You have trouble getting people to believe you."

That, of course, was the root of it. In contrast to Nixon, Rather came across as credible, as a man one *would* buy a used car from. Even more galling from Haldeman and Ehrlichman's point of view was the realization that the Nixon White House was serving as a perfect foil for Rather. Working in that tense and volatile atmosphere, he was becoming a much bigger star than he ever would have become in a more placid setting—and, to a large degree, the Nixon strategists had only themselves to blame for that.

The Dan Rather cult that grew out of the Nixon years was a minor phenomenon that fascinated those who were close to him, primarily because it was so much at variance with the person they knew. In reality, Rather was a far cry from the shin-kicking, anti-Nixon firebrand that so many viewers, on both sides of the political fence, perceived him to be. He was, to be sure, a diligent and aggressive reporter who refused to be intimidated by the various attempts to coerce and control him.

Ever mindful of Elmer Davis's dictum, he did not let the bastards scare him. But as he himself was quick to point out during the Nixon years, there were other White House correspondents (notably, James Deakin of the *St. Louis Post-Dispatch* and Martin Nolan of the *Boston Globe*) who were often tougher on the President and his policies.

Still, Rather was the one with the forum—the most powerful medium and its most powerful network—and he brought to it a dynamism, an intensity of feeling, that set him apart from most other television correspondents. Although he prided himself on his possession of cool and poise, that usually came across as a transparent facade. His personal emotions simmered close to the surface, and his efforts to keep them in check often had the opposite effect. Rather was, in that sense, not a good actor; whether angry or compassionate, solemn or cheerful, viewers *felt* it in an almost visceral way. He brought to his reporting a high-strung, personal intensity that frequently gave it more emotional force than he truly intended.

With the mileage he was getting out of the White House beat, Rather was acquiring a reputation as one of the best reporters in the business. Still, there were those who chose to regard him as little more than a tailor's dummy, and who attributed his success almost solely to his telegenic face. Like Charles Collingwood, he was movie-star handsome, and, like Collingwood, he discovered that this was, at times, a dubious advantage. Thus, goaded in part by his irritation with the pretty-boy image and in part by residual insecurity from his early years, Rather continued to push himself very hard to prove his worth, especially in areas where he felt the greatest need for improvement. One of his mentors was Eric Sevareid, from whom he solicited advice about what books he should read to fill some of his educational gaps. Sevareid, impressed by what he once described as Rather's "refreshing modesty," responded with a tutorial plug for the essays of Montaigne: "A man isn't educated until he reads Montaigne," Sevareid counseled. So Rather's constant striving to improve, to excel, to overcome disadvantages real and imagined also contributed to the tension that characterized much of his on-air persona.

At the same time, his blue-collar Texas background was a conscious source of strength. For one thing, it enabled him to scoff at White House charges that he was a creature of the liberal and elitist Eastern Establishment. Unlike so many other young men from the provinces who rose to journalistic stardom in Washington and New York, Rather remained in close touch with his origins. His own parents were dead by this time, but throughout his years on the White House beat, he regularly returned to Texas for vacation visits with his wife's family. Rather's strong sense of regional identity also surfaced in his casual conversation, which was spiced by Texas colloquialisms. Camera crews he worked with were urged not to hurry but to "move pronto." Producers who suggested a course of action he considered impractical were politely informed that "that dog won't hunt." Once, when a close friend was in serious financial trouble, Rather offered him "an Oklahoma loan"— meaning, presumably, one that did not have to be repaid. And at times when the long hours and the daily pressures of the White House assignment wore him down, he often acknowledged exhaustion with an equine metaphor: "I feel like I've been ridden hard all day and put to bed wet."

What dismayed so many of Rather's friends during the Nixon years was the way his on-camera presence—the frequently grim expression and taut style of delivery—completely overshadowed the natural warmth that, off the air, was one of his most striking characteristics. Whereas most of the big-name correspondents at CBS News were inclined to treat secretaries and other underlings in a perfunctory, even disdainful manner, Rather was unfailingly pleasant and often went out of his way to take a personal, sympathetic interest in their lives and careers. Much of the time, in fact, he was generous and courteous to a fault. With his unceasing flow of "sirs" and "ma'ams," "pleases" and "thank yous," he carried Southern gentility to the point of saccharine overkill. He also suffered from a chronic inability to say no, whether to a celebrity-fawning pest on the street or to a friend requesting a luncheon date. As a result, he was forever running late and overextending himself, a pattern of behavior that irked his wife and others who made futile efforts, from time to time, to impose a modicum of order on his chaotic habits. Washington bureau chief Bill Small once said that, in this respect, Rather closely resembled that notorious people-pleaser, Hubert Humphrey. "If they were women," Small chortled, "they'd be pregnant all the time."

But Rather's more human qualities seldom came across to viewers, least of all to those who habitually watched his reports from within the fortress of the Nixon White House. To Nixon and his cadre, Rather was arrogant and unfair, intense and unrelenting, their Media Enemy Number One. As Washington's resident nightclub comic Mark Russell once put it, "Dan Rather is to Nixon what hiccups are to a glassblower."

20 Kill the Messenger

By the spring of 1971, at the time Haldeman and Ehrlichman were accusing Rather of being excessively credible, the war between the Nixon Administration and CBS was heating up on other fronts as well. In February of that year, CBS News had aired a documentary called *The Selling of the Pentagon.* Written and produced by Peter Davis (who later directed *Hearts and Minds,* the Oscar-winning film about Vietnam), *The Selling of the Pentagon* was an hour-long examination of the Defense Department's public-relations activities. It was a strong and provocative documentary, very much in the Murrow-Friendly tradition. Indeed, just as the famous *See It Now* broadcast on McCarthy was "told mainly in his own words and pictures," so Davis and Roger Mudd—the show's on-air reporter and narrator—relied almost exclusively on the Pentagon's own public-relations programs to make their point: namely, that the Pentagon was not dispensing information so much as cold-war propaganda, and that many of its PR projects were both wasteful and nefarious.

The broadcast touched off a spirited controversy. Pentagon charges that CBS News was guilty of deliberate distortions in its editing techniques led to a Congressional investigation, and that, in turn, brought Frank Stanton into the fray. When Stanton refused to comply with a House subpoena demanding "outtakes" (film not used on the show), the investigating subcommittee moved to have him cited for contempt of Congress. In truth, Stanton and other CBS executives were not entirely happy with the way *The Selling of the Pentagon* had been edited. One interview, in particular, had been manipulated in such a way as to give

301

viewers a mildly misleading impression. But this minor transgression was not crucial to the show's central theme, which was thoroughly and accurately documented. Stanton's main argument, however, was that the government did not have the right to probe into the inner workings of a news organization, especially when the subject in question was a critical report on a powerful branch of the federal government. Compliance with the subpoena, he contended, would have a "chilling effect" on the freedom of the press to cover government activities. As far as he was concerned, the fundamental principle at stake was the Holy Grail of American journalism—the First Amendment.

The fight against government interference was one that Stanton, that suave lobbyist, had been waging for years, ever since the quiz-show scandals of the 1950s. But never before had it escalated to the point where he was threatened with being cited for contempt of Congress. Frank Stanton was now in the twilight of his long reign as president of CBS (in two years he would be sixty-five, the mandatory retirement age at the network for everyone but Chairman Paley), and many of his subordinates on the news division level regarded this uncompromising stand—taken on their behalf—as the high point of his distinguished career. Needless to say, almost everyone in the broadcasting industry was greatly relieved when the House voted to recommit the contempt citation, thus bringing the episode to a close.

The Nixon-Agnew years also brought out the best in Walter Cronkite. Of all the major television correspondents, Cronkite was the most vigorous in his denunciations of the White House assault on the network news divisions, and of course he also brought to the battle the greatest measure of prestige and authority. His most blistering counterattack came in the spring of 1971, when in a speech accepting a trade award as Broadcaster of the Year, Cronkite lashed out at what he called "a grand conspiracy to destroy the credibility of the press." Those were harsh words; perhaps, some of his colleagues thought, a bit too harsh. Veteran producer Joe Wershba, who had been a front-line soldier in Murrow's army in the early 1950s, congratulated Cronkite on his speech, but said that he was troubled by the word "conspiracy." Wasn't that going a little too far? No, Cronkite replied, it sure as hell wasn't. Two years later, when the "White House horrors" (as John Mitchell labeled them) came to light—the elaborate plans to "screw our enemies" and all the rest of it—Wershba went back to Cronkite and apologized.

In addition to its public attacks on the networks, the Nixon White House was also adept at manipulating and exploiting them to serve its political ends. Those tactics were especially evident in the early months of 1972 when Nixon made his historic visit to China, quickly followed by his step-toward-détente trip to the Soviet Union. The two events were timed and packaged in such a way as to induce extensive and favorable media coverage on the eve of Nixon's reelection campaign; and the networks, responding with Pavlovian predictability, pulled out all the stops on both stories. Yet they really had no choice in the matter. Regardless of the media manipulation that went into their planning, and whatever their effect on domestic politics, the Presidential visits to Peking and Moscow were big and important stories, and therefore deserved the saturation television coverage they received. Journalistic judgment had to be the sole criterion then, and it was also the sole criterion a few months later when Walter Cronkite committed the power and prestige of the *CBS Evening News* to a thorough examination of the Watergate affair.

Watergate was not an easy story for television to cover. The scandal was enveloped in shadow and cover-up, and to get to it, reporters had to navigate a hazardous course. But if the networks were slow to move on that story (and they were), so, too, were the wire services and all major newspapers and magazines—save, of course, for the *Washington Post* and its two enterprising reporters, Bob Woodward and Carl Bernstein.

By the fall of 1972, Woodward and Bernstein had pushed well beyond the Watergate burglary itself into the far more explosive area of political espionage and sabotage, exposing a trail of illegal acts that led to the top echelon of the Nixon Administration. Until then, the networks had given only desultory attention to the story, but stirred by the *Post*'s startling allegations, Cronkite and the CBS News management decided to go after it in a big way. The Watergate project was turned over to the most experienced field producer on the *Evening News* staff, the talented and resourceful Stanhope Gould, and in Washington Dan Rather and Daniel Schorr were assigned to help him smoke out the story.

It was, they discovered, both too soon and too late for that. Although Woodward and Bernstein had been able to root out valuable confidential sources, the cover-up was still holding firm, and, indeed, the various reports in the *Post* had the effect of clamping the lid on tighter than ever. Still, in snooping around Washington, Gould and his reporting team came up with enough to convince them that Woodward and Bernstein had the goods. Thus, the decision CBS News faced was whether to put together a full-scale report, almost entirely derivative of the *Post*'s stories, or to abandon the assignment, at least for the time being.

It was not an easy decision to make. Even though any CBS Watergate story would take great care to label its sources and include all White House denials, those journalistic fine points would be forgotten if the *Post*'s allegations were subsequently refuted. The ensuing discredit would reflect almost as much on CBS News as it would on the *Post*. Hence, when they finally did decide to go ahead with the story, Cronkite and his colleagues were saying, in effect, that their faith in the reporting of Woodward and Bernstein was nearly as great as that of Ben Bradlee, the *Washington Post*'s editor.

Derivative sources or no, Gould had assembled a vast amount of material in film, still photos, charts, and other graphics, which he processed and edited into two parts, each running slightly more than fourteen minutes. It was an extraordinary, unheard-of chunk of time for one story, no matter how momentous. For years, CBS News people had been fond of saying that if television had existed when the Ten Commandments were issued, the lead that night on the *Evening News* would have been: "Moses came down from Mount Sinai today with the Ten Commandments, the three most important of which are. . . ." Yet now Gould was proposing that roughly two-thirds of the Cronkite show on two separate nights be devoted to the Watergate story.

Dick Salant and other news executives were already wary of the project, and the inordinate length of Gould's package deepened their apprehensions. "Isn't this awfully long?" Salant wondered. "Do we really need this much?" But after Cronkite screened the material, he was, if anything, more enthusiastic than ever, and it was his vote that carried the day. The report would run in two parts, fourteen minutes each.

Part one was broadcast on October 27, 1972, ten days before the election. Cronkite led into the report with this introduction:

> At first it was called the Watergate caper—five men apparently caught in the act of burglarizing and bugging Democratic headquarters in Wash-

ington. But the episode grew steadily more sinister—no longer a caper, but the Watergate affair escalating finally into charges of a high-level campaign of political sabotage and espionage apparently unparalleled in American history.

A couple of times during the broadcast, Cronkite got out of his anchor chair to point to some graphics in an effort to simplify some of the story's more puzzling details. "That alone was enough to alert viewers to the fact that this was no ordinary news show," a jubilant Gould said the next day. "In living rooms all across America last night, husbands were hollering to their wives, 'Honey, quick, get in here. Something's wrong. *Walter's standing up!*'" As the publisher of the *Washington Post*, Katharine Graham, later told Salant, by way of thanks, "You turned our local story into a national story."

She was not the only one to grasp the significance of the broadcast. The following day, William S. Paley received a telephone call from Charles Colson, who was then the muscle man of Haldeman's antimedia operation. An ex-Marine, Chuck Colson prided himself on his toughness. He once confided to White House cronies that he liked to be thought of as a "flag-waving, kick-em-in-the-nuts, antipress, antiliberal Nixon fanatic." In a stream of abusive obscenities, Colson told the CBS Chairman that the Watergate report on the *Evening News* was the most irresponsible journalism he had ever seen. He went on to characterize it as a cheap and desperate attempt to swing the election to George McGovern, and he warned that CBS would live to regret it.

Even before his conversation with Colson, Paley had been unhappy with the Watergate report. He, too, felt it had been aired uncomfortably close to the election, an election Richard Nixon seemed certain to win by a landslide. Moreover, he thought the mixture of facts and allegations was confusing and not in keeping with the standards of CBS News. And above all, he considered the length of the story grossly disproportionate. The telephone call from Colson did little to assuage Paley's objections, and in a subsequent meeting with Dick Salant, he elaborated on them with considerable force.

Salant had anticipated corporate displeasure with the Watergate report, but he was not prepared for the severity of Paley's rage. In all his years at CBS, he had never seen the Chairman quite so livid. When the subject of the second segment came up, Paley made it very clear that he did not want to see it aired on *his* network. Such was the autonomy of the news division by this time that even Paley, with all his power, stopped short of actually ordering Salant to kill part two of the report. But there was, in Paley's voice and manner, the unmistakable threat of reprisal.

Salant did not know about the conversation with Colson (although he soon began to entertain strong suspicions in that direction), and he left the meeting with Paley both puzzled and shaken. There were still frictions in his relationship with Paley, dating back to 1964 when he was ousted as president of the news division, but in recent years almost all of Salant's corporate dealings had been with his friend and patron, Frank Stanton, or with Stanton's deputy, Jack Schneider. At this stage of his career, it was not like the Chairman to involve himself so directly and so insistently in the internal affairs of the news division. As a matter of fact, the reason Paley was so involved was that Colson had called him only after he had first tried and failed to reach Stanton. If Stanton had been the one to take the call, the clash with Salant surely would have been less heated; indeed, it might not even have occurred. Stanton was accustomed to dealing with Colson and his ilk, and he generally shielded both Paley and the news division from their boorish threats.

After his meeting with Paley, Salant began going over the script of part two, this time with a less indulgent eye. Consciously or not, he was looking for a loophole, and, astute lawyer that he was, he soon found one. A large portion of the second segment dealt with the laundering of illegal campaign money in Mexico, a complicated transaction that was an essential ingredient of the Watergate story. But Salant remembered that this subject had been covered in a Dan Schorr report broadcast during the Labor Day weekend as part of a series of Sunday specials that summer on the 1972 campaign. Therefore, Salant argued, it was an old story and did not need to be repeated on the *Evening News*. In taking that position, Salant conveniently overlooked the fact that a program aired on a summer holiday weekend had neither the audience nor the impact of an *Evening News* broadcast; even more to the point, it did not have the towering authority of Walter Cronkite. As he proposed the cut, Salant confided to his associates that he hoped he was making an honest news judgment. For even in his own mind, there lurked the uneasy suspicion that he was using his legalistic finesse to put a journalistic face on a decision that, in reality, had been prompted by corporate pressure.

Stanhope Gould vigorously protested the cut, and he was supported by Gordon Manning. Their main argument was that Watergate was such a complex story it had to be spelled out in detail, even at the risk of some repetition. But Cronkite went along with the cut, in large part because he fully appreciated the tight spot Salant was in. If there were to be reprisals, Salant's head would be the first to roll, not Cronkite's. So this time it was Salant's vote that carried the day, and the second segment was cut from fourteen minutes to eight minutes. The concession was not enough to placate Paley. When part two was aired on the *Evening News* a few nights later, he flew into another rage, warning Salant that this sort of thing must never happen again.

Dick Salant and the other CBS News people who were involved in the two Watergate reports survived that storm, but there is no telling what might have happened if the Nixon White House had not been put squarely on the defensive by the full flood of Watergate disclosures a few months later. For in the immediate aftermath of Nixon's landslide victory that fall, his antimedia troops were certainly not in a defensive mood. A few days after the election, Colson telephoned Stanton to inform him that from now on, it was going to be all-out war. The Nixon Administration, he said, was going to use its power to destroy CBS on Madison Avenue and Wall Street. "We'll break your network!" Colson shouted over the phone.

Naturally, Stanton was upset by the call, and the more he thought about it, the more depressed he became. His own career at CBS was almost at an end (his mandatory retirement was set for the following March), and in the past few years he had come to love the news division, to regard its protection as his highest duty. Yet he would be forced to leave the battle just when it seemed to be entering its most critical phase. As he prepared to step down, Stanton shuddered to think what the next four years would bring, now that Nixon and his henchmen had a huge electoral mandate to cite as justification for their actions.

In the meantime, Dan Rather's career had reached a critical, even perilous, crossroad. On the surface, at least, the Nixon years were working very much to his advantage. In addition to his regular White House coverage, he was acquitting himself well on periodic specials, most notably an hour-long, prime-time, one-on-one interview with Nixon in January 1972. And having inherited Harry Reasoner's slot on the Sunday night news show, he had moved into that select group of correspondents who anchored their own broadcasts. He now ranked right next to Roger Mudd in the pecking order.

Yet with each advance he made, Rather became increasingly aware of a disturbing fact: within the CBS News power structure, there was a formidable anti-Rather faction that sought, at almost every turn, to thwart his progress. He knew he could still rely on the support and encouragement of two key men: Dick Salant in New York, and his immediate superior in Washington, Bill Small. But by the early 1970s, the chief activist and strong man on the CBS News management team was Gordon Manning, and Rather had what he often described as "a serious Manning problem."

He first became aware of it in 1970 when, following Reasoner's departure, he began to lobby for the Sunday night anchor slot. Rather frankly believed that he had earned a regular anchor assignment, but Manning contended that while he was an excellent field correspondent, he had hardly any studio experience, a consideration he had ignored four years before when he picked Roger Mudd to anchor the Saturday news. Even when he gave his reluctant approval to the move, Manning imposed on it the demeaning condition of a trial period, which lasted for several weeks before he finally, and still with reluctance, announced that Rather was Reasoner's official successor on the Sunday night show.

Then, in the summer of 1971, when Mudd was in the doghouse because of his Washington and Lee speech and John Hart was assigned to anchor the *Evening News* in Cronkite's absence, there were many CBS people who felt that Rather should have been chosen over Hart. Rather, it was argued, had more star quality and was far better known to viewers across the country. Indeed, some insiders thought that Manning purposely passed over Rather that summer because he, much more than Hart, loomed as a serious, long-range threat to Mudd, who was still Manning's top choice for the role of Cronkite's regular backup and eventual successor. Rather was finally given an opportunity to anchor the *Evening News* when Cronkite took a few days off the following spring. Yet even then, he still had ample reason to believe that Manning was trying to stifle his career. For by then, Rather and Manning were embroiled in an angry dispute over another matter.

In the spring of 1972, Rather coauthored an article for *Harper's* magazine on the ominous and all-but-invisible power base Haldeman and Ehrlichman had established within the Nixon White House. It was a project he cared deeply about, for although he was one of the very few reporters in Washington during this pre-Watergate period who had a clear understanding of the profound influence Haldeman and Ehrlichman were exerting on the Nixon Presidency, Rather had been unable to get that story across to viewers. The rise of Haldeman and Ehrlichman had been a subtle process, a gradual accumulation of power, no one step of which had been especially dramatic or newsworthy; as such, it did not lend itself to the "headline" style of Rather's nightly stand-uppers from the White House lawn. In the *Harper's* article, the Haldeman-Ehrlichman story would be given the depth and background it required. At the same time, it also occurred to Rather that such an article, appearing in a magazine like *Harper's*, would enhance his own reputation as a serious and perceptive journalist—and that notion no doubt crossed Gordon Manning's mind as well.

When Rather first proposed the idea, Manning, preoccupied with other matters, gave it his vague and tentative consent. But when the article was written and was ready for submission, Manning decided to play his own version of "kill the messenger." He summoned Rather to his office, and although he did not go so far as to order him not to publish it, Manning made cryptic and menacing remarks to the effect that if the piece were published, it might invalidate Rather's value to CBS News at that summer's conventions and even at the White House itself. He said that he wanted Rather to "cool it" and "keep a low profile."

Rather was furious with Manning, both for retracting his consent and for resorting to threats to prevent the article from being published. Nor was he proud of himself when the rancorous scene in Manning's office ended with his capitulation. The article was pulled, but Rather and his coauthor then decided that there was enough material in the Haldeman-Ehrlichman story to be developed into a book. Out of that decision eventually evolved *The Palace Guard*.

Rather's relations with Gordon Manning were downright cordial compared to the problems he was having with Manning's favorite producer, Paul Greenberg. From the fall of 1971 until the following September, Greenberg produced both Mudd's Saturday show and Rather's Sunday night broadcast, an arrangement that neither he nor Rather found to his liking. Rather, who was strictly a hard-news man in those days, did not share Greenberg's enthusiasm for back-of-the-book features. In addition, he disapproved of the way Greenberg treated people, especially his abuse of low-level operatives who were in no position to fight back. Greenberg, for his part, thought that Rather was "overrated," that he lacked depth and intellectual substance, especially in comparison to Mudd. The Mudd comparison was uppermost in Greenberg's mind, for his career was inextricably linked with Mudd's, and since Rather had become Mudd's chief rival, Greenberg viewed him as a threat to his own future as well.

During the year they worked together on the *CBS Sunday News*, Rather and Greenberg generally kept their hostility under control and avoided any kind of open and ugly confrontation. That came later, in the fall of 1972, shortly after Greenberg became executive producer of the Cronkite show, a promotion that, by definition, made him the most powerful producer in the CBS News organization. In early October, as part of the network's coverage of the 1972 election, Rather filmed a report for the *Evening News* on how the campaign was shaping up in the key state of Michigan. But on the day it was scheduled to run, the report was yanked from the lineup at the last minute. That in itself was no cause for concern; Rather simply assumed that a time squeeze or some other minor complication had forced Greenberg to hold back the Michigan story until another day. But just to make sure there was nothing wrong with the report itself, he telephoned Greenberg from Washington and said, "I notice the Michigan piece didn't play, and I—"

"That's right," said Greenberg, interrupting, "and it's never going to play." Before Rather had a chance to reply, Greenberg went on to say, "And don't ever call me like this again. You are not to deal directly with me." He then added that in the future, if Rather had any complaints or questions about the *Evening News*, he should take them up with one of his deputies. And with that, Greenberg hung up.

Rather couldn't believe it. To be told that he, the network's chief White House correspondent, was not entitled to communicate directly with the executive producer of the *CBS Evening News* was preposterous as well as insulting. Infuriated, he promptly called Manning, who expressed some concern but not nearly as much as Rather thought the situation warranted. Manning told Rather he'd check it out, and a few minutes later he called back and said, "I talked to Paul, and he says you're a liar."

When Rather asked him what in hell that was supposed to mean, Manning replied, "I don't know. He wouldn't elaborate." Then, in the time-honored manner of executives faced with a sticky problem, Manning proposed that Rather fly up to New York the next day and have lunch with him and Greenberg. "I'm sure this is just some silly misunderstanding," he suggested weakly.

As far as Rather was concerned, "lunch" was not the way to handle the matter. Greenberg had stepped out of line and should be reprimanded. Skip the amenities. Even more galling, when Rather flew to New York the next day for lunch, he found Manning, but no Greenberg. "Paul's tied up," said Manning, visibly embarrassed. As they made their way through a tense and awkward meal, Rather had the eerie feeling that Greenberg—the ostensible subordinate who was totally indebted to Manning for his flourishing career at CBS—was, in reality, the dominant partner in their complex relationship. After lunch, Rather, at Manning's insistence, went to Greenberg's office. There he was again told that he was a liar, this time to his face. Rather managed to keep his voice under control as he asked Greenberg to explain precisely what he meant by that. Greenberg replied that he didn't owe Rather an explanation. That ended the conversation.

Rather left Greenberg, and on his way out of the building, he stopped by Manning's office and said, "I don't know what kind of games you guys are playing, but don't think for a moment that I'm going to stand for this shit." Manning responded with a helpless shrug, as if to say, There's nothing I can do about it.

On his shuttle flight back to Washington, Rather was angry, and more than that, he was apprehensive. Until then, he had attributed his problems with Manning and Greenberg to the neurosis of office politics. To be resented and even stymied on occasion because he was viewed as a threat to Mudd, their fair-haired boy, was irritating but hardly cause for alarm. He could deal with that kind of intramural jockeying, and there was no real danger of his not being able to survive it. But the humiliating treatment to which he had just been subjected had far more ominous implications.

Ominous was the word for it. Greenberg's associates on the *Evening News* were aware that he was unhappy with Rather's work. Even before the Michigan story, he had complained about Rather's "cheap shots" and "smart-ass attitude" and his objections to that particular report were more general than specific. Throughout the Presidential campaign that fall, Greenberg delivered frequent and obscene harangues on how Rather was needlessly aggravating the problems CBS was having with the Nixon Administration. "He's fucking up the works," Greenberg said at one point, "and we're all going to suffer for it." Greenberg strongly implied that Rather was exploiting the Administration's feud with the network to serve his personal ends, thereby putting his own career ambitions above the welfare of CBS News.

That was a harsh indictment, but even given Greenberg's appetite for malice, his co-workers believed that he would not have dared launch such a virulent personal attack on a correspondent of Rather's stature unless he was extremely sure of his ground. Those who understood how the Manning-Greenberg alliance worked were convinced that in lashing out at Rather, Greenberg had Manning's tacit approval and even, to some degree, his encouragement. The evidence also suggests that Manning and Greenberg were taking their cue from a strong anti-Rather bias that was seeping down from the corporate sphere. For by the fall of 1972, much of the White House–inspired pressure to get rid of Rather was coming from CBS's own affiliate stations across the country.

In their struggle to resist White House coercion, the networks' weakest point of defense, their soft underbelly, was their affiliates. Unlike the network centers in New York, these individual stations were licensed by the government, and thus were more vulnerable to government threats and harassment. Beyond that, many of the affiliate owners and station managers agreed with the Nixon-Agnew thesis that the concentration of journalistic power in New York and Washington gave the network news broadcasts a built-in, Eastern Establishment, liberal slant. They didn't like the strong and critical reporting on Vietnam and Watergate any more than the White House did. So, partly out of fear and partly out of sympathy with the Nixon Administration, some of the affiliates began to side with the White House against the network news divisions.

The removal of Dan Rather from the White House beat remained a top priority of the Nixon strategists, and some of their allies among the CBS affiliates were now lending their support to that goal. That was a kind of pressure that the CBS management had to take seriously. It was one thing to ignore the crude proposals John Ehrlichman made over breakfast at the Plaza Hotel, but the affiliates had the kind of leverage that counted: the power to refuse to take network programs. Hence, largely in response to the affiliates' lobbying efforts, an anti-Rather atmosphere began to permeate the executive suites of CBS. And although his most loyal supporters on the news division level, such as Dick Salant and Bill Small, remained firm in their defense of Rather, others, such as Manning and Greenberg, did not.

Such, then, were the forces bearing down on Rather, both from within and without CBS, as Richard Nixon moved toward his landslide victory in the fall of 1972. As the network braced itself for the much-heralded "four more years" and the prospect of even more ferocious battles with the Administration, rumors began to spread that Dan Rather was a marked man who would not be able to survive Nixon's second term, at least not as White House correspondent. And that, in essence, was what Paul Greenberg's bullying and bad-mouthing were all about. He sensed that Rather was on the ropes, and since that neatly conformed to his personal bias and best interests, he couldn't resist getting in a few hard licks of his own.

These difficult days were made even more difficult for Rather by the severe strain in his relationship with Roger Mudd. Both men viewed that situation with some regret, for they had formerly been good friends. They had first met in 1961 at the time of Hurricane Carla, when Rather was still working for the CBS affiliate in Houston and Mudd, having recently joined the CBS News Washington bureau, was sent to Texas to cover the story for the network. Then, in 1964, when Rather was struggling through his rookie year as White House correspondent, Mudd was one of the few people in the Washington bureau who went out of his way to befriend him. They became so close in those days that when Rather was pulled off the White House beat and transferred to London, the Mudds gave the Rathers a going-away party.

But by the early 1970s, their friendship was on the rocks. More than anything else, it had become a casualty of the natural rivalry that built up between them in the wake of Harry Reasoner's departure. Mudd felt that Rather was largely to blame for that because of the way he played up the rivalry to outside interviewers, encouraging them to plead his case in newspaper and magazine articles. Rather maintained that he never brought the subject up in interviews, but when it was raised, he candidly discussed it. Besides, he thought that Mudd had nothing to complain about since, with Manning shuffling the cards, the deck was stacked in his favor. But even though they were no longer friends, Mudd and Rather, both having been reared in the tradition of Southern courtesy, were invariably civil to each other—that is, until the spring of 1973, when they had a nasty falling-out over a change in company policy.

Bill Paley issued an edict that spring forbidding CBS News corre-spondents from indulging in any more "instant analysis." The custom-ary practice of following a Presidential speech or news conference with immediate commentary by Sevareid and others had elicited some of the Nixon Administration's sharpest criticisms of television news, dating back to Agnew's first antimedia diatribe in the fall of 1969. Paley's directive seemed to be a delayed reaction to that criticism, and it was widely interpreted as a concession to the Nixon White House. The Chairman was irked by this reading of his motive, and when he put out a subsequent memorandum insisting that the decision had been prompted solely by journalistic considerations, some wit in the news division observed that "fortunately for Paley's nose, the Blue Fairy isn't dealing as harshly with him as she did with Pinocchio."

Unhappy with the edict, five of the network's top Washington correspondents—Mudd, Rather, Marvin Kalb, Daniel Schorr, and George Herman—decided to send a letter of protest to the CBS man-agement. (Significantly, Sevareid did not join in the action. He had long been uncomfortable with the policy of instant analysis on journalistic grounds, believing that it resulted too often in ill-conceived snap judg-ments that were later regretted.) The tone of the letter was quite frank, with Mudd supplying many of its sharper touches. But when the time came to sign it, Rather balked, saying that the language did not accu-rately reflect his feelings on the issue and that he preferred to write his own letter. The other correspondents were annoyed by that, but they were far more provoked by Rather's subsequent behavior. When Dick Salant found out about the letter, he let the rebellious correspondents know that he did not object to their protest. At that point, Rather sent word, through Washington bureau chief Bill Small, that he was willing to sign the letter after all.

His colleagues' response to Rather's change of mind was an em-phatic "No way." As far as they were concerned, Rather had chickened out when the chips were down, and now that Salant's tolerant reaction had reduced the risk involved, he was trying to worm his way back in. All of them were sore, but Mudd was in a special rage. In his opinion, Rather was trying to have it both ways. On the one hand, he reveled in his reputation as the gutsy, hard-hitting reporter who sallied forth each day to do battle with the Nixon White House, and yet behind the scenes, he was just another double-dealing company man who was willing to stand up to his own brass on a point of principle only after being assured of management support. The incident seemed to bring all of Mudd's smoldering resentment toward Rather up to the surface. Over the next several months, he seldom missed an opportunity to make caustic remarks about Dan Rather's character and ambition.

For his part, Rather did not need Mudd or anyone else to tell him that he had behaved badly. "It was not one of my heroic moments," he later admitted to a magazine reporter, and in private conversations he went a lot further than that. Yet most of his many friends at CBS News were inclined to take a more sympathetic view, for they appreciated the enormous pressure he was under. More than any of his colleagues or competitors, Rather was on the cutting edge of the Nixon Adminis-tration's assault on TV journalism. There was also ample evidence that powerful forces within his own network had turned against him, and Rather knew (even if Mudd and the other correspondents did not) that the risks involved in signing the protest letter were much greater for him than for them. The improbable postscript to all this was that the letter, instead of incurring Paley's wrath, apparently helped nudge him toward reconsideration. Five months later, he reversed himself and rescinded the ban on instant analysis.

The Mudd-Rather feud came at a time when the career fortunes of both men were clearly on the upswing. By the spring of 1973, Roger Mudd's period of penance was over, and he was moving into his inheri-tance as Walter Cronkite's regular backup on the *CBS Evening News.* What's more, that assignment suddenly became more of a showcase than it had been during the Reasoner years. Cronkite had a sturdy constitution, but he was now fifty-six and the job of anchoring a high-pressure daily news show was an exhausting routine, both mentally and physically. Needless to say, it was in the best interests of both Cronkite and CBS to keep him in prime condition; and so, like an aging all-star ballplayer who sits out the second games of doubleheaders to preserve his strength, Cronkite signed a new contract with the network in 1973 authorizing him to take three months off a year. Perhaps the main reason he welcomed the arrangement was that it enabled him to devote more time to his favorite off-duty passion—sailing.

Next to Cronkite, the chief beneficiary of the new contract was Roger Mudd. He anchored the *Evening News* for more than two months that summer. And while summer is normally a slow season both for news and for television, this one was hardly typical. Thanks to the Ervin Committee's Watergate hearings and related "bombshells," there was more than enough happening in the summer of 1973 to keep viewers glued to their TV sets.

As for Dan Rather, he was a major beneficiary of the Watergate scandals themselves. The flood of disclosures that began to erupt that spring took the heat off the press in general, and off reporters like Rather in particular, shifting it onto the White House, where it belonged. By the summer of 1973, Haldeman, Ehrlichman, and Colson and their sundry partners in crime were out of the White House and on their way to jail—all of them, that is, save for the "unindicted" coconspirator himself. Still, Rather was not entirely over the hump. In some respects, the controversy he generated with his coverage of the Nixon White House would become even more intense in the months ahead, and the vigorous campaign waged against him by the CBS affiliates would not be repulsed for good until the following spring.

But by the summer of 1973, the worst was over; the deeper Nixon's Presidency sank into disgrace, the better Rather looked. And it was during this period that the Dan Rather cult grew to full flower. Over the next several months, a spate of admiring articles were written about him, including a full-length profile in *Esquire* that speculated on the post-Cronkite future and ended on the glowing note that "this could be the beginning of a beautiful anchorman." (It was precisely this kind of article that set Roger Mudd's teeth on edge.) Yet even as so many external events were breaking his way, Rather continued to brood about his in-house problems. His humiliation at the hands of Manning and especially Greenberg had left him so bitter that he was giving serious thought to cashing in his chips when his contract with CBS expired and trying his luck at another network. Rather had been nurtured in the proud tradition of CBS News, and he still felt a strong sense of loyalty to it. But loyalty can be stretched only so far, and he wasn't at all sure that he wanted to continue working for an organization in which so much power was concentrated in the hands of Gordon Manning and Paul Greenberg.

21 Rooks and Bishops, Knights and Pawns

Paul Greenberg's promotion to the post of executive producer of the *CBS Evening News* was preceded by a series of intricate maneuvers that had a disruptive effect on the show's internal operation and on the careers of some of its key personnel. The elaborate choreography was set in motion in the spring of 1971 when Les Midgley informed Salant and Manning that he wanted to move on to another assignment. He was nearing the end of his fourth year as executive producer of the Cronkite show, and enough was enough. He had never cared for the long hours and daily pressures that the job entailed, and he now insisted that the burden be passed on to somebody else. Faced with the prospect of replacing him, Salant and Manning had to address themselves to the tricky question of what to do with Midgley's chief deputy and heir apparent—Sandy Socolow.

Socolow felt that he had been unjustly passed over in 1967 when Midgley inherited the post from Ernie Leiser, and in the years since then, he had made it clear on several occasions that if he were denied the job the next time around, he would resign. Moreover, Socolow had always believed that the reason Leiser had pushed so hard for Midgley to succeed him was that the way would then be clear for him to step into Midgley's slot as executive producer of the Special Reports unit, a direct exchange of one power base for another. That, to be sure, was one of Leiser's motives, but there was also another reason why he had been reluctant to recommend that Socolow be named his successor.

In Leiser's judgment, the most critical and difficult aspect of producing the *CBS Evening News* was the need to act as a countervailing force to Walter Cronkite. By his sheer presence, Cronkite emanated such stature and authority that he had an intimidating, even oppressive effect on his co-workers, which was not necessarily good for the broadcast. Therefore, the show's executive producer should be someone with enough independent strength and authority to stand up to Cronkite from time to time. Leiser did not have confidence in Socolow's ability to do that. He believed that Socolow was so attuned to Cronkite's moods and preferences that, intuitively, they governed his own journalistic reactions. In the process of becoming Cronkite's friend, confidant, and surrogate, Socolow had sacrificed the independence that, in Leiser's opinion, was a prime prerequisite for the position of executive producer.

There was an exquisite irony in this situation. For years just about everyone at CBS News (including Socolow himself) had viewed his special relationship with Cronkite as a precious asset, and, in fact, some of his colleagues were more than a little envious of his privileged status. Yet when it came to being considered for the top job, the one he lusted after and felt he had earned through diligence and demonstrated ability under fire, the Cronkite connection proved to be more of a detriment than an advantage—and Socolow himself did not even seem to realize that.

But if Ernie Leiser was less than candid in his 1967 conversations with Socolow, he was quite frank about his misgivings in the private talks he had at the time with Dick Salant. As a result, Salant came to share those reservations, and now, four years later, as Midgley prepared to step down, they were very much on his mind. Yet Salant also understood that if Socolow were denied the promotion a second time, he was apt to be angry enough to quit CBS News, and Salant certainly did not want that to happen. For one thing, he was genuinely fond of Socolow (as was Leiser, for there was nothing personal in any of this). More important, he regarded him as too good a man to lose. In addition, Salant realized that if Socolow were passed over again, not only would he have an unhappy Sandy Socolow on his hands, but an unhappy Walter Cronkite as well, and that was a headache he wanted to avoid at all costs. So this time, there seemed to be no alternative.

As it turned out, however, there was another way. For at this point, Gordon Manning displayed his genius for managerial manipulation.

Manning also did not want Socolow to become executive producer of the *Evening News,* but his objections were more convoluted and stemmed, in part, from his own aspirations. Ever since he took over as hard-news vice-president in 1964, Manning had been frustrated—first by Leiser, later by Midgley—in his periodic attempts to assert direct control over the day-to-day operation of the *Evening News*. The fact that he was their titular superior meant very little, for both men had considerable weight and authority stemming from their years of experience at the network and their close association with Dick Salant. Manning had every reason to believe that Socolow, having served such a long apprenticeship under Leiser and Midgley, would be just as resistant to outside interference. More than that, his intimate relationship with Cronkite would be a decided advantage, for it would give him a powerful and trusted ally in any serious confrontations with management. So Manning had his own reasons for not wanting Socolow to become Midgley's successor, and he had a plan to circumvent it. He proposed to Salant that Socolow be moved up to the management level as his own chief deputy. To clear the way for that appointment, Manning would have to oust his present deputy, Ralph Paskman, but he had no qualms on that score. Instead, he had wanted to get rid of Paskman for some time.

Ralph Paskman had been a key member of the CBS News management team since the 1950s, and he had demonstrated, over the years, a remarkable gift for survival. His present title was executive editor and deputy news director, and essentially he provided the coordinating link between the various news shows and the correspondents in the field. Through his subordinates on the Assignment Desk, he orchestrated the day-to-day "troop movements" to and from story locations around the world. Paskman was a journalist of the old school who loved to bark orders and chew people out. Several producers and correspondents considered him to be an anachronism, a rather corny relic from an earlier era when reporters bragged about "scoops" and addressed their editor as "chief." On the management level, Manning and others felt that Paskman was actually a martinet *manqué;* that beneath all his bluster, he ran a fairly lax operation and was too often willing to settle for mediocre and slipshod work.

In Manning's view, Paskman was a man of limited vision and ability whose gruff, swaggering manner was, in reality, a defensive posture assumed to compensate for his own shortcomings. Thus, Manning's motive in wanting to replace Paskman with Socolow was not entirely Machiavellian. He sincerely believed that Socolow would be a big improvement over Paskman in that job. Yet at the same time, moving him into Paskman's slot would neatly eliminate Socolow from consideration for the post of executive producer of the *Evening News*. The problem now was to convince *him* that it was the right move.

To make the position more attractive to Socolow, Manning proposed that it be given a fancier title. As he and Salant discussed that prospect, a far more elaborate plan for managerial upgrading gradually evolved. It was decided that Manning and his vice-presidential counterpart, Bill Leonard, would be elevated to the newly created rank of senior vice-president, and that four other men—Socolow, Washington bureau chief Bill Small, Emerson Stone, head of the radio operation, and Casey Davidson, in charge of camera crews, directors, and other technicians—would be given the title of vice-president. But the promotion of Socolow was the key move, the one that prompted all the others.

When Socolow found out what Manning and Salant had in mind for him, he was both stunned and flattered. His ambition had been focused so intently on the executive producer's job that it had never occurred to him he might be a candidate for a management-level post, much less one with the august title of vice-president. And Manning certainly couched the offer in glowing terms. Socolow was told that not only would he be taking on a much broader range of responsibilities, but the new assignment would also put him on the executive track for future advancement. Manning was operating on the assumption that when Salant retired he would succeed him, and Socolow was encouraged to assume that he was in line for Manning's job and thus in position one day to become president of CBS News.

This was heady stuff for Socolow; at the age of forty-three, he was eleven years younger than Manning and had plenty of future ahead of him. So he readily accepted the offer. If Socolow had any doubts about why Manning and Salant wanted to ease him out of the *Evening News* apparatus into the management structure, he did not betray them in his conversations with friends and colleagues. He chose to view the move solely in positive terms, as a dramatic leap forward in his CBS career. The doubts would come later, along with the regrets.

The various managerial promotions were ready to go into effect by November 1971, but Salant decided to hold off the official announcement until after the question of Les Midgley's successor was resolved. Although he retained the prerogative of final approval, Salant delegated the task of selecting the new executive producer of the *Evening*

News to Manning, and Manning in turn brought Socolow and Cronkite into the decision-making process. Now that Socolow had been upgraded out of contention, the most logical candidate was his coproducer on the show, Russ Bensley. But Manning, Socolow, and Cronkite all felt that Bensley should remain in his present post as the officer in charge of the broadcast's film operation and staff of associate producers. Bensley, they all agreed, was a superb film and production man, one of the best in the business. But Socolow and Cronkite had serious doubts about his feel for hard news, the day-to-day headline stories that formed the nucleus of the *Evening News*. To pull Bensley out of a job for which he was brilliantly suited and put him in one in which he was likely to be much less effective did not make any sense. So Russ Bensley was ruled out.

But if not Bensley, then who? This was the opening Manning had been waiting for, and he jumped in with a spirited pitch for Paul Greenberg. But both Cronkite and Socolow were wary of Greenberg, primarily because of his reputation for mistreating people who worked for him. Faced with the united opposition of Socolow and Cronkite, Manning did not press his case. Instead, he took Greenberg to lunch a few days later and gave him a going-over, telling him that his reputation as an SOB was hurting his career.

So Greenberg's name joined Bensley's on the "no" list. Various other candidates were then considered, and after numerous discussions, the decision was made to entrust the assignment to Chicago bureau manager John Lane. His qualifications for the post were, in some respects, quite dubious. He had never produced a network news show, and, never having worked in New York, he was unfamiliar with the complex infrastructure of the CBS News headquarters. But Lane had other credentials working in his favor. He had a solid background in both print and electronic journalism, and he had earned very high marks over the past three years as Chicago bureau chief.

Like Heywood Hale Broun and Bill Crawford, John Lane was the son of a prominent journalist. His father, Clem Lane, had been city editor of the *Chicago Daily News* in the 1930s and 1940s, and over the years he had come to be regarded as something of a legend in that lively newspaper town. His son worked briefly for CBS News in Chicago during the late 1950s, and then spent six years, from 1959 to 1965, as a reporter and rewrite man at the *Daily News*, where the towering shadow of Clem Lane's reputation loomed heavily over him. In 1965, he went to work for WBBM, the CBS-owned station in Chicago, and two years later, he switched over to the CBS News bureau. Lane was appointed bureau manager in 1968, and the diligence and enterprise he brought to that assignment greatly impressed his New York superiors, most of whom had never heard of Clem Lane. He had become, at last, his own man.

Sandy Socolow telephoned Lane over the Thanksgiving weekend of 1971 to inform him that he was on the verge of being appointed executive producer of the *CBS Evening News with Walter Cronkite.* And now it was Lane's turn to be stunned and flattered. He knew he had been doing an excellent job in Chicago and had earned a promotion of some kind. But executive producer of the Cronkite show, the most powerful and most prestigious producer's job in the CBS News organization—*that* took his breath away. Only later did Lane begin to wonder how his fellow Chicagoan and old friend, Russ Bensley, would view his appointment.

It was a good question. Like everyone else who had worked on the *Evening News* in recent years, Bensley had long assumed that Socolow would succeed Midgley as executive producer. But in the fall of 1971, when he heard rumors that Midgley was preparing to leave the broadcast and Socolow was to be promoted to the management level, Bensley began to nourish his own aspirations. And as the rumors became more frequent and more traceable to reliable sources, his hopes soared to the point where he fully anticipated the promotion. Such, then, was Bensley's state of mind when, a few days after Thanksgiving, he was summoned to Manning's office. Manning's first disclosures—that Midgley was leaving the *Evening News* and Socolow was to become a vice-president—filled Bensley with elation. This is *it,* he thought, savoring in advance Manning's next pronouncement. Then came the crusher: John Lane was the choice for executive producer of the *Evening News.*

Bensley was shocked, and in a subsequent meeting with Manning, Socolow, and Cronkite, he urged them to reconsider the decision. Although he shared their high estimation of Lane's ability, he argued that since the post was not going to Socolow, it should go to him. He was next in line, and it was important that the promotion come from within the show's apparatus in order to preserve the morale and continuity of the *Evening News* operation. Bensley went on to say that his own morale had been dealt a serious blow, and that, frankly, he now had to reassess his commitment to the Cronkite show and CBS in general. He then left the decision-makers to their own counsel.

Manning, Socolow, and Cronkite had assumed that the low-key, soft-spoken Bensley would be a good soldier and accept Lane's appointment with, at most, a slight murmur of protest. They had obviously underestimated him and they now were genuinely concerned that he might resign in protest. That, they agreed, was a most disturbing prospect. The loss of Midgley and Socolow was going to be difficult enough to sustain, and if Bensley were to quit, the Cronkite show would be stripped of all three of its senior producers. What's more, they had to worry about an angry reaction from the associate producers, most of whom felt a strong sense of loyalty to Bensley. Suddenly the entire fabric of the *Evening News* operation appeared to be in jeopardy, and as they discussed the situation, Manning, Socolow, and Cronkite concluded that their most prudent move was to relent and give Bensley what he wanted. They still had reservations about Bensley's ability to handle the job of executive producer, but they decided they could live with them a lot more easily than with the divisive turmoil his rejection was likely to cause.

Bensley, in the meantime, had returned to the *Evening News* area in a high state of agitation. He firmly believed that he had taken the right stand, but he was not at all optimistic about the outcome. He was standing in front of a bulletin board, brooding over the decision his superiors had made against him when, out of the corner of his eye, he caught sight of Cronkite striding toward him with a broad grin on his face. Extending his hand, Cronkite said, "Congratulations, Russ—you're it!"

A few days later, when the sweeping reorganization was announced in a flurry of memoranda, John Merriman, the editor of the Cronkite show, sat at his desk poring over the official verbiage as intently as a Kremlinologist trying to decipher the latest power shift in the Politburo. Finally, another member of the staff asked him, "Well, John, what do you make of it?"

Merriman glanced up and looked around to make sure none of the principals was within earshot. He then chuckled and said, "They've thrown a hell of a lot of window dressing on it to try and confuse us, but it's obvious what the lead is. Midgley is leaving, and Socolow didn't get his job. *That's* the headline." It was not for nothing that John Merriman was esteemed for his editorial acumen.

Others, however, were less perceptive. For example, Cronkite viewed Socolow's promotion as an excellent move, and he had encouraged him to accept it. From a personal point of view, Cronkite would have preferred keeping Socolow on the *Evening News,* but the last thing he wanted to do was stifle his friend's career. The way he saw it, Socolow would have a chance in his new vice-presidential position to extend his skill and authority over a much broader range. Beyond that, he would be in line to inherit Manning's job someday, and eventually move up from that to the presidency of CBS News. Such an opportunity did not come along every day. What Cronkite failed to anticipate was that Socolow's lofty new management position would be worth not much more than "a pitcher of warm spit," as the crusty John Nance Garner once characterized another vice-presidential office, the one he occupied under FDR.

The problem, as Socolow himself soon discovered, was Gordon Manning. He was such an activist, such a bustling eager beaver, that he tended to smother anyone serving as his chief deputy. Unlike Salant, who, ever conscious of his own lack of training in journalism, concentrated on administrative matters and executive decisions, Manning could not resist delving into the day-to-day news operation. His background was in news, and that was his passion. The administrative duties that were part of his job—making out budgets and the like—utterly bored him. So he dumped most of those chores on Socolow while he proceeded to exert direct authority over story assignments and other matters that Socolow had been told would be under his jurisdiction. Thus Socolow became, in his new assignment, little more than a glorified clerk, saddled with paperwork and other administrative trivia. And for that, he had given up his long-cherished dream of becoming executive producer of the *CBS Evening News.*

The tedium and frustration of his new job soon began to have an adverse effect on Socolow's personality. The fire and exuberance that had been the driving force behind the Cronkite show slowly disappeared. No longer having a daily outlet for all that combustion, he bottled it up. He became withdrawn, occasionally even morose, and in his dealings with others, he often adopted a formal, rather pompous manner, as though he were striving to cultivate a vice-presidential comportment. Most of his colleagues did not care much for the "new Socolow," but those who knew him well were sympathetic, for they understood how frustrated he was. What was not easy to understand was how Socolow, who was so shrewd and savvy in other ways, had allowed himself to be euchred into such a situation. It was, of course, a question that crossed Sandy Socolow's own mind more than once. But if this was difficult for Socolow, his plight was nothing compared to what poor Russ Bensley was going through.

The most urgent task that confronted Bensley in December 1971, as he prepared to take over as executive producer of the *Evening News*, was filling the two producer posts he and Socolow had just vacated. For the Socolow job—overseer of breaking news, general nuts-and-bolts man, and, most important, regular liaison with Cronkite—he picked John Lane. Bensley thought that was the least he could do for Lane after he had muscled him out of the top job. As for Lane, he was amenable to the assignment and, in truth, was more comfortable with it. He recognized that with Socolow elevated out of the picture, Bensley was next in line and had earned the right of succession. Thus it was more seemly that he join the *Evening News* staff as Bensley's deputy. An Irish Catholic and graduate of Loyola University in Chicago, Lane had a fine, Jesuitical sense of order and hierarchy. First one becomes a bishop, and only *then* begins to reach for a red hat.

John Lane brought to his new assignment some of the strengths Socolow had given it: energy, diligence, and solid journalistic judgment. But in other respects, he did not measure up to his predecessor. He was new to New York, new to the *Evening News*, and new to Walter Cronkite—and that, in particular, proved to be a difficult adjustment. He did not know Cronkite well and was more than a little intimidated by him. Uneasy in the great star's presence and uncertain of his own authority, Lane was unable, in his first few months on the job, to establish a working rapport with Cronkite. As a result, Cronkite felt Socolow's absence from the broadcast even more acutely than he had thought he would.

It was generally assumed that the other producer slot—the one Bensley had vacated—would go to Ron Bonn, the associate producer who regularly took over Bensley's duties when he was on vacation or out of town on another assignment. But the officious manner he adopted on those occasions antagonized other members of the show's production staff, and, keenly aware of "Ron's unfortunate people problem" (as he was wont to describe it), Bensley decided that Bonn was not the best choice. Instead, he entrusted the post to Ed Fouhy, who for the past three years had been doing a fine job as the Cronkite show's Washington producer. But Fouhy did not find the New York assignment to his liking. He missed the autonomy he had enjoyed in Washington, and as the producer in charge of the film bank—the accumulated enterprisers and other less urgent stories—he was working away from his natural strength, which was hard news. After a few unhappy weeks in New York, Fouhy requested permission to return to his former duties in Washington.

That posed a problem, however, for the Washington job had since been promised to Bonn, as a peace offering. Bonn, who felt he had been unjustly passed over, had been threatening to quit ever since the Lane-Fouhy appointments were announced, and to induce him to stay, Bensley came up with the Washington offer. Although not entirely mollified, Bonn agreed to the move and was preparing to leave for Washington when Fouhy suddenly announced he wanted his old job back. At that point, Bensley, feeling a little like a chess player who has just blundered his own king into check, decided he had no choice but to let Fouhy return to Washington and keep Bonn in New York as Fouhy's successor.

So Ron Bonn became the other New York producer, and after many false starts and stops, the team of Midgley, Socolow, and Bensley was replaced by the team of Bensley, Lane, and Bonn. Comparisons were unavoidable, and it soon became evident that John Lane was no Socolow and Ron Bonn was no Bensley. And that, in turn, made it much more difficult for Russ Bensley to become the kind of executive producer Les Midgley had been.

Even under the best of circumstances, it's unlikely that Bensley would have delegated as much authority to his deputy producers as Midgley had delegated to his, for that was not his natural inclination. He loved to immerse himself in the nitty-gritty of a news broadcast, which had presented no problem when he was working at a local station in Chicago, or even later when his responsibilities on the *Evening News* were limited to film production. But the Cronkite show *in toto* was too rigorous and complex an operation for one person to busy himself with all its copious details, and that was the mistake Bensley now made. Aware that Bonn and Lane were not as experienced or as proficient as he and Socolow had been, Bensley sought to ease their respective burdens by taking on many of their duties himself. He spread himself too thin, and the *Evening News* operation lost much of the cohesion and stability that had characterized it during the Midgley years. Harried and overworked, Bensley left too many key decisions unresolved until late in the afternoon, which only aggravated normal deadline pressures. Day after day, as air time approached, the atmosphere in the *Evening News* area was so tense and chaotic that Bensley's co-workers generally braced themselves for what they called "another crash landing."

At first, the confusion was attributed to the trials of transition. But after several weeks passed and conditions seemed to grow more instead of less hectic, even some of Bensley's friends and admirers began to wonder if he was ever going to get a firm grip on the controls. One person who, by then, was past the stage of wondering was Walter Cronkite. He was not at all happy with the way Bensley was working out, and he made no attempt to conceal his displeasure.

Bensley's performance as executive producer was a confirmation of all the doubts Cronkite had felt when his name was first mentioned for the job. Just as he had suspected, Bensley was proving to be more of a film and production man than an editorial man; he was spending far too much time fretting over production details instead of concentrating on his primary area of responsibility: the lead, the lineup, the news of the day. In addition, Cronkite and Bensley did not communicate well with each other. Over the past few years, Cronkite's two most kindred spirits on the staff had been Socolow and his editor, John Merriman, both of whom were mad shouters and chest-pounders, whose frenzied outbursts when things went wrong seemed to demonstrate that they shared his competitive passion. In contrast, Bensley's natural reserve, his imperturbable cool, his almost eerie serenity in the midst of crisis, seemed to irritate Cronkite. It was as though he equated Bensley's impassive manner with indifference, the unforgivable sin in Cronkite's canon. He also thought Bensley was too indulgent. When Bensley suggested that letters of commendation be sent to bureaus whenever they did outstanding jobs on stories, Cronkite scorned it as "a damn-fool idea." It would be much better, he said, to send them letters of reprimand when they failed to do good work.

"The problem," Bensley later recalled, "was that Walter is a stick man and I guess I'm more of a carrot man. We were never able to resolve that basic difference." Bensley also had trouble dealing with what he called Cronkite's "competitive paranoia," his tendency to complain all the time about "stories that NBC had that we didn't have, while he took for granted all the stories we had that they didn't have."

The frictions in the Cronkite-Bensley relationship might have been ironed out if John Lane, in his role as liaison between anchorman and executive producer, had been able to develop a smooth working relationship with Cronkite. But Lane was a far cry from Socolow in that area, and as Cronkite became increasingly disgruntled with the new team he had to work with, he began to spend more and more time each day in Socolow's new vice-presidential office. He wasn't just dropping by for a little casual conversation. His sense of alienation from the *Evening News* apparatus had reached the point where he was going over the heads of his producers and taking his grievances to management, as represented, in this case, by his old friend and trusted confidant.

Cronkite found in Socolow a most sympathetic listener. He, too, had been dubious of Bensley's ability to handle the job of executive producer, the job for which he, Socolow, had been groomed and which would have been his had he rejected the vice-presidential bait. And now, encountering little but frustration in his role as Gordon Manning's bookkeeper and detail man, he could not help but feel a certain amount of jealousy and resentment toward Bensley. Little wonder, then, that Socolow, spurred by Cronkite's litany of complaints, eventually took steps—cautiously at first and then with ever-increasing boldness—to assert his own direct authority over the *CBS Evening News.*

Inevitably, that brought Manning into the act. Once Socolow had broken the ice on the touchy matter of managerial interference in the internal affairs of the *Evening News* operation, Manning felt free to impose his energetic presence on the show's daily decision-making process. Working through Socolow (and, therefore, with Cronkite's tacit approval), he began to harass Bensley with one memo after another, proposing this, urging that, and frequently second-guessing decisions that had been made without benefit of his prior counsel. It was exactly the kind of meddling that Leiser and Midgley had managed to prevent. But Bensley, lacking their stature and authority, and having no powerful allies to turn to for help, was totally beleaguered. As Stanhope Gould, Bensley's good friend and comrade-in-arms during this difficult period, put it, "There was no way that Russ could have survived that situation. Once Gordon and Sandy began fucking all over him the way they did, he didn't have a chance."

Among those observing Bensley's predicament with more than routine interest was Paul Greenberg. By the summer of 1972, he could see that Bensley was in deep trouble, and he decided the time had come to force Manning's hand. Accordingly, he went to Manning and said he was bored with producing the weekend news shows and he intended to quit CBS News unless he was given a better assignment. Manning was not about to risk losing his favorite producer, and he, too, felt the time was now propitious to put Greenberg in charge of the *Evening News*. He knew that Cronkite and Socolow had reached the point where they would welcome almost any move to replace Bensley. Hence, Manning was confident that they would not oppose Greenberg's appointment as they had the previous fall.

At the same time, Manning realized that Bensley's removal would have to be handled with great care and delicacy. A summary dismissal was out of the question. Whatever his failings, he did not deserve that, and such an arbitrary ouster would be sure to enrage those members of the *Evening News* staff who still felt a strong sense of loyalty to Bensley. The need, therefore, was to find another suitable assignment for him, one that did not bear the stigma of a demotion. As luck would have it, just such a position opened up later that summer when Bob Wussler, the executive producer of the Special Events unit, decided to leave CBS News to become general manager of WBBM in Chicago— the same station where, incidentally, Russ Bensley had begun his career in broadcast journalism twenty years earlier.

Manning was sure he could persuade Bensley to take over the Special Events unit, for there was certainly no disgrace in being asked to replace Wussler. Quite the contrary; by 1972, Wussler had become one of the more powerful barons within the feudal structure of CBS News. His Special Events operation was comparable in size and importance to the Special Reports unit, over which first Midgley and then Leiser had presided during these years. But unlike Leiser and Midgley, whose big years at CBS were behind them by 1972, Wussler was a young baron (thirty-five) whose career was just entering its prime. Having risen rapidly to a position of eminence at CBS News, he was about to go soaring in another direction. For in accepting the offer to manage the CBS-owned station in Chicago, Bob Wussler was moving into a high-level executive post outside the news division and toward a future power base within the corporate sphere of CBS.

Wussler's entire professional life had been spent at CBS in New York. A native of New Jersey, he decided, while a college student at Seton Hall, to go into television. It didn't have to be news, necessarily, but it had to be television, preferably network television. A young man in a hurry even then, he did not want to waste time working at some rinky-dink local station. So, about a month before his graduation in 1957, he made a trip to New York, presented himself to the personnel people at CBS, and was hired as a mail-room clerk.

After a mere five weeks in the mail room, he landed a job in the news department as a production assistant, and soon he was working as one of the minions on the Doug Edwards *Evening News* show, where he came under the tutelage of the Maestro—Don Hewitt. But Hewitt was just one of his mentors. In his eagerness to learn and succeed, Wussler went out of his way to seek guidance from just about everyone. He was a fast learner, too, and by the early 1960s he had risen to the rank of producer. Also by then, he had acquired two powerful benefactors—Ernie Leiser and Bill Leonard—who threw their weight behind his career. The man-in-space flights had just begun, and Leiser, then in his management phase, assigned Wussler to produce the network's live coverage. And when he wasn't immersed in space projects, he worked as Leonard's chief deputy in the newly formed election unit. Then, in early 1965, the decision was made to coordinate the long-range planning of space and political coverage into one operation, to be called the Special Events unit. Wussler, having established his expertise in both areas, was picked to head it. So, at the age of twenty-eight, he already had a powerful domain of his own.

Over the next seven years, Wussler and his Special Events team planned and produced the live coverage of all space shots, all political conventions, all election-night returns, and various other major stories, such as the funerals of Eisenhower and de Gaulle, and President Nixon's visit to China. The job of managing all this was one for which Wussler was extremely well suited. He was, to begin with, a superb organizer and a master of advance planning. He had the ability, when the occasion warranted it, to put everything else aside and focus all his attention on even such tedious details as hotel reservations and car rentals for the horde of CBS News personnel assigned to cover a political convention. In addition, Wussler had a flair for lively production techniques. As a onetime Hewitt protégé, he recognized that news programming could benefit, at times, from an inventive use of graphics and animation and other visual embellishments. Thus, a Wussler-produced broadcast invariably featured bright displays of one kind or another.

He was also an adroit empire builder. Over the years he gathered around him a staff of competent, hardworking deputies and assistants, many of whom felt toward Wussler an intense personal devotion that transcended mere loyalty. Being young and amiable, he encouraged camaraderie, even intimacy, and in that way he helped create and nurture his own personality cult. Almost everyone called him "Bobby," and with his soft, impish face and easygoing manner, he *was* "Bobby" —just as Cronkite, by way of contrast, was clearly "Walter," not "Walt" or, God forbid, "Wally." His subordinates also appreciated the way Wussler allowed them to live high off the hog. Those who worked for him seldom, if ever, had to worry about getting swollen expense accounts approved. It was not indulgence on his part so much as calculation, for he understood, better than most, one of the immutable laws of network television: money is power, and vice versa. Wussler strove to cover stories in a big, even lavish way and to take on extra projects that, inevitably, would push him over budget. He knew that would induce his superiors to give him a larger budget the next time around, which would, in turn, enable him to expand his staff and increase his personal power. He once confided that he operated on the principle that "a huge commercial enterprise like CBS will always give you the money as long as you continue to deliver the goods and give them plenty of drama." No one in those days ever accused Bobby Wussler of failing to deliver the goods or coming up short on drama.

Even so, he had his detractors. A few people at CBS News thought he was overly slick and show-bizzy, all flash and no real editorial substance. They loved to point out that he was entirely a creature of TV production, that he had never worked as a reporter, per se, and had never written a news story. Others resented his transparent, outsized ambition and the cunning way he played the company game. In his adept handling of his superiors, Wussler reminded some of his in-house critics of the engaging but unscrupulous hero in *How to Succeed in Business Without Really Trying*—who, they noted, had also started out in the corporate mail room. And, as was the case with Robert Kennedy, the nickname "Bobby" did not always connote affection.

Even those who liked and admired Wussler could not resist tossing off a disparaging remark from time to time. Harry Reasoner, who enjoyed working with him and had a high regard for his ability as a producer, once described him, nevertheless, as "a Catholic Sammy Glick." Then, alluding to the fact that he was the only Protestant in a large Catholic family, Reasoner added with a smile, "And take it from me, they're the worst kind."

But all hands agreed that given the combination of qualities he had going for him—youth, talent, resourcefulness, and charm—Wussler's career had not yet come close to reaching its peak. Hence, no one was surprised when in 1972 he left CBS News to become general manager of WBBM. It was generally assumed that in a few years time he would be back in New York in a management post on the network level. But nobody, except perhaps Wussler himself, anticipated the meteoric burst that followed. He did such an outstanding job at WBBM that two years later, in the summer of 1974, he returned to New York as a network vice-president in charge of sports. And two years after that, in the spring of 1976, he was appointed president of the CBS Television Network, a promotion that moved him squarely into the top echelon of the corporate hierarchy. Next to his immediate boss, Jack Schneider, who reigned over the entire broadcast operation, Wussler had the biggest and most important job in CBS's vast television empire. As president of the TV network, he was directly responsible for all prime-time programming, the lifeblood of CBS, its chief source of profits and power.

By this time, Wussler's former colleagues at the news division were beyond being impressed—they were awed. Some of them recalled that in years past it had often been said (more or less in jest) that young Bobby Wussler was determined to have Dick Salant's job—president of CBS News—by the time he was forty. Now, at the age of thirty-nine, he had done even better. They were, for the most part, quite proud of him. He was, after all, one of their own—their "Bobby"—although they realized that from now on, should they happen to run into him, they had better refrain from calling him that.

Wussler's departure from CBS News in 1972 cleared the way for Gordon Manning to make the next move in the elaborate chess game he had been playing. As he had suspected, he was able to persuade Russ Bensley to take over as head of the Special Events unit. His only anxious moment came when Bensley demanded to know if the offer reflected management's dissatisfaction with his performance as executive producer of the *Evening News.* Manning, recognizing that this was no time for a lapse into candor, assured Bensley that that was not the case at all. So, satisfied with Manning's "for-the-record" explanation (though not so naive that he swallowed it whole), Bensley agreed to the change. In truth, he welcomed a new assignment. For all his outward cool and low-key manner, he was not impervious to the pressures of producing the *Evening News,* nor was he unaware that his superiors were not all that happy with the way he was running the *Evening News* operation. So he concluded that the better part of valor was to seize this opportunity while it was available.

The move turned out to be a good one for Bensley. Once he adjusted to the new set of circumstances he had to deal with—the long-range planning, the detailed logistics, the unique problems inherent in live coverage of "special events"—he did a solid and professional job. And he found he did not miss being at the center of action and power on the Cronkite show. Like a soldier who has seen plenty of combat (and picked up some shrapnel in the process), Bensley was more than content to let others go out each day into that fire zone.

Once Manning had induced Bensley to take the Special Events job, he was in a position to make his crowning move, and just as he had suspected, Cronkite and Socolow raised no serious objections this time to Paul Greenberg's appointment as executive producer of the *Evening News.* Others, however, were not so equable; when the change was announced in September 1972, it sent tremors of apprehension through members of the show's production staff. They were acquainted with Greenberg's reputation as a Simon Legree, and, even more than their concern about that, they were worried about losing their own slots on the broadcast. During his years as executive producer of the weekend news shows, Greenberg had built up his own able corps of associate producers and film editors, and there was every reason to believe that he would want to bring in his own people.

But Greenberg proved to be a pleasant surprise, at least in the beginning. First of all, he did not dismantle the production staff he inherited. He kept John Lane and Ron Bonn as his chief deputies, even though, since they were Bensley appointees, he would have been entirely justified in replacing them. And the staff changes he did make were gradual and generally in the category of normal turnover. In other ways as well, Greenberg was on his best behavior during the first few weeks of his reign as executive producer of the Cronkite show. Actually, he was quite entertaining when he wanted to be, and he now put that side of his complicated personality on display. A gifted raconteur with a mordant sense of humor, he regaled his new subordinates with gossipy anecdotes and trenchant one-liners.

At the same time, they discovered what a strong and talented producer he was. For years it had been an article of faith within the

insular world of the *Evening News* staff that among hard-news producers at CBS (thus excluding the documentary and *60 Minutes* people),
Russ Bensley was in a class by himself when it came to cutting and
shaping long film stories. But most of the show's associate producers
soon came to regard Greenberg as Bensley's peer in that department;
some thought he was even better. But if Greenberg's forte, like Bensley's, was film and production, he did not allow himself to become
overly absorbed in that area. He was a much more efficient *executive*
producer than Bensley had been, both in terms of delegating duties to
Lane, Bonn, and others, and in terms of maintaining tight control over
the overall operation. In this respect, as well as others, Greenberg's six
years of experience as weekend producer had been an excellent preparation for his present assignment.

There was, however, one big difference: the anchorman Greenberg now had to work with was Walter Cronkite. At the time of his
appointment, he and Cronkite scarcely knew each other (Cronkite, in
fact, had referred to him once as Paul *Gold*berg), and Greenberg realized how important it was for him to establish a working rapport. So he
set out, from his first day on the job, to prove to Cronkite that he was
worthy of his trust and respect. He made sure that Cronkite was kept
informed of all major developments as the news of the day unfolded and
the show's lineup began to take shape, and he generally deferred to
Cronkite's preferences regarding the lead and other editorial decisions.

Greenberg even extended his assiduous wooing of Cronkite to
situations outside the shop. At his suggestion, they began playing tennis
together twice a week. A natural athlete, Greenberg was a superb
player; as for Cronkite, he played the game with enthusiasm, but he was
not nearly as skilled as Greenberg, and if Greenberg had chosen to play
at the top of his form, he would have zapped Cronkite, six-love, almost
every time out. But Greenberg recognized that he had nothing to gain
by humiliating his anchorman on the tennis court, and so he toned
down his game to make their matches less one-sided. He did not go so
far as to baby Cronkite with soft shots (Cronkite, with his fierce pride,
would have furiously resented that), but he usually aimed them down
the middle, where Cronkite could reach them more easily. That way,
even though Greenberg always won, Cronkite was able to leave the
court under the heady delusion that he had given his younger and more
agile opponent a spirited run for his money.

In these and other ways, Greenberg courted and won Cronkite's favor, and as Cronkite became increasingly satisfied with his new executive producer, he began spending less and less time in Sandy Socolow's office complaining about the *Evening News* operation. That deprived Socolow of his direct access into the show's inner workings, and he soon ceased to be a force of managerial interference, as he had been during most of Bensley's troubled tenure. Instead, he lapsed more and more into the frustration of his vice-presidential duties.

Manning's active role, however, was not similarly diminished. He and Greenberg conferred with each other constantly, and that led some insiders to assume that Manning was calling many of the day-to-day shots. But more astute observers of their complex relationship were drawn to the conclusion that it was Greenberg who dominated Manning, instead of the other way around. Yet this topsy-turvy arrangement did not seem to bother Manning one bit. Others might gossip about the strange and mystical power Greenberg had over Manning, but as far as Manning himself was concerned, Greenberg was his boy, his creation, and, as such, he could do no wrong.

Others, however, had plenty of grievances, especially after Greenberg's "nice-guy" phase came to an end. Once he was convinced that he had worked his way into Cronkite's good graces and that he had the rest of the *Evening News* staff firmly under his control, Greenberg began reverting to his old habit of ruling by fear and harassment. Once again, he became caustic and abusive; not all the time, to be sure, and not toward everyone, but often enough and toward enough people to incur widespread enmity at CBS News. And as Dan Rather discovered when he had his bitter run-in with Greenberg, those who were the targets of his harsh and often personal attacks had no satisfactory recourse. As long as Manning was in charge of the network's hard-news operation, Greenberg's position was sacrosanct.

The prevailing assumption during this period, when the Manning-Greenberg alliance was at the height of its power, was that Manning's own position vis-à-vis his superiors was just as secure, and that he was therefore destined to remain in authority at CBS News for many years to come. But that was not the case at all. Indeed, now that he had demonstrated how adept he was at playing chess with the lives and careers of key personnel under his jurisdiction, Manning was about to find out what it was like to be a sacrificial knight in someone else's game.

22 A Little More
Tabloid in the Blood

It was no doubt inevitable that Gordon Manning's style of leadership would arouse discord within the ranks—and that is precisely what happened. By the early 1970s, the line was clearly drawn. On one side were Manning's ardent supporters, who viewed him as a positive force, a strong and enterprising news executive. On the other was a growing and increasingly vocal faction that believed, with equal fervor, that his effect on the news operation had been largely detrimental. Nearly everyone eventually gravitated toward one extreme or the other, for on the subject of Gordon Manning, almost no one was neutral. Even his effusive personality—engaging to some, irritating to others—touched off long and spirited arguments.

Ebullient, humorous, and voluble, Manning was a lively conversationalist who generally dominated any group that gathered around him over lunch or cocktails. He was a man of catholic interests, and there was hardly a subject about which he did not have at least a smattering of knowledge or a strong and usually provocative opinion. He spoke rapidly in sharp, staccato bursts, the words spurting out in great gusts of enthusiasm, and some of his CBS colleagues were put off by his mercurial, almost manic style of delivery, the restless way he flitted about from one topic to the next, allowing no pause for reflection or riposte. Hughes Rudd, for example, once groused that Manning had "the attention span of a hummingbird." But others found his unceasing flow of quips, anecdotes, and once-over-lightly insights stimulating, and were content to sip their drinks in amused silence while he chattered on in an orgy of free association.

Manning's natural effervescence carried over into his work. Even his detractors could not help but admire his industry and his energetic dedication to the welfare of CBS News. If he resorted at times to devious manipulations, he was motivated not only by personal ambition but also by an earnest desire to strengthen the news operation from top to bottom. Moreover, unlike so many television news executives, he was not afraid to take chances. It's true that some of his gambles (such as hiring Joe Benti to anchor the *Morning News*) did not pay off, but others (such as hiring Heywood Hale Broun) did. And even those who detested Paul Greenberg personally had to admit that he was a brilliant producer, and that Manning deserved high marks for having recognized that at a time when most other people at CBS scarcely knew who Greenberg was.

Manning was also bold and outspoken in his relations with the corporate hierarchy. He constantly pushed for larger budgets and more air time. In other ways, too, he fought hard for what he saw as the news division's best interests. At the time of the two-part Watergate report in the fall of 1972, he argued strenuously to dissuade his immediate boss, Dick Salant, from ordering cuts in the second segment, even though he knew that Bill Paley was on the warpath, and that the threat of reprisal was very much in the air. As the producer of the Watergate package, Stanhope Gould deeply appreciated the way Manning went to bat for him, and he came away from that experience convinced that of the three senior news executives—Salant, Manning, and Bill Leonard —Manning was the most fearless when it came to standing up to corporate pressure. Nor was Gould alone in his opinion. But if Manning's tenacious defense of controversial programs and the news division in general endeared him to many of his journalistic colleagues, it did not necessarily endear him to the corporate brass, and least of all to the man in charge of the network's entire broadcast operation—Jack Schneider.

Schneider had been leery of Manning ever since 1966, when, in the period of crisis following Fred Friendly's sudden resignation, he approached him with a tentative offer to succeed Friendly as president of CBS News, and Manning turned him down, citing loyalty to Friendly as the reason. As far as Schneider was concerned, Manning's prime loyalty should have been to CBS, and he decided then and there that he was not a man entirely to be trusted.

Manning's behavior over the years since had only made Schneider that much more suspicious. He recognized that Manning had every right to lobby vigorously on behalf of the news division, but Schneider didn't care for the way he went about it. Like Friendly, Manning was inclined to be a news division "purist" who had trouble concealing his disdain for the more tawdry aspects of network television. As president of the CBS Broadcast Group, Schneider was obliged to traffic in the "impurities"—prime-time ratings, commercials, profits, and so on—and he resented the way Manning seemed to sneer at that, and his holier-than-thou attitude that news was the sole oasis in an otherwise vulgar wasteland. The way Schneider saw it, if his career was a form of prosti-tution, then Manning was no less tarnished as long as he continued to draw his sizable paycheck from the swollen coffers of commercial tele-vision.

Manning's tactics also infuriated Schneider. On some occasions, when he wasn't being supercilious, Manning seemed to pander to what he considered to be Schneider's crass sense of values. In arguing for a budget increase or special air time for some news venture, Manning would launch into a spirited sales pitch, depicting the proposed project as a cinch to attract a large audience and rake in maximum advertising revenue. It was as if he thought Schneider could not be trusted to judge a news proposal on its own merits, and that the safest way to win his approval was to give him a snow job. Schneider, who happened to be a very shrewd customer, was insulted to the point of rage by such maladroit attempts to con him. In his view, if there was one thing worse than being scorned as a huckster, it was to be treated as a *dumb* huck-ster.

So, by the early 1970s, Schneider was totally disenchanted with Manning. In particular, he was determined to disabuse him of the notion that he was destined to become president of CBS News when Salant retired. And the most emphatic way to get that message across was to remove Manning from his present post, for as long as he re-mained hard-news vice-president, he had a certain right to assume he was Salant's heir apparent. But deposing Manning was easier said than done. As long as he had the support of Salant and other key news division people, Schneider was reluctant to make a move to oust him. He still bore deep scars from the 1966 furor, when he was portrayed (not altogether inaccurately) as the corporate heavy who made the decision to broadcast *I Love Lucy* reruns instead of the Fulbright hear-ings on Vietnam, thus precipitating Friendly's dramatic resignation.

Schneider certainly did not want to stir up that kind of mess again, with Manning this time cast in the martyr's role. Hence, it was imperative that Manning's removal be handled in such a way that nobody—inside or outside CBS—would interpret it as an attempt by Schneider to disrupt or undermine the news operation. So Schneider prudently chose to play a waiting game, confident that, in time, Salant and Bill Leonard (with both of whom he had a generally cordial relationship) would come around to his view of Manning. And by 1973, Schneider could sense that the period of patient waiting was nearing an end. Manning was losing the support he needed to survive.

Salant and Leonard had long been steadfast in their defense of Manning. He was, they acknowledged, overly zealous and disdainful at times, and, indeed, there were occasions when they found him almost as exasperating as Schneider did. Nevertheless, they believed that his virtues as an aggressive and innovative news executive more than compensated for his faults. But as time went on, Salant and Leonard gradually changed their minds. Salant, in particular, came to regard Manning as erratic, even flighty, and seriously lacking in managerial discipline. He thought that when Manning had to make an important decision, he often was either too impetuous or, at the other extreme, that he temporized too much. For example, Salant was not at all happy with the way Manning had handled the choice of Les Midgley's successor as executive producer of the *Evening News.* That untidy sequence of events and irresolute shifting around offended Salant's sense of order and precision.

For others, the chief aggravation was Manning's zest for dispatching memos. His passion for bombarding his subordinates with story ideas was, if anything, even more excessive than it had been during his years at *Newsweek;* and as had been the case there, many of his suggestions were so obvious that those on the receiving end often took umbrage at the implied insult that they were editorial cretins. Most of the recipients rarely did more than grumble about the barrage of "Gordograms" (as Manning's missives came to be called), but Washington's maverick producer, Bill Crawford, once took it upon himself to try to set Manning straight. In response to a particularly redundant Gordogram, Crawford fired off a terse and impertinent note to Manning, informing him that "in case you're not aware of it, we get copies of the *New York Times* down here, too." Moreover, in the memo area as well, Manning sometimes displayed his confusing tendency to combine spontaneity with indecision, boldness with equivocation. Even on those occasions when he did come up with a striking story suggestion, he often went on, in the next few sentences, to give detailed reasons why it probably wasn't such a good idea after all. This generally left the recipients in a bit of a quandary: Should they take their cue from the proposal itself, or should they accede to Manning's own arguments for not pursuing the story? As Ralph Paskman and his Assignment Desk cohorts were fond of saying during the Manning years, "His question mark is our command."

Still others soured on Manning because of the high-handed way he played favorites, overtly promoting the careers of certain producers and correspondents (notably Greenberg and Mudd) at the expense of others. Those who had no use for Greenberg, in particular, resented the way Manning pampered him. Such front-line correspondents as Dan Rather and Hughes Rudd, both of whom had been involved in bruising, personal scraps with Greenberg, extended some of the animosity they felt toward Greenberg onto Manning, and that, too, gave impetus to the anti-Manning sentiment that, by the early 1970s, was gaining strength throughout the various domains of CBS News.

But the harshest indictment came from those who had reached the conclusion that Gordon Manning, on occasion, fell far short of the mark in the precise area where his credentials were supposed to be impeccable: journalistic judgment and integrity. One of Manning's favorite topics of conversation was his pre-CBS background at United Press, *Collier's,* and *Newsweek*—which, he implied, gave him a professional, even a moral, edge over those CBS News people who had spent all or most of their careers in broadcasting. It was a sore subject, for there was a tendency among his colleagues to accept that assessment as valid. Many television journalists continued to be plagued by a sense of inferiority, a feeling that they still did not measure up to their lodge brothers who toiled in the presumably less tainted milieu of print journalism. Hence, their disillusionment was all the more severe when they discovered the flaws in Manning's professional character. And the flaws were there, no question of that. In his dealings with Jack Schneider and other corporate executives, he presented himself as a news purist, a man of high principles, a staunch defender of the true journalistic faith. But those who worked with him on the news-division level sometimes saw another, less appealing side of Gordon Manning.

At the time of Mary Jo Kopechne's death at Chappaquiddick, correspondent David Culhane and producer Bobby Wussler were assigned to cover the inquest that had been ordered to determine whether criminal charges should be brought against Edward Kennedy. The legal proceeding in Massachusetts naturally attracted a swarm of journalists, and while they were waiting for the inquest to begin, they were startled by the sight of a familiar face, or what *seemed* to be a familiar face: that of Robert Kennedy, who had been killed a little more than a year earlier. The Kennedy look-alike was an Italian actor who, it was claimed, was to star in a new movie about Bobby Kennedy. He had been brought to the scene of the inquest by some PR genius in the hope of drumming up a little free publicity for the film.

Both Culhane and Wussler found the actor's presence there repellent and firmly agreed that under no circumstances would they allow CBS News to be dragged into that kind of cheap exploitation. Shortly after they settled that question, Wussler received a phone call from Sandy Socolow in New York, who at that time was still a producer on the Cronkite show and was calling to discuss the film piece on the inquest for that night's broadcast. He mentioned that he had heard a rumor about an uncanny ringer for Bobby Kennedy being "up there with you guys" and wondered if that angle should be included in the story. Wussler explained that it was a cheap publicity stunt. He said that he and Culhane had decided to steer clear of it, and Socolow seemed to concur with that decision.

A few minutes later, Wussler received a second phone call, this one from Manning. He did not ask about the inquest; instead, all his questions dealt with the Kennedy look-alike. Why weren't Wussler and Culhane making an effort to get him on camera, to put him in the story? Wussler explained the situation, but Manning persisted; it was a terrific human-interest angle, he said, and they should go after it. But Wussler held firm; he and Culhane had been assigned to do a story on the inquest into the death of Mary Jo Kopechne, and he had no intention of mucking it up with a flack job on some movie. He and Manning continued to bicker for the next several minutes, and finally Manning said, "You know what your problem is, Bobby? You need a little more tabloid in your blood."

Wussler didn't know quite how to counter that particular charge, and so he agreed to include the Kennedy look-alike angle in the CBS story, but only on the condition that Culhane be allowed to brand it as a publicity stunt. After he got off the phone, he explained the compromise arrangement to Culhane and told him what Manning had said about his tabloid deficiency. The two men stared at each other in silent wonder, then Wussler smiled and said, "Our peerless leader." That remark triggered a release of rollicking laughter, and, their good humor restored, they proceeded to film the report in accordance with Manning's wishes.

For David Culhane, it was an eye-opening experience. Like Manning's, his background was in print journalism (he had worked on the *Baltimore Sun* for ten years before joining CBS News in 1967), and he also tended to believe, with Manning, that his years of newspaper experience gave him an edge over his colleagues who had spent their entire careers in broadcasting. In particular, he thought that someone like Wussler, who was strictly a child of television and a slick production man to boot, did not have the values that were conducive to sound journalistic judgment. Yet on this most revealing occasion, it was Wussler who had taken a stand in defense of taste and principle, while Manning, the ex-print man, had insisted they jazz up a sensitive story with a tacky sideshow. Thus was Culhane induced to revise, radically, his opinions of both Wussler and Manning.

John Hart experienced a similar disenchantment. It occurred in the summer of 1972, not long after disclosures of Senator Thomas Eagleton's medical history prompted a harried George McGovern to dump him as his vice-presidential candidate. A Democratic conclave, dubbed a "mini-convention," was scheduled to rubber-stamp McGovern's subsequent choice for running mate, Sargent Shriver, and Hart was picked to anchor CBS's live coverage of that event. A few days beforehand, Manning, Hart, and the producers assigned to work on the broadcast met to discuss the way to handle the coverage. Since this was an unprecedented occurrence in American politics, it was suggested that an outsider—a professional politician who understood the rules of the mini-convention—be invited to assist Hart. Several qualified Democrats were proposed (Larry O'Brien, Joseph Califano, and others), and then Manning blurted out a suggestion: "What about Tom Eagleton?"

Hart assumed that Manning was indulging in a bit of gallows humor, and he started to laugh. But when he noticed the expression on Manning's face, Hart suddenly realized that he was serious. "Gordon," he exclaimed, "that's a terrible idea!" After all that Eagleton had just gone through, CBS could not ask him to help report on the nomination of his own replacement.

"I know what you're saying, John," Manning replied, "but that's not the way to look at it. The difference between us is that you're talking news business and I'm talking show business."

Hart just stared at Manning, and one of the producers present quickly changed the subject. The idea of having a politico co-anchor the broadcast was quietly dropped, but Manning's impulsive pitch for Eagleton—and the rationale he gave to justify it—made a lasting impression on Hart. He was indebted to Manning for his present position as anchorman on the *Morning News,* but from that point on, although he still liked Manning personally (Hart was among those who found Manning to be an extremely engaging luncheon companion), he no longer had any professional respect for him. He became, in fact, one of Manning's more outspoken critics, even saying on one occasion that something had to be done about Manning and "his flaky ideas before he wrecks the company."

Something was about to be done. By 1973, Salant and Leonard were picking up anti-Manning vibes from all directions, and, given their own instinct for survival, they began putting more and more distance between themselves and Manning. Salant, indeed, went further than that. The various grievances against Manning that were percolating up to the management level only deepened his own misgivings about him. Accordingly, he quietly passed the word to Jack Schneider that if a move were made to oust Manning, he, Salant, would not oppose it.

Schneider was delighted to hear that. But having waited this long to settle Manning's hash, he was willing to wait a little longer, until he was absolutely sure of his ground. Ever mindful of the fracas he went through in 1966, Schneider was determined to avoid, at all costs, another open quarrel with the news division over a change in its management. What he needed was a dramatic reason, a cause célèbre, a Manning blunder of such magnitude that even his most fervent loyalists would be hard pressed to make a case in his defense. And in the summer of 1973, Schneider was given the cause célèbre he was looking for. Her name was Sally Quinn.

On the surface, it seemed as if Manning were at the height of his power. With Paul Greenberg entrenched as executive producer of the *CBS Evening News* and Roger Mudd serving as Cronkite's regular backup on the show, Manning was reshaping the news operation to suit his personal preference and building toward a future when (as he envisioned it) he would succeed Salant as president. And in almost every respect, CBS News was riding high. The Cronkite show still held a firm grip on the ratings lead in the nightly news field, and the weekend news programs also consistently outdrew their competitors. In addition, *60 Minutes* was far and away the most successful show of its kind on television, and in keeping with the Murrow-Friendly tradition, CBS News continued to set the pace in the airing of provocative documentaries. The one sore spot was the *Morning News*. Thus, as part of his energetic effort to strengthen every department under his jurisdiction, Manning had recently been focusing most of his attention on that program.

The *CBS Morning News* was still mired in the rut into which it fell in 1965 when it was taken out of its 10:00 A.M. time slot and shoved into direct competition with NBC's *Today* show. It could be argued, of course, that it was not necessary to be the leader in *every*thing, and that, in view of all its other triumphs, CBS News could have accepted with good grace NBC's domination of the early-morning audience. But that was *not* in keeping with CBS tradition. Once, in the late 1960s, when Mike Dann, then in charge of programming for CBS, joyously informed Bill Paley that CBS had nine of the ten top-rated daytime shows, the Chairman's only reaction was to frown and grumble, "That goddamn NBC always hangs in there for one." Needless to say, Paley was not at all happy with the way the *Morning News* had been floundering, and he had his own remedy for improving it, as Manning discovered when, in the spring of 1973, he and Paley traveled to China.

China had been opened up to American visitors by Richard Nixon's historic trip there a year earlier. On that occasion, the travel quota was extremely tight, and the networks were instructed to send only essential, working personnel; executives whose duties were supervisory were not supposed to go. But Manning was determined to circumvent that restriction, and so, having himself listed as a "sound technician," he joined the select group of CBS News people who accompanied Nixon to China in February 1972. While there, Manning's intrusive attempts to make himself useful imposed an additional burden on the harried producers and correspondents who were responsible for CBS's coverage of the story. But at least he had been there, and now, a year later, when Paley decided to visit China, Manning was asked to go along as his escort.

Even before that trip, Manning and Salant had been contemplating a change on the *Morning News*. John Hart, the show's present anchorman, had been unable to make an appreciable dent in *Today*'s powerful hold on breakfast viewers, and there were signs that the dreary combination of poor ratings and middle-of-the-night hours was having a debilitating effect on his morale, just as it had previously sapped the spirits of Joe Benti and Mike Wallace. By the spring of 1973, Manning and Salant had taken the trouble to alert Hart that he should start thinking of his future beyond the *Morning News,* and Hart more or less agreed that it was probably time for him to move on to another assignment. So the revamping of the *Morning News* was very much on Manning's mind when he and Paley went to China. He knew Paley was an inveterate viewer of the show—its fabled "audience of one"—and in between visits to the Great Wall and other tourist attractions, Manning brought the subject up. Paley agreed that it was time, once again, to give the program a new face, and he asked Manning who was being considered for the anchor assignment. Manning casually tossed out a few names—Roger Mudd, Dan Rather, Charlie Kuralt, even Heywood Hale Broun—but Paley had his own candidate. In the course of one of their conversations, he suddenly asked Manning, "By the way, how is my old friend Hughes Rudd doing these days?"

Perhaps it was his presence in an exotic and/or Communist country that made Paley think of Rudd. A few years earlier, when Rudd was Moscow correspondent for CBS News, Paley had visited the Soviet Union. It was a sentimental journey for Paley, the son of Russian-Jewish immigrants, and he and Rudd hit it off very well, in large part because Rudd, who would not know how to be obsequious to anyone, even if his life depended on it, treated the Chairman like a regular guy, a drinking buddy, and took him around to some of Moscow's more raffish night spots. Paley, accustomed to dealing with overly decorous hosts who never allowed him to forget that he was a VIP, relished the opportunity to let his hair down a bit. But beyond that, as he now told Manning in China, Paley admired the offbeat feature stories Rudd had been doing on the *Morning News* in recent years, and he gently suggested that perhaps Rudd's grouchy humor and other talents were being wasted as a field correspondent. That was all Manning needed to hear, and by the time they left China, it was decided: Hughes Rudd would replace John Hart as anchorman on the *Morning News.*

But when Manning returned to New York, he walked smack-dab into the tumult of a Women's Lib uprising at CBS News. The women's movement had been building up steam at CBS over the past couple of years, as it had been at many other large corporations throughout the country, and in response, a few more female reporters and middle-level producers had been hired. But all the top jobs—in management, production, and on the air—were still occupied by men. As a major step toward rectifying that, leaders of the CBS News women's group held an acrimonious meeting with Dick Salant (while Manning and Paley were in China) at which they demanded that the next opening in an anchor position be filled by a woman. Salant, who was clearly out of his depth (nothing in his studies at Harvard Law School or his subsequent experiences in the legal and broadcasting spheres had prepared him for anything like this), felt he had no choice but to accede to their demand. Thus, he and Manning now faced a dilemma. Feminist fury or no, Manning certainly could not renege on his promise to Paley; the *Morning News* assignment was going to Rudd, and that was that. But Salant could not go back on his word, either, and therefore the only peaceful solution was to replace Hart with a male-female anchor team—Rudd and Ms. X. That was the tough part of the decision: Who should they pick to become the first anchorwoman in the history of network journalism?

If all these developments had come to a head a year earlier, the choice would have been a talented young black woman named Michele Clark. Another graduate of WBBM in Chicago, Clark joined CBS News in the late summer of 1971 and quickly established herself as the best and the brightest female reporter on the network's payroll. By the spring of 1972, she was out on the campaign trail, covering major primary races for the Cronkite show and other broadcasts. That summer, she was promoted to correspondent, and it was quite evident by then that the CBS News management had large plans for her. Indeed, as though in anticipation of future Women's Lib demands, Clark was given a kind of quasi-anchor assignment that summer and fall. She frequently took over the Washington slot on the *Morning News* when that show's regular Washington correspondent, Nelson Benton, was on vacation or was filling in for Hart in New York. Thus, in just a little more than a year, Clark had gone further than any other female *or* black reporter ever had at CBS News and was now on the verge of moving into the top echelon of network correspondents. But in December 1972, while flying home to Chicago for Christmas vacation, Michele Clark was killed in a plane crash. She was only twenty-nine, and Salant expressed the feelings of just about everyone at CBS News when he issued a statement that said, in part: "Her untimely death is not only a personal loss. Our profession suffers as well. And so does the public, who would have come to admire her as greatly as we do." Five months later, as he and Manning addressed themselves to the task of selecting a suitable anchorwoman for the *Morning News,* Salant felt that loss more acutely than ever.

Among the women reporters and correspondents working at CBS News in the spring of 1973, the most promising was Lesley Stahl, who had joined the Washington bureau the previous year. But when Manning sounded her out about the *Morning News* assignment, Stahl wisely told him that she did not think she was ready, quite yet, to take on that kind of challenge. So Manning turned his attention to outside candidates, women who had made their reputations in print journalism. Gloria Steinem and Nora Ephron were among the names mentioned, as was Sally Quinn. Manning had been impressed by Quinn's work as a feature reporter for the *Washington Post.* Also in her favor was the fact that both he and Salant knew her. Back in the summer of 1968, Quinn had worked for CBS News at the political conventions (as a low-level minion who ran errands for both Salant and Manning), and Manning had pleasant memories of her from that experience. So did Salant, which is one reason why he gave his approval when Manning made up his mind to go after Quinn for the *Morning News.* But the decision to hire Sally Quinn was far more Manning's than Salant's, a point that would not be forgotten in the months ahead.

The daughter of a retired three-star general, Sally Quinn wound up in journalism entirely by accident. Following her graduation from Smith in 1963, she spent the next six years drifting through a number of odd jobs, giving little or no thought to a permanent career. For the most part during these years, she worked in Washington, where she had spent part of her childhood as a self-described "Army brat." ("Being a general's daughter," Quinn once wrote, "is like being a princess.") Her briefly held jobs were generally clerical and secretarial in nature, but having been a debutante and member of the Junior League in the Washington area, she had entrée into Washington's rather insular social world. That, in fact, was what brought her to the attention of the *Washington Post*'s editor, Ben Bradlee. One day in the spring of 1969, Quinn received a call from Bradlee, inviting her to come in for a job interview. Assuming that he planned to offer her a secretarial position, she was not particularly excited by the prospect. When she arrived for the interview, however, Bradlee told her he was looking for a young woman reporter to cover Washington parties and other social news, and, since he knew she was personally familiar with that turf, he had thought of her. Quinn was both surprised and delighted, but when Bradlee asked her to leave some stories she had written for him to look at, she had to confess that she had never written anything. Philip Geyelin, the editor of the *Post*'s editorial page, overheard the confession. Looking over at Bradlee, he volunteered, "Well, nobody's perfect." Bradlee, nodding in agreement, then turned to Quinn and said, "You're hired."

Bradlee's instincts were right on target. Quinn did know the Washington social turf, and, despite her lack of training, she quickly developed into a good reporter. She had an excellent ear for picking up lively and embarrassing quotes, and her breezy, often bitchy writing style was tailor-made for that cocktail- and dinner-party world of self-important government officials and their social-climbing wives. (Once, when Henry Kissinger was asked to comment on women reporters in Washington, he replied that Maxine Cheshire, the *Post*'s gossip columnist, "makes you want to commit murder. On the other hand, Sally Quinn makes you want to commit suicide.") In addition to her journalistic skills, Quinn was physically attractive—honey-blonde and willowy— and that naturally influenced Manning's decision. So, having settled on Quinn as his choice and having obtained Salant's approval, Manning flew down to Washington to woo her away from the *Post*. Or, as he put it to Quinn when they met for dinner one night in early June 1973, "We're going to revamp the *CBS Morning News*, and we're looking for a woman who can knock Barbara Walters off the air. We think you're the one who can do it."

That extravagant, throw-down-the-gauntlet remark set the tone for the heavy promotional blitz that followed. After Manning, through adroit appeals to Quinn's considerable vanity, succeeded in persuading her that she was ready for the big time—instant stardom on national television—the CBS publicity mills went into action, touting her as the new wonder woman of network journalism. Among the first to respond to the bait was *New York* magazine, and Manning was delighted when he learned that it was planning to do a cover story on Quinn. He was far less pleased, however, when the article was published in mid-July, three weeks before the Rudd-Quinn team was scheduled to make its debut. Written by Aaron Latham (a former colleague of Quinn's at the *Post*), it played up the impending competition between Quinn and Barbara Walters, strongly implying, erroneously, that there was a personal feud between the two women. (Since Walters, whose forte was interviewing, never broadcast the news, she was not classified as an anchorwoman, per se. Nevertheless, as the female star of the *Today* show, she was viewed as Quinn's natural rival.) Even worse, Latham portrayed Quinn as a spoiled, selfish, and ruthless vamp who slept around a great deal, especially with men in a position to help her career. As a hatchet job, the piece bore a certain similarity to the kind of spicy profiles Quinn herself had written for the *Post;* and, like many of the "victims" of her feature stories, she now hollered foul, claiming that she had been misquoted and that Latham's article was filled with flagrant and malicious distortions.

The damage, however, was done. Not long after the piece was published, Rudd and Quinn were sent out on a week-long, coast-to-coast promotional tour. Latham's profile had preceded them, and, as Quinn now discovered, media critics across the country took their cues from it. In one city after another, she was described as CBS's new "blonde bombshell," "femme fatale," and "sex symbol." One reporter's idea of a relevant question was to ask Quinn who she thought was "the sexiest politician in Washington," while another felt compelled to assure his readers that "at no time during our interview did Sally lay a hand on me." Even if Quinn had been a brilliant broadcasting natural, a female equivalent of Edward R. Murrow, it would have been extremely difficult for her to overcome all that misleading ballyhoo, and the CBS people were largely responsible for burdening her with that. It's true, of course, that neither Manning nor the network's PR staff had any control over Latham's article or the lurid press notices it inspired, but the lavish buildup they engendered made her an inviting target. So Quinn was, to some extent, an innocent victim of overpromotion. But she had only herself to blame for the dismal and thoroughly inept performance that followed.

In her own apologia for her CBS ordeal, a book entitled *We're Going to Make You a Star,* Quinn chose to make much of the fact that she had not been properly trained for the role of anchorwoman. It was a grievance she arrived at only by hindsight. In December 1973, as her brief and ignominious career at CBS was coming to an end, Quinn and Manning had an angry confrontation, at which she asked him why he had put her on the air in a big show-case, cold turkey, without any training. Manning responded by asking her what her reaction would have been if he had insisted that before she took on the *Morning News* assignment, she had to spend a few months working as an anchorwoman at one of the network's local stations. When Quinn haughtily replied that she would never have given her consent to that, Manning snapped back, "That's why." In other words, when the *Morning News* offer was made, Quinn herself thought she was ready for stardom. After all, she had succeeded in a big way on the esteemed *Washington Post* without having paid any prior journalistic dues, and she wasn't about to submit to a demeaning apprenticeship for television.

But, in fact, it wasn't Quinn's inexperience that did her in so much as it was her on-air personality. To her credit, she carefully eschewed the "femme fatale" image, even going so far as to appear overly prim and proper at times, but in other respects, she seemed to go out of her way to vindicate Aaron Latham's unflattering portrayal. The self-centered, frequently bitchy tone that had given some of her *Post* features an appealing zest was completely out of place on a straight news program. The Rudd-Quinn format was structured to include occasional ad-libs, and her impromptu remarks on various news stories were, at times, so insensitive that they almost seemed calculated to offend. On the morning of its debut in early August 1973, the show featured a grim film piece on child-labor abuse among migrant workers, to which Quinn's ad-lib response was a glib comment that when her parents had made her clean her room, she thought that was child labor.

That lapse, admittedly, could have been attributed to opening-day jitters, but unfortunately, similar gaffes occurred over the next several weeks, with appalling regularity. On one occasion, when Rudd read a tell story about a decompression mishap that had caused a man to be blown out of an airplane at 39,000 feet, Quinn thought it was funny and burst out laughing. These were not errors of inexperience so much as flaws in taste and sensibility, reflecting a built-in attitude that no amount of local-station seasoning was likely to correct. In short, she often came across as shallow and snobbish, a spoiled and arrogant Army brat. Nor was that impression merely an on-camera aberration. Most of her *Morning News* co-workers found Quinn to be a prima donna, although those who took the trouble to befriend her generally came to recognize that her "Princess Sally" hauteur was, to a large extent, a defensive posture she assumed to conceal the misery and humiliation she was experiencing in her new career.

Quinn's CBS colleagues might have been more sympathetic if she had demonstrated greater journalistic talent. But there, too, she was a big disappointment. Her on-air interviews were extremely uneven in quality; even at her best, she was no threat to Barbara Walters in that department. And unlike others who have made the transition from print to broadcast journalism, Quinn could not get the hang of writing for television. Her problems in that area were further aggravated by the fact that she was paired with Hughes Rudd, one of the strongest writers in the business. The inventive and irreverent sidebars he wrote for the show, as well as his all-around professionalism, only made her look that much worse.

By the fall of 1973, Sally Quinn had become nothing less than the laughingstock of the television industry. Her on-air flubs had become so notorious that wherever TV executives and their toadies gathered for lunch or cocktails, it was not unusual to overhear a group at a nearby table chortling over "Sally's latest." To add injury to insult, the *Morning News* ratings, dismal to begin with, had dipped slightly since she and Rudd had begun co-anchoring the broadcast. By December, Quinn herself realized that the situation had deteriorated to the point where her only move was to get out, and fast. She knew it was the only hope she had of salvaging her reputation, or what was left of it. Accordingly, she told Manning that she wanted out of her contract, and a few weeks later, she quit CBS News and returned to the *Washington Post.* Needless to say, no one at CBS tried to dissuade her from leaving.

One day back in August, after the Rudd-Quinn team had been on the air for about three weeks, Jack Schneider was having lunch with one of the network's top correspondents, who, at one point, asked how the new version of the *Morning News* was doing.

"It's a disaster," Schneider replied in a tone that made it clear he did not regard it as *his* disaster.

"Well," asked the correspondent, "what are you going to do about it?"

"Nothing, yet," said Schneider. "Just wait."

By December, the period of waiting was over. The jury was in with its verdict: Gordon Manning's decision to hire Sally Quinn and give her a big Hollywood buildup had turned into a fiasco, a travesty. Schneider knew he now had the specific blunder, the cause célèbre, he needed to justify Manning's dismissal, and, accompanied by Salant, he took the matter to Arthur Taylor, Frank Stanton's successor as president of CBS. It wasn't just the Sally Quinn mess, Schneider explained (although that was probably reason enough), but in all kinds of other ways, he contended, Manning had become a "discordant" influence, both in his dealings with the corporate management and within the news division as well. Between them, Schneider and Salant presented the case against Manning in detail, and even before they were through, Taylor indicated his sanction. As he had just recently taken over as president of the huge CBS empire, Taylor was still at a point where he relied heavily on the counsel of his various deputies; hence, if Schneider and Salant thought a managerial change was in order, he had no objections.

Paley also gave his approval, although at first he was reluctant to do so, for he was fond of Manning and they had got along very well when they visited China earlier that year. As Schneider later said to one of his associates, "Gordon apparently was at his ass-kissing best on that trip, and that didn't help matters any." But when Paley was reminded that Sally Quinn had been Manning's idea, he fell into line with the others. Business was business, and the person responsible for having inflicted *her* on CBS did not deserve to remain in a key management position, congenial traveling companion or no.

When Salant broke the news to Manning, he urged him to accept, as compensation, a top-level producer's job, either in New York or perhaps overseas, in London. But Manning, who felt he was being made a scapegoat and was deeply bitter about it, said to hell with that. He had his own notion of appropriate compensation. In a few months, he would complete his tenth year at CBS News, at which point he would be eligible for a pension. His intention, he said, was to clear out as soon as he passed the ten-year mark, and all he wanted was a window-dressing position to tide him over until then. In the meantime, Washington bureau chief Bill Small had been picked to succeed Manning, and in early February 1974, the changes went into effect. Small was appointed senior vice-president in charge of the hard-news operation, and Manning, in accordance with his request, was given the fancy but utterly meaningless title of "vice-president and assistant to the president of CBS News."

As it turned out, Gordon Manning stayed on at CBS News for a little more than a year. During the first few weeks following his downfall, he sulked around in his new, supernumerary post, nursing his grievances. But Manning was far too restless to endure such a quiescent existence for very long, and in the spring of 1974, he decided to try his hand at a little producing. What's more, he hit the jackpot on his very first try. Through his numerous contacts (one of Manning's strengths was that he seemed to know just about every journalist and news source worth knowing), he was able to line up Aleksandr Solzhenitsyn for a Walter Cronkite interview that June. The Nobel Prize-winning author and Soviet dissident had been a prominent figure even before he was exiled from Russia in early 1974, and in the weeks following his banishment, he had become a full-blown international celebrity. But, unlike most celebrities, Solzhenitsyn was media-shy, and inducing him, through intermediaries, to submit to a television interview was no small achievement.

Manning went on from there to produce other good stories, and by the fall of 1974, he was working full-time as a producer. He still evinced flashes of bitterness from time to time, complaining to friends about the way Salant had sold him out to "that cutthroat," Schneider. But for the most part, Manning became, once again, his old glib and chipper self. He was almost always ebullient when talking about his new line of work, telling luncheon companions, in his rat-a-tat-tat, lickety-split style of delivery, that the producing racket was the only way to fly, and if he had only known how much fun it was, he would have gone into it years ago instead of wasting his time in management. Longtime Manning observers could not help but smile at that, for as they clearly remembered it, his entire executive style had been that of a frustrated producer who could not resist meddling in other people's work.

So, at the age of fifty-seven, Manning was thoroughly enjoying his new career as a *bona fide* producer. By December 1974, when he completed his tenth year at CBS, thus passing the pension milestone, his spirits were so buoyed by his recent success that he had no intention of leaving the network. But then, in his zeal to come up with a dramatic coup, Manning once again made the mistake of overreaching himself, and the result was another public embarrassment for CBS News.

In the aftermath of President Nixon's resignation and the subsequent Watergate trial of the "big enchiladas"—Mitchell, Haldeman, and Ehrlichman—Manning proposed to Bill Leonard that they try and line up Haldeman for an exclusive CBS television interview. Of all the high-level officials in the Nixon Administration, Haldeman was in many ways the most powerful and certainly the most inaccessible. He loathed the press, and even during the years when he wielded so much power in the Nixon White House, he almost never gave interviews. But in early 1975, as his lawyer moved to appeal his conviction in the cover-up trial, Haldeman indicated to Manning and Leonard that he was receptive to the idea of a CBS interview. He emphasized, however, that if he did give his consent, he expected to be paid, and paid handsomely. Convinced that a Haldeman interview would make big news, Manning and Leonard talked Salant into approving the project, and after all the negotiations were completed, CBS paid Haldeman $100,000 for the privilege of interviewing him on television. When news of that transaction was disclosed, the network became the target of some rather pious criticism as the phrase "checkbook journalism" suddenly came into vogue. That, actually, was the least of it.

The two one-hour interviews were aired on successive Sundays in the *60 Minutes* time slot in the spring of 1975. The "interrogator" was Mike Wallace, regarded by many as the hardest hitter in TV journalism. But this time Wallace was outmaneuvered; he wasn't able to lay a glove on Haldeman. The former advertising man and renowned media expert knew exactly how to play the interviews to his own advantage. He came across as bland and soft-spoken (which is hardly how his former associates at the White House remember him), and he parried Wallace's queries with the same kinds of evasive answers he had given at his trial, stopping well short, obviously, of telling all he knew about the Watergate cover-up. Thus, the biggest news to come out of the Haldeman interviews was CBS's folly. The network had shelled out all that money for a huge load of nothing, and in addition to all the sanctimonious scolding, there now was the sound of mocking laughter in the air.

Salant, Leonard, and Wallace absorbed most of the public heat for the Haldeman interviews, but within the world of CBS News, there were many who felt that Manning—as the instigator and producer of the project—was the chief culprit. Once again, as in the Sally Quinn affair, he was accused of having blundered CBS News into an embarrassing fiasco. As far as the anti-Manning faction was concerned, it was a case of *twice* bitten, *thrice* shy, and few were surprised when, soon thereafter, he left CBS to take on a producer's job at NBC News.

Specifically, Manning was hired to organize and produce NBC's coverage of the 1976 political conventions and elections. That assignment pitted him against Russ Bensley, who, as head of the Special

Events unit, would be in charge of CBS's political coverage. At both conventions in the summer of 1976, CBS won the ratings battle, the first time in twenty years it had been able to pull off such a sweep. The many CBS News correspondents and producers who worked at the conventions naturally deserved most of the credit for that achievement, and, as the man who planned and produced the coverage, Bensley was singled out for special congratulations. But there were those who contended that if Bensley were truly a gentleman, he would send a note over to Manning at NBC, thanking him for everything he had done to make CBS's victory possible. After all, they pointed out, Manning himself had always been so thoughtful about writing memos to others, it seemed only fair to let him know that his work had not gone unnoticed.

23 Small Reward

On the day it was announced that he had succeeded Gordon Manning as senior vice-president in charge of hard news, Bill Small was setting himself up in Manning's old office when an outside reporter called to get his reaction. "I've only been at this desk for six hours," Small told the reporter, "and I'm just trying to find out where the men's room is and where they keep the key to the liquor cabinet." When that quote appeared in print the next day, no one at CBS was misled into thinking that such an idle pleasantry reflected Small's true feelings. During the eleven years he served as Washington bureau chief, he had acquired a reputation for being a strong administrator who ran a tight ship. It was obvious that, in the wake of the Sally Quinn disaster and Manning's other misfortunes, Small was being brought into New York to shape things up. In some ways, the situation was analogous to the one he had faced back in 1963 when he assumed command of the Washington bureau.

Small's predecessor then had been David Schoenbrun, whose stint as Washington bureau chief was brief but memorable. Hired by Murrow in Europe in 1945, he spent the next sixteen years as the network's Paris correspondent, during which time he became a recognized authority on French politics and culture. Bill Paley was fond of saying in those days that David Schoenbrun owned Paris, and that was, perhaps, only a slight exaggeration. Indeed, his Francophilia was such that even Charles de Gaulle, normally so aloof and mistrustful of Americans, warmed up to him.

But the heady years in Paris spoiled Schoenbrun. When, in late

1961, he was picked to replace the recently fired Howard K. Smith in the dual role of top Washington correspondent and bureau chief, the Kennedy Administration was in full flower, and Schoenbrun assumed that the cachet he brought with him from France would give him entrée into the inner circles of Camelot. The Kennedys, however, had their own carefully cultivated set of influential journalists, in both print and broadcasting, and they saw no reason to accord preferential treatment to Schoenbrun. That blow to his outsized ego only made him more determined to prove that he was every bit as important as he claimed to be. He began riding around the city in a chauffeured limousine, in an obvious attempt to impress official Washington. That could have been dismissed as an extravagant frivolity, but in other, more damaging ways Schoenbrun began to use his position as bureau chief to trumpet his own cause, to promote himself as the Washington headliner, the CBS counterpart of David Brinkley.

In Paris, Schoenbrun had been a one-man show, but now he had to share the on-air action with such other front-line correspondents as George Herman, Bob Pierpoint, and a young and talented new man named Roger Mudd. Still, that did not deter him from trying, on many occasions, to hog the best assignments for himself, a practice that did not exactly endear him to his colleagues. Even more than the intrabureau competition he had to put up with, Schoenbrun resented the prevailing CBS News system under which all decisions regarding what went on the air were made by producers in New York, and he frequently fought with them and with his superiors on the management level. At one point, in a fury of frustration, Schoenbrun called a staff meeting and announced that if New York did not give the bureau (by which he meant primarily himself) more air time, he intended to stop giving New York film feeds of Washington stories. "We'll go on strike!" he fumed.

After Schoenbrun had been on the job only a few months, the New York management had seen enough to conclude that whatever he had been in Paris, he was causing serious problems in Washington. In the spring of 1962, Schoenbrun received a call from Blair Clark, then general manager under Salant, informing him that the news director for the CBS affiliate in Louisville, Kentucky—a bright fellow named Bill Small—would be flying down to Washington the next day. Clark said that he was thinking of offering Small a deputy managerial position in the Washington bureau, and he suggested that Schoenbrun have lunch with him so they could get acquainted. Schoenbrun had no inkling that he was about to meet his eventual successor.

Bill Small's journalistic background differed radically from David Schoenbrun's. During the years when Schoenbrun was wining and dining with French notables, Small was earning his stripes in the decidedly unglamorous world of management on the local-station level. Following his graduation from the University of Chicago in 1951, he went to work for a Chicago radio station, WLS, and soon became its news director. After five years at WLS, he landed a job as news director at a much larger radio and television station, WHAS in Louisville. Small spent the next six years there, during which time he became increasingly active in various trade organizations and in that way began to build a national reputation, at least within the clubby confines of broadcast journalism. He served as president of the Radio-Television News Directors Association in 1960, and over the years he wrote articles for *The Quill*, the magazine put out by Sigma Delta Chi, the professional journalism society. Also, since WHAS was a CBS affiliate, Small had numerous contacts at CBS News in New York, and one of his closest friends there was Blair Clark. Clark had been primarily responsible for inflicting Schoenbrun on the Washington bureau, and by the spring of 1962, he was ready to rectify that. Accordingly, he summoned Small to New York, apprised him of the problems he was having with Schoenbrun, then offered him the deputy slot in Washington. Schoenbrun would stay on as bureau chief, at least for the time being, but Clark made it clear that he was counting on Small to bring the Washington operation under his managerial control. Small accepted the offer, and the next day he flew down to Washington for his get-acquainted lunch with the man he was destined to replace.

Schoenbrun did almost all the talking at lunch, and thus Small was mildly startled when Schoenbrun suddenly said to him, "You must be damn good. I'm impressed."

"Oh, why is that?" asked Small.

"Because Blair Clark turned down an invitation to Kay Graham's party to have dinner with you."

Until that moment, Small had found all the stories he had heard about Schoenbrun's ravenous yearning for social acceptance a little hard to believe. Now he knew better. As for Schoenbrun, he should have been impressed. A few months later, he was eased out and Bill Small was appointed Washington bureau chief.

Small was in a highly advantageous position. Almost anything he did would be viewed as an improvement over Schoenbrun, and he quickly set out to play up the contrast between himself and his predecessor. He had done some on-air work in Louisville, but whatever ambitions Small once had in that area were now well behind him. Therefore, unlike Schoenbrun, he concentrated all his energies on running the bureau, and, as a result, the CBS News correspondents who worked in Washington no longer had to worry about competing with their boss for air time. That alone was enough to boost staff morale.

Small's appointment as Washington bureau chief could not have come at a better time, for this was the period when CBS was taking steps to enlarge and strengthen its entire TV news operation. As part of that effort, Small was given a green light to beef up the Washington bureau, and he made the most of it. More than anyone else, it was Bill Small who deserved the credit for transforming the CBS News Washington bureau into the powerhouse it became in the 1960s.

Under his aegis, "Roger Mudd on Capitol Hill" and "Dan Rather at the White House" became familiar sign-offs to millions of Americans who previously had never paid much attention to who covered what in Washington. At Small's request, Marvin Kalb was transferred from Moscow to Washington in 1963 and assigned to cover the State Department. The following year, he heartily welcomed Eric Sevareid's decision to move from New York to Washington, and they soon became frequent lunching companions, in large part because Small proved to be a patient sounding board for the commentaries Sevareid had to write each day for the Cronkite show. He was also instrumental in getting Daniel Schorr and John Hart transferred to Washington from other bureaus, and he lured good people away from major newspapers, such as Fred Graham from the *New York Times* in 1972 to cover the Supreme Court for CBS News. (He also tried on several occasions to hire Sally Quinn away from the *Washington Post,* but although Quinn later said yes to Manning, she always said no to Small.) Finally, he recruited promising young reporters without reputations, such as Bruce Morton and Bob Schieffer, and groomed them to the point where they were ready to step into the showcase beats vacated by Mudd and Rather.

Beyond all that, Small constantly served as a buffer between the strong staff he assembled in Washington and his superiors in New York, who sometimes tried to pressure him into doing things their way instead of his. Small would have none of that. He insisted on having absolute control over his own domain, and the correspondents who worked in Washington during those years were appreciatively aware that Small was not only protecting them from second-guessing executives in New York, but also from government officials who often called to complain about their reporting. Such correspondents as Rather and Schorr, who frequently were embroiled in controversy, might not have survived the Nixon years as well as they did if Bill Small had not backed them up as firmly as he did.

This is not to suggest that Small was an easy man to work for. On the contrary, he was tough and demanding and he drove his people very hard. A rather short and heavyset man, Small had a square-jawed face with an unusually high forehead that made his favorite expression —a glower of disapproval—that much more intimidating. His idea of a generous compliment was to remind someone who had just done a good job on a story that there was still plenty of room for improvement. When Bob Schieffer joined the bureau in 1969, Small showed him around the shop, pointing out where the various "star" correspondents sat when they were in the office. So Schieffer pleasantly inquired, "And where will I be sitting?" Small fixed him with a baleful stare and replied, "I don't expect *you* to be sitting." To go along with his cold and rigorous manner, Small was obsessed, almost to the point of paranoia, with the question of loyalty. Several correspondents were convinced that he assigned various deputies to serve as his eyes and ears around the bureau, with instructions to report back to him all gossipy complaints, especially those comments that were in any way critical of Bill Small.

Nevertheless, Small was, on balance, a fair bureau manager, as well as a thoroughly able one, and, as a result, staff morale was generally high in Washington during the twelve years he ran the operation there. He did lose good people from time to time, but for the most part, he somehow managed to keep all those restless and clashing egos in check, if not altogether in harmony, and next to the impressive array of talent he gathered around him, the Washington bureau's most striking feature during those years was its stability.

By the early 1970s, Small ranked high in the eyes of the CBS management, with the notable exception of Gordon Manning, who resented Small's stubborn resistance to New York's hegemony over his bureau. Manning's anti-Small bias also reflected apprehension. He knew that both Jack Schneider and Dick Salant had a high regard for

Small, and he sensed (quite accurately, as it turned out) that Small loomed as a threat to his own position.

In addition to the outstanding job he was doing in Washington, Small helped his own cause in other ways. He was, at all times, properly deferential to his superiors in areas outside his jurisdiction, an attitude that contrasted sharply with Manning's as well as with that of his Washington predecessor, David Schoenbrun. Whenever Schneider went down to Washington on network business, Small gave him the red-carpet treatment and always made sure he was available for lunch or dinner that day in the event that Schneider wished to dine with him, which he frequently did. Small also scored points by writing two books in the early 1970s defending television news on the network level. Since they were published at the time when the Nixon-Agnew assault on the networks was going full blast, Small's strong and well-documented case for the defense was deeply appreciated, not only within CBS but throughout the industry.

It all came together for Small when Schneider and Salant, once they had decided to dump Manning, agreed that Small should be the one to replace him. It was a promotion that, by definition, would put him in line to succeed Salant when he retired as president of CBS News. Salant informed Small of the decision in late January 1974, and two weeks later, he moved into his new office in New York and began his search for the men's room and the key to the liquor cabinet.

Like many executives who suddenly find themselves in a new position, Small inherited a batch of problems, and the most pressing headache he had to cope with was what to do with an investigative report called *The Trouble with Rock*. The situation was extremely sensitive, for the report raised some disturbing questions about the probity of a member of the corporate family: the CBS records division, which, at the time, was grossing over $300 million a year, enough to make it the world's largest record company.

Several months earlier, in the spring of 1973, the president of CBS Records, Clive Davis, had been abruptly fired. In the civil complaint it brought against him, CBS charged that Davis had padded his expense account the previous year to the tune of $94,000, of which $20,000 allegedly went to stake his son to a lavish bar mitzvah at the Plaza Hotel. But that, apparently, was the least of it. Shortly before Davis was fired, federal narcotics agents disclosed that they had come up with evidence linking Davis's right-hand man, David Wynshaw, to the drug scene and the Mafia; and that, in turn, touched off a grand jury investigation into charges that employees at CBS Records and other record companies had used drugs, a highly valued commodity in the rock music world, as a form of payola. All of a sudden it seemed as though CBS was about to become enmeshed in a major and ugly scandal. This being the spring of 1973, the Watergate revelations were then in full eruption, and columnist William Safire, having recently begun his new career as the chief Nixon apologist for the *New York Times,* challenged CBS News to investigate the corruption inside its own house for a change. Safire was hoping to hit a nerve, and he did. The very day his column appeared, Manning decided, with Salant's approval, to go after the CBS Records story in a big way.

The project was assigned to a special new investigative unit headed by Stanhope Gould. Over the past few months, Gould and another associate producer on the Cronkite show, Linda Mason, had been putting together investigative reports, and with impressive results. They won an Emmy for their story on the Soviet wheat deal in the late summer of 1972, and Gould quickly followed that up with his two-part enterpriser on Watergate, which caused so much commotion in the fall of that year. Both those stories had been bell-ringers, and as a reward, Gould and Mason were given permission to form their own separate unit, independent of the *Evening News* staff, and work exclusively on investigative reporting.

As the officer in charge of the new operation, Gould was eager to score another big coup, a dramatic, headline story that would justify the decision to set up a full-time investigative unit. So, in the spring of 1973, when Manning proposed that he delve into the drug payola story, Gould responded with enthusiasm, and he and Mason promptly went to work on the assignment. The story, needless to say, was not an easy one to track down, and they spent the next several months pursuing it. But finally, in early 1974, just as Manning was being eased out of his senior vice-presidential post, Gould had a script ready to show to the management of CBS News.

In the meantime, executives at CBS Records were in a rage over the news division's decision to sic its new investigative team on the record industry, and they were taking their complaints to the new president of CBS, Arthur Taylor. It was Taylor's first major test in a matter concerning the integrity and autonomy of the news division since Frank Stanton's retirement in the spring of 1973, and more than a few insiders were intensely curious to see how he would handle it. For Taylor was, in many ways, still a stranger to them, an outsider whose appointment as Stanton's successor had taken the entire broadcasting industry by surprise.

For years, those who were privy to the inner workings of CBS's complicated corporate structure had assumed that Jack Schneider was the crown prince, the man destined to succeed Stanton and eventually inherit the throne of Chairman Paley Himself. At one point, in 1969, he was even given an impressive new title—executive corporate vice-president—and that, all observers agreed, was the official signal: Paley had settled on Schneider, and that was that. But Schneider's savvy in the broadcasting field did not extend to other spheres. In particular, he was out of his depth in the world of Wall Street and high finance, and that made him something less than an ideal choice for president of the entire corporation. So, in 1971, Schneider was quietly returned to the post of president of the Broadcast Group, and a few months later, Paley brought in Arthur Taylor to become Stanton's successor.

At the age of thirty-seven, Taylor had a reputation for being a financial wunderkind. He had distinguished himself as an investment banker in Boston, and had gone on from there to become executive vice-president of the International Paper Company. Still, Taylor was utterly new to broadcasting and journalism, and none of his experiences in the tidy and decorous world of finance had prepared him for the awkward position he now found himself in as the corporate president of both CBS News and CBS Records. It was, he thought, a most unseemly situation, one that could be likened to a decision by General Motors to hire Ralph Nader and give him carte blanche to unleash his "raiders" on its engineering department. In other words, Taylor was not at all happy with the news division's investigation of the drug payola story, and he and Salant had a few heated exchanges on the subject.

As the middleman between Salant and Taylor, Schneider warned his new boss that if the news people felt that corporate management was trying to pressure them into abandoning the story, they just might leak their concern to the outside press; and, he said, that kind of clamor was the last thing that Taylor and CBS needed. He strongly recommended that, in a situation like this, the most prudent course of action was to give the news division its head and rely on its good judgment. Taylor was also influenced by the discovery that Paley did not seem to object to the news division's investigation. Indeed, there were indications that the Chairman viewed the project as an astute and classy move, proof positive that CBS News reported *all* the bad news, not just Watergate and other stories critical of the Nixon Administration.

Thus, Taylor eventually came around to the position that CBS News had the right—perhaps even the obligation—to go after the drug payola story, even if the result turned out to be a public embarrassment (or worse) for another member of the corporate family. As a matter of fact, by the time it was finally ready to go on the air, Taylor had given the report his cautious blessing. After it was all over, Schneider, who had a wry appreciation of what Taylor had gone through, would refer to the experience as "the greening of Arthur Taylor."

Meanwhile, back at the news division, where good judgment was supposed to prevail, the report had become the subject of a fierce debate. During the months that he and his investigative team were pursuing the story, Stanhope Gould sent periodic memos to his increasingly impatient superiors, assuring them that he was on the trail of some "very explosive material." But when he finally came up with a script in January 1974, it fell considerably short of that promise. The report went into the problems that had beset CBS Records, but that story was old hat by now, and in the several months that had passed since it first broke, it had not led to bigger headlines. The juicy scandal that many anticipated and those inside the record industry feared had not materialized. By now, in fact, there were clear signs that the grand jury investigation was petering out, presumably for lack of hard evidence.

That was also the problem with Gould's script. It included allegations that unnamed employees at CBS Records and similar companies had served as "connections" between the Mafia-controlled drug traffic and various rock stars and disc jockeys. But almost all the charges came from unidentified sources, and their information was vague and specious. There was no real corroboration, no firm evidence to back them up. Sandy Socolow, who had been overseeing the project, was furious. He told Gould that he had done an unprofessional job, that all his work over the past few months had been a waste of company time and money, and that he, Socolow, was going to recommend that the story be scrapped.

Now it was Gould's turn to be furious. He conceded that the allegations dealing with drug payola were largely unsubstantiated, but he caustically reminded Socolow that his Watergate report in 1972 had also been built around uncorroborated charges. Socolow, however, was adamant, and he passed Gould's script on to Manning with the recommendation that it be killed. Manning, having fallen into a lame-duck status, promptly passed it on to Salant, who, in turn, dumped it back on the man who had just succeeded Manning, Bill Small. That was typical of Salant, who had a genius for recognizing when it was to his advantage to remind everyone that his background was not in journalism. While the buck usually crossed his desk, it did not necessarily stop there.

So the task of deciding what to do with *The Trouble with Rock* devolved on Small, and he began having regular meetings with Gould in an effort to arrive at a mutually satisfactory solution. The meetings, which extended over several weeks, into the spring of 1974, did not go well. Small began by proposing certain cuts in the report, and Gould noted that almost all the suggested deletions had to do with those portions that dealt with CBS Records. "Let's give them a sanitized version," Small said at one point with a conspiratorial wink that Gould resented almost as much as the suggestion itself. "What the hell, no one will know the difference."

Gould soon developed an intense dislike for Small. He regarded him as an inflexible and uptight company man who had none of Manning's flair and courage when it came to resisting corporate pressure. Nor did Gould respect Small as a journalist. In his view, Small, having spent almost his entire career in management, had no real understanding of what it took to be a good reporter, no appreciation of the risks and difficulties involved in tracking down the kind of story he was now desperately trying to salvage. Gould also sensed that Small was personally antipathetic toward him as well, and he was right about that. In particular, Small did not approve of Gould's raffish appearance—the shoulder-length hair and the shaggy, villainous-looking beard—and the hippie life-style that went with it. Small had a clearly defined image of what a CBS News producer should be, and Gould did not exactly conform to it. Thus, even under the best of circumstances, it was unlikely that Small and Gould would have hit it off.

Small finally realized that he and Gould were never going to agree on what cuts should be made in the script. So he told Gould the report was not suitable for broadcast, and that he had decided to kill it. Gould, having anticipated that, promptly launched a campaign of defiance. He passed out copies of the script to various influential friends, such as Dan

Rather and John Hart, and induced them to intercede with Small on his behalf. He also began spreading the word around that he planned to resign and take his case to the outside press, thereby triggering a public row that would put Small and CBS News in one hell of a fix. Small was incensed; he summoned Gould to his office and accused him of trying to stir up a rebellion. But although he was angry, he was not all that concerned about Gould's threat. For Small, having reassessed the situation, knew precisely how to put the kibosh on that.

Gould's assumption all along had been that if the report survived Small's cleaver, it would run as a two- or three-part series on the Cronkite show. His two previous investigative blockbusters—the Russian wheat deal and Watergate—had been aired that way, and the rock story had originally been assigned with that end in mind. But now Small had what he called a better idea. He suddenly decided that instead of being unsuitable for broadcast, *The Trouble with Rock* was worthy of a one-hour special report, to be aired on a Sunday evening in August with David Culhane as the on-air correspondent.

Gould was wise to that stratagem. He knew that a one-hour report narrated by David Culhane on a midsummer weekend would have neither the audience nor the impact of a featured series on the *Evening News* narrated by Cronkite himself. Yet Gould also realized that this was a subtle distinction that people outside the business were not likely to grasp. Were he to try to make a public issue out of it, Small or some other CBS spokesman would simply point out that as a one-hour special report, Gould's story was being given far more air time than the fifteen or twenty minutes it would have been allotted as a series crammed into the crowded format of the *Evening News.* In short, Small had come up with a brilliant ploy, and Gould knew there was no way he could counter it. But even in his rage and frustration, he could not help but admire Small's cunning. "It was a master stroke," Gould grudgingly conceded to friends. "It was more than shrewd, it was downright Jesuitical."

So *The Trouble with Rock* was broadcast as a one-hour special at 6:00 P.M. on Sunday, August 11, 1974, more than fourteen months after the project had been assigned. And, aired in that inconspicuous time slot, it elicited scarcely a ripple of viewer reaction. Moreover, the report was the victim of another piece of unfortunate timing that could not be blamed on Small. It was broadcast just two days after Richard Nixon's resignation, and with the entire country caught up in the high drama of a disgraced President's fall from power, who cared about allegations of a little graft in the record industry?

Having outfoxed Gould on the resolution of the rock story, Small's next move was to discipline him. A few days after the report was aired, he informed Gould that he was taking him off the investigative unit because he had to have in that sensitive position someone he could trust and who would not betray his confidence. He told Gould that he was free to return to his former job as an associate producer on the Cronkite show. But Gould naturally interpreted Small's action as a demotion, a slap in the face, and he refused to go along with it. He now realized that as long as Small was in charge of the hard-news operation, he had no future at CBS. So he resigned, and a few weeks later, he went to work for NBC News as an investigative producer.

Thus, the long, drawn-out quarrel over Stanhope Gould's rock music story remained an internal dispute. Thanks in large part to Small's finesse, it never escalated into a public fracas. But on another internal matter that flared up that summer, Small and his associates would not be so fortunate.

Ever since the Watergate dam broke in the spring of 1973, Dan Rather had been riding the Nixon whirlwind for all it was worth. His stock was rising in direct proportion to the President's unrelenting slide into ignominy, and he became a kind of cult hero in the eyes of countless Nixon-haters across the country. Although he had not set out to cultivate his reputation as an anti-Nixon firebrand, and was to a large degree puzzled by it, Rather now seemed to be going out of his way to live up to it. His questions at Presidential news conferences became harder and more penetrating than ever. For his part, Nixon, who had long viewed the press as his natural enemy and was now privately blaming reporters like Rather for his present tribulations, seemed even more eager to exacerbate the friction in his relationship with the CBS News White House correspondent.

At a press conference in San Clemente in August 1973, for example, Rather prefaced his query with these words: "Mr. President, I want to state this question with due respect to your office, but also as directly as—"

Nixon chopped him off in mid-sentence. "That would be unusual," he snapped.

Another memorable moment occurred two months later during

Nixon's first news conference following the firing of Special Prosecutor Archibald Cox and related events that had been part of what was quickly labeled the "Saturday Night Massacre." Taking a somewhat philosophical tack, Rather asked, "Mr. President, I wonder if you could share with us your thoughts, tell us what goes through your mind when you hear of people who love this country and people who believe in you say reluctantly that perhaps you should resign or be impeached?"

It was the first time a reporter had dared to broach the dread subject of impeachment at a Presidential news conference. Nixon's face went through the familiar contortions that, over the years, had so often turned his public appearances into intriguing exercises in psychodrama. Then, scowling at the reporters assembled before him, he replied, "Well, I'm glad we don't take the vote of this room, let me say."

Yet in truth, Rather was growing weary of being on the cutting edge of Nixon's antipathy toward the press; and for all its morbid fascination, he was also getting tired of the Watergate story. Nevertheless, he continued to pelt Nixon with questions about bribes and cover-ups and personal thoughts about impeachment, and some habitual viewers of the televised press conferences confessed that they instinctively braced themselves whenever Rather's face appeared on the screen with what one critic called "that gleam of attack in his eye." And it was against this volatile background that, in March 1974, Dan Rather and Richard Nixon had their most celebrated confrontation.

The occasion was the convention of the National Association of Broadcasters in Houston. It was essentially a staged news conference, one that had been carefully orchestrated by the White House in an effort to present the harried President in the best possible light. Most of the station owners and managers in the audience that night were assumed to be sympathetic toward Nixon (or, at the very least, the sort of people who would show "due respect"), and sure enough, their questions, for the most part, were softballs that Nixon pounced on with barely concealed glee. But in order to negate charges that the event had been completely rigged, the three network White House correspondents—Rather, Tom Brokaw of NBC, and Tom Jarriel of ABC—were also allowed to participate. When Rather's turn came and he introduced himself, the audience responded with a burst of applause, accompanied by quite a few of boos as well. Rather, blessed with selective aural equipment, did not hear the catcalls, only the applause. Nixon also apparently heard only the favorable reaction, for he now asked Rather in a tone of heavy sarcasm, "Are you running for something?"

If this were fiction, it might be written that at this dramatic moment Rather's entire past life flashed before his mind's eye, which focused, in particular, on a day when, as a young college student, he had been taught to revere the Elmer Davis dictum: "Don't let the bastards scare you." But in reality, no thoughts of any significance passed through his mind. More than anything else, his response was intuitive and visceral. Glaring up at Nixon, Rather replied, "No, sir, Mr. President, are you?" That touched off another commotion, and this time there were a few gasps as well as more boos and applause. When it subsided, Rather asked a typically tough question about the House impeachment investigation, which Nixon, just as typically, parried with an evasive answer.

It did not take Rather long to discover that this time he had stepped into it up to his ears. Not all the reaction from viewers and fellow journalists was hostile, but a great deal of it was, and even some of Rather's admirers thought that he had gone too far. Various CBS executives, who had been grumbling for months about Rather's abrasive and controversial reporting, now became more open and insistent in their criticisms, and once again, as in the dark days following Nixon's landslide victory in 1972, rumors began to spread through the company that he was on the verge of being taken off the White House beat.

But then a very unexpected thing happened. A week or so after the Nixon-Rather exchange in Houston, the episode came up at a high-level meeting at Black Rock, the CBS corporate headquarters. Almost all the comments were predictably censorious until Bill Paley had his say. The way he saw it, Paley said, Nixon had tried to embarrass "our guy in front of his peers" (by whom he meant, presumably, the assembled broadcasters) and on national television as well. "I know how some of the rest of you feel," Paley added, "but *I* think Dan had every right to defend himself, and that he held his ground very well."

Paley approved. Like a wire-service bulletin, that message quickly crackled through the CBS grapevine, and one could almost hear the muscles strain and bones snap as the long gray line of executives, from the corporate heights down to the news-division level, wrenched and churned to bring themselves into line with the Chairman's view of the Houston incident. Thus, Paley's imperial blessing served to take most of the heat off Rather, at least within the company, but he still had one more formidable hurdle to clear: the wrath emanating from some CBS affiliate stations.

Several pro-Nixon affiliate owners and station managers had been trying to run Rather off his beat ever since the White House launched its personal campaign against him, and now, in the aftermath of the Houston news conference, they were more determined than ever. The annual affiliates' meeting was scheduled for May in Los Angeles, and the anti-Rather forces began pushing hard to have the "Rather question" become a top-priority item on the agenda. Dick Salant was so alarmed by this prospect that he prevailed upon Rather to put in a personal appearance at the affiliates' meeting. Rather had no stomach for such a mission. As far as he was concerned, he had nothing to apologize for, and he did not care to be put in a position where he would have to be pleasant and conciliatory toward people who were trying to wreck his career. But Salant pleaded with him, and so, more out of personal loyalty to Salant than company loyalty to CBS, he agreed to do it.

As it turned out, Rather's appearance at the affiliates' meeting—a demeaning and distasteful ordeal that lived up to all his glum expectations—did help quell the recall move against him. But ironically, the station owners and managers who were clamoring for his removal from the White House beat were about to get their wish, anyway. Indeed, if Rather had known then what was destined to take place later that summer, he might have been tempted to twit his detractors a bit, to assure them that their worries would soon be over because in just a few weeks they would not have Dan Rather to kick around anymore.

About a week after Nixon's resignation, Rather received a call from Bill Small, inviting him to fly to New York for lunch. Rather did not attach any special significance to the invitation until he arrived in Small's office the next day and discovered that he was going to break bread not only with Small but with Salant and Bill Leonard as well. Rather did not need to consult his agent to know that if the three top executives of CBS News—the president and his two senior vice-presidents—had all arranged their schedules to have lunch with one correspondent, they had more on their minds than good food and casual conversation. At lunch, it was Salant who brought the subject up. He said he wanted to talk about Rather's future, and the next thing Rather heard was that a plan was already in the works for him to leave the White House and move to New York to become the regular anchorman and correspondent on *CBS Reports.*

CBS Reports was the celebrated offspring of the equally celebrated *See It Now.* Created by Fred Friendly in 1959, the program went on to become, under Friendly's brilliant and vigorous guidance, the finest documentary series on television. But in the years since Friendly's departure, *CBS Reports* had lost much of its luster, due largely to the general decline of the documentary format and the corresponding rise in importance of the evening news broadcasts and such magazine-style programs as *60 Minutes*. The be sure, the *CBS Reports* unit had turned out several fine documentaries in the late 1960s and early 1970s, but they generally suffered from a lack of continuity, having been aired, for the most part, in weak and irregular time slots. Nor did they have a clearly defined identity.

Documentary programming at CBS News was under the jurisdiction of Bill Leonard, and now, in the summer of 1974, he and Salant were seeking ways to upgrade the *CBS Reports* operation. As part of that effort, they decided that the show needed its own regular anchorman—a correspondent of proven stature—and Rather, they agreed, had just the right combination of talent and star quality to fill that bill. In the conversation over lunch, Salant and Leonard made much of the fact that Rather would be the first CBS News correspondent since Edward R. Murrow to be honored with a regular assignment on a prime-time documentary series. They neglected to add, however, that Murrow had come to no small amount of grief in that role. Still, all that had happened many years ago, and times had clearly changed. Having gone through the fires of Vietnam and the Nixon-Agnew years, CBS was now more accustomed to living with all the furor caused by its news division—a dramatic case in point being Dan Rather's own career. Through his coverage of the Nixon White House, he had become even more embroiled in controversy than Murrow, and yet he had come out of that experience in good shape.

Or had he? That was the question that troubled Rather. In truth, he had no strong objections to leaving the White House. He had been working that beat for more than ten years, and he agreed that it was probably time to move on to another assignment. He sensed that after Lyndon Johnson and Richard Nixon, covering Gerald Ford's Presidency was likely to become a bland and uneventful routine. Moreover, Salant and the others portrayed the new job—"the promotion," as they kept calling it—in the most glowing terms. As Rather later joked to friends, it was very flattering to sit there at lunch and be told that he was about to become "the Son of Ed Murrow."

What Rather found disturbing, however, was the timing of "the promotion." The floors of the White House had hardly been mopped up following Nixon's lachrymose farewell, and yet he felt he was already being pressured into making a change. Leonard claimed that Bud Benjamin, the executive producer of *CBS Reports,* was putting together his schedule and budget for the forthcoming season, and various decisions in that area depended on Rather's commitment to the new assignment. But even if that was the real reason, Rather knew how such a hasty move would be interpreted by others. Now that Nixon was gone, critics would say, CBS could not wait to reassign his notorious gadfly, the well-known troublemaker. His antagonists at the affiliate stations, in particular, would no doubt choose to claim credit for the move, and Rather certainly did not relish the prospect of their gloating. Yet as he sat there listening to his superiors, none of these sensitive matters seemed to concern anyone but him. He had the feeling that Salant and the others were discussing the new assignment as a *fait accompli,* that he was being given no real choice in the matter—and that was the most disturbing part of all. Therefore, as the luncheon drew to a close, Rather told Salant, Leonard, and Small that he needed some time to think it over. Or, as Small later put it, with a sigh of exasperation, "Dan then went into his Hamlet act, and the world went mad."

That was only a slight exaggeration. News of Rather's lunch with the executive triumvirate quickly made the rounds, and the inevitable conclusions were not only drawn, they were also leaked to the outside press. Television critics on several major newspapers, quoting "informed network sources" as saying that Rather was about to lose his White House assignment, wrote indignant stories that CBS had finally succumbed to anti-Rather pressures. When the first reports appeared in print four days after the now-infamous luncheon, the CBS management was furious. At a luncheon meeting of news executives and top-level producers, Salant revealed that his corporate superiors at Black Rock were so incensed by the "Rather leaks" that they were threatening to send a special group over to the news division to track them down and root out the culprits. Even though the Watergate story was still fresh in everyone's mind, no one had the moxie to ask Salant if the Black Rock leak-pluggers were, perchance, going to be called "Plumbers."

The situation was made all the more distressing by the fact that Rather's contract with CBS was running out, and rumors began to drift back to Salant that Rather's agent, Richard Leibner, had entered into negotiations with both NBC and ABC. NBC News had, in fact, come up with a highly attractive offer, in terms of both money and position, and Rather, disturbed and confused by the sudden turn of events at CBS, was giving it his most serious consideration. And to make matters still more complicated, the CBS brass had lost contact with Rather. Feeling the need "to air out my mind," he had abruptly taken some vacation time due him and gone off on a fishing trip with his son, Daniel.

Small was finally able to locate Rather, and, conveying his concern that the situation was getting out of hand, he suggested that he and Salant fly down to Washington and meet with Rather at his home in Georgetown. When they arrived, Rather was still under the impression that he had been given no real choice in the *CBS Reports* decision, and he was plagued by the suspicion that pressure had been brought to bear on his bosses to yank him off the White House beat. Salant proceeded to set him straight on all that. The *CBS Reports* job, he emphasized, was strictly an *offer*, one that, in his judgment, Rather would be well-advised to accept. But he was free to stay on at the White House if he so desired or, said Salant, "you can suggest to me whatever else you might like to do." Salant and Small also assured Rather that the *CBS Reports* offer had not been dictated in any way by politics or pressure from the affiliates. After all, said Salant, if that was how the game was played, Rather would have been pulled off the White House beat sometime ago, when his presence there was causing problems.

Rather was greatly relieved to hear all this, and the more they talked, the more he warmed up to the idea of the *CBS Reports* assignment, especially after he was told that his new contract would include a very large raise, one that would propel his income to well over the $100,000-a-year mark. So the matter was resolved. Bob Schieffer left his Pentagon beat and replaced Rather as chief White House correspondent for CBS News, and Rather went on to New York to commence his new career as the Son of Ed Murrow.

But it had been a very close call. Perhaps only Rather's most intimate friends at CBS fully appreciated how upset he was, and how close he came to accepting the NBC offer. It was, in fact, so close that it was fortunate for CBS that Gordon Manning was no longer in power. Had he been actively involved in the abrupt decision to reassign Rather, Rather's suspicions of foul play almost surely would have sent him flying to NBC. For it was no secret that Rather did not trust Manning, especially when it came to matters concerning his career. But Small was another story. During their years together in Washington, Small had been unfailingly steadfast in his support of Rather, at times at considerable discomfort and even some risk to himself, and Rather was deeply indebted to him for that. Furthermore, he trusted Small and respected his judgment. In the end, it was Small's assurances, even more than Salant's, that convinced Rather that the move to *CBS Reports* was an honorable one as well as a positive step in his career.

So Dan Rather's view of Bill Small differed radically from that of Stanhope Gould. Yet, unfortunately for Small, the tide of opinion was clearly moving in the direction of Gould's estimation. By the fall of 1974, Small had managed to alienate many of his new subordinates, and he was rapidly becoming, in his own way, as much of a discordant influence as Manning had been.

One of the major grievances against Small was the personnel changes he made. During his first few months in New York, he brought up a number of people from the Washington bureau and moved them into key managerial positions. This was, of course, his privilege, and it would be misleading to suggest that all of his appointments were resented. But two, in particular, did spread dismay through the ranks of the New York staff: those of Don Richardson and Sylvia Westerman as deputy news directors. (To make room for them, Small appointed Sandy Socolow to his former post of Washington bureau chief, a lateral move that enabled Socolow to retain his vice-presidential title.) During their years in Washington, Richardson and Westerman came to be regarded by many of their colleagues as junior executives of limited ability whose chief claim to distinction was their personal loyalty to Bill Small. They were suspected of being the nucleus of "Small's spy system" (as it was sometimes called), and there was now concern that they had been brought to New York to serve as his eyes and ears there, and report back to him all murmurs of discontent about the way he was running the hard-news operation. And during their first few months in New York, Richardson and Westerman were referred to as "the Washington Junta" by some New York staffers who found their presence as intrusive and irritating in its way as Manning's mania for writing memos had been in its.

Another criticism of Small was that his basic approach to news was limited and unimaginative, reflecting the bias of someone who had spent too many years in Washington. He was, by his own admission, a stickler for hard news, and he had no use for the kind of back-of-the-book features that Manning had encouraged. For example, Small let it be known that he viewed Heywood Hale Broun's sports essays on the weekend news shows as a waste of precious air time; and Broun, a proud and sensitive man, became so disheartened by Small's lack of enthusiasm for his work that he eventually left CBS News. Another target of Small's displeasure was the *Morning News,* which, like the weekend shows, was prone to airing plenty of feature stories. Not long after he succeeded Manning, Small called the top producers of the *Morning News* into his office and coldly informed them that "you have interviewed your last transsexual." By the fall of 1974, it was being said of Small that if the Loch Ness monster were discovered, he would not bother to send a correspondent and camera crew to Scotland to film a report on it. Instead, according to this extravagant conceit, he would wait until a Senate committee began to hold hearings on the question of what effects the Loch Ness "beastie"—and sea monsters in general —were having on governmental efforts to curb water pollution.

Covering the story that way would not only give it a more dignified, hard-news tone, it would also be much less expensive, and that was yet another rap against Small. It was said that he was a penny pincher who was more interested in keeping a tight rein on the budget than in going after difficult and costly stories. Some producers felt they were no longer as free as they had been to go out on field assignments, and that long-range projects, in particular, were being stymied because Small thought they would cost more than they were worth. In addition, Small instituted niggling economic measures, such as cutting back the news division's daily newspaper subscriptions, and that was also viewed as an ominous sign. "The days of the high rollers are over," proclaimed Stanhope Gould shortly before he resigned. Then, sliding out of the Vegas argot and into a historical metaphor, he added, "The Roundheads are in command, and the Cavaliers are being put to flight." Gould had a reputation for being one of the most profligate Cavaliers, and the strong indications that Small was determined to keep a tight lid on production expenses was one reason why he chose to leave CBS News.

Gould's sudden departure, and the long and bruising conflict over the drug payola story that led to his resignation, also fueled the resentment that was building up against Small. Gould's supporters were the first to concede that he was erratic and headstrong, but they also insisted that at his best he had few, if any, peers as a field producer, and that he was far too good a man to lose. What rankled many New York staffers was their suspicion that in punishing Gould by taking him off the investigative unit (and thereby precipitating his resignation), Small had acted more out of personal pique than professional judgment.

Nor were Gould and Woody Broun the only ones to leave CBS News during this period. In the summer of 1974, the veteran Washington producer for the Cronkite show, Ed Fouhy, went to work for NBC News, and a few months later, John Hart made his move to that network. By the spring of 1975, when Manning followed Gould, Fouhy, and Hart over to NBC, that network had replaced ABC as the favorite refuge for disgruntled CBS News personnel. In fairness, not all these departures could be blamed on Small. Nor were they all permanent; Fouhy, for example, returned to the CBS News fold in 1977. Nevertheless, the loss of so many able hands in such a short span did not exactly reflect credit on Small, who, during his years in Washington, had prided himself on his ability to retain good people and keep them relatively satisfied. In the eyes of his detractors, the rash of defections in 1974–75 was yet another indication that in making the jump from Washington to the higher executive post in New York, Bill Small had plunged in over his head.

Finally, more than a few New York staffers had trouble adjusting to Small's personality. For all his faults, Manning, with his constant banter and rapid-fire quips, was chipper most of the time. But Small, by way of contrast, had a dour and forbidding manner, and when he walked through the newsroom with his habitual glower of disapproval, his presence often had a chilling effect. Even his occasional attempts at humor and camaraderie tended to rub people the wrong way. One day, for example, he walked up to a writer named Bill Overend, who was sporting a very full and rather unkempt beard, and said with a frosty smile, "Overend, you look like an armpit." Small's intent was facetious, but Overend did not take the remark that way, and Small would soon have occasion to regret it. Shortly thereafter, Overend left CBS News and wrote a hatchet job on Small that was published in the *Village Voice*. In his article, Overend recounted the various grievances against Small and contended that "morale has sunk to an all-time low at CBS since Small's arrival in New York." That particular issue of the *Village Voice* had an unusually high readership at CBS, not only within the news division but also at Black Rock, where most of the corporate executives had been under the impression that the change from Manning to Small was having a beneficial effect on staff morale at CBS News.

One night in the late fall of 1974, as Small was nearing the end of his first year in New York, several staffers were imbibing at The Slate, the bistro situated around the corner from CBS News. At one point, in the midst of their shoptalk, a veteran producer blurted out a confession: "Goddamnit, I never thought I'd hear myself say it, but I miss Manning. Gordon may have been an asshole, but at least he was a *cheerful* asshole." He then raised his glass in a mock toast and added, "So let's give Small credit for that much, at least. He's managed to pull off the greatest miracle since Richard Nixon transformed Lyndon Johnson into an object of instant nostalgia."

24 Character Studies

If Gordon Manning had become an object of instant nostalgia, his protégé, Paul Greenberg, had become an object of morbid curiosity. From the moment it was announced that Bill Small had succeeded Manning, just about everyone at CBS News assumed that Greenberg's days as executive producer of the *Evening News* were numbered. After all, Small had been brought into New York to correct Manning's mistakes, and Greenberg's rise to power, while not necessarily a mistake, had been one of the more overt developments of the Manning years. But more than that, it was known within the world of CBS News that there was very bad blood between Small and Greenberg. The two men had, in fact, engaged in several bitter and personal disputes over the years. In the days following Small's appointment, the story made the rounds that in the midst of one such quarrel, Greenberg told Small that he couldn't "find his ass with both hands." That, however, was a canard. That particular line happened to be an old favorite of LBJ's, one he frequently used to describe Senator Fulbright and various "Harvard smarties," such as Kennedy biographer and historian Arthur Schlessinger. Greenberg had his flaws but he was no plagiarist, and when it came to dishing out invective, he didn't need to steal material from Lyndon Johnson. According to those who were present during the altercation, what he actually said to Small was: "You couldn't find a news story if it was stuck up your ass and somebody shoved your fat head up there to look for it."

So in the weeks following Small's promotion, Greenberg was viewed as a marked man. Greenberg himself clearly sensed that he was living in a state of Damoclean peril, but he had no intention of making things easy for Small. He was not about to give up his *Evening News* post voluntarily. Small would have to depose him arbitrarily, and that just might serve to inflame the resentment that was already building up against him. For the problem, from Small's point of view, was that Greenberg was doing an excellent job. The Cronkite show's ratings were as robust as ever, and if Small made a move against him, Greenberg felt he could rely on the support of Cronkite and other members of the *Evening News* staff. In particular, he was confident that he had the solid support of his two chief deputies, John Lane and Ron Bonn, with each of whom he had developed a sound and productive working relationship.

Both Lane and Bonn were now thriving in their roles as coproducers of the *CBS Evening News*. Greenberg, aware that his abrasive personality antagonized people, generally delegated to Lane the daily task of motivating and placating correspondents and others who were working on stories in the field. Dealing with people was one of Lane's strengths, and he gradually became more decisive and more sure of his own authority. He was still inclined to be overly deferential in his relations with Cronkite, but in every other respect he was proving to be a worthy successor of Sandy Socolow. Bonn was also making impressive strides in his job as the producer in charge of the broadcast's film operation. Greenberg was a good (though demanding) tutor in the craft of cutting and shaping film stories, and Bonn learned a great deal from him. And as he grew more secure in his position, Bonn became less priggish in his relations with his staff of associate producers, although they still grumbled from time to time about the way he scolded them for tardiness and other niggling transgressions.

The dean of that staff was now Sam Roberts, who had been working on the *Evening News* since the early Les Midgley years. In those days, he had been largely overshadowed by Bonn, Stanhope Gould, and Paul Soroka, the heavy hitters on Russ Bensley's production team. But by 1974, with Bonn in Bensley's old job and both Gould and Soroka gone, Roberts was finally getting the recognition he deserved. Another associate producer whose work consistently received high marks was Joel Bernstein, who had been Lane's right-hand man in Chicago. There were also three women on the staff—Linda Mason, Rene Burrough, and Janet Roach—and that represented a sharp departure from the Midgley years, when the corps of *Evening News* producers had been exclusively male.

The makeup of the show's editorial staff had also changed considerably. The lone holdover from the Midgley years was Charlie West, the national writer and Harry Reasoner's frequent lunching companion. Both John Sumner, the veteran foreign writer, and John Mosedale, the "all-else" stylist, had left the broadcast in the waning months of Midgley's tenure, and since then, no less than five writers had followed them into those two slots. The most grievous loss, however, occurred in September 1974 when Cronkite's editor, John Merriman, was killed in a plane crash. More than anyone else except Cronkite himself and possibly Socolow, Merriman was regarded as almost indispensable to the inner harmony and sustained success of the *Evening News* in the late 1960s and early 1970s. His successor, Tom Phillips, never came close to establishing the kind of authority that Merriman had wielded over the editorial operation, and the subsequent period of adjustment was not an easy one.

Because of all the changes that had taken place in such a short time, the in-house consensus in 1974 was that the production staff and especially the editorial staff of the *Evening News* had declined in quality since the Midgley years. All the more reason why a strong hand was needed at the helm, and that was the trump card that Greenberg held. Even those who had been stung by his vitriolic temper and couldn't stand him personally were inclined to agree that his combination of executive strength and creative skills was such that it would probably be a mistake to pull him off the Cronkite show. Thus, when Small replaced Manning and the rumors began to circulate that he was out to get Greenberg, there was a tendency among members of the *Evening News* staff to rally around their executive producer. Small quickly became aware of this sentiment, and, in fact, he may have overestimated it; in any event, it was enough to dissuade him from making an immediate move to oust Greenberg.

By the fall of 1974, many CBS News people were convinced that Small had decided to overlook his past differences with Greenberg and keep him on as executive producer of the *Evening News*. And that, in turn, generated a subtle shift in attitude among some members of the show's staff. His considerable talents as a producer aside, now that they had to face the prospect of being stuck with him indefinitely, they began, once again, to gripe about his temper tantrums and his generally nasty disposition. In the past, such complaints had fallen on deaf ears —Manning's—but now they were reaching Small's ears, and they led him to the conclusion that Greenberg's support wasn't all that solid, after all. Thus emboldened, he decided to act.

In early January 1975, Greenberg began to notice that Cronkite was spending an unusual amount of time in Small's office. As omens go, that was not an encouraging one. So the next time they played tennis (with Greenberg, as always, toning down his game to make their match less one-sided), he asked Cronkite if there was anything going on that he should know about. Cronkite dismissed the question, saying that his recent meetings with Small had dealt with "basically routine" matters. He then quickly changed the subject.

The next day, Cronkite was in and out of Small's office all morning and much of the afternoon. Then, around four o'clock, Greenberg received a call from Small, who said he wanted to talk to him. As he left the *Evening News* area, he ran into Cronkite, who was returning from Small's office. Staring at Cronkite intently, Greenberg asked, "Well, do we have a problem?"

Cronkite, staring back just as intently, replied, *"You* have a problem."

With those words of encouragement ringing in his ears, Greenberg proceeded on to Small's office, where he was brusquely informed that Bud Benjamin, the executive producer of *CBS Reports,* was going to take over as executive producer of the *Evening News.* Small said he was making the change because the *Evening News,* under Greenberg's leadership, had become "unimaginative"—whatever that meant. At that point, Bill Leonard, who was in Small's office, announced that there was an opening for a documentary field producer on the *CBS Reports* unit, which was under his jurisdiction. Leonard told Greenberg that the position was his if he wanted it. It was a demeaning offer, an unequivocal demotion. Yet Greenberg had the distinct impression that if the opening had been in Small's department instead of Leonard's, even that modest life preserver would not have been thrown to him.

So for the third time in three years, the *CBS Evening News with Walter Cronkite* had a new executive producer. But unlike his many predecessors, all of whom had worked extensively in the hard-news area before taking on that assignment, Bud Benjamin's entire television career had been spent in the documentary field. At CBS, that operation existed off by itself, and there was only a tenuous link between it and the rest of the news division. Therefore, even though Benjamin had been around CBS since the mid-1950s, the *Evening News* people knew him only by name and had no idea what working for him was going to be like. The one notable exception was Cronkite himself. He and Benjamin had worked together on numerous projects over the years, and, in fact, it was largely because of his close association with Cronkite that Benjamin was picked to replace Greenberg.

Benjamin started out in print journalism, first at the University of Michigan (where another student named Arthur Miller wrote theater reviews for the school paper), and later, following his graduation in 1939, as a reporter for the Newspaper Enterprise Association. Then, in 1948, he went to work for RKO Pathé as a writer and producer of documentaries. After seven years there, Benjamin left RKO and began writing and producing historical documentaries for television on a free-lance basis. During this same period, Cronkite was appearing on the pseudohistorical *You Are There* show and its successor, a documentary series called *Air Power*. Then, in 1957, CBS decided to give Cronkite a new program in that Sunday time slot, to be called *The Twentieth Century*. A straightforward historical series, it would feature newsreel and TV footage instead of the hokey dramatizations that had characterized *You Are There*. Benjamin was hired to produce the new show, and *The Twentieth Century* made its debut in the fall of 1957 with a profile of Winston Churchill. Thus began Bud Benjamin's working relationship with Walter Cronkite, a weekly collaboration that would continue over the next twelve years.

The Twentieth Century did not stir up the kind of controversy that *See It Now* and *CBS Reports* did. Nor did the Cronkite-Benjamin alliance scale the creative heights Murrow and Friendly had reached in their television documentaries. But it was a creditable historical series, and it attracted a large enough following to keep it on the air until 1966, when it was replaced by a look-into-the-future documentary series called *The 21st Century*. Cronkite and Benjamin also worked together on that program and after it went off the air in 1969, Benjamin went on to produce and oversee various other documentary projects. Then in 1974, when the decision was made to structure *CBS Reports* around one correspondent, Dan Rather, Benjamin took over as executive producer of that broadcast. By January 1975, Benjamin, Rather, and the rest of the *CBS Reports* team were off to a promising start on the new season and were busily working on future programs when, out of the blue, Benjamin received a call from Bill Small, offering him the *Evening News* post.

Despite his enthusiasm for the new, upgraded version of *CBS Reports*, Benjamin felt he could not pass up Small's offer. He was now fifty-six years old, and he recognized that the job of executive producer of the Cronkite show could provide the crowning touch to his career in TV journalism. It was an opportunity he had not anticipated. Having worked exclusively in the documentary sphere, he was not exactly a logical candidate for the *Evening News* assignment. Moreover, being tucked away in the *CBS Reports* enclave, he was only vaguely aware of the animosity between Small and Greenberg. Hence, Benjamin had no clear idea why Greenberg was being sacked or why he had been selected to replace him. He strongly suspected, however, that his long and harmonious relationship with Walter Cronkite had a great deal to do with the latter decision.

He was right. The choice of Benjamin was dictated in large part by Small's desire to win Cronkite's approval of his decision to dump Greenberg. Small knew that Cronkite admired Greenberg's ability and the job he was doing, and that he was also only mildly concerned about the morale factor, all the personal grievances against Greenberg. But Small was confident that while Cronkite might feel obliged to defend Greenberg up to a point, he was not likely to go the extra mile for him, especially if it meant blocking the appointment of his old friend and colleague, Bud Benjamin. That proved to be the case. As Cronkite later confided: "If it had been anyone else but Bud, I probably would not have endorsed the move.

On his first day as executive producer of the Cronkite show, Benjamin went around the *Evening News* area with a cheery smile and introduced himself to everyone. "It was like Liberation Day in Paris during World War Two," one staffer later said. "We were so accustomed to Greenberg that we didn't quite know how to respond to Bud's easygoing nature." Indeed, Benjamin's benign manner was so pronounced that in the weeks ahead, some people made the mistake of assuming he was a pushover. "It reached the point where I had to caution them not to confuse civility with weakness," Benjamin later recalled. "Still, I don't believe you get the best results out of people by shouting and screaming at them all the time." Then, in an implicit allusion to his predecessor, he added, "I know there are others who choose to operate that way, but that has never been my way."

When it came to supervising a news program, Benjamin's way was similar to Les Midgley's. As an executive producer of documentaries, it had long been his habit to delegate plenty of responsibility to his deputies; and now, having moved over to the hard-news operation where he inherited a staff that had more experience than he did in that area, he relied even more on his subordinates. Like Midgley, Benjamin preferred to concentrate on the broad, overall picture, and as a result, the show's other producers began to take on more authority in the day-to-day decision-making process than they had been allowed to exercise under Greenberg. This was especially true of John Lane. Under Benjamin, Lane soon became as powerful a force as Sandy Socolow had been under Midgley: the nuts-and-bolts man who kept all the engines going, day in and day out. The show had flourished under Greenberg's leadership; now under Benjamin, there was no noticeable falling off in quality, and that was a net plus inasmuch as the *Evening News* staff no longer had to work in an atmosphere of fear and intimidation. In other words, Benjamin demonstrated that, Leo Durocher and Paul Greenberg notwithstanding, nice guys don't necessarily finish last.

Bud Benjamin's appointment to the post of executive producer of the *CBS Evening News* was a popular move, one that reflected favorably on Bill Small. As a matter of fact, most of the apprehensions about Small that had been formed during his first year in New York were now in the process of being dispelled. The Washington Junta was no longer perceived as the meddlesome presence it had earlier appeared to be. Don Richardson turned out to be a harmless and amiable man who devoted almost all his time to routine administrative details, and Sylvia Westerman served primarily as Small's intellectual guru and sounding board. In their respective roles as deputy news directors, they had a certain amount of influence on Small, but their direct authority over the news operation as such was minimal.

There were also signs that Small was breaking out of his Washington straitjacket and coming around to the view that back-of-the-book features, if judiciously aired, had a place on hard-news broadcasts. Nor was the portrayal of him as a tightwad proving to be all that accurate. In the fall of 1975, a veteran producer who a year earlier had been one of Small's harshest critics now conceded that he could not cite one instance in which a worthwhile story had not been covered because of budgetary considerations. "That fear, like most of the others, turned out to be groundless," he said. "In fact, I must admit that I've changed my mind about Small, and so have a lot of other people. He's doing a good job."

There were, to be sure, several producers and correspondents who continued to resent Small's blunt and austere personality, and his obsession with loyalty. But by February 1976, as he completed his second year as senior vice-president, the tide of opinion had shifted to the view that, warts and all, Small was still a better news executive than Gordon Manning had been. Yet, just when it looked as if Small had all his major worries behind him, he and Dick Salant had to wrestle with a new and particularly vexatious problem. Actually, it was an old problem, but one that had taken on a new and thorny twist. The name of the problem was Daniel Schorr.

Dan Schorr made his first big plunge into the hot water that was destined to become his natural habitat back in 1964, when he was the CBS News correspondent in Germany. On the eve of that summer's Republican convention in San Francisco, Schorr broadcast a report that Barry Goldwater planned to take a vacation in the Bavarian resort of Berchtesgaden immediately following his expected nomination. Schorr went on to note that Berchtesgaden had once been Hitler's favorite retreat, and that various right-wing groups in Germany were eager to make his acquaintance. Schorr's story was essentially correct in its facts, but the Hitler angle was a cheap shot; Berchtesgaden had long since been transformed into an American Army recreation center, and there was nothing untoward in Goldwater's intention to spend a few days there. (Incidentally, he was to be the guest of Lieutenant General William Quinn, commander of the U.S. Seventh Army—the same General Quinn whose daughter, Sally, would later become the hapless heroine of another CBS episode.)

Goldwater, infuriated by Schorr's story, proclaimed in San Francisco that he would never again speak into a CBS microphone. Moreover, the Goldwater camp focused much of its wrath on Bill Paley, charging that because of his close friendship with Eisenhower (who was known to be opposed to Goldwater's nomination), Paley was using his network as a partisan weapon against the senator from Arizona. There was no truth to that allegation, but Schorr's inflammatory report was, for Paley, a personal embarrassment, and he was livid. He told Fred Friendly, who had just recently taken over as president of the news division, that he thought Schorr should be fired, although Paley did not go so far as to demand his dismissal. Friendly did not fire Schorr, but he did send him a cable of reprimand, and, in the meantime, he filled the San Francisco air with his own special brand of fulminations. ("Dan

Schorr has given me a clubfoot at this convention!" he bellowed at one point.) Schorr eventually worked his way back into Friendly's good graces, but Paley never really forgave him. In later years, long after Friendly had gone and Salant had been restored to the presidency of CBS News, he often had to defend Schorr against Paley's charges that he was not to be trusted.

Schorr spent most of his career in Europe, first as a stringer for the *New York Times* and other news organizations, and then, since 1953, as a correspondent for CBS News. But in 1966, at the age of fifty, he was brought back to the States and assigned to the Washington bureau, where he would remain for the next ten years. When Schorr joined the Washington staff, the most desirable beats—the White House, Capitol Hill, and the State Department, among others—were occupied, and so he was assigned to report on the various social issues encompassed by LBJ's "Great Society" programs. Later, following other trends as they developed, he shifted his attention to environmental problems and economic stories.

Working in that amorphous, unstructured way—covering subjects instead of governmental institutions—a less aggressive reporter might easily have gotten lost in the shuffle, with most of his reports consigned to the *Morning News* and other back burners. But Schorr was unusually skilled and tenacious in the fierce scramble for air time. Since he was older and less telegenic than the likes of Mudd and Rather, he felt he had to make up the difference in hustle and chutzpah, and he did. "When you're not pretty and your voice isn't especially good, then your entire career is forced into attention-getting," he told an interviewer from the *Washington Post* in 1974. But his pushy attitude and tactics antagonized many of his colleagues. In particular, they resented his outsized ego, his obvious view of himself as being brighter and better than most other CBS News correspondents. Nor did they appreciate his peevish, self-pitying complaints on occasions when his stories failed to make the *Evening News* lineup. "He's a goddamn crybaby," one colleague said of Schorr in 1973, reflecting what had become, by then, a fairly common sentiment within the Washington bureau. "To hear him talk, you'd think there was some dark and sinister conspiracy at work to keep him off the air and undermine his career. What a load of crap that is. Hell, in the past few months, he's been on the tube more than anyone else around here."

That last part, at least, was true enough. Except for Sevareid and his nightly commentaries, Schorr logged more air time on the Cronkite show in 1973 than any other correspondent reporting out of Washington. But there was a special reason for that, and the reason was Watergate. It became Schorr's full-time assignment in the summer of 1972, a few weeks after the "third-rate burglary" occurred, and he stayed with the story as it grew from caper to scandal to staggering crisis. The abrasive tenacity that made him an irritant to many of his co-workers also made him a first-rate reporter, and Schorr pursued the Watergate story with verve and diligence. Much of the time, it's true, he was obliged to follow the scent of the *Washington Post*'s Woodward and Bernstein, the trailblazers who probed most deeply into the elaborate cover-up. Still, Schorr did come up with a few fresh leads of his own. And thanks to Watergate, he became an almost nightly fixture on the Cronkite show. The story brought him more recognition by far than any of his previous assignments for CBS News. Thus, as was the case with Dan Rather, the Nixon years served to elevate Dan Schorr to journalistic stardom. He was even accorded the ultimate honor—inclusion on the White House "enemies' list"—a circumstance that Schorr himself reported to CBS viewers in the lively summer of 1973, when the Watergate affair exploded into a scandal of epic proportions.

By the following summer, the story had undergone another escalation, from scandal to Presidential crisis, from the crimes of Watergate to the specter of impeachment. As the story moved toward a Constitutional showdown between the White House and Congress, it drifted away from Schorr into the hands of other correspondents, notably Rather and Mudd. Finally, there came the night of reckoning when Nixon went on television to announce his resignation. The CBS News correspondents assigned to take part in the instant analysis following Nixon's speech that night were Cronkite, Sevareid, Rather, and Mudd. Schorr had participated in similar panel discussions at other critical junctures in the story, but now, on this climactic night, he was not invited to join in, and he was not at all happy about that. He was even less happy when he saw how his colleagues responded to Nixon's resignation speech. Except for Mudd, who frankly and accurately pointed out that the speech "did not deal with the realities of why he was leaving," the correspondents showered praise on Nixon's valediction. Cronkite called the speech "conciliatory," Sevareid described it as "magnanimous," and Rather, of all people, said Nixon gave "to this moment a touch of class—more than that, a touch of majesty." The collective performance of his three colleagues reeked of bathos, and Schorr, for one, thought he knew why.

In the hours leading up to Nixon's speech, Schorr detected a strong sense of apprehension on the part of the CBS management, reflecting its concern over recent charges that Nixon was being hounded out of office by a hostile press. At one point that day, Sandy Socolow, having recently taken over as Washington bureau chief, personally urged Schorr not to be "vindictive." When Schorr protested that such an admonition seemed to question his professional integrity, Socolow assured him that similar words of caution were being passed to all correspondents. That, along with the subsequent on-air comments by Cronkite, Sevareid, and Rather, was enough to set Schorr's fertile, conspiratorial mind whirling. He began to see an insidious connection between the management's nervous attitude, the way the postmortem to Nixon's speech had been handled, and his own exclusion from the broadcast. And he proceeded to brood about all that over the next several weeks.

Five months later, in January 1975, the question of CBS's coverage of Nixon's resignation came up at a "rap session" Schorr was having with students at Duke University. According to published accounts of that exchange (which appeared first in the college newspaper, *Duke Chronicle,* and later in *New York* magazine and a Washington newsletter called *Media Report*), Schorr told the students that Cronkite, Sevareid, and Rather had gone easy on Nixon out of deference to management's wishes. He was also quoted as saying that the reason Mudd had not gone along with the kid-gloves treatment was that he had flown into Washington late in the day, and thus did not get the word. (This was not true; Mudd had been in Washington all that day, and the reason he did not get the word was that there was no official word or edict, as such.) Schorr further implied that management's desire to avoid critical analysis of Nixon's speech was the main reason why he, the intrepid Watergate reporter, had not been allowed to participate.

The published reports of Schorr's remarks at Duke did not exactly improve his standing in the eyes of his superiors and colleagues. Sevareid, in particular, was furious. He had interceded with Paley on Schorr's behalf back in 1964, at the time of the Goldwater controversy, and had gone to bat for him on other occasions in more recent years when officials in the Nixon Administration sought to discredit Schorr's reporting. "And this," he now thundered, "is the goddamn thanks I get!" At Sevareid's instigation, he, Cronkite, and Rather signed an angry letter to *New York* magazine following its account of Schorr's comments at Duke. Charging that a "slander" had been committed, the letter went on to assert: "The notion that executive orders at CBS News were handed down to 'go soft on Nixon,' and that those of us who felt constrained from whipping an obviously beaten man behaved in response to such orders, is false." Sevareid also vowed, in a private letter to Schorr, never to speak to him again unless he received "your personal apology and your public retraction of your remarks about me and the others." Instead of complying with that demand, Schorr offered a clarification that Sevareid found unacceptable, and, to this day, three years later, he still has not spoken to Schorr.

In clarifying his position, Schorr stated that the published versions of his exchange with the students were inaccurate. While acknowledging that he made statements critical of management and its attitude, he contended that he did not directly malign his fellow correspondents. That explanation did little to console the CBS News management, especially Dick Salant and Bill Small, both of whom had also defended Schorr over the years, shielding him from the complaints of Paley and other corporate executives, as well as from the wrath of the Nixon White House. Now, like Sevareid, they felt betrayed, but more than that, they were eager to find out what it was, precisely, that Schorr had told the Duke students. Therefore, when Schorr informed them that his remarks had been taped and that he was willing to submit the tape as evidence, Salant asked him to send it up to New York so that he and Small could listen to it.

In light of Schorr's close association with the Watergate story and the White House tapes, which were such a significant part of that story, what happened next was almost eerie. When Salant and Small sat down to listen to the Duke tape, it reeled along until it approached the portion dealing with CBS's coverage of the Nixon resignation, and then, suddenly, there was a gap—a *gap,* just like the one in the White House tape that, several months earlier, had caused such a public uproar. Schorr naturally insisted, with self-righteous fervor, that the gap was accidental, a bizarre coincidence, and Salant and Small, having no evidence to the contrary, were perfectly willing to believe that. But Sevareid, that stern Norseman, took a less charitable view when he found out about the gap. "I'm sure the son of a bitch erased it himself," he confided to friends.

Thus had Dan Schorr managed, over the years, to antagonize Bill Paley, Fred Friendly, Dick Salant, Bill Small, Dan Rather, Walter Cronkite, and Eric Sevareid—not to mention a goodly number of less formidable CBS associates. Like Richard Nixon, he was running out of crises, and now, in 1976, he blundered into his own mini-version of Watergate, an affair that, in its own way, was also characterized by deceit and an ill-advised cover-up.

In the months following Nixon's resignation, Schorr became immersed in another provocative headline story: Congressional investigations into assassination plots and other covert abuses of power committed by the CIA over the past three decades. Schorr pursued that assignment throughout 1975 with his customary perseverance, and by January 1976, the story was approaching its climax. The House Intelligence Committee, chaired by Representative Otis Pike, had completed its investigation and was preparing to release its 340-page report on the CIA. By then, choice excerpts from the Pike report were being leaked to various newsmen, and Schorr was the recipient of the biggest leak of all. In late January, he obtained a complete copy of the report from a confidential source and began extracting material from it for stories he reported on the *Evening News* and other broadcasts. Then, four days later, the full House, many of whose members were upset by all the leaks to Schorr and others, voted to lock up the report, thereby reversing the committee's earlier decision to release it to the public.

As a journalist protected by the First Amendment, Schorr did not feel bound by the House action. Indeed, given the peculiar situation he was in—he was, so far as he knew, the only reporter who had a copy of the suppressed document—he felt more strongly than ever that his primary obligation was to the public and its right to know. Accordingly, he proposed to Salant that the Pike report be published in a paperback edition under the auspices of CBS. Salant passed on the proposal to publishing executives at CBS, who said they wanted nothing to do with such a project. But even before Salant informed him of the company's negative reaction, Schorr had decided to act on his own, while neglecting to inform his superiors of his intention. Through a lawyer associated with the Reporters' Committee for Freedom of the Press, he arranged to have the report published in the *Village Voice*, where it appeared in mid-February 1976. And the day after its publication, the *Washington Post* ran a story linking the report to Schorr, in effect fingering him as the man who had turned it over to the *Voice*.

The initial reaction was quite hostile: the *New York Times* and other newspapers denounced Schorr in editorials (accusing him, unfairly, of selling the report, when, in fact, the transaction merely called for a voluntary contribution to the Reporters' Committee), and the House Ethics Committee announced its plans to investigate him. All of a sudden, Schorr was faced with the prospect of being cited for contempt of Congress unless he revealed his source—that is, the identity of the person who leaked the Pike report to him. Then came what appeared to be the unkindest cut of all: CBS News suspended him from all reporting duties (though with full pay) pending the outcome of the committee's inquiry into what had now become the Daniel Schorr case.

To the outside world, it looked as if CBS was punishing Schorr for having passed the report on to the *Village Voice,* and, worse, that it was succumbing to Congressional pressure. That was, to be sure, a large part of it. Salant and other CBS executives were angry with Schorr for what he had done, on his own, with a "secret" government document he had obtained as a CBS employee. Nor were they eager to put CBS in a position of having to defend Schorr's action in hearings before a House committee. Still, even with those grave reservations, Salant and the others might have been willing to bite the bullet on Schorr's behalf had it not been for another aspect of the affair, a sordid internal matter that raised disturbing questions about Schorr's character and integrity.

Schorr's original intention, when he set out to get the Pike report published, was to write an introduction to it. It was, after all, his scoop, and he wanted to get the credit for it. But when it wound up going to the *Village Voice,* he changed his mind and opted instead for anonymity. The *Voice,* he knew, was regarded in some circles as a slightly disreputable, anti-Establishment paper, and, sensing trouble, Schorr wanted to put another layer of protection between his confidential source and publication of the report. Nor did he feel comfortable about having his by-line appear in the *Village Voice,* which had recently published unflattering articles on both him and his boss, Bill Small. So the Pike report appeared in print with an introduction written by Aaron Latham, the author of the celebrated hatchet job on Sally Quinn that ran in the *Voice*'s sister publication, *New York* magazine, back in 1973. Within the CBS News Washington bureau, however, Latham was known not so much as the reporter who had carved up Quinn, but as the current boyfriend (and later husband) of Lesley Stahl—who, in a neat irony, was now CBS News's top woman correspondent, a status that would have been Quinn's had she been able to make the grade in television.

The morning the Pike report was published, Schorr took a copy of the *Village Voice* into the office of Washington bureau chief Sandy Socolow. According to Schorr, Socolow looked at it, fastened his gaze on Latham's by-line, then glanced up at Schorr and said, "Are you thinking what I'm thinking?" It was evident, Schorr later recalled, that Socolow was suggesting the possibility that Stahl had Xeroxed Schorr's copy of the report and then had smuggled it to Latham. Schorr, of course, knew better, but his only response to the query was an elaborate shrug. Later that day, he had lunch with an associate producer named Don Bowers, and, said Schorr, "I kind of led him to think that Lesley had something to do with it. I realized later in the afternoon that I was playing games for no reason at all. So I went to Sandy and said, 'Before you start any investigation of the Xeroxing, I know Lesley had nothing to do with it.' "

Even accepting Schorr's version, his conduct was reprehensible, and his version was singularly lacking in corroboration.

"That is a fucking rearrangement of what happened of the worst sort," said Socolow when informed of how Schorr had recounted the events of that day. "It is just an absolute rewrite of history." Socolow went on to say that when Schorr came into his office with the *Village Voice, he* was the one who proposed that "we check where Lesley and/or Aaron were while the Xeroxing was going on." As for Don Bowers, he was so alarmed by Schorr's comments at lunch that he later called Stahl and told her that Schorr had flatly accused her of stealing the report from him. Finally, as Socolow remembered it, Schorr did not make his about-face later that afternoon but the next morning, *after* the *Washington Post* had come out with its story, which, based on independent confirmation, pointed to Schorr as the agent through whom the Pike report reached the *Village Voice*. What's more, Socolow and others strongly suspected that if the *Post* had not blown Schorr's cover, he would have continued his campaign to implicate Stahl and Latham. For many of Schorr's colleagues were aware of his personal resentment toward Stahl, dating back to 1973 when she was assigned as his regular backup on the Watergate story. At the time, there were some CBS people who dared to suggest that she was showing him up, and Schorr, with his morose sense of not being fully appreciated, saw that as another example of the gross injustice peculiar to TV journalism: the preference for a less talented and less experienced reporter simply because she was younger and better-looking—and, in this case, a woman to boot.

When Schorr's suspension was announced a few days later, the CBS management made no mention of his attempt, directly or indirectly, to pin the rap on Lesley Stahl. Schorr, it was felt, had enough problems, and besides, there was nothing to be gained by dragging Stahl and her private life into the controversy. But in the weeks ahead, the story gradually leaked out, and Schorr, already bitter toward his employers for having suspended him, regarded that as part of a CBS-inspired campaign to smear him. In his view, the Stahl episode was a trivial side issue, "a piece of office gossip" (as he labeled it) that clearly paled in comparison with his impending First Amendment confrontation with the House Ethics Committee.

In truth, Salant and other CBS executives were duly concerned about the First Amendment questions involved in the Schorr case: a reporter's right to protect his confidential sources, and the further journalistic right to publish a government document without government sanction. Even though it disapproved of the furtive way Schorr had gone about getting the Pike report published, the CBS management supported his position on the general Constitutional principle, which was why it agreed to pay the $150,000 in legal fees he incurred over the next few months. Yet, at the same time, Salant and the others did not view the Stahl matter as an irrelevant side issue. As far as they were concerned, it could not be overlooked—and that, more than anything else, was what impelled them to take such strong punitive action against him in February 1976.

Cut adrift from his day-to-day labors at CBS News, Schorr entered into what he called "the full-time martyr business." He hit the lecture circuit, presenting his case before sympathetic college audiences, and in between his performances on the podium, he prepared for his encounter with the House committee. When the showdown came in September, he was ready. Ably assisted by his lawyer, prominent Washington attorney Joseph Califano (soon to be named Health, Education and Welfare Secretary in Jimmy Carter's Cabinet), Schorr proved to be an effective and eloquent witness at the hearing. In his opening statement, he told the committee that "to betray a source would for me be to betray myself, my career and my life. And to say that I refuse to do it isn't quite saying it right. I cannot do it." Also working to Schorr's advantage was the fact that the furor over the CIA leaks had died down during the intervening months, and (thanks in large part to the CBS suspension, which cast him in the role of lonely underdog), the tide of press and public opinion had shifted in his favor. By September, the prevailing mood on Capitol Hill was that it would be a lot easier to live with Schorr as an exonerated journalist than as a martyr nailed to the cross of the First Amendment. So, taking its cue from that mood, the House Ethics Committee voted not to recommend a citation for contempt. That matter finally settled, Schorr and his CBS employers now addressed themselves to the question of his future.

Back in February, when Schorr was caught trying to wriggle out of his ill-conceived deception, his superiors were so furious that their first impulse was to demand his resignation right then and there. But Schorr protested, with much justification, that a public dismissal coming at that time would only serve to whet the appetites of those congressmen who were clamoring for his scalp. As an alternative, he proposed that he merely be suspended for an indefinite period while he was under investigation. After consulting with their bosses on the corporate level, Salant and Small agreed to that, but only on the condition that Schorr sign an undated letter of resignation—a kind of secret "interlocutory decree" that would not become final (or public) until after the House proceedings had been resolved. Yet now, in September, with the investigation over and Schorr's resignation set to become official, Salant was warming to the idea of a reconciliation.

When he discussed the question with Arthur Taylor and Jack Schneider, they promptly offered opposite views: Taylor recommended reinstatement, while Schneider contended it was in the best interests of CBS to let Schorr go, as planned. As for Paley, his attitude had also softened a bit. Despite his long-standing mistrust of Schorr, Paley, like the other CBS executives, had been impressed by his performance before the House committee, and, shrewd showman that he was, he recognized that Schorr, having emerged from the controversy a hero, now had a higher box-office value than ever before. Hence, even though he still bore a personal grudge against Schorr and felt that his dismissal was long overdue, he was willing to acquiesce in the event that Salant and the others decided to put him back on the air.

As it turned out, that decision was not theirs to make. The CBS management assumed that Schorr was yearning to be reinstated, but that was not the case at all. For one thing, he was still seething with resentment toward his employers for having suspended him when the heat was on. For another, he had received a very generous financial settlement under the terms of the interlocutory decree—full salary for the remaining three years of his contract, plus severance pay—and thus had no pecuniary need to return to active duty at CBS. More to the point, with the CIA row coming so soon after the squabble over his comments at Duke University, there simply had been too much blood spilled in the past two years. Whereas he once had been viewed as merely an abrasive nuisance, Schorr was now regarded by several of his colleagues—Sevareid, Stahl, Socolow, and others—as a disruptive menace.

Then, too, Schorr was now sixty, just five years away from the company's mandatory retirement age. In recent years, with the Watergate and CIA assignments, his career had reached its peak; a stormy peak, to be sure, but a peak, nonetheless. Even if the in-house climate were less hostile, the road ahead still pointed to a gradual, anticlimactic fade into the sunset, and Schorr, who brought such a heightened, theatrical sensibility to his view of himself and his career, clearly did not find that prospect appealing. But if he quit now, at his moment of triumph as the fearless defender of the First Amendment, he would go out in a blaze of glory. Finally, he had signed a contract to write a book about his CBS experiences, and he obviously could proceed on that project with far less restraint if he were no longer working at the network. So, for all these reasons, when Salant mentioned the possibility of reinstatement, Schorr's reply was thanks ! 'it no thanks: he preferred to take the money and run.

Schorr's book, *Clearing the Air,* was published in the fall of 1977. In its more dispassionate sections, the book had much to recommend it. In particular, Schorr's accounts of his coverage of the Watergate and CIA stories, especially during the early stages when he had to dig into dark corners to come up with fresh leads, could serve as a valuable guide for aspiring journalists—a worthy companion piece to Woodward and Bernstein's *All the President's Men.* Anyone reading those chapters could not fail to appreciate that Dan Schorr was one of the best reporters in the business. But most of the book dealt with his personal problems with his CBS employers and colleagues, and his attempts to come to grips with that subject brought out the less attractive side of Schorr's professional nature: that of the self-serving propagandist. Indeed, his recollections of his various run-ins at CBS were so flawed by glaring omissions that after reading *Clearing the Air,* some of his former co-workers thought the title he chose was a master stroke of unconscious irony.

In writing about the dispute over the statements he made at Duke, for example, Schorr neglected to inform his readers about the tape recording of those remarks that was sent to Salant and Small, the one with the intriguing gap. No doubt he decided that to bring that up would only cloud the air instead of clear it. Similarly, in his passing reference to the Lesley Stahl incident, Schorr greatly minimized his own role, barely conceding that he had anything at all to do with that affair. From his book, one would never know that Sandy Socolow and others have steadfastly insisted that Schorr was the one who planted the calumny about Stahl in their minds. Here, too, he must have concluded that, in the interests of clarity, too many cooks would only spoil the pristine broth of his own version. Throughout the book, in general, Schorr portrayed himself as more sinned against than sinning, a lonely, misunderstood Galahad whose difficulties with his colleagues would never have occurred if in moments of crisis they had been endowed with his kind of courage and lofty sense of principle. As J. Anthony Lukas wrote in his review of Schorr's book in the *New York Times Book Review:* ". . . he seems less to be clearing the air than settling old scores."

That title, incidentally, was a substitute choice. Schorr came up with *Clearing the Air* after he was forced to abandon a prior inspiration because William Safire had selected it for the title of his Washington novel, which was published a few months earlier. If Safire had not beaten him to the punch, Schorr's book would have been published under an even more ironic title—*Full Disclosure.*

25 "We Are No Longer Starvelings..."

The Daniel Schorr imbroglio was an unsettling diversion, but nothing more than that: a temporary disturbance that had no lasting effect on the internal affairs of CBS News. In the meantime, other, more significant changes were taking place, for by the mid-1970s, the leadership of CBS News was going through a gradual yet definitive transition. Gordon Manning's downfall in 1974 was merely the first break in the Salant-Manning-Leonard chain that governed the news division through most of the 1960s and early 1970s. The next member of the triumvirate to depart was Bill Leonard, the vice-president in charge of the soft-news operation, who left in the fall of 1975 under circumstances far more agreeable than those Manning had experienced. As a reward for his years of faithful service to CBS, Leonard was promoted to the rank of corporate vice-president and assigned to Washington, there to work primarily as a lobbyist for the network. It was a very cushy post, one that would provide him with a limousine, a lavish expense account, and all the other trappings, but would not burden him with a great deal of pressure. Given Leonard's age, fifty-nine, it was an ideal way to wind down his long career at CBS.

As a news executive, Leonard had managed to avoid the glaring misjudgments and internal strife that helped wreck Manning's career at CBS and, more recently, seemed to jeopardize Bill Small's. This was, to a great extent, a triumph of temperament. There were those who found fault with Leonard's low-key and deliberate style, claiming that he was overly content to rely on the initiatives of the many talented producers under his command, while at the same time he did not

397

hesitate to take a full measure of credit for their achievements. But that was a minority view. Those who worked most closely with him, the various soft-news producers themselves, were staunch boosters of Leonard, in large part because he *did* give them free rein. Moreover, when a documentary report or a *60 Minutes* piece was edited, polished, and ready to be screened by Leonard, they valued his comments and criticisms, which were invariably fair and often incisive. "You can always tell when a story is too long or badly paced," Bud Benjamin once commented. "When Leonard complains that in the middle of screening a piece, his fanny began to itch, then you know it needs to be cut or restructured or at least *something* is wrong with it." As was once said of Hollywood tycoon Harry Cohn, the taste and attention span of the national viewing public was somehow wired to Bill Leonard's ass.

Most aspects of the soft-news operation had flourished under Leonard's supervision, but his greatest pride and joy was, without question, *60 Minutes.* Although Don Hewitt was the one who came up with the idea for the show and nurtured it through its formative stages, it is no exaggeration to say that *60 Minutes* would never have gotten off the drawing board in 1968, or survived the lean years when it was beset by feeble ratings, had it not been for Leonard's vigorous lobbying. Therefore, it was only fitting that at the time of his departure from CBS News in late 1975, *60 Minutes* was on the verge of becoming the most successful show of its kind in television history, the first news program to score consistently high in the competitive jungle of prime-time ratings. "He's the best executive I've ever worked for," Hewitt said the day he learned about Leonard's Washington appointment. "I feel sorry for the guy they pick to replace him."

To ease that burden, the CBS management decided to divide Leonard's empire and parcel it out to two men. For several years, Leonard's chief deputy had been a former *Variety* reporter and columnist named Bob Chandler who worked primarily on the political side of Leonard's domain, helping plan and coordinate convention and election coverage. So the job of supervising political coverage was given to Chandler, while the rest of Leonard's empire—overseeing *60 Minutes* and the documentary units—was entrusted to a veteran producer named John Sharnik. Both men were accorded the title of vice-president, but Sharnik had clearly inherited the choicest plums.

John Sharnik was among the group of bright young journalists who had worked on *Stars and Stripes* in Europe during World War II, and after spending a few years at the Sunday Department of the *New York Times,* he joined CBS News in 1954. By the late 1950s, he was working as a producer for Les Midgley on the instant specials that soon evolved into *Eyewitness.* Sharnik became, in fact, the prime creative force on *Eyewitness,* and from there he went on to produce a long and impressive documentary series on World War I, followed by several years as a top producer of news documentaries for *CBS Reports* and other programs. So, in 1975, having built up a formidable reputation as a writer and producer over the past twenty years, Sharnik welcomed the opportunity to show what he could do as an executive.

The move turned out to be a mistake. Sharnik was such a strong producer in his own right that he had difficulty adjusting to the more detached and noncreative role of managerial overseer. Like many gifted writers, he was inclined to be a heavy-handed editor, and before long, Hewitt and various producers on the documentary units were grumbling about Sharnik's captious criticisms and talking about how they missed Bill Leonard even more than they had thought they would. Sharnik was aware of these complaints and made a sincere effort to become less arbitrary or more Leonardian in his approach. But that only increased his sense of frustration, for in truth, he was not happy in his new job, which, for all its status, was too far removed from the creative process to suit his natural bent.

In 1977, when CBS News tried out a new prime-time, magazine-style broadcast in the *60 Minutes* vein, a frothy offshoot called *Who's Who,* Sharnik jumped at the chance to serve as its executive producer, while still hanging onto his vice-presidential post. *Who's Who* remained on the air only a few months, but Sharnik's brief return to the playing field was enough to convince him that he belonged in production, not in management. So, in the late summer of 1977, he relinquished his managerial slot to become senior executive producer in charge of all prime-time documentaries. Succeeding him as soft-news vice-president was Bob Chandler, which meant that he now had jurisdiction over all of Leonard's former territories. The move also signaled a return to Leonard's executive style, for as Hewitt remarked shortly after the change was announced, "There should be no problems with Chandler. He's cut from the same cloth as Bill Leonard."

The departures of Manning and Leonard left Dick Salant as the only remaining member of the management team that came to power at CBS News in the 1960s, and by 1978, he had moved into the twilight of his long reign as president of the news division. His retirement was officially set for the spring of 1979, when he would turn sixty-five, but there was a strong possibility that he would be replaced even before then in order to effect a smooth and orderly transition.

Whenever the time did come for him to step down, Salant would be able to do so with a deep sense of satisfaction. Except for the two years he spent in limbo, when Fred Friendly was running the show, Salant had been president of CBS News since 1961, and thus had guided it through the critical years of growth and development in TV journalism. When he took over in 1961, CBS News had 469 full-time employees and an annual budget of about $20 million. By 1978, the number of full-time employees had swelled to just under a thousand, and the yearly budget was close to $100 million. More to the point, perhaps, CBS News, which for years had operated in the deep red, causing it to be scorned by the corporate Babbitts as a constant drain on network profits, was now taking in almost as much in advertising revenue as it was spending to gather and broadcast the news. That in itself was an impressive indication of how successful, as well as important, television news had become.

But mere numbers scarcely begin to tell the story. In 1961, TV journalism was still struggling through its awkward adolescence, and CBS News in particular had lost its early initiative to NBC and the bright new team of Huntley and Brinkley. Under Salant, however, all that changed dramatically. He deserved much of the credit for the single most important programming advance of the 1960s—the expansion of the *Evening News* to a half hour—and he presided over the advent of such other shows as the *Morning News,* the weekend editions of the *Evening News,* and *60 Minutes.* Under Salant's aegis, Walter Cronkite took over as anchorman on the *Evening News,* and Harry Reasoner was brought out of the shadows and given his opportunity to shine. Salant was also responsible, directly or indirectly, for hiring such star correspondents as Mike Wallace, Roger Mudd, and Dan Rather, and for moving others, such as Eric Sevareid, Charles Kuralt, and Hughes Rudd, into slots where their respective talents could be used to full advantage. And it was during Salant's reign that CBS overtook NBC and firmly established itself as the dominant voice in television news. Finally, Salant himself emerged as a forceful and, at times, eloquent spokesman for broadcast journalism.

Still, the record was not entirely flawless. Salant was largely to blame for the contract stalemate that precipitated Reasoner's departure to ABC in 1970. And, with Gordon Manning, he also helped bring on the Sally Quinn fiasco. A more general criticism was that Salant too often remained aloof from the journalistic process, a detachment that reflected his sincere belief that since his own background was in law and not news, his various deputies were better equipped to make purely editorial decisions. Nevertheless, there were times when it seemed that his retreat behind the "I'm-just-a-lawyer" cloak was essentially a stratagem to avoid direct involvement in internal controversies, such as the prolonged dispute over the drug payola story in 1974. In the final analysis, however, Salant's mistakes and shortcomings clearly paled in comparison with all that had been accomplished during his years as president of CBS News.

Given the volatile nature of the business and the political storms that buffeted the networks (and CBS News in particular) during the 1960s and early 1970s, it's a wonder that he lasted in the job as long as he did. Indeed, there were many CBS people who believed that Salant would not have survived, especially during the Nixon-Agnew years, had it not been for the unflagging support of his friend and patron, Frank Stanton. Hence, it was hardly surprising that in the aftermath of Stanton's retirement in 1973, rumors began to circulate that Salant was in trouble. By 1975, they had become so rampant that Stanton's successor, Arthur Taylor, felt obliged to put in a special appearance at one of the regular luncheon meetings of news executives and producers, at which he assured everyone present that Salant's job was not in jeopardy. "At that point," said Don Hewitt, who had attended the luncheon, "Bill Small stabbed himself in the chest with his fork."

Hewitt's fanciful observation reflected the general assumption that Small was destined to succeed Salant and was having trouble keeping his impatience under control. When he was picked to replace Manning as hard-news vice-president in 1974, Small was given to understand that he would eventually move up to the top post. But he had damaged his chances with his rocky start in New York, and although he had made some progress since then toward tempering the rancorous mood of that first year, there were strong indications that anti-Small forces were exerting enough influence to prevent his becoming the next president of CBS News. The situation was further complicated by uncertainty over who, when the time came, would be empowered to resolve the question of Salant's successor. For by the mid-1970s, the winds of change were also blowing through the corporate sphere and causing turmoil there.

One day in the fall of 1974, Bill Paley, now seventy-three yet still very much in command of his giant "candy store," ran into Mike Dann, who, until he left the network in 1970 to go into public television, had been in charge of programming at CBS. Paley greeted Dann cordially, and at one point, while he was bringing him up-to-date on recent developments at CBS, he went out of his way to say that young Arthur Taylor was doing very well as Frank Stanton's successor. But as David Halberstam later wrote in his lively magazine account of that conversation, "Dann knew Paleyology well enough to translate that: it meant that Arthur Taylor was doing well but the jury, composed of twelve Bill Paleys good and true, was still out."

Two years later, the jury came in with its verdict, and it was thumbs-down on Taylor. In October 1976, he was ousted as president of CBS and another corporate officer, John Backe, was elevated to that post. The sudden move startled most industry observers. Wall Street analysts in particular were taken aback, for Taylor had been appointed president of the huge corporation in 1972 because of his financial acumen, and his performance in that area had been outstanding. Corporate sales and earnings were soaring to record highs in 1976, and the company's future loomed more bullish than ever. And although Taylor had a long way to go before he would be recognized as a worthy successor to Stanton in the demanding role of high-minded spokesman for broadcasting policy and chief guardian of the CBS image, he was making impressive progress on that front as well.

As part of that effort, Taylor had entered into a love affair with the news division. He had come to regard CBS News as the class act in his vast repertory, and he began to use much of his authority to defend and promote its best interests. His boldest move in that direction came in the spring of 1976 when he committed himself, in public, to an expansion of the *CBS Evening News* from a half-hour to a one-hour format. Salant had been pushing that proposal for the past several years, but had always run into stiff opposition from his corporate superiors, who insisted that the affiliates would never agree to give up thirty minutes of their lucrative local news time to clear the air for a one-hour version of network news. Yet now the president of the entire corporation had suddenly come out in favor of the one-hour format, and, more than that, he told Salant he was prepared to use the full power of the network to pressure the affiliates into going along with it. Salant was ecstatic. He had long been convinced that expanding the *Evening News* to a full hour would be as significant an advance in network journalism as the 1963 shift to a half hour, and, in more personal terms, he saw it as the perfect capstone to his own career, a chance to go out with a bang and a flourish. Taylor's abrupt dismissal in the fall of 1976 brought an end to that dream. The embryonic campaign for a one-hour version of the *Evening News* was scrapped, at least for the foreseeable future.

But having friends and admirers on Wall Street and in the news division availed Taylor nothing so long as he failed to retain the support of the one presence that mattered most: that jury composed of twelve Bill Paleys good and true. There was, from the beginning, a notable lack of rapport in the Paley-Taylor relationship, and Taylor aggravated the situation by overplaying the role of crown prince. Since he was, at forty-one, thirty-four years younger than Paley, Taylor thought he had a free hand to impose his style and personality on CBS, and start building toward the post-Paley future. Bill Paley bitterly resented that. Never mind that he himself had often said over the years that television was a young man's business, and never mind that he was now ten years past the company's mandatory retirement age. Those who were schooled in Paleyology clearly understood that such policies and attitudes were never meant to apply to Paley himself. As one insider put it shortly after he lowered the boom on his would-be successor, "Taylor made the horrendous mistake of acting as though Paley had died and he had inherited the company."

Ironically, it was Taylor himself who had recruited John Backe, the obscure newcomer who was suddenly picked to replace him as president of CBS. Backe had spent several years in various managerial positions at General Electric, then moved into publishing, first as marketing director and later as president of Silver Burdett Company, a textbook firm. Taylor brought him to CBS in 1973 to head its Publishing Group, which was then the weak link in the corporate chain. CBS's publishing ventures flourished under Backe's leadership; the group's earnings jumped from $3.2 million in 1973 to $24.3 million in 1976. His biggest coup was the $50 million acquisition of Fawcett Publications Inc., a transaction that impressed Paley and greatly influenced his decision to make the forty-four-year-old Backe his new heir apparent.

Backe's position was further strengthened in the spring of 1977 when Paley, whose extraordinary reign over CBS was now approaching its fiftieth year, finally made a partial move toward retirement. At the CBS annual meeting that spring, he stepped down as chief executive of the corporation and turned the operational reins over to Backe. But significantly, Paley held onto the title of Chairman (and the ultimate power of that office), and he made it clear that he intended to remain in the picture as a kind of patriarchal overseer for the next several years —which meant, as one longtime associate put it, "until he draws his last breath."

Still, as long as he remained in the Chairman's good graces, Backe had authority over the day-to-day affairs of the vast conglomerate, and he soon began to exercise it. The most pressing problem he had to confront was the sharp decline in the network's ratings. For twenty years, dating back to the days of *I Love Lucy*, CBS had led the opposition, season after season, in the annual battle for prime-time ratings. But a remarkable surge by ABC, for years the weakest of the three networks, enabled it to soar past both its rivals in 1976 and relegate CBS to the unaccustomed indignity of second place. In the fall of 1977, with the start of a new television season, CBS fared even worse, dropping to third and last place in the ratings. And in October, Backe, prodded in part by Paley's personal, almost visceral chagrin, decided the situation had become critical enough to warrant a sweeping change in structure and personnel. It also, not incidentally, presented Backe with a golden opportunity to remove top executives he had inherited from Taylor and replace them with his own people, who would be personally beholden to him.

Bob Wussler, the resourceful hustler who had risen so rapidly from the middle-level ranks of the news division to become president of the Television Network, now experienced the first serious setback of his meteoric career. His domain was carved up into three divisions—entertainment, sports, and network (the latter's function now largely confined to sales and affiliate relations)—and he retained jurisdiction over only one-third of it: the sports operation, which, eighteen months earlier, had served as his stepping-stone into the network presidency. Two of his deputies, Robert Daly and James Rosenfield, were picked to run the other two divisions. But the biggest loser in the October 1977 shake-up was Wussler's immediate boss and patron, Jack Schneider. After eleven years as head of the Broadcast Group, he was kicked upstairs to the post of corporate senior vice-president, a fancy-sounding title that in no way obscured the fact that he had been eased out of the mainstream of power. The big winner in the upheaval was Schneider's successor, Gene Jankowski, who had been with CBS since 1961. Jankowski's early background, like Schneider's, was in sales, and he moved up to the top echelon through a variety of positions, mainly in administration.

Prior to all the disruptions in the corporate hierarchy, Bill Small had been pinning his hopes for the presidency of CBS News on Schneider, who, in the past, had been his champion. But that was wishful thinking on his part, for by 1977, Schneider had soured on Small. Indeed, shortly before his own ouster that fall, Schneider had reached the conclusion that the man for the job was not Small, but Bud Benjamin. Moreover, he imparted his preference to both Backe and Jankowski, the two men who would now be making the decision regarding Salant's successor.

Benjamin was also Salant's personal choice. He, too, had become disenchanted with Small, and in private conversations with Backe and others, he made it clear that if the decision were his to make, Benjamin would be named to succeed him. Another scenario had Bill Leonard being brought back from Washington to become the next president of CBS News. Since both Leonard and Benjamin were only a few years younger than Salant, the appointment of either man would obviously be an interim move designed to buy the new management more time to scrutinize various long-term candidates. Within the executive suites of CBS, that alternative was being referred to as "our Pope John ploy." Nor were the above-mentioned names the only ones being bandied about as 1977 drew to a close. Clearly, the question was still very much in the air, and yet on one point all hands agreed: whoever was designated to take over the post would find Dick Salant a tough act to follow.

Some of the network's most respected correspondents had also reached or were nearing the point of retirement. Eric Sevareid's long and distinguished career at CBS came to an end in November 1977 when he turned sixty-five. He did not choose to lapse into inactivity, however. His postretirement plans included writing and narrating an independently produced television series on American and European diplomacy during the years between the two World Wars. But Sevareid was, he admitted, ready to leave the rigors of daily journalism. His many friends and colleagues had long been accustomed to listening to his complaints about his health. "The trouble with you," he once told Fred Friendly, "is that you don't realize hypochondriacs get sick, too." And to a luncheon companion in the fall of 1976 he mournfully confessed, "I'm now just living defensively. This is a young man's game, and it's time for me to get out of it." Then, his eyes brightening, even though his words continued to come out in a sepulchral hush, he added, "But at least I've stayed the course. Forty-odd years in this lunatic business, and somehow, incredibly, I managed to survive it all. So, whatever else they care to say about me, they have to grant me that: I've stayed the course."

Charles Collingwood, Sevareid's comrade from the early Murrow years, was also entitled to make that boast. By 1977, he was no longer working out of London as the network's chief foreign correspondent. He had returned to New York two years earlier, in part because he, too, had grown weary of the daily journalism grind ("chasing around airports and all that bother"), and even more so because his wife was seriously ill and he wanted her home, in the care of American doctors. His CBS assignment in New York was to anchor occasional specials and documentaries, but that was hardly enough to keep him busy. He was still very much the Duke, still as elegant and as debonair as ever, but his days of glory as a topflight correspondent were well behind him, and, like a baseball team that's no longer in the pennant race, he was simply playing out the season. In the summer of 1977, shortly after his sixtieth birthday, Collingwood anchored a documentary dealing with the problems of retirement. His friends were not surprised when he chose to conclude the broadcast that night on a personal note, confessing to viewers that his interest in the subject transcended mere journalistic curiosity.

On the other hand, Walter Cronkite, who was a few months older than Collingwood, did not care to dwell on that particular subject. As a matter of fact, he was known to be irritated by the many speculations about who was going to succeed him as anchorman on the *CBS Evening News*. To judge from all the talk, one would think that Cronkite was on the verge of packing it in, when, in reality, he had every intention of clinging to that slot until November 1981 when he would make the big turn past sixty-five. He was still, far and away, the preeminent figure in broadcast journalism, as he had been for the past decade or so, and he continued to drive himself to maintain that position. As was the case with Sevareid and Collingwood, his laurels stretched back to the years when he was a young reporter covering World War II, but unlike them, Cronkite was not yet content to rest on them.

His one major concession to advancing age was the contract agreement he worked out in 1973, whereby he could take three months off a year. But the combination of events and his own restless need to be at the center of all the important action prevented him from taking full advantage of the new arrangement. In the summer of 1974, the House Judiciary Committee's impeachment debate kept him on the job until the end of July. After anchoring CBS's live coverage of that, he took off for Martha's Vineyard, planning to squeeze in a little vacation time before the full House assembled to vote on the articles of impeachment. But then came the swift and unexpected denouement: the disclosure of the "smoking-gun" tape that left no doubt of Nixon's personal involvement in the Watergate cover-up, and the President's subsequent decision to resign. Idly sailing the waters off Martha's Vineyard, Cronkite was frantically summoned to shore and hustled down to Washington to preside over the CBS coverage of Nixon's speech. It was almost as if the CBS executives feared that Nixon's resignation might not be accepted as official unless Cronkite appeared in his customary anchor slot to give it his imprimatur.

The following summer, Cronkite interrupted his vacation only briefly, to be the guest of honor at a company party celebrating his twenty-fifth anniversary at CBS. But his vacation in the summer of 1976 was almost a total washout. Not only were there the two political conventions to anchor, but that was also the summer of America's bicentennial gala, and there was no way that Walter Cronkite was going to miss out on CBS's participation in that. Indeed, old "Iron Pants" was at the top of his form on July 4, 1976, when CBS News took over the network all day and all evening for its live-coverage program called *In Celebration of US.*

Cronkite anchored the entire broadcast, from 8:00 A.M. until midnight, once again demonstrating that when it came to that particular form of TV journalism—marathon coverage of a live, spontaneous event—the old warhorse was still in a class by himself. Moreover, he visibly rejoiced in every aspect of the celebration, from the spectacle of the tall ships in New York Harbor to the rousing displays of fireworks that brought the long national birthday party to a close. Like the first moon landing seven years earlier, it was Cronkite's kind of story: a flag-waving tribute to America the Wonderful, and he once again seized the opportunity to embrace and embody the old-fashioned verities. As one overwrought viewer later wrote, "It was a great day for the country's two Uncles—Sam and Walter."

In the weeks leading up to the bicentennial broadcast, CBS aired a slew of promotional spots, exhorting viewers to tune in on the Fourth of July. During one of them, an announcer's voice proclaimed that this was a once-in-a-lifetime opportunity, noting that the next big splash of this kind would not occur until the tricentennial in 2076, "and by then, none of us will be here." At that point, Cronkite's face reappeared on the screen, and, in that hearty tone of reassurance so familiar to millions, he delivered an ad-lib that quickly put all apprehensions to rest. "Of course I'll still be here," he chortled, "doing the *Evening News.*" A few days later, when a mutual friend passed Cronkite's remark on to Harry Reasoner, Reasoner responded with a merry laugh, then said, "Don't bet against it."

For the most part, Harry Reasoner did not have much to laugh about in 1976. Up until just the year before, he had been performing wonders at ABC News. Reasoner's move to that network in 1970, to co-anchor the *ABC Evening News* with Howard K. Smith, gave that broadcast an enormous boost in both prestige and ratings. For the first time in the history of TV journalism, ABC became competitive in the nightly news field. It was still running third, but by the end of 1974, its share of the evening-news audience had shot up from 15 percent (at the time of Reasoner's arrival) to 23 percent, just a point or two less than NBC. Reasoner's original contract with ABC was expiring in 1975, and in negotiating a new one, he said he wanted, in addition to more money, a chance to anchor the show by himself. Under the terms of the proposed arrangement, Howard Smith would be relegated to the Sevareidian role of commentator.

Reasoner's bosses were all set to comply with that demand, until they were presented with an unexpected alternative. Roger Mudd's contract with CBS was also expiring that year, and the ABC brass learned from his agent that Mudd might be receptive to the right kind of offer from another network. All of a sudden, the intoxicating vision of a Reasoner-Mudd anchor team began dancing through the heads of ABC executives. They felt that Mudd, with his youthful appearance, his political savvy, and his crisp, straightforward broadcasting style, had the ideal characteristics to complement Reasoner's middle-aged look and his more urbane and casual approach to the role of anchorman. Such a combination had, the ABC people thought, the potential of becoming the best marriage in television news since Huntley and Brinkley. Beyond that, the ABC management contemplated, with relish, the coup of enticing another top-stakes horse away from the rich and smug CBS News stable.

But Reasoner was, to put it mildly, far less enthusiastic about the idea. Like his superiors, he had a high regard for Mudd's ability, and he would have welcomed him to ABC with open arms as the network's chief Washington correspondent or in any other high-ranking post— save that of co-anchorman on the *Evening News.* In addition to the professional respect they had for each other, Mudd and Reasoner were also good friends. Even during Reasoner's last years at CBS, when the weekend news operation was sharply divided between his Sunday night coterie and the Mudd-Greenberg Saturday faction, the two correspondents did not allow that discord or their respective career ambitions to impair their friendship. Thus it was, in the spring of 1975, that Reasoner appealed to Mudd as a friend. He invited him to lunch at the Oyster Bar, and there, over drinks and crustacea, he earnestly explained his position. He had been striving for many years for the opportunity he now had to anchor a network evening news show by himself, and it was not likely ever to come his way again. Reasoner said that he would be elated if Mudd should decide to come over to ABC News in some other capacity worthy of his talents, but he hoped that Roger understood how much the solo anchor job meant to him.

Mudd's response was gracious and amicable. He assured Reasoner that he would never dream of accepting such an offer unless it were made with his, Reasoner's, full approval—and that was that. Yet at the same time, he hoped that Harry understood that he would have nothing to gain by going over to ABC in a job other than that of co-anchorman on the *Evening News* since he was already entrenched in the number two slot at CBS News. Or, to put it another way, as long as he had to remain in the role of backup, better to sit in regularly for Walter Cronkite than Harry Reasoner. When all this was subsequently explained to the ABC executives, they were more than a little miffed at Reasoner for the way he had exploited his friendship with Mudd to protect his own roost. As far as they were concerned, he had acted entirely on behalf of his own ego and ambition instead of on behalf of what was best for ABC News.

Still, Reasoner was, without question, the reigning star of the ABC news operation, and with Mudd out of the picture, his bosses now gave him what he wanted. That turned out to be a mistake. Reasoner took over as sole anchorman on the *ABC Evening News* in the fall of 1975, and the show soon lost the ratings momentum it had been building up over the past five years. By the spring of 1976, it was once again floundering in the depths of last place, seven points behind the *NBC Nightly News* and ten points behind the Cronkite show. And just as Reasoner deserved most of the credit for the big boost that occurred in the early 1970s, he now had to bear most of the blame for the sharp reversal. In anchoring the *Evening News* alone, without a "heavy" to play off of, he often seemed to lack sufficient weight and presence; and his wry charm, so effective when he was paired with a "straight man," began to wear thin.

By the spring of 1976, his superiors decided that drastic action was needed to remedy the deteriorating situation. Accordingly, in April, ABC announced that it had lured Barbara Walters away from NBC's *Today* show, and the size of the lure sent shock waves through the broadcasting industry: a five-year contract at $1 million a year. For that queenly sum, Walters would co-anchor the *ABC Evening News* with Reasoner (thus becoming the first anchorwoman on a network evening news show) and, in addition, would interview celebrities on several prime-time specials over the course of each television season. It was, by far, the biggest bundle ever bestowed on a TV journalist, although there was even some question as to whether that term accurately described Walters's professional status.

Reasoner was furious when he learned about the deal. Along with his disappointment over being demoted back to a co-anchor slot, he thought the choice of Walters as his new on-camera partner smacked of desperation and the worst kind of show-biz ballyhoo. In his view, she was not a journalist so much as a TV personality, a talk-show "hostess," and that clearly did not conform to his idea of television news. What's more, Reasoner felt the money ABC had agreed to pay her was scandalous, although his objections on that score were considerably mollified when the network consented to renegotiate his contract and increase his salary to about $500,000 a year. Yet even as he accepted that raise, thereby pledging his cooperation, Reasoner had the sour feeling that he was being squeezed into a demeaning, no-win situation. Even if the ratings of the *ABC Evening News* did improve—and he did not regard that as a likely prospect—Walters would get all the credit.

Barbara Walters made her debut as an anchorwoman in October 1976, and it would be an exaggeration to say that she was a total failure in that role. Male chauvinists who gleefully anticipated another Sally Quinn fiasco were deprived of that pleasure. After all, Walters had plenty of television experience behind her, and, unlike Quinn, she knew what camera to look at and how to comport herself on the air. But she had no real training or background in news, and that—just as Reasoner had feared—proved to be a large part of the problem. Over the years, the best anchormen—as Cronkite, in particular, so ably demonstrated—did not merely read the news, but conveyed a clear sense of being on top of it, of being acutely aware of its nuances and complexities. Beyond that, some of them—such as David Brinkley, Hughes Rudd, and Reasoner himself—were gifted writers who knew how to grace their copy with deft personal touches. Walters, however, was not strong in either of those areas, and, as a result, she came across as lacking in journalistic authority. Her forte was interviewing, and, not surprisingly, she fared much better on her prime-time specials, which were interview programs. But that skill was not integral to the job of anchoring an evening news broadcast.

Nor was Walters's broadcasting style conducive to the role of anchorwoman. Her rather harsh voice and her unfortunate speech impediment inspired crude and often cruel parodies that further undermined her credibility. Worst of all, from the standpoint of the ABC management, which had invested so much money in her, Walters failed to live up to all the advance hoopla regarding her presumed star quality. She did not attract millions of new viewers to the *ABC Evening News;* instead, the show's ratings actually dropped a bit during her first few months in the co-anchor slot.

Walters's presence on the *ABC Evening News* also brought out the worst in Harry Reasoner. His snide looks and innuendos made it clear, to even the most casual viewer, that he had no use for her and that he loathed the situation he now found himself in. Some of his friends and colleagues were disappointed in his behavior; they felt that no matter how trying the circumstances, he had a professional obligation to display, on the air at least, a little more class. But Reasoner literally could not help himself. He viewed the whole experience as such a humiliating ordeal that he was unable to disguise his true feelings. He did not entirely lose his sense of humor, however. Once, when a friend asked him how he was coping with the Walters situation, Reasoner replied,

"It's very simple. I've explained to them that all they're going to get out of me is my nine thousand dollars a week and not a penny more."

As time went on and it became evident that the pairing with Walters was never going to work, Reasoner began making preparations to leave ABC. When his contract was renegotiated, following ABC's decision to hire Walters, it included an oral agreement which would permit him to leave the network with no strings attached in June 1978, should he choose to do so. And by the end of 1977, Reasoner had decided that, barring a dramatic change in ABC policy, he would exercise that option, which he privately referred to as "my Barbara Walters escape clause." He was confident that he could negotiate a return to CBS, although he realized that in doing so, he would have to accept "a severe reduction in both money and ego." For Reasoner now had to face the glum reality that at the age of fifty-four his career in TV journalism had crossed its crest. The road ahead no longer pointed up, toward the summit, but was veering off toward a more modest plateau. As he adjusted to that reality, Reasoner could not help but reflect on what might have been if he had played his cards differently in 1975 when ABC had a chance to hire Roger Mudd as his co-anchorman, and he intervened to prevent that.

Roger Mudd's career, on the other hand, was in fine fettle. Although he had shopped around in 1975 (at NBC as well as at ABC), he chose to stay at CBS, and shortly after he signed his new contract there, Mudd embarked on a new assignment. He had been covering Capitol Hill since 1962, and that beat had long since ceased to be a challenge. Indeed, he had become so conversant with the convoluted rituals and procedures of Congress that he was, at times, a bit of a bore on the subject. Mudd himself recognized the need for a change, and so in 1976 he requested and was granted permission to move into a larger sphere. Taking on the title of National Affairs Correspondent, he was allowed to roam across a broad landscape and pick his spots at random as long as he didn't encroach on someone else's beat. Even more to his liking, he was given the freedom to venture into the delicate area of interpretation, to infuse his reports with an editorial point of view. This was contrary to accepted practice; for years, Salant and other news executives had nervously insisted that a clear line be drawn between reporting and commentary. Yet now, in Mudd's case, they were willing to make an exception. The result was that several of his pieces, especially during the 1976 political campaigns, were trenchant and witty, a re-freshing departure from the rigid and bland objectivity of most televi-sion reporting.

Mudd was also spending a great deal of time in Walter Cronkite's anchor chair. By the summer of 1977, he was in his fifth year as Cron-kite's regular replacement; and since that summer was a relatively quiet one, Cronkite chose to remain on Martha's Vineyard without journalistic interruption, and Mudd anchored the *CBS Evening News* from early July until the middle of September. All that steady action enabled him to sharpen his skills as an anchorman, and he was now far more polished and self-assured than he had been when he first tried his hand at anchoring back in the mid-1960s. Thus, with each passing year, Roger Mudd seemed to strengthen his unofficial position as Cronkite's heir apparent.

His principal rival for that honor was still Dan Rather, whose career had undergone another major change since he left the White House beat in 1974 to become the regular anchorman and correspondent on *CBS Reports.* That move had been calculated to transform him into the Edward R. Murrow of the 1970s, but it didn't quite work out that way. Rather and the various producers he worked with put together several good documentaries in 1975, and his full-time commitment to the pro-gram gave it the kind of specific and strong identity that had been missing in CBS documentaries since the Murrow years. But the network still adhered to the policy of airing *CBS Reports* broadcasts in irregular and generally weak time slots, and the lack of continuity made it all but impossible for the program to attract a large audience of habitual view-ers. Compared to what he had been accustomed to at the White House, Rather found himself working from a position of low visibility and minimal impact; and that, in turn, rekindled suspicions that CBS had pulled him off the White House assignment to stifle him. By the time he finished his first season on *CBS Reports,* Rather was seriously con-cerned about the course his career was taking, although he did manage a brave laugh when a CBS friend suggested that he would soon qualify as a candidate for one of those American Express commercials that featured vaguely remembered has-beens. ("Do you know me? I used to cover the White House for CBS News.")

It was, therefore, a fortuitous break for Rather when, in the fall of 1975, he was asked to join Mike Wallace and Morley Safer as a regular correspondent on *60 Minutes.* For Don Hewitt's magazine program was about to make television history, and Dan Rather was destined to share in that triumph.

During the first three years of its existence, from 1968 to 1971, *60 Minutes* was a biweekly broadcast aired on Tuesday nights in prime time. In that slot, it became a *succès d'estime,* but that was all. Like almost every news show that has been thrown into the arena of entertainment programming, *60 Minutes* did not fare well in the ratings. It remained in the prime-time schedule as long as it did only because Dick Salant and Bill Leonard persisted in their efforts to keep it there, arguing that *60 Minutes* brought a much-needed touch of prestige to the network's regular lineup. But in 1971, their superiors decided that three years of prestige were enough, and that fall, *60 Minutes* was shifted to the 6:00 P.M. Sunday slot, which, over the years, had been occupied by *The Twentieth Century* and other news or public-affairs programs. There it became a weekly broadcast, except during football season when it was often preempted. Salant and Leonard protested the decision, but as it turned out, the switch was exactly the tonic the show needed.

In its new Sunday time period, *60 Minutes* gradually began to attract a larger and larger audience. At the same time, the program continued to grow in critical esteem; some reviewers, in fact, went so far as to laud it as the best show of any kind on commercial television. By the fall of 1975, its ratings had improved to such an extent that network executives were encouraged to give *60 Minutes* another chance in prime time, and in early 1976, it was moved up to 7:00 P.M. on Sunday. And by then, the network brass no longer viewed *60 Minutes* with condescension as a "throwaway" news program that would bring to the CBS schedule a smidgen of prestige, and nothing more. That was the season when ABC launched its big push to overtake CBS in the prime-time sweepstakes, and *60 Minutes* was pressed into action as part of the network's counteroffensive. "I've waited twenty years for this," an exultant Dick Salant declared. "I always knew that if I survived in this job long enough, the day would come when those characters would turn to me to help them out with a ratings problem." Nor did *60 Minutes* let them down. Its success as a prime-time program exceeded even Salant's expectations, for it went on to become one of the ten top-rated shows on network television. Nothing like it, or even close to it, had ever happened before in the thirty-year history of TV journalism.

The show's correspondents and the redoubtable Don Hewitt received nearly all the credit for the evolution of *60 Minutes* into a prime-time blockbuster, but they, in turn, were quick to acknowledge the importance of the large and talented corps of field producers that Hewitt had assembled. By 1976, there were seventeen full-time producers assigned to *60 Minutes,* and some of them, like Palmer Williams, Hewitt's second-in-command, Joe Wershba, and Phil Scheffler, brought a wealth of experience to their duties. Along with the veterans, there were a dozen or so younger hands, such as Barry Lando, Harry Moses, Norm Gorin, and Grace Diekhaus, who also produced consistently strong pieces.

But the main creative force behind the show was still Hewitt, and the triumph of *60 Minutes* as a prime-time showcase carried him to the apex of his long and brilliant career at CBS. For years he had been guided by the conviction that entertainment values were not anathema to news programming; that, on the contrary, a judicious use of show-business techniques was needed to lure viewers "into the tent." With *60 Minutes* he conclusively demonstrated that slick entertainment and journalistic quality could be combined to achieve a highly positive effect. The program's best and most memorable pieces were its hard-hitting, investigative reports on political corruption and other front-page subjects. But what gave the show an extra dimension—and accounted for much of its appeal—was its back-of-the-book features on popular personalities. Thus, the old disparity that critic John Lardner once defined as "Higher Murrow and Lower Murrow" was fused on *60 Minutes.* In its stories on serious, controversial subjects, the program was every bit as strong and provocative as *See It Now* had been, and yet it also attracted the kind of mass audience that Murrow had been able to reach only with his gossipy interview show, *Person to Person.* "I always knew we'd get the documentary freaks," Hewitt once remarked. "But with the other stuff, we draw in viewers who couldn't care less about news and who otherwise never watch a television news show. That's the difference between us and conventional documentaries."

In early 1976, when *60 Minutes* was reinserted in the prime-time schedule and Dan Rather joined the broadcast as its third correspondent, one of his first assignments was to do a story on actor Robert Redford. That decision was vintage Hewitt: Dapper Dan meets the Sundance Kid. Around this time, producer Bill Crawford, who had been a Hewitt apprentice back in the 1950s and who, in more recent years, had worked with Rather in Washington, ran into a CBS friend from

New York and asked him, "How does brother Rather like being in the clutches of the Maestro?"

"He likes it just fine," the friend replied. "Of course, he is a little nervous about the show-biz side of Hewitt. This Bob Redford assignment, for example. Dan has misgivings about that. He's not sure that it qualifies as serious journalism."

Crawford let out a hearty laugh and said, "Yeah, I bet, and I can hear Hewitt's answer to that: 'Fuck journalism, Dan, just find out what he wears to bed at night.' "

Rather refrained from asking Bob Redford about his bedtime attire. Actually, such a question would not have been at all appropriate, for the interview ranged over a number of thoughtful and serious subjects. It was yet another example of how Hewitt, through shrewd judgment, managed to have it both ways on *60 Minutes:* marquee value *and* more substance than such a personality piece normally offers.

Dan Rather, Mike Wallace, and Morley Safer made a formidable trio. In the years since Safer joined the broadcast in 1970, he and Wallace had worked out a smooth and appealing on-air relationship, and Rather blended nicely into that pattern. All three men had been through severe professional trials—Rather during the Nixon years, Safer in Vietnam, and Wallace in the pitfalls of his early career—and they had acquired the kind of authority that comes from having performed well under fire. Diligent and perceptive reporters, they were at their best in the probing, one-on-one interviews around which most *60 Minutes* stories were structured. And not to be overlooked, especially in light of the show's prime-time status, was the fact that all three had star quality—and they were treated like stars. Each of them had his own entourage of producers, researchers, and secretaries, and they had star-sized egos that required constant solicitude. When Rather joined *60 Minutes* and new, spacious offices were constructed to accommodate the three correspondents, Hewitt had tape measures and similar devices brought in to make sure that the size and shape of each office were precisely the same.

But if there was a first among equals, it was definitely Wallace. He was the veteran, the correspondent who had been with *60 Minutes* since its inception, and it was his presence that dominated the show. He was generally assigned to the biggest and most controversial stories, and the tone of most *60 Minutes* broadcasts clearly reflected his aggressive style and personality. "He's my Kojak," Hewitt told an interviewer from *People* magazine in 1977. But whereas Safer and Rather, both in their mid-forties, had many years ahead of them, Wallace was approaching the end of his career at CBS. He turned fifty-nine in 1977, and, like Cronkite and Collingwood, he was at a point where he had to start thinking seriously about retirement.

Ever mindful of the need to build for the future, CBS News continued to replenish its ranks with quality correspondents. In April 1976, just a few days after ABC announced that it had hired Barbara Walters away from NBC, CBS disclosed (though with far less fanfare) that it had signed up Bill Moyers to succeed Dan Rather as the regular anchorman and correspondent on *CBS Reports*. It was an impressive acquisition, for Moyers was widely esteemed as a man of many parts. A Lyndon Johnson protégé, he served as deputy director of the Peace Corps in the Kennedy Administration and later became the most powerful member of the White House staff during the early years of LBJ's Presidency. But his training had been in journalism; that was his major at the University of Texas, and while a student there, he worked at the Austin television station owned by Lady Bird Johnson. The years in Washington followed, and then, in 1967, Moyers resumed his journalistic career on an unusually high level: as publisher of the Long Island newspaper *Newsday*.

His stint at *Newsday* ended in 1970 when the paper was sold, and Moyers spent the next few months writing a book, *Listening to America*. He then ventured into public television, and over the next five years, his widely acclaimed documentary series, *Bill Moyers Journal*, appeared regularly on PBS. Moyers's reports were distinguished by his penetrating intelligence and his strong, personal point of view; and in 1976 he brought to CBS all the gifts that had characterized his performance on public television.

During his first year on the new job, Moyers and his *CBS Reports* colleagues came up with several commendable documentaries, including a two-hour probe into the CIA's clandestine military activities in Cuba. Broadcast in July 1977, *The CIA's Secret Army* was the most explosive documentary aired on CBS since *The Selling of the Pentagon* six years earlier. Yet Moyers was plagued by the same frustration that had beset Rather when he undertook the job of anchoring *CBS Reports*. The programs were still consigned to weak and irregular time slots, which made it difficult to build up a large and loyal audience. Moreover, dazzled by the success of *60 Minutes*, some CBS executives, on both the corporate and news-division levels, were arguing that the long documentary—one or more hours devoted to a single story—had become a dinosaur, a stodgy throwback to an earlier era, that should be scrapped in favor of a breezier, multisubject format.

"That's a lot of bullshit," Moyers told an interviewer in the fall of 1977. "The problem is not the format, it's the scheduling. If they would give us more air time on a regularly scheduled basis, we'd show them that we could have just as much impact and influence as *60 Minutes* or the *Evening News* or any other news program on television." He paused a moment, and then added, "I suppose that sounds awfully immodest, but that's the way I honestly feel."

Clearly, Moyers was having trouble adjusting to the rigid policies of a huge commercial network. He sorely missed the freedom and flexibility he had enjoyed at PBS, and in January 1978, he informed Salant that he would probably leave CBS at the end of the current season. His plans were not yet definite, he said, but as matters then stood, he intended to return to public television. Salant did everything within his power to persuade Moyers to stay, but unfortunately, he did not have the power to give Moyers what he wanted: a regularly scheduled documentary program in a strong time slot. And those who did have that power—Salant's corporate superiors—didn't give a damn whether Bill Moyers remained at CBS or not.

There were, by this time, other new faces in various anchor chairs. When Mudd and Rather took on more ambitious and more time-consuming assignments, their weekend slots became available to other correspondents. By 1977, the Saturday edition of the *CBS Evening News* was being anchored by Bob Schieffer, who had been doing a solid job covering the White House since replacing Rather on that beat three years earlier. Schieffer's counterpart on Sunday evening was Morton Dean, in many ways the best of the New York–based correspondents. And the headliner on the Sunday night news show, Harry Reasoner's old domain, was Ed Bradley, the first black correspondent to move up to the anchorman level at CBS News, a promotion he earned with his excellent coverage of Jimmy Carter's Presidential campaign.

And in 1977, the *CBS Morning News* was given yet another new look. For the past three years, ever since Sally Quinn's abrupt departure, the program had been co-anchored by Hughes Rudd in New York and Bruce Morton in Washington. Since both Rudd and Morton were excellent writers, the *Morning News,* during this period, may well have been the most literate news show on television. And that, in turn, may explain why the program's ratings shot up a couple of notches in 1975. It continued to lag far behind the *Today* show, but its ratings were now better than they had ever been since the *Morning News* was sentenced to the 7:00 A.M. dungeon ten years earlier. What's more, staff morale during the Rudd-Morton years was higher than it had been in quite some time.

But the upbeat trend did not last. In 1976, the show's ratings began to drop again, and the slide continued over the next several months. Then, in the summer of 1977, Morton, having grown weary of the early-morning hours and the desk-bound rigidity of a five-day-a-week anchor assignment, asked to be taken off the program. In accordance with his wishes, he rejoined the corps of Washington field correspondents, and replacing him on the *Morning News* was Lesley Stahl.

But Rudd's departure from the New York anchor slot was definitely not voluntary. The recent decline in the ratings clearly contributed to his downfall. Beyond that, some of Rudd's superiors felt that his grouchy style, which once seemed so appealing at that hour, had grown stale. Finally, there was the age factor. At fifty-six, Rudd no longer figured prominently in CBS's future plans; and since the *Morning News* was intended, among other things, to serve as a training ground for correspondents and producers on the way up, it was decided that the time had come to move a younger man into Rudd's anchor slot, one who might better complement the youthful and attractive Lesley Stahl. So, in the fall of 1977, Richard Threlkeld, whose reporting from Vietnam and the West Coast had impressed the CBS management, took over as the male and New York half of the new anchor team.

To avoid antagonizing his loyal viewers and to spare Rudd the embarrassment of a public ouster from the *Morning News* anchor slot, Dick Salant and Bill Small instructed their public-relations people to put out the story that he was tired of doing the show and had requested a less arduous assignment. In point of fact, Rudd was deeply hurt by the decision to replace him, but believing that it was also in his best interests to put a positive face on the move, he chose to go along with the PR sham. They got away with it, too; one press account after another echoed the company line that Rudd had asked to be relieved of his co-anchor duties. As deceptions go, the Rudd "cover story" was not an especially sinister one. Nevertheless, it stands as a fitting example of how a news organization's pious commitment to "the public's right to know" tends to weaken when the matter in question concerns its own internal affairs.

Schieffer, Dean, Bradley, Morton, Stahl, and Threlkeld formed the next wave of CBS News stars, and gathered behind them, in bureaus around the world, were other correspondents on the rise. The most dramatic change in their ranks was in minority representation. In the late 1960s, there was just one black correspondent (Hal Walker) and one woman (Marya McLaughlin) on the CBS News payroll. But by the end of 1977, there were fourteen women and ten blacks working as full-time correspondents or reporters. And for all of them—black and white, male and female—the name of the game was still time on the air, and, in particular, time on the nightly showcase, the *CBS Evening News with Walter Cronkite*.

In the fall of 1977, a milestone in TV journalism was quietly passed; so quietly, in fact, that even within the industry, it was scarcely noted. That fall, the Cronkite show completed its tenth year of sustained supremacy in the nightly news field. A full decade had passed since the *CBS Evening News* edged ahead of *The Huntley-Brinkley Report* in the ratings and went on to open up a commanding lead over its competitors. But the opposition was not exactly dormant. Over the course of several months in 1976 and 1977, both NBC and ABC took major steps to try to close some of the gap between their evening news programs and the Cronkite show.

In addition to hiring Barbara Walters, ABC's senior management turned the reins of the news operation over to Roone Arledge, who, in the past decade or so, had built that network's sports department into the best in the business. Flamboyant and erratic, Arledge took over as president of ABC News in the spring of 1977, and he promptly set out to infuse it with his own energy, ideas, and taste. To beef up the operation, he hired several good correspondents and producers away from the other networks. And in a more drastic move, he revamped the format of the *ABC Evening News*, steering the show away from its anchor team to feature a bevy of field correspondents, who often introduced each other's reports, employing a technique called "whiparound." By the fall of 1977, Reasoner and Walters between them were averaging only about three minutes a night on camera, compared to Cronkite's six or seven minutes. The initial effect of the ABC whiparound approach was jerky and disorienting, a lot of flighty motion with no fixed center of identity or authority. Still, for better or for worse, Arledge was at least trying something different.

But he was also imposing on the ABC News operation a tabloid mentality that many of his colleagues and competitors found disturbing. When the "Son of Sam" murder suspect was arrested in New York in the summer of 1977, Arledge pulled out all the stops, and the *ABC Evening News* devoted twenty minutes—practically the entire broadcast—to that one story. That kind of sensationalism was rare in network journalism, and some of ABC's senior correspondents, having been schooled in another tradition, were deeply embarrassed by it. To his CBS friends, with whom he still had lunch two or three times a week, Harry Reasoner characterized Arledge as "a clown, a buffoon." Indeed, Arledge's presence at the helm, coming on top of the problems he was having with Walters, hardened Reasoner's resolve to exercise his "Barbara Walters escape clause" and leave ABC in June 1978.

Numerous changes were also taking place at NBC. For five years, starting in 1971, John Chancellor had been the sole anchorman on the *NBC Nightly News.* But then, in the spring of 1976, David Brinkley, who had been devoting his efforts to commentary and occasional documentaries, returned to the anchor role he had shared for so many years with Chet Huntley. Teaming up with Chancellor, Brinkley soon demonstrated that he had not lost his wry touch. The night after Barbara Walters made her debut on the *ABC Evening News,* Brinkley, going on the assumption that curiosity had induced some regular NBC viewers to check her out, opened his broadcast with a terse remark addressed to them: "Welcome back."

In September 1977, Brinkley and Chancellor introduced a new format on the *NBC Nightly News,* featuring in-depth coverage of fewer stories. It meant that some of the day's news was given short shrift, but even so, it was a worthy attempt to negate the frequent complaint that network news shows were nothing more than visual headline services. It was also a far more effective and appealing innovation than the revved-up whip-around format ABC had adopted earlier in the year.

The Chancellor-Brinkley team was destined to be short-lived. Later that fall, Chancellor disclosed that he had asked to be relieved of his co-anchor duties. He said that after seven years of doing the *Nightly News,* he wanted to shift his attention to commentary and other assignments. Chancellor insisted that the decision was entirely his own, but some NBC insiders contended that, at the very least, he had been nudged in that direction by network executives who were piqued by the chronic inability of the *Nightly News* to pose a serious threat to Cronkite's firm grip on the ratings. The change was due to occur sometime in 1978, and the candidate most frequently mentioned as Chancellor's successor was Tom Brokaw, the engaging host on the *Today* show.

While all those upheavals were occurring within the other two shops, the attitude at CBS News was not unlike that of a poker player who, having been dealt a full house, watches with smug amusement the hapless struggles around the table to put together straights and flushes. Clutching its winning hand, the Cronkite show chose to stand pat. Moreover, the prevailing view throughout the industry was that neither NBC nor ABC had a realistic chance of overtaking the *CBS Evening News* as long as Cronkite remained in the saddle. But most observers agreed that following his retirement in 1981, it would be a brand-new ball game, and the three-way competition was then likely to become quite close and intense.

By 1978, the *CBS Evening News* staff had expanded considerably. There were now eleven associate producers working on the show in New York alone, plus several more in Washington and other bureaus. And the editorial staff had been enlarged to four writers; now, in addition to national, foreign, and "all else," there was an economics slot. The broadcast's various operations were still under the benevolent supervision of Bud Benjamin. As 1977 came to an end, Benjamin completed his third year as executive producer, and he was thriving in that post. Thanks in large part to his calm, low-key manner and his willingness to delegate so much of his authority to John Lane and other deputies, the daily grind was not wearing him down the way it had some of his predecessors. He had every intention of presiding over the *CBS Evening News* for another few years—assuming, of course, that he wasn't summoned to a higher post. For by this time, the word was seeping out that Benjamin might be appointed the next president of CBS News.

But even if he did not move up to the management level, it was unlikely that Benjamin's reign would extend beyond the Cronkite era. Like Don Hewitt, Ernie Leiser, and Les Midgley, the three producers who guided the Cronkite show through its critical period of development in the 1960s, Benjamin had been around since the early days of TV journalism; and, like them, he was now in the waning years of his CBS career. Other producers who made significant contributions to the

Evening News during the 1960s and 1970s were now ensconced in different spheres of the CBS News operation. Sandy Socolow was in his fourth year as Washington bureau chief, Russ Bensley was in his sixth year as head of the Special Events unit, and Paul Greenberg was rebuilding his shattered career as a producer for *CBS Reports.* As Benjamin's chief deputy, John Lane was the probable choice to become the next executive producer of the *CBS Evening News,* but there was no guarantee of that. His rivals for that honor included the show's other veteran producers, Ron Bonn and Ed Fouhy, the executive producer of the *Morning News,* David Horwitz, and the woman in charge of the weekend news programs, Joan Richman. They and many others represented the future, and on them would devolve the task of meeting the challenge of the post-Cronkite years.

So throughout the world of CBS, from the executive suites on the corporate level down to the various command posts within the news division, a definitive transition was taking place, a gradual passing of the torch from the old order to the new. Members of the CBS family were never more conscious of this generational change than in November 1977 when Eric Sevareid's career at the network came to an end; for more than anyone else who was still around, Sevareid was the keeper of the flame, the embodiment of the Murrow tradition. Sevareid himself had an acute sense of having been part of an important and evolutionary epoch in American journalism. As a matter of fact, he touched on that subject in a speech he gave at the Washington Journalism Center a few months before his retirement.

It was, for the most part, a testy, quarrelsome speech. Sevareid had been highly irritated by some of the things that had been written about CBS in recently published books and magazine articles, and the bulk of his speech was an effort to set the record straight. He lashed out at various "myths" that had been promulgated: "the myth that since the pioneering, ground-breaking TV programs of Murrow and Friendly, CBS News has been less daring, done fewer programs of a hard-hitting kind . . . the myth that the corporation is gradually de-emphasizing news and public affairs . . . the myth that Fred Friendly resigned over an issue of high principle." On he went, covering numerous other points as well in what he described as "this litany of complaint."

But toward the end of his speech, Sevareid's mood suddenly grew mellow. He was aware that the occasion might turn out to be the last chance he would have to address his peers as one of them, an active member of the working press, and he did not want to conclude on such a sour and petulant note. Instead, he seized the opportunity to deliver an eloquent epitaph for his craft and generation:

"Let me say now only that we are not the worst people in the land, we who work as journalists. Our product in print or over the air is a lot better, more educated, more responsible than it was when I began some forty-five years ago as a cub reporter. This has been the best generation of all in which to have lived as a journalist in this country. We are no longer starvelings and we sit above the salt. We have affected our times."

Author's Note

This book evolved out of a casual conversation I had with Winthrop Knowlton, the president of Harper & Row, in the late summer of 1974. *The Palace Guard* was about to be published that fall (under Harper & Row's imprimatur) and Knowlton, oblivious to the state of exhaustion I was in following the fifteen months of hard labor that went into that book, proposed that I commence work —at once!—on a new project. Not being content to leave it at that, he specifically suggested that I undertake a book on the internal affairs of CBS News— the off-camera world that viewers are never privileged to see. Knowlton insisted that the time was ripe for such a book and that it was a natural one for me to write, if only because I had a firsthand familiarity with the subject. Even in my groggy condition, I had to admit that he had a point there.

For nearly four years, from late 1969 until the spring of 1973, I worked as a writer at CBS News. When I joined the staff there, I was thirty-four years old and had twelve years of professional journalism behind me, first as a correspondent for UPI (yes, like Walter Cronkite and so many others, I received my early training in that arduous vineyard, an experience I've never regretted), then later as a free-lance magazine writer. Or to put it another way, I was among those who were slow to recognize the rising importance of TV journalism. During the years I worked at UPI and later, when I was hustling to make ends meet as a free-lancer, I shared the traditional disdain so many print journalists have felt toward television. It was primarily economic need plus a certain vague curiosity that induced me to enter that world, yet another refugee from print washed up on the electronic beach, an innocent abroad in a confusing land of roll-cues and satellite feeds and videotape. But once inside that world, I soon became fascinated by the complex craft of television news and an admirer of those who had mastered the various skills peculiar to it.

I was also fortunate to have worked at CBS News during a momentous period in its own history. I signed on just a few weeks after Spiro Agnew delivered his famous anti-media speech in Des Moines, which ushered in the Era of Confrontation between the networks and the Nixon Administration; and my last major assignment for CBS News was to help write a special report on the Watergate disclosures that erupted in the spring of 1973. Because I was there, on the inside, during those years, many of the events and conflicts recorded in *Air Time* stem, at least in part, from personal observation. Such matters as Harry Reasoner's contractual problems in 1970 and the various pressures Dan Rather had to contend with were experiences that the principals themselves shared with me and other confidants. Nor was it necessary for me to ask others about the Walter Burns side of Walter Cronkite's personality, the competitive fire that often flashed across his anchor desk when he was not on camera. For like everyone else who has ever written for Walter, I had my share of copy flung back at me with his concise instructions on how to improve it. Indeed, there are several passages in this book in which I appear as an invisible participant—an off-camera voice, as it were—although I was determined, from the outset, to avoid the indulgence of the first-person singular. Even now, as I venture forth from the woodwork, I do so with some reluctance.

But although I was privy to a thousand and one daily triumphs and disappointments that occurred within CBS News during the years I worked there (and countless others from the past that veteran colleagues reminisced about), it never occurred to me then that I might be gathering material for a future book on the subject. Having made the jump from print to broadcasting, I was more than content to make my home in that brave new world. What changed my plans—and drastically changed my life—was my association with Dan Rather.

Among other duties, I wrote for Dan on the *CBS Sunday News* after he succeeded Harry Reasoner as anchorman on that program. Out of that experience, a close friendship developed. As I have written elsewhere, *The Palace Guard* grew out of a series of far-into-the-night conversations Dan and I had at P. J. Moriarty's, the bistro to which members of the *Sunday News* staff repaired after the broadcast every weekend. Shortly after we agreed to collaborate on a book about the Nixon White House and had lined up a publisher, I concluded that, Dan's hectic, day-to-day schedule being what it was, the book would never get done unless I left CBS to work on it full time. And that, in turn, eventually led to that summer day in 1974 when, with *The Palace Guard* set for publication, Win Knowlton informed me that, my obvious need for a long rest notwithstanding, I was to get cracking on a book about CBS News.

As part of my preparation for that task, I read numerous books on broadcasting in general and CBS News in particular. Almost all of them were helpful in one way or another, but I am especially indebted to the following works. First and foremost, I must acknowledge Eric Barnouw's comprehensive three-volume study, *A History of Broadcasting in the United States*, a towering achievement that was an invaluable source of information to me as it has been to others who have written about the growth of radio and television in this country. Two other general books I feel obliged to mention are Les Brown's *Television: The Business Behind the Box* and Martin Mayer's *About Television.* On the subject of CBS News itself, there are two books that are deserving of my special thanks: *Prime Time,* Alexander Kendrick's biography of Edward R. Murrow, and *Due to Circumstances Beyond Our Control,* Fred Friendly's spirited account of his years at CBS.

In addition to those and other books, I read hundreds of newspaper and magazine articles on television news that have been written over the past thirty years. Again, at the risk of being overly selective, I should like to acknowledge my gratitude to two in particular. One is William Whitworth's 1968 *New Yorker* profiles of Chet Huntley and David Brinkley, which opened the door to my understanding of the early Huntley-Brinkley years at NBC. The other is David Halberstam's two-part essay on CBS, which appeared in the *Atlantic Monthly* in early 1976. Since Halberstam's articles were published at a time when I was immersed in interviews for this book, his strong reporting served as an informal guide into a few areas I was then exploring, even though, based on my own information and experience, I found myself disagreeing with some of his interpretations.

But the richest vein of source material for *Air Time* was, without question, the hundreds of personal interviews I conducted from early 1975 until the fall of 1977. The members of the CBS family, from William S. Paley on down, were extremely generous in the time they granted me. As the interviews progressed, I began to get a clear picture of CBS News in historical terms, and to feel confident that I could relate that history in a narrative form, replete with interwoven plots and character conflicts; in short, that the book could be written as a *story* and not just a series of unrelated events. That narrative approach would have been impossible to carry out if it had not been for the excellent cooperation I received from most of the CBS people I interviewed.

I should note at this point that journalists tend to be marvelous interviewees. Wise to the tricks of the trade, many of them took a perverse delight in being on the other side of the cat-and-mouse game for a change. Since they know from experience what a reporter yearns for, they often stretched themselves to recall the kind of telling anecdote or colorful quote that brings a story to life. At the same time, because of their own professional commitment to rooting out the facts, many of my former CBS colleagues were remarkably forthright and candid, even when discussing matters that cast themselves in an unfavorable light or reflected discredit on close friends and associates. I appreciate how difficult that was, and to them, above all, I am deeply indebted.

I also am grateful to several CBS friends of mine who took the time and trouble to read large portions of this book when it was still in manuscript and gave me the benefit of their comments and criticisms. To identify them might only serve to embarrass them, to saddle them with part of the responsibility for interpretations that is entirely my own. But they know who they are, and I thank them for their counsel and encouragement.

One person I can and must identify is my researcher, Harriet Rubin Roberts. It is no exaggeration to say that this book would never have left the starting gate as quickly and as easily as it did had it not been for her thoroughness in tracking down vast quantities of printed material and her judicious sifting through it to separate the relevant from the superfluous. A special word of thanks should also go to Ann Morfogen of the CBS News Information Office, whose cooperation in providing the documents I needed and overall interest in this project went well beyond the routine call of duty.

In addition to Win Knowlton, who came up with the idea for the book, there are several other people at Harper & Row who made important contributions to *Air Time*. At a time when some writer friends of mine have complained that they cannot find one good editor to oversee their work, I was blessed, on this book, to have no less than three hovering over me. First, I must thank Kitty Benedict, who, undaunted by the ordeal she was put through with *The Palace Guard*, guided the progress of *Air Time* from its inception to its point of completion. Then, after Kitty left Harper & Row to grace another publishing house with her presence, I inherited Buz Wyeth, whose calm professionalism and personal warmth turned what promised to be a jarring disruption into a smooth transition. And I'm especially indebted to Burton Beals, whose skill and patience during the final stages of cutting and revising significantly helped to make *Air Time* a better book. I also want to thank Mel Zerman and Roger Strauss for the kind encouragement they offered at critical points along the way, as well as my copy editor, Buddy Skydell, and his chief, Dolores Simon, for the labors performed, under the pressure of a tight deadline, in transforming an untidy manuscript into a handsome book.

Last but far from least, a word of gratitude to my agent, Owen Laster. Due to a regrettable oversight, his role in the survival of *The Palace Guard* at a hazardous juncture was not acknowledged when that book was published. So let me now thank him for that and for negotiating the terms of *Air Time* in a way that allowed me to write it at the leisure it required.

And to all my friends and former colleagues at CBS News, a final word: those of you who could not resist the temptation to begin this book at the index, with the letters of your choice, be advised that you are now back where you started.

—GARY PAUL GATES

March 1978

Index

Aaron, Johnny, 30
ABC, rivals surpassed by, 404
ABC Evening News, 237, 238–241, 277,
    408–412, 420–421
ABC News, 76, 93, 115, 252, 272–273
  anchor team sought by, 408–410
  CBS alumni at, 39, 48, 170, 240, 253,
    376
  ratings of, 75, 239, 278, 408, 410, 411
  Reasoner's move to, 234–241, 267, 278,
    285
  third-network role of, 236, 239,
    253–254, 410
  upgrading efforts of, 236, 238–239,
    277–278, 408, 410, 414, 420–421
About Television, 200
advertising revenue, 53–54, 123, 126,
    239, 338, 400
Agnew, Spiro, 266, 267, 296, 302, 312,
    314, 361
Air Power, 89, 382
Alaskan earthquake, 109–110
Ali, Muhammad, 195–196
Allbritton, Louise, 45
All the President's Men, 395
Alsop, Joseph, 42
American Week, The, 41
anchormen, 79, 198
  ad-libbing of, 88, 102, 111, 113, 207,
    208, 225, 262, 350
  first use of, 74, 87–89, 198, 217
Andrea Doria, sinking of, 69–70
Apollo 11 flight, 199, 212–213
Arledge, Roone, 420–421
Arlen, Michael, 163
Associated Press (AP), 9, 196

Aubrey, James T., 97, 125, 174
audience research, 26–27, 236

Backe, John, 402, 403–404, 405
Ball, Lucille, 23
Baltimore Sun, 173, 342
Banow, Joel, 149
Barker, Eddie, 2, 11–12
Benjamin, Bud, 372, 381–384, 398, 405,
    422
Benny, Jack, 23, 210
Bensley, Russ, 64, 181, 185–187,
    188–189, 190, 191, 192, 193, 203,
    260
  as Midgley's successor, 321, 322–323,
    325–329, 332–333
Benti, Joe, 168, 280–283, 337
Benton, Nelson, 170–171, 346
Bernstein, Carl, 303–304, 387, 395
Bigart, Homer, 66
Birnbaum, Bernie, 187
Blank, Ben, 240
Bliss, Ed, 2–3, 193–194
Bonn, Ron, 191–192, 203, 220, 325, 326,
    333, 334, 379, 423
Boulton, Milo, 52
Bowers, Don, 392
Bradlee, Ben, 304, 347–348
Bradley, Ed, 418, 420
Brasselle, Keefe, 174
Brinkley, David (see also
    Huntley-Brinkley Report), 6, 72–79,
    91, 101, 104–105, 114, 116, 153, 154,
    236, 357, 400, 421
  background of, 73–74

Brinkley, David *(cont'd)*
  Huntley paired with, 74–77
  wit and talent of, 77, 78, 225
Brokaw, Tom, 270, 368, 422
Broun, Heywood Hale, 67, 257, 258, 259,
  321, 337, 345, 375, 376
Buksbaum, David, 240
Burdett, Winston, 157–158, 294
Burke, Stan, 158
Business of Health, The, 107–108

Calendar, 104, 219–221, 222, 223, 227,
  241, 271, 274, 276
Califano, Joseph, 393
Calmer, Ned, 270
Cambodia, coverage of war in, 262–263
Camel News Caravan, 70, 72, 74
cameramen, 63, 94
Canadian Broadcasting Corporation
  (CBC), 158
Can the World Be Saved?, 203
Captain Kangaroo, 271
Carter, Jimmy, 418
Cassirer, Henry, 51–52
Castan, Sam, 164
CBS (Columbia Broadcasting System):
  Broadcast Group of, 124–125, 237, 338,
    404
  Columbia Group of, 124
  entertainment vs. news programming
    at, 23–24
  expansion and reorganization of, 124
  news as early commitment of, 22–23
  1977 shake-up in, 404–405
CBS Evening News (see also Cronkite,
  Walter; Edwards, Douglas):
  under Benjamin, 381–384, 422
  under Bensley, 321, 322–323, 325–329,
    332–333
  breaking news on, 143, 183, 184, 185
  competition for getting pieces on, 171,
    386–387
  Cronkite backup on, 168, 213, 221,
    230, 244, 267, 268, 284–286, 287,
    308, 315, 409, 413
  editorial staff of, 193–197, 204, 206,
    285
  enterprisers on, 143–144, 183, 186,
    188, 189
  expansion to half-hour of, 5, 93, 94–95,
    104, 139–140, 143–144, 147, 152,
    183, 276
  expansion to seven nights of, 260
  field producers of, 187–191
  film portion of, 143–144, 184, 185–187,
    190–191, 193, 194, 204

CBS (cont'd)
  under Greenberg, 263, 310–312, 317,
    333–335, 343, 378–381, 383, 384
  under Hewitt, 55–70, 91–93, 119–122,
    139, 140–141, 143, 149, 153, 182,
    218, 222, 422
  last-minute frenzy on, 151, 184–185,
    204
  under Leiser, 104–105, 119, 121, 136,
    137–145, 147, 149, 152, 153, 175,
    183, 185, 186, 209, 210, 317–318,
    319, 422
  lineups for, 150, 181, 183–187,
    194–195, 202, 310
  under Midgley, 145, 148–153, 166,
    171–172, 181, 183, 184, 185, 187,
    193, 194, 195, 203, 206, 228, 326,
    328, 379–380, 383–384, 399, 422
  Midgley's replacement on, 317–335
  proposed one-hour format for, 402–403
  Vietnam reporting on, 160–161, 180,
    208–211, 295
  Washington correspondents and,
    171–172, 295
  Watergate story on, 303–307, 362, 365,
    387
  weekend editions of, 249–263, 375,
    400, 418
CBS Morning News, 136, 172, 179–180,
  252, 271, 280–287, 386
  with Benti, 168, 280–283
  with Hart, 168, 170, 180, 199, 268,
    269, 283–284, 286–287, 343, 344–345
  with Rudd and Morton, 418–420
  with Rudd and Quinn, 179–180, 287,
    345–352
  time shift and decline of, 277, 419
  with Wallace, 104, 221, 223, 249, 254,
    271, 274–277, 278, 280–281, 282
CBS News *(see also specific shows):*
  ABC vs., 235–240, 404, 414
  Assignment Desk at, 63, 94, 110, 150,
    184, 186, 216, 217, 250, 319
  back-of-the-book concept in, 139, 144,
    148, 256, 258–260, 374–375, 380,
    415
  "bulletin fever" in, 110
  in corporate reorganization (1966), 124
  editorial staff of, 64–66
  election unit of, 111, 118, 132, 133
  film reporting advanced in, 60–64
  front-of-the-book concept in, 139, 144,
    259
  graphics in, 60–61, 203
  NBC rivalry with, *see* NBC News

CBS News *(cont'd)*
"newsroom-studio" concept in, 92–93, 140
New York correspondents and reporters for, 172–173
in 1964 upheavals, 78, 95–96, 97–117, 118–122, 248–249
Nixon Administration vs., 296–303, 307, 311–316, 367–372, 389
pride and tradition of, 97–98, 129, 235, 237, 316
producer's role in, 59–60
production units as feudal fiefdoms in, 133–134, 136, 145
regional bureaus of, 104, 139, 291
reporter-contacts of, 217–218
salaries in, 233–234, 242, 247, 281
Special Events unit of, 329, 330–331, 332, 333, 354–355
Special Reports unit of, 145, 148, 317, 329
"strong bench" of, 104–105, 154
technical vs. editorial staff of, 59–60
Washington bureau of, 166, 167–172, 192, 222, 246–248, 251, 283, 293–300, 312–313, 314, 356–361, 374, 386–387, 391
women and blacks in, 420
Women's Lib uprising at, 345–347
CBS Radio Network, 124
CBS Records, drug payola story and, 361–367
CBS Reports, 7–8, 31–33, 37–38, 41, 107–108, 118, 131–132, 148, 187, 370–374, 380, 382, 383, 399, 413, 417–418
CBS Sunday News, 226–227, 230, 231, 242, 252, 307–308, 309, 310, 418
CBS Television Network, 97, 124, 174, 332
CBS TV News, 55
Chancellor, John, 153, 167, 236, 239, 269, 287, 421–422
Chandler, Bob, 398, 399
Charnley, Mitchell, 215–216
Chester, Ed, 57
Chicago Daily News, 321–322
Chicago Seven trial, 165, 189
China, People's Republic of, 39, 150, 279, 303, 344–345, 352
Church, Wells, 53–54, 99–100
Churchill, Winston, 159, 382
CIA, Pike report on, 390–395
CIA's Secret Army, The, 417
civil rights legislation, 114, 247–248

civil rights movement, 9, 37–38, 95, 189, 218, 247–248, 291–293
Clark, Blair, 103–104, 118, 119, 138–139, 140, 357–358
Clark, Michele, 346–347
Clearing the Air, 395–396
Cobb, Buff, 271–272
Cochran, Ron, 238
Collier's, 134, 135, 146, 156, 340
Collingwood, Charles, 4, 32, 36, 43–48, 50, 80, 87, 138, 147, 157, 221, 294, 406
CBS bypass of, 46–48
as chief foreign correspondent, 48, 155, 157, 158–159
personality and style of, 44–45, 46–47, 48, 155, 243, 286, 299
in Southeast Asia, 155–156, 158
Colson, Charles, 305, 306, 307, 316
Columbia University, 127, 183
commercials, 54, 143, 269, 274
communications satellites, 56, 94, 184
congressional beat (Capitol Hill), 168, 170, 246, 264, 287, 386, 412
Connal, Scotty, 120
Connor, "Bull," 38, 292
convention coverage, *see* political conventions
Cosell, Howard, 253
Cox, Archibald, firing of, 368
Crawford, Bill, 64, 249–252, 255, 256, 276, 321, 339, 415–416
Crawford, Kenneth, 250, 251
Cronkite, Walter (see also *CBS Evening News*), 48, 49, 64, 82–96, 128, 151, 172, 176, 178, 198–213, 286, 406–408
assassination coverage by, 1–7, 93, 211–212, 281
background of, 82–86
Benjamin and, 381–382
bicentennial coverage by, 407–408
buildup of, in 1950s, 89–90
editorial role of, 181, 183, 195–196, 202, 204–207, 275
emotions expressed by, 199, 200, 212
Friendly and, 111–116, 119, 121, 133, 142
Greenberg and, 334–335, 379, 381
Huntley-Brinkley vs., 78, 91, 95, 101, 104–105, 116, 119, 144–145, 153, 154, 197, 198
as interviewer, 199–200, 353
Midgley's replacement and, 318, 321, 323, 324, 325, 327–329
as *Morning Show* host, 90, 182, 270

Cronkite, Walter *(cont'd)*
  Mudd-Trout as replacement for,
    112–116, 118, 133, 142, 248–249
  Murrow and, 84, 86, 101–102, 112, 198
  as new star (1952 conventions), 72, 74,
    75, 87–89, 100, 113, 198, 217
  at 1960 conventions, 78, 91, 111
  at 1964 conventions, 78, 111–112,
    115–116
  at 1968 conventions, 199–200, 208
  Nixon, Watergate, and, 302, 303,
    304–305, 306, 307, 387, 388, 389,
    407
  Paley and, 95–96, 112–113, 114, 115,
    119
  Rather and, 11, 288–289, 290
  Reasoner and, 8, 46, 47, 213, 221,
    225–226, 228, 230–231, 233, 234,
    235, 237, 285, 408
  recent competition of, 420–422
  retirement and successor of, 230, 231,
    235, 244, 280, 285, 288, 406, 413,
    417
  selected for *Evening News*, 6, 46, 80,
    82, 91, 104, 139, 174, 183
  Socolow and, 181–185, 187, 195, 203,
    204, 317–318, 324, 327, 328, 335
  space exploration and, 90–91, 191, 199,
    212–213
  "Uncle Walter" image vs. off-camera
    personality of, 200–207
  Vietnam and, 122–123, 208–211
Cronkite, Walter Leland III, 83
cue cards, 62, 64
Culhane, David, 173, 192, 258, 341–342,
  366
Cunningham, Hugh, 290
Cushing, Richard Cardinal, 107

Daley, Richard J., 199–200
Daly, John, 51, 90, 98, 238
Daly, Robert, 404
Dann, Mike, 344, 402
Davidson, Casey, 320
Davis, Clive, 361–362
Davis, Elmer, 17, 21, 98, 99, 290, 299,
  369
Davis, Peter, 301
Deakins, James, 299
Dean, Morton, 173, 418, 420
Defector, The, 156
de Gaulle, Charles, 356
Democratic conventions, 101, 112–116,
  165, 178, 199–200, 212, 224,
  248–249, 270
Diamond, Ed, 167–168
Diekhaus, Grace, 415

Diem, Ngo Dinh, 156, 162–163
documentaries, 118, 187, 344, 371, 382,
  397–399, 414–418
  evening news vs., 33–34
  hard news vs., 121
  Hewitt's role in, 122, 222–225, 243,
    244, 278, 415
Downs, Bill, 30
Downs, Hugh, 269
drug payola story, 361–367, 375–376,
  401
*Due to Circumstances Beyond Our
  Control*, 25
Duffy, Warren, 9
Duke University, Schorr's comments at,
  388–389, 395, 396
Dulles, John Foster, 39
Dunning, Bruce, 166
Dylan, Bob, 165

Eagleton, Thomas, 342–343
Edwards, Douglas, 46, 48–49, 50–70, 87,
  238, 271
  background of, 50–52
  downfall of, 78–81, 91, 95, 104, 115,
    139, 174, 198
  evening news show of, 55–70, 76, 78,
    91, 92, 169, 174, 182, 186, 218, 221,
    250, 330
  Huntley-Brinkley vs., 76, 78–79, 144
  Swayze vs., 70, 71, 72
  TV as viewed by, 53–54
Ehrlichman, John, 297–298, 301,
  308–309, 312, 316, 353
Eisenhower, Dwight D., 23, 37, 385
election and campaign coverage, 116
  computer techniques for, 120, 132
  in 1966, 232–233, 278
  in 1968, 212, 224, 231, 232, 264–265,
    278, 279, 281, 283, 295–296
  in 1972, 170, 306, 310, 311, 346
  in 1976, 354–355, 412–413, 418
enterprisers, 140, 143–144, 183, 186, 188,
  191
Ephron, Nora, 347
Ervin Committee, 315–316
Esquire, 316
Eye on New York, 131
Eyewitness, 46, 80, 90, 146–148, 150,
  174, 183, 186, 187, 218, 399

Face the Nation, 169
"FFI guys," 63
Fickett, Mary, 219, 271
film reporting, 56, 60–64, 69–70, 184,
  185–187, 190–191, 204, 334
  "bank" for, 185, 326

film reporting *(cont'd)*
  double projector system for, 61–62
  effect of videotape and satellites on,
    93–94
  enterprisers and, 143–144, 186–187
  lead-ins and, 193, 194
  silent (MOS), 61, 63
  "talking heads" in, 62
  tell stories vs., 64, 183, 193
First Tuesday, 127, 224
Flanner, Janet ("Genet"), 48
Ford, Gerald, 371
Ford Foundation, 126–127, 277
foreign correspondents, 35–49, 83–84, 86,
    89, 137–138, 155–166
  in Vietnam, 122, 155–157, 158–166,
    180, 243, 262–263, 283, 294, 419
  in World War II, 7, 15, 16–17, 36,
    40–41, 44–45, 84, 99, 157
Fouhy, Ed, 171–172, 325–326, 376, 423
Frank, Reuven, 34, 74, 75, 76–77, 78, 87,
    205
Friendly, Fred, 37, 100, 106–113, 137,
    158, 222, 283, 301, 382, 406
  as CBS News president, 106, 108–128,
    142, 148, 160, 175, 247, 248, 251,
    277, 293–294, 385–386, 390, 400
  as *CBS Reports* producer, 31–32, 37,
    107–108, 118, 131–132, 148, 187,
    370–371
  Cronkite and, 111–116, 119, 121, 133,
    142
  deputies appointed by, 118–119, 121,
    130–136, 152
  Hewitt replaced by, 119–122, 140,
    222
  Murrow and, 18–19, 31–32, 106–107,
    108–109, 121
  resignation of, 122–128, 135, 142, 277,
    337, 423
  as *See It Now* producer, 18–19, 21–22,
    25, 31–32, 107, 108, 118, 272
  Vietnam coverage under, 122–128,
    160, 161, 162
Fulbright, J. William, 123, 125, 378
Full Disclosure, 396
Furness, Betty, 74, 148

Gabriel, Ralph Henry, 245
Gandolf, Ray, 284
Garroway, Dave, 90, 269, 270
Geyelin, Philip, 348
Gleason, Jackie, 23
Godfrey, Arthur, 90, 220
Goldwater, Barry, 2, 111, 385, 388
Good Morning, 270–271

Gould, Jack, 41, 53, 75, 78, 219
Gould, Stanhope, 188–191, 192, 225, 250,
    303–305, 306–307, 328, 337, 362,
    364–367, 374, 375, 379
Graham, Fred, 169, 359
Graham, Katharine, 135, 305
Greenberg, Paul, 231, 423
  Evening News and, 252–255, 258–263,
    267, 310–312, 317, 321, 328,
    333–335, 343, 378–381, 383, 384
  Manning and, *see* Manning, Gordon
  personality of, 260–261, 321
  Rather and, 309–313, 316, 335, 340
  Small and, 378–381, 383

Halberstam, David, 162, 163, 211, 402
Haldeman, Bob, 296, 297, 298, 301, 305,
    308–309, 316
  CBS interview deal with, 353–354
Haley, Hal, 231, 252, 255
Hamilton, Don, 234
Harriman, Averell, 45
Hart, John, 168, 170, 180, 199, 268, 269,
    283–287, 288, 342–343, 344–345,
    359, 366
Hartz, Jim, 269
Harvest of Shame, 32, 33–34, 107, 187
Hear It Now, 18
Hearst, Patty, 166
Hearst newspapers, 58, 98
Hecht, Ben, 58
Heggen, Tom, 216
Henry, Bill, 74, 75
Herman, George, 169, 314, 357
Hewitt, Don, 56–70, 76, 79, 100, 101,
    110, 251, 275, 330, 399, 401
  background of, 57–58
  Evening News and, 55–70, 91–93,
    119–122, 139, 140–141, 143, 149,
    153, 182, 218, 222, 422
  firing of, 78, 119–122, 222
  personality and spirit of, 58–59, 66–69,
    79, 119, 120–121
  as *60 Minutes* creator, 122, 222–225,
    243, 244, 278, 398, 413, 415–417
  as technical innovator, 60–63, 143
Hitler, Adolf, 36, 385
Horwitz, David, 423
House Ethics Committee, 391, 393, 394
House Intelligence Committee, 390
Howe, Quincy, 53
Hubbell, Richard, 52, 86
Humphrey, Hubert H., 212, 224, 300
Huntley, Chet, 6, 72–79, 91, 101,
    104–105, 114, 116, 153, 154, 400,
    421

Huntley-Brinkley Report, The, 7, 75–79,
    93
  beginnings of, 74–75
  CBS Evening News vs., 109–110, 119,
    144–145, 153, 197, 205, 420
  end of, 153, 197
  success of, 77–78, 95–96, 144
  tag line of, 77, 87, 205

I Can Hear It Now, 18
I Love Lucy, 27, 123, 126, 130, 277, 338
investigative reporting, 107, 362–367,
    376, 415

Jackson, Allan, 12
Janowski, Gene, 405
Jarriel, Tom, 368
Jencks, Richard, 267
Jennings, Peter, 238
John, Mr., 272
Johnson, Lyndon B., 4, 34, 110, 116, 148,
    160, 200, 371, 377, 378, 417
  Cronkite's Vietnam coverage and,
    122–123, 161, 211
  Rather and, 242, 293, 294–295, 296

Kalb, Bernard, 169
Kalb, Marvin, 168, 169, 314, 359
Kalischer, Peter, 156–157, 158, 159, 294
Kaltenborn, H. V., 98
Kaphan, Norma, 273
Kempton, Murray, 78
Kendrick, Alexander, 294
Kennan, George F., 123, 125
Kennedy, Edward, 341
Kennedy, Ethel, 265
Kennedy, John F., 33, 37, 101, 103, 209
  assassination of, 1–13, 93, 148, 169,
    247, 253–254, 292–293
Kennedy, Robert F., 211, 264–265, 283,
    331, 341–342
  assassination of, 10, 211–212, 265, 281
Kennedy Administration, 162–163, 169,
    357, 417
KHOU (Houston), 290
Khrushchev, Nikita S., 218
King, Martin Luther, 9, 211, 247
Kintner, Robert, 40, 95, 115
Kissinger, Henry, 169, 348
Klauber, Ed, 98–99, 129
KMBC (Kansas City), 85, 86
KNXT (Los Angeles), 280, 281, 282–283
Kopechne, Mary Jo, 341
Korean War, 18, 86–87, 181–182
Kovacs, Ernie, 226
KTLA (Los Angeles), 274

Kuralt, Charles, 100, 147, 154, 179, 182,
    217–218, 219, 221, 345, 400
  On the Road with, 64, 173–177, 187,
    243

Lamas, Fernando, 65
Lamoreaux, Bud, 259, 260
Lando, Barry, 415
Lane, Clem, 321–322
Lane, John, 321–323, 325, 326, 328, 333,
    334, 379, 384, 422, 423
Lardner, John, 30, 415
Latham, Aaron, 349, 350, 391–392
Laurence, Jack, 163–165, 189, 225, 294
Leibner, Richard, 372
Leiser, Ernie, 158, 178, 188, 240,
    250–252, 291, 293, 329, 330
  background of, 104, 137–138
  Cronkite replacement resisted by,
    112–113, 133
  editorial role of, 143–144
  Evening News and, see *CBS Evening
    News*
  Manning and, 142–143, 152, 328
  Midgley and, 137, 139, 145, 146, 147,
    148–149, 151, 317
  personality and reputation of, 104,
    141–142
Leonard, Bill, 111–112, 130–134,
    232–233, 238, 273, 320, 330, 339,
    343, 353, 354, 370–372, 381, 405
  as Friendly's deputy, 118, 128,
    130–131
  Mudd-Trout affair and, 112, 113, 115,
    116, 133
  60 Minutes and, 223, 224, 243, 278,
    398, 414
  Washington appointment of, 397–398,
    399
Life, 222–223
Lippmann, Walter, 42
London, CBS correspondents in, 15, 17,
    155, 157, 158–159, 165
Lone Ranger, The, 51, 271
Look, 135, 146, 164, 201
Los Angeles Times, 155
Lowe, David, 187
Lower, Elmer, 236, 240

MacArthur, Charles, 58
MacArthur, Douglas, 86–87, 156
McCarthy, Eugene, 170, 211, 296
McCarthy, Joseph R., 14–16, 20–22,
    24–25, 29–30, 33, 106, 108, 161
McCarthyism, 21, 24, 73, 157
McGee, Frank, 153, 269

McGovern, George S., 170, 305, 342
McLaughlin, Marya, 170–171, 420
magazine format, 122, 127, 222–223
Mann, Ralph, 234–236
Manning, Gordon, 121, 130–131,
    134–136, 164, 165, 175, 177, 231,
    233, 238, 243, 307, 360–361, 365,
    374, 375
    CBS critics of, 336–343, 354, 385
    downfall and departure of, 351–354,
        361, 362, 376–377, 378, 397, 399
    Evening News and, 136, 142–143,
        152–153, 249–250, 251–255, 257,
        259, 261–263, 317–325, 328–335
    Greenberg and, 252–255, 256, 259,
        261, 263, 309, 310–313, 321,
        328–329, 333, 335, 340, 343, 378,
        380
    Morning News and, 136, 280, 282,
        286–287, 344–352, 401
    Mudd and, 231, 233, 249, 263, 268,
        310
    print background of, 134–135, 146,
        340, 342
    Rather and, 308, 309–313, 316, 335,
        373
    Schneider and, 128, 135, 337–339, 343,
        351–352, 353, 361
March on Washington (1963), 9, 247
Mason, Linda, 362, 379
Maxwell, Elsa, 272
Mayer, Martin, 200
Meredith, James, 292
Merriman, John, 141–142, 150, 151, 168,
    181, 193–197, 204, 205, 227,
    228–229, 241, 323, 327, 380
Metalious, Grace, 272
Mickelson, Sig, 100, 101, 104, 113, 118,
    131, 138, 173–174, 175, 215, 216,
    217, 218, 250
    Cronkite and, 87–89, 207, 217
    firing of, 102, 217
Middle East, 48, 51, 145, 155, 157
Midgley, Les, 134, 137, 139, 145–153,
    174, 240, 329
    Evening News under, see *CBS Evening
        News*
    replacement of, 317–335
Mike and Buff, 271–272, 275
Mike Wallace Interview, The, 272
Miller, Gerald, 262
Mitchell, John, 302, 353
Monroe, Marilyn, 30–31
Morning Show, The, 90, 182, 270
Morton, Bruce, 169–170, 171, 173, 359,
    418–419, 420

Moscow, CBS correspondents in, 169,
    282
Mosedale, John, 197, 220, 227, 241, 380
Moses, Harry, 415
Moyers, Bill, 417–418
Mudd, Emma Jeanne, 264
Mudd, John Dominic Kostka, 245
Mudd, Roger, 8, 9–10, 48, 154, 200, 231,
    232, 233, 234, 285, 301, 400
    ABC interest in, 408–409, 412
    as anchorman, 262, 264, 265–266,
        315–316
    background of, 244–246
    as Cronkite's regular backup, 267, 315,
        409, 413
    as Cronkite's successor, 231, 244, 263,
        288, 413
    Greenberg and, 256–257, 260–261,
        262–263, 267, 309–311, 409
    Kennedys and, 264–265, 283
    in Mudd-Trout plan to replace
        Cronkite, 112–116, 248–249
    as National Affairs Correspondent,
        412–413
    Rather and, 288, 308, 309–311,
        313–316, 413
    Washington and Lee speech of,
        266–268, 284, 288, 308
    in Washington bureau, 168, 170, 171,
        246–248, 251, 264, 313, 357, 359,
        387, 388, 412
    on weekend editions of *Evening News,*
        249, 255, 256–257, 259, 261–263
Mudd, Samuel, 244–245
Muggs, J. Fred, 269, 270
Murrow, Edward R., 6, 7, 14–34, 35–37,
    39, 40, 53, 75, 78, 79, 99, 106, 173,
    187, 249, 253, 288–289, 301, 382,
    415, 423
    background of, 16–17, 50
    CBS disputes with, 21–33, 91, 97, 102
    Cronkite and, 84, 101–102, 112, 198
    departure of, 13, 32–33, 37, 91, 102,
        103
    Friendly's relationship with, 18–19,
        31–32, 106–107, 108–109, 121
    illness and death of, 13, 34, 35, 108,
        109
    legacy of, 35, 98, 301, 371, 415, 423
    vs. McCarthy, 14–16, 20–22, 24–25, 29,
        30–31, 33, 160
    personality and style of, 14, 15, 19–20
    Rather as "son of," 371, 413
    as talent recruiter, 35–49, 51, 84, 86,
        294, 356

Murrow, Edward R. *(cont'd)*
  TV Industry as viewed by, 26, 33, 34,
    53, 87, 266
  as wartime broadcaster, 16–17, 32, 161,
    193
Murrow, Janet, 19

Nader, Ralph, 226
NBC, 34, 40, 56, 115, 127, 372–373, 417
NBC News *(see also specific shows)*, 34,
    39
  CBS alumni at, 287, 354, 367, 376
  CBS rivalry with, 7, 8, 38–39, 70,
    72–79, 90, 91, 95–96, 98, 101, 104,
    112, 114–115, 116, 119, 130,
    144–145, 153–154, 171, 197, 206,
    224, 248, 250, 268, 269–271, 277,
    281, 327, 344, 400, 419
  evening news expanded by, 5, 93
  upgrading efforts by, 421–422
NBC Nightly News, 153, 206, 287, 410,
    421–422
Newman, Paul, 174
Newsday, 417
newspapers, 155
  film reporting vs., 70, 94
  shift to TV from, 5–6, 94, 291
Newsweek, 105, 134, 135, 147, 250, 251,
    339, 340
New Yorker, The, 48, 73
New York Herald Tribune, 57, 137, 146
New York magazine, 348–349, 388, 391
New York Times, 36, 41, 53, 66, 75, 98,
    150, 155, 157, 162, 219, 359, 362,
    386, 391, 399
Night Beat, 272, 275
Nixon, Richard M., 34, 167–168, 198,
    266, 278, 330, 344
  "enemies list" of, 387
  impeachment and, 368, 387, 407
  in 1968 election, 212, 279
  in 1972 election, 303, 305, 313
  press conferences of, 367–369
  Rather and, 242, 288–289, 295–300,
    301, 303, 307, 308, 312–316,
    367–370, 371, 387, 388, 389
  resignation of, 366–367, 370, 371, 372,
    387–390, 407
Nixon Administration, 167, 266, 364
  press attacks by, 266, 267, 296–298,
    299, 300, 301–303, 307, 311–312,
    361
Nolan, Martin, 299

On the Road series, 64, 175–177, 187,
    243

Oppenheimer, J. Robert, 22
Oswald, Lee Harvey, 4, 8–9, 253–254
outlook, defined, 184
Overend, Bill, 376
Overseas News Agency (ONA), 137

Paar, Jack, 90, 270
Palace Guard, The, 309
Paley, Barbara Cushing "Babe," 29
Paley, Sam, 22
Paley, William S., 22–33, 35, 120, 124,
    125, 126, 128, 267, 302, 352
  CBS tradition as viewed by, 97–98, 129
  China and Soviet trips of, 344–345, 352
  "instant analysis" edict of, 314–315
  Morning Show and, 284, 345, 346
  Murrow and, 23–26, 29, 35, 98,
    107–108
  1964 upheavals and, 95–96, 97, 105,
    112–113, 114, 116, 119, 133, 248
  on Nixon-Rather exchange, 369
  Salant and, 105, 128, 129, 305–307
  Schorr and, 385–386, 388, 389, 390,
    394
  Sevareid and, 39–40, 42
  Smith and, 38, 39, 41
  Stanton's successors under, 363–364,
    402–404
  Watergate report opposed by,
    305–307, 337
Pappas, Ike, 166, 173
Paris, CBS correspondents in, 156–157,
    158, 356
Paskman, Ralph, 94, 158, 159, 250, 291,
    319–320, 340
PBS, 417, 418
Perigord, Lorraine, 273
Person to Person, 28–31, 35, 46–47, 89,
    101–102, 253, 272, 415
Pierpoint, Bob, 169, 293, 357
Pike, Otis (report), 390–395
Plante, Bill, 166, 173, 180, 258
PM (talk show), 273, 275
political conventions, 5, 6, 46, 231
  of 1948, 18, 52–53, 56, 57, 72, 87, 88
  of 1952, 72, 74–75, 87–89, 100, 131,
    198, 217
  of 1956, 72, 74, 75, 101, 131, 270
  of 1960, 78, 91, 100–102, 129, 250, 273
  of 1964, 78, 111–116, 119–120, 133,
    248–249, 385–386
  of 1968, 165, 179, 199–200, 208, 212,
    224, 279, 281, 347
  of 1976, 354–355
prompting techniques, 62–63, 64
Proxmire, William, 5–6

Public Broadcasting Laboratory (PBL),
126–127, 277

Quinn, Sally, 180, 287, 343, 347–352,
354, 359, 385, 391–392, 401, 411,
418
Quinn, William, 385
Quint, Bert, 166
quiz-show scandals, 26, 27, 28, 29–30, 31,
302

radio news, 71, 163, 169, 193
commercial fee system in, 53–54, 84
transition to TV news from, 36, 40–41,
45, 48–49, 52–55, 88, 114, 163
TV impact vs., 17–18, 24, 88
Rather, Dan, 48, 139, 154, 168, 171,
199–200, 251, 288–300, 400
anchorman role of, 307–308, 316
background of, 289–290, 299–300
CBS power structure vs., 308–316,
369–370, 413
CBS Reports and, 370–374, 382, 413,
417
as Cronkite's successor, 288, 316
Greenberg and, 309–313, 316, 335, 340
Haldeman-Ehrlichman story of,
308–309
JFK assassination and, 1–2, 3, 10–12,
169, 292–293
Johnson and, 242, 293, 294–295, 296
London transfer of, 294, 313
Mudd and, 288, 308, 309–311,
313–316, 413
Nixon and, *see* Nixon, Richard M.
promoted from White House beat,
370–374, 413
on *60 Minutes,* 413–417
Small and, *see* Small, Bill
South covered by, 291–293
on Sunday *Evening News,* 242,
307–308, 309
Vietnam coverage and, 294, 295
as White House correspondent, 170,
232, 288–289, 293–300, 307, 310,
312–313, 359, 360, 367–370, 387
Rather, Jean, 291
ratings, 281, 284
ABC rise and fall in, 75, 239, 278, 404,
408, 410, 411
CBS leadership in, 23, 24, 70, 75,
144–145, 197, 344, 422
CBS as third in, 404
CBS-NBC battle for, 70, 72–79, 95–96,
101, 104–105, 112, 116, 119,

ratings: CBS-NBC *(cont'd)*
144–145, 153, 197, 217, 419, 420,
422
Reasoner, Harry, 7–9, 46, 47, 48, 79, 93,
100, 154, 172, 214–241, 275,
293–294, 380
anchorman role of, 8, 46, 213,
221–222, 225–227, 228, 229, 230,
235–236, 249, 420
background of, 214–217
on *Calendar,* 104, 219–221, 222, 271,
274
CBS critics of, 231–233
contract negotiations of, 233–236,
408–410, 412
Cronkite and, *see* Cronkite, Walter
in move to ABC, 234–241, 267, 278,
285
Mudd and, 231, 408–410, 412
personality and style of, 225–229
replacement of, 242–244, 307, 308
on *60 Minutes,* 222–225, 233, 278, 279
Wallace and, 274, 275, 278, 279
Walters and, 410–412, 420, 421
Reasoner, Kay, 216–217
Redford, Robert, 415–416
Republican conventions, 88, 101, 102,
111, 116, 119–120, 208, 248, 385
Reynolds, Frank, 239, 277, 294
Rhee, Syngman, 156
Richardson, Don, 374, 384
Roach, Janet, 379
Roberts, Sam, 190, 379
*Rock Springs Daily Rocket and Sunday
Mirror,* 178
Rogers, Will, Jr., 270
"roll cue," 58
Rome, CBS correspondent in, 157–158
Rooney, Andy, 220–221, 223, 240
Roosevelt, Franklin D., 52, 245, 324
Rosenfeld, James, 404
Ruby, Jack, 8, 254
Rudd, Hughes, 139, 173, 258, 260–261,
262, 291–292, 336, 340, 400
on *Morning News,* 177–180, 345, 346,
350, 351, 418–420
Runyon, Damon, 7
Rusk, Dean, 123
Russell, Mark, 300
Russell, Richard, 9

Sack, John, 220
Safer, Morley, 48
on *60 Minutes,* 243, 279, 413, 416, 417
Vietnam and, 158–165, 243, 294
Safire, William, 362, 396

St. Louis Post-Dispatch, 299
Salant, Richard, 118, 119, 133, 135, 139,
    165, 175, 250, 267, 268, 274, 338,
    339, 343, 354, 360–361, 412, 418
    background of, 102–103
    career record and successor of,
        399–402
    drug payola story and, 362, 363, 365,
        401
    Evening News and, 143, 149, 152, 205,
        288, 304, 305–307, 317–321, 339,
        400
    Morning News and, 275–276, 286–287,
        344–347, 352, 400, 419
    mistakes and firing of, 103–106, 108,
        118, 140
    Rather and, 293, 297, 308, 312,
        370–374, 400
    Reasoner and, 219, 223, 229, 231, 232,
        235, 237, 238, 400
    restoration of, 128–131
    Schorr and, 385, 386, 389, 390, 391,
        393, 394, 396
    60 Minutes and, 223, 224, 243, 410,
        414
    Stanton and, 32, 102–103, 105–106,
        128–130, 306, 401
    successor of, 405
    Watergate report and, 304, 305–307,
        337
salaries in broadcast journalism, 53–54,
    233–234, 236, 239, 242, 247, 281,
    410
Salisbury, Harrison, 84
Sandburg, Carl, 25
San Francisco Chronicle, 120
Sarnoff, David, 23
Schakne, Bob, 173
Scheffler, Phil, 63, 94, 150–151, 187, 415
Scherer, Ray, 294–295
Schieffer, Bob, 169, 170, 171, 359, 360,
    372, 418, 420
Schneider, Jack, 134, 236–237, 267–268,
    285, 306, 332, 360–361, 363–364,
    394
    background of, 124–125
    in Friendly resignation fracas, 124–126,
        127, 128–130, 277, 337, 338
    Manning and, 128, 135, 337–339, 343,
        351–352, 353, 361
    in 1977 corporate shake-up, 404–405
Schoenbrun, David, 356–359, 361
School of the Air, 16
school segregation, 22
Schorr, Daniel, 168, 171, 303, 306, 314,
    359, 360

Schorr, Daniel *(cont'd)*
    background and personality of,
        386–387
    in Goldwater controversy, 385–386,
        389
    Nixon speech coverage criticized by,
        387–389, 395, 396
    Pike Report and, 390–395
Schoumacher, David, 170, 171, 173
See It Now, 14–16, 18–22, 24–26, 30,
    31–33, 46, 58, 106, 108, 182, 269,
    272, 301, 382, 415
Selling of the Pentagon, The, 301–302
Senate Foreign Relations Committee,
    Vietnam hearings of, 123–126, 127,
    128, 130, 277, 338
Serafin, Barry, 170–171
Sevareid, Eric, 21, 32, 36, 39–43, 44, 45,
    47, 50, 75, 77, 80, 87, 111, 128, 146,
    221, 232, 299, 386, 400
    CBS disputes with, 39–40, 97
    early career of, 40–41
    Establishment role of, 167–168
    as news analyst, 41–43, 104, 208, 314,
        359
    personality and style of, 40, 41, 42–43,
        167–168, 264
    retirement of, 405–406, 423–424
    Schorr and, 387, 388–389, 390, 395
Sharnik, John, 187, 398–399
Shriver, Sargent, 342
Shulman, Max, 216
Simon, Bob, 166
Sirhan Sirhan, 281
60 Minutes, 127, 162, 165, 233, 242–244,
    278–280, 295, 344, 354, 398, 399,
    400, 413–417
    creation of, 122, 222–225
    evolution and success of, 414–417
Slate, The, 151, 207, 377
Small, Bill, 268, 320, 356–361, 397, 405
    appointed D.C. bureau chief, 359–361
    background of, 357–358
    as hard-news vice-president, 352, 356,
        361, 365–367, 370–377, 378–381,
        383, 384–385, 419
    Rather and, 300, 308, 312, 314, 360,
        370, 372, 373–374
    resentments toward, 374–377, 401
    Schorr and, 385, 389, 390, 394, 396
Smith, Howard K., 32, 36–39, 40, 41, 42,
    44, 45, 46, 48, 167, 246, 277
    departure from CBS of, 37–39, 97, 104,
        357
    Reasoner and, 236, 238–240, 278, 408

Snyder, Joan, 259–260, 274–275, 276
Socolow, Sandy, 64, 270, 364–365
  background of, 181–182
  Evening News role of, 181–185, 186,
    187, 190, 193, 195, 196, 197, 201,
    341, 380
  in Midgley replacement maneuvers,
    317–325, 327, 328, 335
  as Washington bureau chief, 374, 388,
    392, 395, 396, 423
Solzhenitsyn, Aleksandr, 353
Soroka, Paul, 192, 276, 379
sound cameras, 61
Soviet Union, 85, 345
Soviet wheat deal story, 362, 366
space technology, 60–61, 90–91, 191,
    199, 203, 330
Spillane, Mickey, 30
sports news, 257–258
Sputnik, 60–61, 90
Stahl, Lesley, 347, 391–393, 395, 396,
    419, 420
"stand-upper," defined, 61
Stanford, Leland, 82–83
Stanton, Frank, 26–33, 38, 41, 54–55,
    100, 120, 134, 267, 352, 363, 402
  background of, 26–27
  Friendly and, 123, 124, 125, 126
  in Mudd-Trout affair, 112, 113, 116,
    119
  Murrow and, 28–33
  Nixon threats and, 306, 307
  in Pentagon controversy, 301–302
  Salant and, 32, 102–103, 105–106,
    128–130, 306, 401
  Vietnam coverage under, 123, 124,
    125, 126, 161–162
Stars and Stripes, 137, 146, 398
State Department beat, 169, 359, 386
Steinem, Gloria, 347
Stevenson, Adlai, 2
Stone, Emerson, 320
Strawser, Neil, 63, 169
Suez crisis (1956), 37, 146
Sullivan, Ed, 90
Sumner, John, 196, 197, 227, 380
Sunday News Special, 80, 90
Supreme Court beat, 168, 169, 359
Swayze, John Cameron, 70, 71–72,
    75–76, 81, 153, 238
Swing, Raymond, 193
Syvertsen, George, 262

Taft, Robert, 62
talk shows, 272–273, 275

Taylor, Arthur, 352, 362–364, 394, 401,
    402–403
Telenews, 56, 63
television journalism:
  beginnings of, 52–53
  early quality of, 55–56
  impact of JFK assassination on, 4–6,
    93
  1960s events as suited to, 95
  powerful effect of, 24
  purity of print vs., 340
  show-biz side of, 17–18, 121, 205, 233,
    265–266, 271
  technology of, 58–62, 93–94, 143, 147,
    291
  transition from radio to, 36, 40–41,
    48–49, 52–55, 88, 114, 163
Tell Me About Women, 214–215, 216
tell stories, 56, 64, 109–110, 183, 193,
    194
Theis, Bill, 9
This Is New York, 131, 134
Thomas, Lowell, 50, 55
Threlkeld, Richard, 166, 419, 420
Time, 144, 147, 281
Tito, 36
Today, 153, 219, 268, 269–271, 276, 277,
    344, 345, 349, 410, 419, 422
Tonight, 90
Trouble with Rock, The, 361–367
Trout, Robert, 16, 51, 87, 88, 98, 99, 112,
    113–116, 248–249
Trujillo, Rafael, 132
Truman, Harry S, 45, 86, 173
Twentieth Century, The, 89–90, 382, 414
21st Century, The, 382

United Press (UP, UPI), 2, 9, 11, 36, 40,
    43–44, 72, 73, 82, 83–85, 99, 101,
    134, 156, 194, 230, 259, 340
United States Information Agency
    (USIA), 13, 33, 37, 103, 108, 216

Van Dyke, Dick, 270
Vanocur, Sander, 116
Variety, 95, 127, 288, 398
Vatican, 157–158
videotape, 41–42, 56, 93–94
Vietnam, Vietnam War, 34, 48, 148, 220,
    225, 243, 266
  CBS correspondents assigned to, 122,
    155–157, 158–166, 180, 243,
    262–263, 283, 294, 419
  Cronkite's evolving views on, 208–211
  Friendly's resignation over reporting
    on, 122–128, 338

Vietnam *(cont'd)*
  protests against, 95, 145, 189
  reactions to coverage of, 159, 160–162,
    163, 211, 295, 296, 312
  Tet offensive in, 164, 209, 211
Village Voice, 376, 390–392
voice-over narration, 61, 63, 64

Walker, Hal, 170–171, 420
Wallace, Chris, 280
Wallace, Mike, 51, 154, 172, 200, 232,
    234
  background of, 271–274
  interview shows of, 272–273
  Morning News and, 104, 221, 249, 254,
    271, 274–277, 278, 280–281, 282,
    345
  on *60 Minutes,* 162, 223–225, 242,
    243–244, 278–280, 295, 354, 413,
    416–417
Wallace, Peter, 273–274, 280
Walters, Barbara, 270, 348, 349, 351
  as ABC anchorwoman, 410–412, 417,
    420
Warren Commission, 148
Washington bureau, *see* CBS News
Washington Post, 180, 303–304, 305,
    347–348, 349, 350, 351, 359, 386,
    387, 390–391, 392
Watergate *(see also* Nixon, Richard M.),
    34, 198, 279, 296–298, 309, 312,
    367–368, 372, 387–390, 407
  CBS beneficiaries of, 315–316, 387
  CBS report on, 303–307, 362, 365
  "checkbook journalism" and, 353–354
WBBM (Chicago), 186, 188, 189, 322,
    329, 332, 346
WCAU-TV (Philadelphia), 125
WCBS (New York), 114, 173
WCCO (Minneapolis), 216
Webster, Don, 262–263
Weel, Alice, 64–66, 92

We're Going to Make You a Star, 349
Wershba, Joe, 20, 302, 415
West, Charlie, 196, 197, 227, 228, 237,
    380
Westerman, Sylvia, 374, 384
Westin, Av, 56, 240, 275–276, 277–278
Westmoreland, William, 209
WHAS (Louisville), 358
White, E. B., 73
White, Paul, 98, 99, 129
White House beat, 168, 169, 170, 222,
    242, 278, 288–289, 293–294,
    295–300, 312–313, 386
Who's Who, 399
Williams, Palmer, 415
Wilson, Edmund, 205
WMAQ (Chicago), 271
Women's Liberation Movement, 192,
    226, 345–347
Woodward, Bob, 303–304, 387, 395
World in Crisis, The, 146
World News Roundup, 36, 54, 160
World Tonight, The, 103, 138
World War II, 23, 36, 52, 83–85, 137,
    208
  CBS reputation in, 24
  radio coverage of, 7, 15, 16–17, 32, 36,
    40–41, 44–45, 84, 99, 157
  writers, CBS, 90, 193–197, 284, 285
    all-else, 196–197
WRNL (Richmond), 246
WSB (Atlanta), 50–51
WTOP (Washington), 86, 246, 264
Wussler, Bob, 329–332, 341–342, 404
WXYZ (Detroit), 51, 271
Wynshaw, David, 362

You Are There, 6, 89, 182, 382
Young, Bob, 238

Zelman, Sam, 141
Zousmer, Jesse, 30, 253–254, 255